Yajna

A Comprehensive Survey

With kind regards, ॐ and prem

Swami Niranjan

Yajna

A Comprehensive Survey

Sannyasi Gyanshruti
Sannyasi Srividyananda

Yoga Publications Trust, Munger, Bihar, India

Published by Yoga Publications Trust
First edition 2006

ISBN: 81-86336-47-8

Publisher and distributor: Yoga Publications Trust, Ganga Darshan, Munger, Bihar, India.

Website: www.yogavision.net

Printed at Thomson Press (India) Limited, New Delhi, 110001

Dedication

In humility we offer this dedication to
Swami Sivananda Saraswati, who initiated
Swami Satyananda Saraswati into the secrets of yoga.

Contents – at a glance

List of Tables

Preface

There are certain classical systems, the revival of whose pure form can bring about a spiritual revolution. Yajna is one such system. Yajna is a science as well as an act of faith. As a science, it is a precision-based series of rituals that have been part of the Indian psyche for over 4000 years through the medium of the Vedas. The classical literature, assiduously preserved, contains the methodology as well as the philosophy of yajnas. It also forms the basis of this book.

It is, however, faith that makes the experience of yajna spontaneous and elevating, and this is achieved only when we attempt to invoke and surrender to the divinity inherent in the practice of yajna, or when the experience descends to us from realized masters.

One such master is Swami Satyananda Saraswati, who inspired the yogic renaissance in the twentieth century. Since the early 1960s, Sri Swamiji has unveiled to the world many sciences from the ancient Indian scriptures, previously considered secret and esoteric.

As an exponent of yoga, Sri Swamiji integrated the different systems of yoga and showed how they could be adapted and applied to meet the needs of all. He also introduced recitation of *Saundarya Lahari* and chanting of the *Bhagavad Gita* and Upanishadic verses. In 1990, a landmark year, Sri Swamiji began Panchagni sadhana. From an ardent proponent of yoga and a (supposedly) strict guru, he transformed into a soft, compassionate and serene person who now talked only of bhakti, the importance of surrender and the ecstasy of seva.

Since 1995, Sri Swamiji has taken us through yet another important aspect of Vedic lifestyle – yajna. He has presented the Rajasooya Yajna in a rediscovered form, with Sat Chandi Yajna as its base. As he says, "Yajna is a very powerful tool for inspiring and enlightening human consciousness. It includes the body, mind, faith, mantra, ritual as well as your entire life. This combination makes yajna a very potent tool for metamorphosis and transformation. The body, mind and mantras all unite to produce a special effect which changes your thinking and your life. When this total participation takes place, you can know yourself and converse with your inner being."

Every satsang by Sri Swamiji is a special experience of learning and bliss. But the happiest moment of my life came when he mentioned, in a satsang, that I should undertake a study of the yajna processes contained in the Vedic literature.

As a physics student working on matters relating to atomic radiation protection, I had always been fascinated by the two approaches to understanding the structure of the universe: the matter-centric approach of scientists and the spirit-centric belief of philosophers – and the two approaches always seemed to run parallel!

Both approaches use the smallest entity to understand the largest. The scientific approach uses matter, particles, atoms and the structure of matter to understand the universe. The other follows the subtle path, using the mind, intellect, senses, etc. to reach extrasensory perception. One employs research tools, systematic experiments, deductive logic, and the other prefers contemplation and meditation. The first school of thought postulates the 'Big Bang' theory for the creation of the universe, and the second believes that creation issued forth from the Supreme's desire to become many from one.

In yajna, both approaches find congruence. As Sri Swamiji says, "Yajna is a scientific process which includes a most important thing—faith."

Furthermore, Sri Swamiji has also given a significant definition of yajna. Speaking about the importance of yajna in the life of a householder, he said, "Yajna does not just mean a ritual where pooja items are consigned to the flames and dedicated to God. The word yajna consists of three syllables – ya, ja and na, which refer to the three processes involved in every act we perform—*utpadana*, *vitarana* and *uparjana*, i.e. production (ya), distribution (ja) and assimilation (na). There has to be a balance between these three components. Sharing one's wealth with other members of society is of topmost value."

With this understanding of combining the material with the spiritual, science with faith, the microcosmos with the macrocosmos, I have made an attempt to discover their meeting points through the medium of the most ancient ritual connecting human beings with the divine essence – yajna.

– Sannyasi Gyanshruti

1

Yajna – A Celebration of Life

Before beginning our presentation, we will quote from the invitation by Swami Satyasangananda Saraswati to the 2004 Sat Chandi Mahayajna held in Rikhia, in order to understand that in reality yajna is a symbol of life and consciousness evolving as they pass through different phases of existence.

> Expansion of mind is that state when you begin to perceive a different dimension in relation to your existence, which until that moment remains unknown or concealed from you. The precise moment when man recognized fire was the moment of his greatest insight. It was the split second when his consciousness took an evolutionary leap from the instinctive to the intelligent and intuitive plane.
>
> This must have then led to a chain reaction, because after that there was no stopping man. His realization of a difference between himself and other living creatures led him to a further insight into how he could live apart from them nurturing his home, growing his own food, and rearing his cattle and livestock. Fire and grain thus signify that precise moment of insight into a world which, until then, was unknown to the primitive man who existed billions and trillions of years ago – a discovery that catapulted him into what he is today.

It is not surprising therefore that the *Rig Veda*, the oldest written text of a most ancient civilization, begins with a tribute to this awesome manifestation of nature. *"Agni meede purohitam"* is a statement that gives agni or fire the status of divinity or one that illumines the path. One can thus clearly see how the ceremony of yajna evolved as a commemoration of this historic event, a salute to the foremost quantum leap made by man.

This is the utilitarian aspect of his discovery. But beyond that there is another deeper esoteric aspect, which relates to that expanded state of mind that tantra talks about. For in that state of mind, fire and grain assume a different role, one that elevates them to the role of catalyst of creation, signifying that we owe our existence to fire and grain.

In the *Bhagavad Gita* Lord Krishna says to Arjuna:

अन्नाद्भवन्ति भूतानि पर्जन्यादन्नसम्भवः ।
यज्ञाद्भवति पर्जन्यो यज्ञः कर्मसमुद्भवः ॥3:14॥
कर्म ब्रह्मोद्भवं विद्धि ब्रह्माक्षरसमुद्भवम् ।
तस्मात्सर्वगतं ब्रह्म नित्यं यज्ञे प्रतिष्ठितम्॥3:15॥

All living beings spring forth from anna, which is a product of rain. Rain is caused by yajna, which in turn takes place due to karma. Karmas manifest out of knowledge, which is the essence of Parabrahma or the Supreme Self. On account of this, that supreme immortal Paramatma is forever enshrined in yajna.

Until we can grasp the profundity of these words, yajna will remain just a fire ceremony for us. It will not expand the mind and give us that sublime experience of unity with the source of our creation. The Bible tells us of just such an event in the life of Moses, who in a similar expanded state of mind saw that highest reality as fire, which revealed to him the Ten Commandments, a revelation which gave birth to one of the foremost religions in the world. That was no ordinary fire; it was the cosmic light born out of the divine vibration, an experience which tantra developed through the ritual of yajna, highlighting how an exoteric act can become an uplifting esoteric experience.

In the physical body this cosmic light manifesting as the inner fire or prana is the link between annamaya kosha and manomaya kosha. It is the mythical missing link that transported man from the physical animal dimension to the intelligent and creative being of the twenty-first century. In the slokas mentioned above, the Gita hints at yajna being the medium of his further evolution from man to superman, for that supreme knowledge is *pratishthit* or established in this rite just as heat is established in fire or light in the sun.

Swami Satyananda has said that yajna is a celebration of man's first awakening. It was not recorded by any race, nationality or civilization. Then man was the true example of a universal human being. We are fortunate, as that moment is forever enshrined in the ritual of yajna, which was developed by the Vedic seers. The ritual of yajna therefore is designed to establish man's connection with the cosmic properties abounding in the universe.

2

Introduction to the Yajna Tradition

Yajna, translated in English as sacrifice, has been preserved as a science and philosophy in the Vedas and Vedic literature. Compiled over 4000 years ago, these texts have been the reference-point for the performance of all yajnas from then to now. For those who have witnessed a yajna, mention of the word may bring to mind the picture of an altar, a sacred fire with flames rising from it, the chanting of mantras and offering of oblations. This is the gross form of yajna. The mantras are symbols of praise and gratitude. The offerings represent sacrifice. However, there is also the subtle, experiential aspect of yajna, which is inherent in its gross form.

Yajna is also a concept, and can be viewed from various perspectives covering, for example, the principles of creation and sustenance. Further, as a science, yajna has the proven ability to rejuvenate an environment. The expanse of yajna is indeed vast, and it touches life in many different ways. The aim of this book is to introduce yajna, to appreciate how it was used during Vedic times, the traditional methods of performing yajna that are prevalent even today, and its possible application in modern life.

Genesis of yajna

The term 'yajna' appears in the opening hymn of the *Rig Veda Samhita*, acknowledged as the oldest text in the world, without any prior definition. This would indicate that yajna existed even before the creation of textual material and was also known to the pre-Vedic people. However, the concept of yajna was shaped, developed and perfected in the Vedic period. Different parts of the Vedic literature, in their own characteristic way, have touched upon the subject. For example, the *Rig Veda* treats it as a concept. The *Yajur Veda* describes it as a ritual. The *Kalpa Sutras* treat it as a conduct, and argue that it is the best of all conducts. The Upanishads and the *Bhagavad Gita* give a Vedantic or philosophical version of yajna, whereas the Itihasas and Puranas give it a human form and weave interesting legends around it. It is interesting to see how yajna is viewed in important Vedic works.

Rig Veda: According to the *Rig Veda*, Prajapati created the gods. The gods performed a sacrifice, and yajna was the outcome of this first and foremost sacrifice made through will and contemplation. The gods visualized the creator, Prajapati, in the form of yajna, and through the yajna worshipped him too – that is, yajna itself. For the gods, yajna was an instrument as well as an objective. This concept may be slightly intriguing, but it is brought out beautifully in *Purusha Sukta*, a hymn from the *Rig Veda* (R 10.90,1–16).

Yajur Veda: In the *Taittiriya Samhita*, the most popular part of the *Yajur Veda*, there is a story that alludes to the principle of yajna. Prajapati created *devas* (gods) and *asuras* (demons). Thereafter, for their livelihood, he created yajna and chandas (metres such as Gayatri, etc.). To begin with, yajna and chandas were residing with the devas, but when the devas ceased to be united in their approach to life, yajna was displeased and frustrated, and moved to the asuras. Chandas followed him. Eventually, realizing that they no longer enjoyed the prosperity and wealth that yajna had brought them, the devas asked him to return, but he refused. The devas also understood that the solution now lay with Prajapati, and so they asked him to resolve the situation. After a series of prayers, Prajapati acceded to their request. He extracted the essence of the chandas from the collection of mantras in the custody of the asuras and granted it to the devas. With the essence gone, the chandas returned to the devas and yajna also followed them. Thereafter, the devas expanded the rituals of yajna. The asuras imitated them, and *rishis* (seers) also earned yajna through their austerities. From the rishis, yajna reached ordinary human beings. In essence, the *Taittiriya Samhita* relates the birth of yajna to the need for a livelihood by the devas and others.

Shatapatha Brahmana is a monograph that deals with the procedural part of yajna. Its version of yajna is similar to that of the *Rig Veda*. It states that the gods performed yajna to express their gratitude, and also to secure the favour of their creator, Prajapati. In this yajna they offered their mind and soul as sacrifice. Pleased with their devotion, Prajapati offered himself as a sacrifice in their yajna. This is how Prajapati became yajna, creating a model of himself (SB 11.1, 8,3). Again, we see yajna as an instrument as well as an objective.

Bhagavad Gita is said to be the essence of the Upanishads. It gives at least three shades of meaning to yajna. To begin with, it views yajna as a practical means of livelihood. Yajna as sacrifice is shown to be the principal base of everything in the universe. The Gita equates dispassionate acts *(karma)* with yajna and recommends that throughout life, one should perform every act with full vigour, enthusiasm and devotion, but develop a dispassionate attitude towards the outcome. This, in its opinion, is the yajnic way of life.

In another context, the *Bhagavad Gita* says that Prajapati created devas, human beings and other entities. He also created yajna to be used by his creation as the means of satiating all desires. Yajna is equated with the mythological divine cow, Kamadhenu, who spontaneously fulfils every desire. The fulfilment of desires is, however, based on the give and take principle, adds the Gita, indicating an essential aspect of yajna. Human beings are to offer oblations to the devas. Pleased with the offerings, the devas would reciprocate. After completing all the oblations in a yajna, only the leftovers should be used by human beings. This cycle of sacrifice should continue without any breach by either party.

The third shade of meaning of yajna in the *Bhagavad Gita* is contained in the statement that all sentient beings originate from food and are also sustained by food. Food has its root in the rains, and rains are due to yajna. Thus, yajna is at the base of everything. Also, yajna is not possible without karma.

Puranas are classic texts that have simplified the knowledge contained in the Vedas for easy use by all. According to the *Bhagavata Purana*, yajna is an incarnation of Lord Vishnu. Akuti and Ruchi had twins named Yajna and Dakshina. Ruchi was Lord Brahma's foster son and Akuti was Svyambhava Manu's daughter. Manu adopted Yajna. Once, when Manu was in deep meditation, his enemies, the demons, wanted to take that opportunity to destroy him. Yajna fought with them and killed them all, thus saving his father. For his valour, Yajna was rewarded with the kingdom of heaven. Therefore, to earn fame and heaven, the *Bhagavata Purana* recommends the propitiation of yajna.

In the *Vayu Purana* there is a story about the origin of yajna related to the third of the ten incarnations of Lord Vishnu. Once Mother Earth was drowning in the depths of the waters. Lord Vishnu, assuming the form of a huge boar (Varaha avatara), lifted her up and restored her to her rightful place. Having accomplished the purpose of this incarnation, the divine rescuer decided to leave the body of the boar. So Lord Shiva came in the form of Sharabha, and remorselessly killed Varaha. The body fell down into the waters, and from this 'falling body', yajna emerged. Brahma, Vishnu, Shiva and the other gods, with the help of their attendants, carried the body up into the sky. While Lord Vishnu was dissecting Varaha with his discus, 1008 forms of yajna emerged from the body along with the implements and ingredients of yajna. From the bodies of Varaha's three assistants, three forms of fire were created, known as *garhapatya agni, dakshinagni* and *ahavaniya agni*, which filled the entire universe. From them, the three parts of the universe – *prithivi* (earth), *antariksha* (space between earth and sky) and *dyu loka* (sky), came into existence. The fires were pacified at a point said to be the abode of the gods, beyond the three lokas. Only yajna, in its essence, could transcend the lokas and reach the gods. Therefore, external or physical yajna is performed using the three forms of fire and articles of oblation to contact the gods.

The story is a metaphor, but it gives an idea of how yajna originated, and also underlines the basis of yajna, which is sacrifice. It is also mentioned in the *Kalika Purana* albeit with minor differences.

These examples from a cross-section of Vedic literature illustrate that yajna was the most popular and important concept of the Vedic period. A deeper look into the Vedas will create a better appreciation of the concept.

Vedas, Vedic dharma and yajna

The Vedas uphold the traditional wisdom and culture of ancient Indian society. This wisdom shaped the way of life in the Vedic society. A code of conduct called Vedic dharma prescribed the norms of behaviour for managing individual interests. In particular, it emphasized that individuals should work for personal aspirations in an appropriate manner, so that self-interest was not at the cost of other members of society, the lower species, or Nature. Vedic dharma fostered a development that was conducive to individual spiritual upliftment and created a grateful approach towards Nature.

However, it was imperative for the society to continually update these prescriptive and normative measures in order to keep the governing structure flexible in relation to time and development. This flexibility gave Vedic dharma its eternal character *(Sanatana dharma)*, and also made it the subject matter of the Vedas as indicated in the following sloka:

तस्मात् धर्म इत्येव शास्त्र विषयो न वेदार्थ इति।

Tasmaat dharma ityeva shaastra vishayo na vedaartha iti.

Therefore, dharma is the subject matter of Veda, not its import.

The concept of yajna possibly originated from the Vedas in relation to commandments that one should adhere to the principles of dharma. According to Swami Niranjanananda Saraswati, "Dharma is awareness of the sense of justice, righteousness and goodness inherent in one's personality, and living accordingly." Dharma provides the 'do's' and 'don'ts' for one's actions and behaviour. Keeping within the boundaries of dharma therefore gives a direction to individual aspirations.

Yet the Vedics who expounded on dharma in the Samhitas stated *what* should be done in life, but did not elaborate *how*. Where to go was clear, but how to go was conspicuously absent. This vacuum was filled by the addendum of the Vedas, the *Brahmana Granthas*, which gave techniques of dispensation (of dharma), described the procedures and rites that would enable one to follow the dharmic path, and bound the mantras from the Samhitas with procedures for actions (rituals or *vidhis*)[1].

The Brahmana Granthas, in turn, are comprised of three parts: the injunctions of the mantras for various types of actions *(yajnartha ajna),* the exact procedures to be followed *(vidhi)* and the significance of the injunctions *(arthavada).*

Purushartha and kratvartha: Given the goal fixed by dharma, actions in life became equivalent to efforts in pursuit of this goal. The aspirations were thus grouped into four types: *dharma*, the duty or obligation to oneself, one's family and society; *artha,* material needs related to our external social life; *kama*, emotional fulfilment; and *moksha*, liberation, the desire to attain transcendence. These are the four main aims to be pursued in life and are known as *purushartha*. All individual actions amount to fulfilling these four goals, which give us the motivation to fulfil our natural obligations and to pursue our innermost desire to find a state of contentment and peace.

The Vedic seers envisaged that these goals should be pursued while following the righteous path, *ritasya panthah*.

---

[1] See Chapter 2 and Annexure 1 for a detailed explanation of the structure of the Vedas

Rita means righteous behaviour. More specifically, it means that one's actions should not cause harm to others, one's thoughts should not spread negative vibrations, and one's interactions with Nature should not disturb its dynamic equilibrium. Corruption in one's approach at any of these levels amounts to moving away from rita towards unrighteous action, *anrita* or non-rita.

Rita is a feature of an ideal world. In the imperfect world that we live in, it is very difficult, almost impossible, to completely adapt to rita. Our aspirations do not cease. The solution lies in striving to be as close to rita, righteous behaviour, as possible. To achieve this, the Vedas give detailed procedures for righteous actions. Such actions are known as *kratvartha*. If anrita or inappropriate action is the dominating factor in one's life, putting in continuous efforts to move away from anrita (rather than being in rita) is desirable. So purushartha is to be performed the kratvartha way.

Birth of the Vedic concept of yajna: Gods (devatas) represent and illustrate rita. To be like the devatas is man's natural tendency. A methodology or technique was necessary to enable society to move away from anrita to rita, so that godliness could be achieved. The Vedics believed that this could be achieved by constantly purifying oneself through ritualistic action, or kratvartha. This gave rise to the concept of a ritual based on sacrifice. It is known as yajna. Yajna is the bridge to cross from the path of 'rite' to the path of 'righteousness' (rita).

The development of the Brahmana Granthas provided a ritualistic way of fulfilling aspirations. Everyone works to achieve everlasting happiness, for example, but dharma expects individuals not to achieve it at the cost of others. To accomplish both, the Brahmana Granthas prescribed an elaborate ritual called *darshapoorna yajna*. It is particularly recommended for those who aspire for a confirmed reservation in heaven! Heaven being the superlative degree of happiness, this ritualistic approach attracted people. Similarly, the yardstick of wealth and prosperity was an abundance of cattle and rich agricultural produce. To achieve this, the Brahmanas provided rituals like *chaturmasya yajna*, *agnishtoma*, etc. In this way, the textual part of the Vedas had relevance to people's lives, hence their acceptance.

The performance of ritualistic actions according to the injunctions of the Brahmanas amounts to doing kratvartha, which offers an easier way to accomplish purushartha within the dictates of dharma. The elaborate Vedic rites based on sacrificial principles are called *kratu* or yajna. The action-oriented part of yajna is called *karma kanda*. It is based on the Brahmanas, and is meant for material prosperity and overall welfare.

Yajna as a concept, therefore, is ritualistic action. It should be performed to achieve purushartha within the framework of dharma. Yajna promises to take one to the righteous path. This assumes that the aspirant has: (i) a positive mental approach (resulting from the mantra chanting), (ii) an understanding of the mechanics of the rituals (vidhi), to be followed faithfully, and (iii) an understanding of the significance of the rituals (from the arthavada of the Brahmana Granthas).

The first assumption is the most important, as it gives the mind the strength to raise its potential so it can convert a 'rite' to the 'right path'. In the absence of such an approach, one would fall away from rita, make the rituals a merely mechanical process and cease being ecologically friendly. To develop a proper understanding of yajna would then amount to:

- Appreciating the ritual
- Understanding its deeper or internal form
- Visualizing the ecological aspect of the process (as a by-product).

Etymology of the term 'yajna'

The Sanskrit word 'yajna' is derived from the root verb *yaj*, which means 'to worship', 'to unite/congregate' and 'to give unconditionally *(daan)*'. The beauty of the word lies in the fact that all three meanings of 'yaj' apply to it individually as well as jointly. All action-based processes of worshipping, congregating and giving[2] are called yajna, and the gross form of yajna, which includes all three actions jointly, is also yajna. *Katyam Shrauta Sutra*, a text on sacrifice, defines yajna as: *Dravyam devata tyagah* – Sacrifice of articles for divine figures (devatas) through the sacred fire is yajna.

Swami Satyananda Saraswati has said, "Yajna has three essential aspects. The first aspect is the ritual, adorning the yajna area, invoking the higher forces through the chanting of mantras, kindling the fire and offering oblations into it. The second aspect is satsang or association with sadhus and saints. Being in the presence of truth is a vital part of yajna. The third aspect is daan, which means giving away or offering what belongs to you. The act of daan glorifies a yajna."

Universal principle of give and take

The sacrifice in an external or physical yajna is the offering of special items called *dravya* or *havi* to the devata. Pleased by the oblation, the devata is believed to reciprocate with a blessing or boon. Yajna then becomes a process of give and take, which is also the rule of life. Indeed, in everyday life most of our interactions are based on this principle.

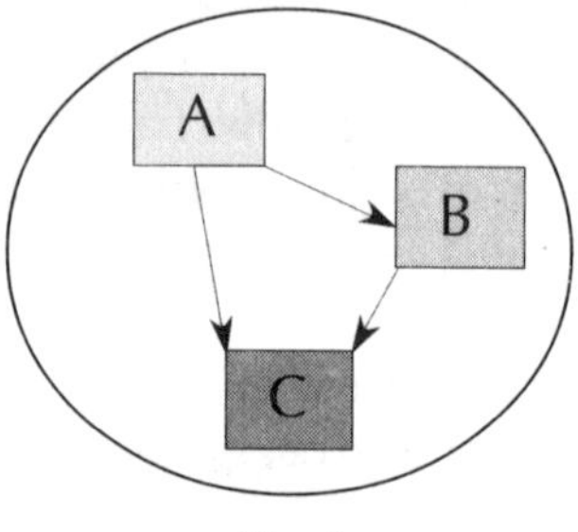

Fig. 1

Giving and taking are occurring continuously in the universe. Take the simple principle of energy transfer. Energy travels from higher to lower levels. Suppose there are three points A, B and C, at different levels – one below the other. B receives energy from A and gives it to C. A cannot receive from B nor can B from C due to their positional levels. But A will receive

[2] See Chapter 4

energy from someone who is at a higher plane, and the cycle continues. Give and take (or the GnT law) is thus a universal law, and yajna symbolizes it.

We can look at the GnT principle and yajna from another point of view. All living beings are composed of a mortal and an immortal component. To develop and sustain the mortal part (the body), the principle of 'take' is necessary, and to develop and sustain the immortal part (the soul), the principle of 'give' is required. Since the body is individual specific, it can 'take' at an individual level. However, the soul is part of the universal consciousness, and so the 'giving' must have a collective quality. What is being given, or sacrificed, also assumes various levels.

At the physical level, the sacrifice means renouncing material articles, *swahakara*. At the mental level, it amounts to giving up the right to materialistic articles acquired, *idam na mama*. At the spiritual level, it amounts to renouncing 'I-ness' with the purpose of merging into the supreme consciousness from where the soul journeys to occupy the mortal body. The individual soul and thereby the individual being can evolve following collective giving (service or seva).

Every individual should then be occupied in actions that lead to the achievement of sacrificial principles at all three levels. If one cannot achieve them fully in this lifespan, one has to take birth repeatedly until convergence takes place.

Whether or not one believes in the hypothesis of rebirth, there is not likely to be a difference of opinion on two other hypotheses: (i) everyone has aspirations, and (ii) everyone desires to achieve all that they aspire for in this lifespan. However, what is to be aspired for differs from individual to individual, and so does the yardstick for measuring achievements. So how do we strike a commonly acceptable solution?

Since yajna and the principles of Vedic dharma show: (i) what is the appropriate thing to aspire for (rita, or righteousness), (ii) how to divide our lifespan to categorize and prioritize aspirations into the four purusharthas, and (iii) how to make efforts to fulfil aspirations by following the kratvartha path in the beginning and switching over to the ritasya path at an appropriate time, it readily follows that yajna provides a common solution.

The first two points above – aspiring for righteousness and categorizing our aspirations as purusharthas – cover the aspect of knowledge or the science of life. The third gives the technique of dispensation or the art of using this knowledge. Knowledge without dispensation is futile. The greatness of yajna lies in the fact that it teaches us the science *(shastra)* of life and also enables us to deploy it through the art of living. On this account, we can broadly postulate that yajna refers to the actions of individuals as members of society, as part of a group. Sacrifice of self-interest in the legitimate and larger interest of society is also yajna. In return, benefits such as security and reciprocal help automatically come.

It is evident then that yajna as a way of life is based on two principles – sacrifice and righteousness. Both are easier to talk about than to follow. Swami Sivananda, whose life is an example of these principles, gives an easy way of practising them. His simple words represent what the Vedas too prescribed: "We are here as passing pilgrims. Our destination is God. Life is service and sacrifice. Righteousness is the rule of life. Human life is not human without virtues." (This covers the knowledge part or science of life. What follows covers the art of life.) "Have a simple, unassuming way of life. Live not to eat but eat to live. Bear no envy. Commit no slander. Speak no falsehood. Practise no deceit. Harbour no malice. You will be ever joyful, happy and peaceful. Serve, love, give, purify, meditate. All creation is an organic whole. No one is independent of that whole. Man makes himself miserable by separating himself from others. Separation is death. Unity is eternal life."

Swami Sivananda has listed the do's and don'ts for our behaviour as individuals and as members of society. They are no different from what the Vedas have said. (i) *Yajno vai shreshtha tamam karma* ("The superlative righteous karma is yajna"), (ii) *Aa no bhadra kratavo yantu vishvatah* ("Let noble thoughts come to us from the whole universe"), (iii) *Sam gacchha dhwam, sam vadad dhwam* ("May you all be united in speech and action"), and so on.

Relevance of yajna today

Why elaborate this ancient concept today? There are two arguments in support of yajna in the current age. Firstly, yajna cleanses the atmosphere, helps to restore the seasons and ecological balance. This could mean a reduction in pollution levels, adequate and timely rainfall, increased ground water levels and control over rising temperatures.

Secondly, yajna induces self-development. Righteous behaviour and sacrificial principles are the most needed attributes for creating a harmonious and benevolent society, and they appear to be dwindling away today. Sometimes, unknowingly or due to our arrogance or ignorance, we indulge in negative actions. The result is disharmony, loss of serenity and ecological damage. To correct our attitude, the philosophy of life supported by yajnic principles could be the answer. Indeed, actions speak louder than words, and righteous actions speak sweeter! The modus operandi for developing a positive attitude to life, guidelines for following harmonious principles, actions for self-purification and spiritual development are some of the things that go into the substance called yajna.

To bring the principle of yajna into our lives, we can start by practising karma yoga, the technique of selfless service. Practising the five simple maha yajnas and, if possible, undertaking to do agnihotra ritual could also be a good way to get into the yajna stream[3].

Vastness of yajna

In order to understand the scientific basis of yajna, two sections of the Vedas, the Samhitas (the mantra part) and the Brahmana

---

[3] See Chapter 11

Granthas (the procedural part) need to be studied intently. The first section deals with prayers and their chanting, which is important from the point of view of vibrational and other subtle effects on an individual and the environment. The second section deals with practical procedures and the physical act of dropping articles of oblation into the sacrificial fire. This is important from the point of view of impact on the environment.

The peculiarity of the Brahmana texts is that they have given multiple definitions of the single term 'yajna'. Some definitions from the *Shatapatha Brahmana* are:

- *Agnirvai yajna*: Agni is yajna.
- *Yajno vai Vishnu*: Vishnu is yajna.
- *Prajapateh yajna*: Prajapati is yajna.

What do such simultaneous definitions indicate? Is yajna Agni or Vishnu or Prajapati? The three definitions of yajna and many additional ones are probably (and at best) attribute-based, lop-sided expressions. They only indicate that the sway of yajna is very vast. Its size can be compared to a giant as seen by a dwarf – any definition will describe only one part of the whole body. If yajna is not studied totally, we are like the proverbial seven blind men who felt they were describing an elephant, but in reality were confined only to its individual parts. The meaning of the multiple definitions is revealed clearly when we refer to the 'partial equation theory'[4].

Yajna – foundation of life

Today, there is a growing interest in and acceptance of a particular technique from Vedic literature – yoga. Swami Sivananda presented the principles of Patanjali yoga in a rediscovered form that would be easy to practise within a stressful modern lifestyle. Swami Satyananda restructured yoga through a synthesis of hatha yoga, kriya yoga, karma yoga and bhakti yoga to give a capsule that works as a solution to life itself. Yajna is another Vedic science that

---

[4] See Chapter 4

holds great promise. In fact, it can play a pioneering role in reshaping our lives and helping us to evolve.

Vedic literature is amazingly vast in magnitude, rich in thought and astonishingly scientific in approach. It is conceded that one needs to spend a long time in contemplation and comparative study of the entire treasury of this literature as well as the various commentaries, etc. before becoming eligible to express a point of view. However, based on the study done so far, the authors would like to postulate the following with a fair measure of confidence.

✧ *If yoga has to become the way of life, yajna has to be the foundation of life.*

This is singularly due to the fact that yajna enables one to understand:

✧ *What is 'desirable',* ishta, *and how to achieve it, and what is 'undesirable',* anishta, *and how to stay away from it.*

To sum up, yajna is a means of purushartha, helping us to work for personal interests within the accepted norms of society, so that in our pursuit of happiness we do not disregard our responsibilities and duties towards society. The Vedas give this mantra of purushartha through kratvartha, ritualistic actions.

The Vedas offer the theory or science of life. The application of the theory is yajna – the art of life. What branch of knowledge can be superior to the one that gives the science of nothing less than *life* itself? And what applied art can be superior to the one that gives the art of life?

This book attempts to give an elementary exposure to yajna. In the process it tries to sort out some of the important definitions, present the philosophy and suggest its application in modern life. It also touches upon two burning problems faced by society – the vulnerability to atmospheric disorders caused by ecological imbalance, and the growing unrest in individual minds and society. It is hoped that this book will be a helpful aid for the reader who witnesses or participates in a yajna in the future.

3

Vedic Foundations of Yajna

The nomenclature 'Vedic' has been acquired by ancient Indian society, as the Vedas and Veda-based literature formed the basis of its culture, religion, behaviour, etc. This literature is the result of creations over centuries and includes all the important texts, monographs, etc. of Vedic society. Naturally, during the course of time, Vedic society did not remain static in its beliefs, values, or lifestyle. A quick look at the Vedic literature allows us to understand how the transition took place, and provides the appropriate understanding of the values of this civilization, in particular, its most important ritualistic conduct – yajna.

There are abundant articles, journals, books and Internet sites that give expansive accounts of the glory of the Vedic civilization, and describe the Aryan civilization, Vedic society, Vedic literature and the Vedas. The focus and coverage of such studies differ depending on their objective and purpose. However, we are not interested in scholarly inferences. We will simply take an overview of the literature so that we can appreciate how yajna was conceptualized, and how the concept was cultivated, developed and its benefits reaped.

We shall use four parameters – culture, civilization, religion and literature – to form an idea of the values nurtured by Vedic society. These four aspects are interrelated and interdependent, and their links provide the clues to the state of a society.

Culture

Culture is a complex word, replete with terminology. It is used frequently, but understood only broadly (and therefore vaguely). Culture is considered to be the basis of individual behaviour in diverse circumstances. *Samskriti* is its equivalent word in Sanskrit. Other words associated with samskriti are 'samskara' as a noun, samskara as a verb and 'samskrit' as an adjective. *Samskara* as a verb means rite, a process of purification of the soul. As a noun it denotes a particular rite like *upanayana* samskara (thread ceremony) or *vivaha* samskara (marriage). *Samskrit* means one who has been purified through the application of samskaras. There are many samskaras. *Vyasa Smriti* mentions sixteen samskaras to be done for the soul from its arrival in the world to its departure. *Manu Smriti*, the principal treatise defining the code of religion, mentions thirteen, and some others forty.

What do the Vedic beliefs say about the raw material – the impure soul – for these samskaras? *Purusha Sukta*, which reflects the culture of Vedic society in a subtle manner, is found in the tenth *mandal* or chapter of the *Rig Veda* (R 10,90.1–16: Rig Veda, mandal 10, sukta 90, richas 1 to 16). It puts forth the idea that a society is formed of four parts: brahmin, rajanya (kshatriya), vaishya and shudra, respectively. While explaining this in the twelfth richa, the composer rishi uses the word *ajayata*, meaning 'one who takes birth', only for the shudra aspect. It implies that the other three parts are not born; they are states of the soul, and these states are attained through samskaras. Thus, of the four parts of society (personified as 'Purusha'), only one takes birth again and again. The other three are the outcome of the process of 'culturing' on the soul.

Manu Smriti mentions that every single being, man or woman, is a shudra by birth. This is the raw material, and it is purified using samskaras. Depending on the evolution achieved, individuals attain one of the three states or varnas. Thus, every human at birth is *asamskrita* or shudra – 'non-purified'. In Vedic times, samskaras were performed to transform the 'shudra being' into a cultured one and to place them in one of the three varnas, taking into account their capacity, attitude, mentality, etc. Those who were either service-oriented or not capable of undertaking any of the three responsibilities (brahmin – pursuit of knowledge, kshatriya – protective and other productive work, vaishya – trade and commerce) were employed in service-oriented work such as general labour, agricultural labour and the like.

The process of 'culturing' was considered the second birth of an individual, who afterwards would be called *dvija* (twice-born). Clearly, categorization of an individual in Vedic society was based on their merit or nature, rather than birthright. In the course of time, the categorization started being accepted as a right descending from the profession of the father, and thereafter as a birthright. Also, the meaning of *varna* as a class of society changed to *jati* (caste) of individuals.

Samskriti as conceived in the Vedas then can be said to be an environment that was conducive for individuals to evolve to the fullest capacity of their souls.

The etymological definition of the word 'culture' augurs well for the Vedic interpretation of 'samskriti'. The English word 'culture' comes from the Latin root *colere*, which means 'to till' or 'to worship'. It is interesting that the process of tilling is embedded in the process of worship. Prayer stems from the desire to evolve. In other words, the mind is being prepared or tilled to produce positive actions. Tilling is a process whereby the potentialities of a seed are actualized. Agriculture is a process of bringing forth the tree that exists in a dormant form in a seed. If the tree blossoms, it is good agriculture. Similarly, culture can be said to include all things, big or small, which contribute towards the actualization of a sentient being's potentialities, helping them to grow to the fullest extent and be useful to society.

In the Vedas, a culture that helps its members to realize their potential is regarded as of the highest quality, and worthy of emulation by the whole universe. A notation in the *Yajur Veda* (Yaju 7.14) says:

सा प्रथमा संस्कृतिः विश्ववारा

Saa prathamaa samskritih vishvavaaraa.

Such a culture ranks topmost among all civilizations and is respected by the whole world.

Culture and civilization

Culture is very closely associated with civilization. However, the two terms are distinct and different from each other, and cannot be used interchangeably. A special aspect of a high culture can be termed 'civilization'.

If people desire to be benefited by society, it is imperative that they care equally for the benefits others receive from them. To sacrifice one's personal interests for others is the basic social rule among members of a culture that gives birth to a civilization. The evolution of a civilization is also based on the same principle. The principle, in turn, is reflected in words like *sabhya*, *sabhyata*, *sabhachara*, etc., which the river of Vedic civilization collected on the way to its convergence with the Absolute, to reach the pinnacle of its achievements.

The Vedic civilization held public servants in high regard. Even a king was supposed to be the servant of society. Cooperation and tolerance were esteemed values. Such qualities, which reflect the need for self-restraint and discrimination, point to highly developed and cultured minds. All the major parts of the Vedic civilization like agriculture, industry, language, literature, etc. reflected its faith in morality and respect for religion. Normally, culture and civilization are the two planks of evolution for a society. In Vedic society, they were the result of conscious creativity and creative action by the members of the society.

Civilization is related to the broad etiquette and style of living. Culture can be transmitted only among people possessing a similar attitude. Culture brings beauty and civilization brings utility. It can be said that civilization is a part of culture only until such time as it becomes a medium for bringing creativity to the surface and aids in the process of beautifying society. It separates from culture as soon as it aims only at utility.

The Vedic civilization was also based on the principles of spirituality and humanity. Its social scientists displayed great consideration for the animal kingdom and micro-biosphere. Even the inanimate was respected. Naturally, they were highly concerned about ecology. Their prayers included the desire to have peace in the universe, the botanical world, the mental sphere and even the medicinal world.

Culture gives rise to self-improvement. A 'society' is a place where people cooperate with each other and sacrifice self-interest for the benefit of others. In a healthy society the common objective is the welfare of everyone. Where there is no trace of cooperation, it is not a society but merely a group of people. Animals come together instinctively and for safety. Human beings form a society for development and evolution. This point is abundantly demonstrated in the Vedic culture, which is indestructible, as it implements the law of give and take through deliberate practice.

The principal mantra giving strength to this is from the *Rig Veda* (R 10.191.2):

सं गच्छध्वं सं वदध्वं सं वो मनांसि जानताम् ।
देवा भागं यथा पूर्वे संजानाना उपासते ॥

Sam gacchadhvam, sam vadadhvam, sam vo manamsi jaanataam,
Devaa bhaagam yathaa poorve samjaanaanaa upaasate.

Just as your ancestors were unanimous in thought and action, you too be of one mind, thought and speech, and evolve together with society.

This prayer aims at diffusing differences among group members, and promoting unity and interpersonal love. To be united means to live together, compromising with differences in thought, but to be unanimous means there is no difference in thought or action (everybody in the group thinks in exactly the same way about the solution to a problem). The Vedic society displayed such fundamentally strong principles. The feeling behind the desire for unanimity in thought, speech and action gave birth to such a healthy and positive culture that it could absorb all the tribes and foreign invaders, and achieve a unique and special state of evolution called the 'Vedic culture'.

Culture and religion

The basis of the culture of a society is a set of supporting principles. Religion can provides this support to the human race. In the Vedic tradition, religion was not restricted to a narrow set of precepts. Vedic dharma referred to the sense of righteousness inherent in the personality. When we act with this awareness, we follow the dharma of humanity – manava dharma or sanatana dharma. Therefore, the *Mahabharata* describes dharma as a code of conduct that holds society together, and at the same time cautions that the basis of dharma is utterly complex, deep and secret – *Dharmasya tatvam nihitam guhaayam.*

Manu Smriti has identified four fundamental pillars of dharma in the context of Vedic society: (i) recommendations of the Vedas, (ii) commandments of the Smritis for individual behaviour with respect to interactions with others, (iii) righteous behaviour, and (iv) fulfilment of desires through the use of discrimination *(viveka)*.

It can be seen that these principles are fundamental to civilizations and culture. They hold good even today. Swami Niranjanananda Saraswati emphasizes that individual dharma boils down to three interdependent and interrelated qualities – *sat vichara* (positive thinking), *sat karma* (righteous action) and *sat vyavahara* (balanced behaviour). A person's behaviour reflects their thought process. A thought *(vichara)* originates in the mind *(chitta)*. The analytical faculty of the mind, intellect *(buddhi)*, vets it, and on receiving internal approval, it is translated into action *(karma)*. When action bccomes part of one's natural behaviour, it is called *vyavahara*.

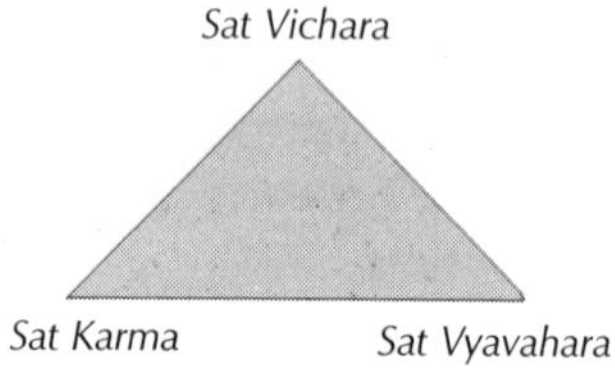

Fig. 2

To avoid duality between thought and action, the prefix *sat*, meaning true or positive, ensures there is harmony in manifestations of the head, heart and hands. In other words, Swami Niranjanananda has simplified the presentation of an old concept to make it easy to understand and (still) easier to practise. This principle is being practised at the Bihar School of Yoga and is also in line with the principles of the Vedic society.

A corollary of this definition is that every positive action results in purifying one's thought and progressively develops discrimination (between desirable 'good' and avoidable 'evil') and dispassion (non-attachment or non-I-ness), thus taking one a step forward in the process of evolution. In other words, Vedic dharma makes one positive and proactive.

Clearly, Vedic dharma is an individual's personal issue. Its aim is to help one to raise the spiritual level of the soul, thereby liberating one from the shackles of worldly attachments. At the same time, it helps to build a cooperative, positive and loving society that is in harmony with the universe and God.

At this juncture, it is appropriate to look at some important tenets of Vedic society. The first and foremost is that dharma has an eternal characteristic *(sanatana)*. Other important beliefs are:

- Law of karma
- Soul as a manifestation of the universal consciousness in all living beings
- Periodic incarnation of god
- Multiple forms of god (function based)
- Journey of the soul through innumerable species
- Rebirth of a human being
- A four-tiered structure of society based on the four varnas, divided on the basis of qualities and capabilities
- Rita or righteous behaviour
- Religion as an individual's personal issue, and full freedom to choose the path found suitable to reach the supreme
- Belief in a divine power and its hand in every universal event
- Guna, karmic division of human nature, and so on.

Culture and literature

Literature is the collective treasure of the wealth called knowledge. The Vedas, Puranas, Ramayana, Mahabharata, etc. are the jewels of Vedic society. They were held intact even in the absence of paper or other means of documentation, only through a process of recitation. So that they did not become vitiated, ingenious methods were invented, known as the *ashta vikriti* or eight systems of recitation. If the texts had not been safeguarded in this manner, any inference about the form and body of Vedic culture would be impossible.

Culture transforms with time, but literature, being a snapshot, remains unaltered. It is literature alone that can reflect a culture. It is the mirror of a culture, depicting not only its external features but also reflecting its internal beauty – through the feelings and sensibilities contained within the texts. As a result, when a society takes a look at itself in the mirror called 'old scriptures', it sees its total personality. In addition, literature is also the guide for a society, directing its progress along the right track. Culture looks to literature as the means of progress, social and spiritual, and as its spokesperson. Vedic culture too is exhibited through its literature, which is very rich both qualitatively and quantitatively.

Below is a bird's eye view of the different texts that fall under 'Vedic literature'. It is also customary to include the *Bhagavad Gita* and *Brahma Sutra Bhashya* of Adi Shankara under Vedic literature. The trio of Upanishads, *Bhagavad Gita* and *Brahma Sutra Bhashya* is known as *Prasthan Trayee*, a journey from *shreyas* (material way) to *preyas* (spiritual way).

Table 1: Vedic literature at a glance

Vedas (4)	Rig Veda, Yajur Veda, Sama Veda, Atharva Veda
Vedangas (6) (Shat Shastras)	Shiksha, Kalpa, Vyakarana, Nirukta, Chandas, Jyotish
Upavedas (4)	Ayur Veda, Dhanur Veda, Gandharva Veda, Artha Veda
Upanga (2)	Puranas (18 main), Dharma Shastra Smriti (22), Itihasa – Ramayana, Mahabharata
Vedic Darshan (6)	Nyaya, Vaisheshika, Poorva Mimamsa, Uttara Mimamsa, Samkhya, Yoga
Non-Vedic Darshan (3)	Charvaka, Baudha, Jain

PLINTH OF THE STRUCTURE OF YAJNA

The extent of Vedic literature is vast. Let us look at the parts that are relevant to yajna. We begin with the meaning of the word 'ved' or 'veda'.

The Vedas collectively (Veda vidya): Etymologically, the word *veda* has many synonyms: wealth, treasure, knowledge, etc. The most appropriate meaning, however, is 'knowledge'. With the passage of time, the term acquired a certain shade of meaning – 'sacred knowledge', and thereafter – 'knowledge about religion'. However, unlike the Koran, the holy scripture of the Muslims, the Vedas are not a single book, neither are they a monograph like the

Bible, nor a collection of books like the *Tripitak* of the Buddhists. Then what are they?

The Vedas are a library, but not one that is merely a collection of *all kinds* of books. They are the storehouse of the knowledge that leads to wisdom. 'Veda' is a generic term for the treasury of knowledge that was built over many centuries and passed on – intact – from generation to generation by word of mouth *(shruti parampara)*. In this faithful transmission, however, possibly at some point of time, the memory of the origins of the knowledge was lost, and subsequent generations developed a belief that the Vedas are eternal, immortal, beyond human creation, etc.

The Vedas are not a collection of codes of conduct or dictates of religion accepted by society after due deliberation in meetings of social scientists and the wise. They have been handed down more as an ancient tradition. That the Vedas are sacred books and worthy of worship has probably come to be the faith due to the wisdom they contain and the reverence that the elders of each generation displayed towards them.

Most Indians, understandably proud of their rich heritage, believe that the Vedas have no beginning, no end, and required no human touch in their creation, i.e. they are *apaurusheya*. Just as Jews and Christians believe that the writing in the Bible is sacred and has come from Him, Indians believe that the Vedas have originated directly from Him. They existed eternally in space, and the seers and visionaries (rishis), in their superior state of consciousness, saw them vividly. It was their darshan.

A form that takes shape in front of the internal visionary organs and thus becomes 'visible' is *darshan*. This darshan could be of a specific subject or an overwhelming, all encompassing principle, like Vedanta darshan, yoga darshan or darshan of the existence of the omniscient power that controls everything (*Tat Twam Asi* – Thou art That). By this definition, the knowledge that dawned upon Buddha was a darshan (Buddha darshan). Similarly, there could be various darshans like Gandhi darshan (of non-violence), Nanak darshan of unity (*Tu hi ek nirankara* – Thou art the only one; or *Sat sri akala* – Truth is beyond time). One can even stretch this link further to add Newton's gravity darshan, Rutherford's atomic darshan, Einstein's relativity darshan, Bill Gates' DNA (Digital Network Architecture) darshan, and so on.

Parts of the Vedas: The Vedas consist of four types of scriptures. Each type is composed of separate (but not independent) monographs called *granthas*. Some are available, but many have been permanently lost. Each Veda is comprised of four parts: (i) Samhita, (ii) Brahmana, (iii) Aranyaka, and (iv) Upanishad.

Samhita means a collection of suktas (a *sukta* is a verse consisting of hymns called richas. A richa is authored by a rishi, is in praise of a devata, and has a metre). A Samhita contains hymns, prayers in praise of devatas, poetic mantras, suktas seeking blessings, prayers for the remedy of evils, etc.

Brahmanas are voluminous texts describing the rules, injunctions, procedures and their dispensation in the yajnic processes, as well as the materials to be used, and the spiritual importance of season-based rituals and karmas.

Aranyakas contain thoughts about the relation of man with this world and God, expressed by the wise (senior citizens who would renounce the material world and go into seclusion). Here, the emphasis is on concentrating on the internal aspects of the yajna process.

Upanishads contain the oldest philosophy. Since they are the culmination of Vedic principles, Upanishads are also known as 'Vedanta' (culmination of the Vedas).

The Vedics believed that He could be approached through humble prayers for prosperity. They also believed in rebirth, going to heaven or hell after death – in other words, in the existence of another world. Their prayers sought happiness here as well as in the other world.

The Vedas contain prayers and poems in praise of various forms of God. However, their uniqueness lies not in their poetic form but in perhaps two other aspects: (i) the deeper and hidden meanings of the mantras and suktas of the Veda

Samhitas, in particular the *Rig Veda*, and (ii) the purpose for which the devatas were requested to shower grace. Elevated thinking and wisdom are revealed in the reflections on material and heavenly happiness, and the theories postulated on the origin and formation of the universe show the depth of their quest for knowledge.

What are the Vedas? If the Vedas are equated with a library, which collection of books are called the Vedas? The Vedas should be understood through their definition, characteristics and subject.

धर्म ब्रह्म प्रतिपादकम्, अनादि, अपौरुषेय, प्रमाणं वाक्यम् वेदः ।

Dharma Brahma pratipaadakam, anaadi, apaurusheya, pramaanam vaakyam vedaha.

That which gives a base to both dharma and knowledge of super-consciousness (Brahma), whose beginning and end are beyond visible limits and have manifested directly from Him, and which is the authority of real knowledge, is called Veda.

The characteristics of the Vedas are described in the following sloka:

इष्ट प्राप्त्यनिष्ट परिहारयोः अलौकिकमुपायम् यो ग्रंथः वेदयति स वेदः ।

Ishta praaptyanishta parihaarayoh, aloukikamupaayam, yo granthah vedayati sa vedah.

It gives supernatural ways and the means of disposing of the undesirable and achieving what is most desirable.

The Vedas are composed of richas.

मंत्र ब्राह्मणयो : वेद नामध्येयम् ।

Mantra braahmanayoh veda naamadhyeyam.

The Vedas contain hymns or powerful poetic expressions in praise of the divine, and dispensation techniques for yajna.

When the richas are sung following prescribed procedures, they become mantras. The mantras and Brahmanas together form the Vedas. Thus, the Vedas describe actions and dharma defines the domain of actions. It provides a direction to actions and norms for variations within permissible limits. We have already seen that dharma means being established in rita (righteous behaviour), and that kratvartha (ritualistic action) leads to it. Yajna is the recipe for kratvartha. In this way, the Vedas are related to yajna. This also proves the point that the Veda Samhitas are made for yajna: *Vedaa hi yajnaartham abhipravrittaha.*

Why study the Vedas? The answer is found in the Upanishadic part of the Vedas. A seeker asked a learned person what it is that, when studied, leaves nothing further to be studied? The answer was *para vidya,* knowledge that enlarged one's wisdom to the level of ultimate truth. The Vedas contain knowledge of both para vidya and apara vidya, and that is why they should be studied.

In order to get the full benefit from the Vedas, a good understanding of their content has to be developed. However, Vedic culture cannot be appreciated through mere intellectual study, because a deeper, intrinsic and perpetual meaning is embedded in the mantras and suktas. They may seem like mere prayers, but once a spiritual approach is incorporated, the underlying philosophy of life, the glory of the universal truth and the convergence of individual consciousness with universal consciousness starts appearing in front of the researcher's contemplative eyes. Such projections reveal the glory of the Vedas. Intellectual exercise starts to take a back seat and revelation takes over. Yogi Aurobindo discovered this, not by a scholarly study of the Vedic mantras, but through inner vision. He was a seer like those who visualized the mantras.

According to Prof. S. K. Ramachandra Rao[1], "Veda has a secret meaning, which alone is of ultimate and real value.

[1] *Internal Yajna,* S.K. Ramachandra Rao, Kalpataru Research Academy, Bangalore, 2002

As against this import, there is the external meaning, the apparent one. It consists of mere grammatical meaning reflected by words, which is conventional and transactional in nature. The latter is meant for the common folk, to help them in their religious aspirations, while the former is deliberately concealed, intended to guide the advanced aspirants. Veda employs this double language method, because there are distinct approaches prevalent among human beings: one that relies on the senses, employs reason and holds intellect in high regard; the other that depends on revelation and inspiration, and employs intuition and insight. The two approaches may be designated 'practical' and 'spiritual'."

That every richa of the Vedas contains such a hidden treasure is declared in the Vedas themselves (R 1,164.39):

ऋचो अक्षरे परमे व्योमन् ।

Richo akshare parame vyoman.

The words of the richas contain the divine powers responsible for driving the universe and are also the cause of its being.

Subjects of the Vedas: The three principal subjects of the Vedas are 'karma', 'upasana' and 'dnyana': *vedashcha karmopasana gyana pratipadakah*. All three words have specific meanings, which are different from their colloquial meanings.

Karma: *Tatra dev-dravyobhayasadhyo yagadih karma*. Here, karma does not mean actions driven by the sensory organs or actions relating to daily routine, but that which the Vedas expect. The Vedas expect a person to perform yajna for the attainment of God as well as for material benefits. They are described in the Vedas. Therefore, Vedic karma means shrauta yajna (based on injunctions from Shruti).

Upasana: *Brahma jivayorupasakatva drishtirupasana*. This is the effort to understand the relationship between Brahman and the individual soul. First is the object *(upasya)* and second the subject *(upasaka)*. The feeling that expresses the relationship between Shiva and jiva as master and servant is known as upasana.

Dnyana (also written as gyana or jnana): *Jiva Brahmanora-bheda evatra dnyanam*. To realize the congruence of jiva with Shiva is knowledge or dnyana.

The above three definitions point out that the principal subject of the Vedas is knowledge about the secret of life. It can be achieved through karma, upasana and dnyana. This, however, does not mean that the Vedas do not contain knowledge of material sciences or about the creation of this universe. There are ample references to both but in connection with some other principal subject, which only means that they are not the main subjects of the Vedas.

Manu Smriti also mentions that the Vedas were formed from agni, vayu and akasha for the purpose of yajna. *Purusha Sukta* mentions that the Vedas are the outcome of the cosmic yajna performed by the devas, through which developed the Vedas, religion and civilization.

Original form of the Vedas: When knowledge unfolded in the inner vision of the rishis, their experiences were given an expression through hymns called mantras, which constituted the Vedas. Initially, there was only one Veda, which contained four types of hymns – *rig, yajus, sama* and *atharva* mantras. All these types were intermixed and the whole conglomeration was used in yajna. This is how it was at the beginning of Satya yuga and it continued to be the same throughout Dwapara yuga[2].

Towards the end of Dwapara yuga, however, a change in the Vedas became inevitable, as the lifespan decreased, and the lifestyle and mindset changed. Pursuing learning and

---

[2] According to Hindu mythology, the age of the world, i.e. the time span between creation and dissolution, is divided into four periods, each called a *yuga*. The first period or yuga is Satya yuga, the second Treta yuga (Lord Rama belongs to this period), the third Dwapara yuga (Lord Krishna belongs to this period), and the fourth Kali yuga (of which the modern period is a part).

practising the Vedas and their use in yajna was becoming progressively difficult. A situation arose wherein the existence of the Vedas came into doubt. Destruction of the Vedas was feared, which would mean the collapse of the yajna system and the eventual end of the civilization.

In order for the yajna system to continue smoothly, sage Krishna Dvaipayana Vyasa undertook the work of sifting through the heap of mantras to separate them into orderly compilations. The work started about a century prior to the famous Mahabharata war and continued for almost fifty years. The Vedas available today in the form of orderly Samhitas, which we know as the *Rig Veda*, *Yajur Veda*, *Sama Veda* and *Atharva Veda*, are the outcome of the herculean efforts of Vyasa, his four disciples Paila, Vaishampayana, Sumantu and Jaimini, and their followers[3].The stupendous work put in by Vyasa was acknowledged by addressing him as Veda Vyasa. Krishna Dvaipayana was an acknowledged rishi and a highly respected figure of the time. That such a personality should have taken the lead in saving yajna speaks of the importance Vedic society attached to the yajnic process. Therefore, once again, it is not unrealistic to call yajna the way of life of Vedic society, and the Vedas the guide.

Origin of the Vedas: The Vedas have attracted scholars and researchers in all ages, and they have attempted to unearth the import of the verses and the origin of the Vedic people. There have been both passionate and impartial approaches to the studies. Unfortunately, they have given rise to widely divergent views on the origin of the Vedas and the Vedic people.

The teachings of the Vedas and Vedic culture are continuous, ruling the lives of people everywhere in India, indicating that the Vedas have taken firm root over the centuries. When exactly the Vedas manifested is a matter of historic interest. For the purpose of understanding yajna as

---

[3] For details of this history see Chapter 12 of the *Srimad Bhagavatam*.

a theme of life, it suffices to say that the Vedas are ancient enough to be the driving force of material and spiritual life in India[4].

The Vedas individually

Rig Veda: When the Vedas were given an orderly form, all the rig mantras were compiled into a single Samhita called the *Rig Veda Samhita*. The mantras and suktas are in adoration of devatas. Different rishis visualized different parts of the 'knowledge'. Such parts were considered to be under the control of different devatas, so the suktas are dedicated to different devatas. The external form of each sukta is the same: it is authored by a rishi, is in praise of a devata and has a metre. But the subjects covered are varied.

The *Rig Veda* is voluminous in terms of mantras/suktas, and expansive in coverage. The total number of mantras is close to 10,500. Rig mantras are used in physical or dravya yajnas. A group of priests called *hotri* who specialize in chanting the mantras must pick out different mantras/suktas, depending on the purpose of the yajna, the sankalpa of the yajamana (the host or sacrificer), the devata to be invoked, etc. Therefore, yajna-specific workbooks have been compiled for easy dispensation of the mantras during the yajnic processes.

Yajur Veda: The process of yajna is very complex in terms of procedures and processes. Descriptions of these processes and details of the procedures are given in the *Yajur Veda Samhita*. Perhaps for this reason, unlike the *Rig Veda*, the structure of the *Yajur Veda* is not hymnal. The mantras of the *Yajur Veda* are in prose form, and are called *yajus*. A group of priests called *adhvaryu* uses the procedures given in this Veda to proceed with the actual physical actions of dropping the oblationary materials into the sacrificial fire and other related activities. Interestingly, the method adopted by the *Yajur Veda* to explain the significance of the steps of

---

[4] A short note on this subject is given in Annexure 2. More serious readers may refer to the original works of scholars.

the yajnic processes is highly spiritual in nature. The Veda clarifies that Brahman has arrived in this world in the form of a human body for a specific purpose. It takes the form of a soul in the body. The soul has brought with it all the devatas, and they have positioned themselves in various parts of the human body. As such, while a person is quite capable of performing any activity, he should realize that the body is a temple of devatas and therefore choose to perform only righteous acts following sacrificial principles. The acts should maintain the purity of the body temple. In other words, a person should perform yajnas. In fact, the *Yajur Veda* says that everyone should be a *shata kratu,* a person who has performed a hundred yajnas in the active span of their lifetime. It assures that by doing so, one will rise spiritually and attain Brahman in the current life itself. All types of yajna find a detailed explanation in the *Yajur Veda*.

Sama Veda: This Veda contains mantras, called sama mantras, which are to be sung (not chanted) in praise of devatas. A group of priests of shrauta yajna (yajnas based on injunctions), known as udgatri, specialize in singing the sama mantras. They sing the sama mantras to praise the devatas invoked by the hotri group and in whose honour the adhvaryu group offers oblations in the sacred fire.

Atharva Veda: This Veda contains two types of mantras called *atharvan* and *angiras* mantras. Atharvan mantras are used in shrauta yajna. A priest called brahma uses the mantras in discharging his duties in a shrauta yajna. This Veda also contains information useful in the yogic sciences[5].

Usage of the word 'brahman': The Sanskrit word 'brahman' is used in the masculine as well as neuter gender. When it is used to denote a person, the gender is masculine (here, brahman or brahmin means the one who devotes his life to the study of the ultimate truth – the Brahman). When these words are used in English, a little ambiguity arises due to similar spellings. To avoid this, we have used the following spellings:

[5] Information on the Vedas other than yajna is given in Annexure 1.

- 'Brahmana' to mean the Brahmana text – Brahmana Grantha.
- 'Brahmin' to mean a person who knows the details of yajnic procedures and performs yajna karma – brahmin manushya.
- 'Brahman' to mean the ultimate truth – Brahman.
- Brahma, one of the priests in shrauta yajna, and also Brahma the Creator.

Brahmana Granthas: We have seen that each Veda treatise is comprised of four parts: Mantra Samhita, Brahmana text, Aranyaka and Upanishad. So each Veda has its own Brahmana text. The Brahmana of the *Rig Veda* gives details of the use of mantras for invoking Vedic devatas. The *Yajur Veda*, being the Veda that elaborates the yajnic processes and procedures, its Brahmana speaks of the ritualistic details to be followed by the adhvaryu group of priests. The Brahmana of the *Sama Veda* is about worship of Vedic devatas through the singing of Sama suktas.

These granthas are subdivided into three parts: (i) injunctions for yajna, (ii) procedures performed in yajna, and (iii) significance and meanings of the rituals performed in yajna. To support the third part, stories in the form of *akhyan* (praise), historical information and importance *(gatha)* are included in these texts.

Aranyaka: After the Brahmana Granthas, the next part of the Vedas is Aranyaka. The Brahmana portion starts where the mantra portion ends. The Brahmana Granthas in turn usher in the Aranyakas. Dravya (physical) yajna as kratvartha or ritualistic action to help in achieving the purusharthas is discussed and described in the main part of the Brahmana treatises. At their end are found appendixes covering the aspects of the yajnic process beyond the physical or external level, i.e. the internal aspect of yajna, and the general philosophy of life. They are the Aranyakas.

After having lived that part of life where one enjoys the fruits and worldly benefits of kratvartha (performing yajna, yagas, etc.), the Vedics would take up the third phase of life

– *vanaprastha ashrama*. Secluded places such as forests away from civil habitation would provide an environment conducive to contemplative life. After discharging the responsibilities towards family and society as householders, they would hand over the reins of family affairs to the next generation and move to an isolated place. Here, time would be spent in understanding the nature, essence and philosophy of yajna. Having performed yajnas throughout their lives, the Vedics were well-conversant with their effects. Now, the yajnic process would be studied in an introverted state for its subtle impressions on the mind and soul. The secrets of yajna were also studied. The knowledge gained in this manner was documented in the Aranyaka textbooks.

Like the Samhitas and Brahmanas, there should also have been 1130 Aranyakas, but today only seven are available. Aranyaka granthas are mostly written in prose form, but they are filled with poetic beauty. The sentences are short and worded well with a distinct lyrical quality.

In the Aranyakas, *karma kanda* (physical processes) is transformed into subtle activities at the mental level. Yajna is the creator and controller of the whole universe. The world is established in yajna. Yajna yields heavenly pleasure on earth and a place in heaven after death. But heaven is not an eternal state, and can come to an end. Therefore, yajna done for the self or for a specific personal desire is of less importance than yajna done with a selfless desire. This would imply that the path of knowledge *(gyana marga)* is superior to the path of action *(karma marga)* to attain the state of Brahman. Aranyakas are treatises that give the meaning and spiritual significance of all the technical and other terms in the physical or external yajnic process.

Upanishads: The Vedic concept of yajna originates in the Samhitas. It is developed through ritualistic processes in the Brahmanas. This leads to the introverted activity of understanding the inner form in the Aranyakas. The Upanishads also provide the spiritual significance of yajna. Aranyakas are the base from where Upanishadic development starts. The final parts of the Aranyakas deal with subjects that are commonly covered in gyana marga. These are called Upanishads.

The Upanishads deal with subjects relating to soul, atman, jivatma, Brahman, etc. They are highly philosophical, but have great relevance to human life and the approach to it. Due to the significance and importance of the subject matter, the Upanishads are popularly called *Vedanta* – 'culmination of the essence of the Vedas'. Indeed, if yajna is equated with a beautiful lotus, then the mantras form the stem, the Brahmanas its structure and the Aranyakas the petals. And the Upanishads are its charm, beauty and fragrance.

The Aranyaka texts created an interest in the quest for knowledge among the younger generations of Vedic times. Some of these aspirants would visit the woods where the wise elders were residing. Discussions-cum-lectures would then take place between the knower and the aspirant – guru and disciple. Such sessions resulted in the development of a philosophically deep subject – *Brahma Gyana,* knowledge of Brahman. The discussions would be question and answer sessions, like a satsang. Upanishadic literature is mostly in the question and answer format, unlike other theoretical treatises. Upanishads such as *Prashnopanishad* and *Kenopanishad* use this format overtly, although this form is not directly apparent in other Upanishads like *Ishavasya*, *Katha* or *Mundaka*. However, their inherent form is the same. A glance reveals that the text is recorded in the form of an answer by a guru to an assumed or implied question from a seeker. Multiple answers to a single question ratify the question and answer style.

During satsangs, the rishis (also called *mantra drashtrah*, meaning 'seers of mantras') revealed the knowledge they experienced in their inner visions. They had minute and complete knowledge of the procedures and rites of yajna. They also had first-hand experience of the changes occurring in the state of mind as a result of performing a series of yajnas and remaining in a yajnic environment. Therefore, during the stages of transformation of the yajnic process from the physical to the mental level, they discovered, for example, that the ritual of animal sacrifice in advanced soma yajnas was nothing but a symbol of sacrificing the baser tendencies of the human mind.

In order to understand and adopt many such revelations and discoveries, they had an ever-ready audience in the form of a modest, gracious and credulous group of followers. This points to the aptness of the term 'upanishad' ascribed to these discussions. A small exercise in Sanskrit grammar will clarify this. *Upa* is a prefix meaning 'without' or 'intervention'. *Ni* means 'total' or 'complete'. *Sad* is a root which means 'to destroy', 'to acquire' or 'to exhaust'. Therefore, Upanishad would mean that branch of knowledge (Brahma Vidya) which:

- destroys worldly karmas that create negative effects or undesirable outcome.
- loosens the shackles of ignorance
- enables the acquisition of true knowledge (Brahma Gyana).

In other words, the word 'upanishad' is formed by weaving together all the three shades of meaning of the root 'sad'.

To sum up, Samhitas, Brahmana texts, Aranyakas and Upanishads are all relevant to yajna. The *Rig Veda* gives the mantras to be used in a yajna. Therefore, the Brahmana texts related to it give details of how to employ these mantras in various yajnas. Similarly, the *Yajur Veda* gives the dispensation techniques of yajna, and, therefore, its Brahmana texts give dispensation techniques. Aranyakas and Upanishads are useful for internalization of the physical yajnic processes for spiritual evolution.

Vedangas: As we have seen, the Vedas are a collection of a huge number of mantras, yajus, etc., beneath which is embedded information on various subjects. In order to properly understand the mantras and to correctly interpret them, six faculties of the arts and science have been developed, known as Vedangas: *Shiksha*, *Kalpa*, *Vyakarana*, *Nirukta*, *Chandas* and *Jyotish*. Their knowledge enables one to correctly interpret the Vedas for spiritual development in general and yajna in particular.

Shiksha is the science of phonetics. It helps in the proper and exact pronunciation of consonants, vowels and their combinations in richas and mantras. Chandas explains how to bind richas and mantras into metre, and describes the details of various metres (chandas), for example, the famous Gayatri chanda. Vyakarana and Nirukta deal with the grammatical aspect, and Jyotish deals with astronomical aspects, the almanac, auspicious times, etc. Kalpa contains the procedures, injunctions and rules, given in a cryptic but unambiguous way, and has four parts – *Shrauta Sutras,* giving details of shrauta samskaras, *Shulba Sutras,* giving the mechanics of yajna, *Grihya Sutras,* giving the samskaras required for householders, and *Dharma Sutras,* giving details of the codes of conduct, duties, etc. for members of society.

All Vedangas are very important from the point of view of yajna. Their deep knowledge and mastery over the dispensation techniques are essential for the priests and the host of a yajna. It is said that fructification of the host's sankalpa, the outcome of yajna and other accruable benefits all depend on the extent of exactitude displayed by all the participants of a yajna. Therefore, great emphasis is given on learning the Vedas, chanting of mantras and carrying out procedural details.

Puranas: A very extensive and verbose explanation of the contents and teachings of the Vedas is given in this part of Vedic literature. The Puranas took knowledge from the Vedas to the average person in novel ways. They give historical accounts of various dynasties of Vedic times, and also introduce bhakti as a new and easier method of self-evolution. They made the performance of yajna a much easier and less cumbersome activity. Yajnas based on Puranas are popularly known as smarta yajnas (based on the injunctions of the Smritis)[6].

---

[6] Details discussed in Chapter 8

SUPPORTIVE ARTICLES OF THE YAJNA STRUCTURE

Mantras

'Mantra' has been defined in the description of the internal structure of the *Rig Veda*. It is an important supportive ingredient of the yajna structure. Mantras are found in all four Veda Samhitas. Rig mantras are found in the *Rig Veda Samhita*, yajus mantras in the *Yajur Veda Samhita*, sama mantras in the *Sama Veda Samhita*, and atharva mantras (called 'atharve') in the *Atharva Veda Samhita*. The details of the structure of sukta, mantra, etc., the way of using them and their benefits *(phala)* are given in a small text called the *Rigvidhana*.

In order to use mantras during the various processes of yajna, they are sometimes reorganized to enable proper chanting. It is likely that the same mantra will be chanted differently by the hotri, adhvaryu or other groups of priests. Their way of chanting and positioning, along with the actions of the adhvaryu and others, are written down by the priests who perform the yajna. Such books, known as *Prayoga*, are practical guides for priests to carry out a yajna according to the prescriptions of the Brahmana Granthas, Kalpa Sutras, etc. Prayoga books are like notes jotted down by a lecturer to enable him to develop the subject while lecturing, and hence there is no standard method of preparing them.

Devatas

Devatas are the cause of the mantras. Hence, from the point of view of yajna, they are even more important than the mantras. We have seen that every sukta of the Veda Samhitas is aimed at offering prayers and adoration to devata(s) by referring to their qualities. However, the origin of the concept of devata, its definition, qualities, classifications, etc. are not found in any of the Veda Samhitas or Brahmanas.

Vedic devatas are defined and described in the treatise *Brihad Devata*, written by Rishi Shaunaka. The set of devatas adored in a shrauta yajna is a subset of the 'brihad devata' (*brihad* means 'very large' or 'total'). The devatas worshipped in smarta yajnas are described mostly in the Puranas. Although the Puranas describe Vedic devatas too, the authentic descriptions of devatas for a yajna is taken only from *Brihad Devata*.

According to A. A. Macdonell[7] (who has translated *Brihad Devata* into English), the Vedic concept of devata has far too many overlapping qualities and a lack of individuality. This is so mainly because most devatas represent some part of the natural phenomenon (all possess the quality of munificence). With the passage of time, human qualities were also added to their description.

According to the Vedic concept, gods were born and reborn, implying that in between they also died. Qualities such as immortality, supremacy, kindness, the ability to use and exhibit occasional discretion in behaviour, etc. were ascribed to them at a later date. And this changed the quality of the prayers too. But for the Vedics, the devatas had a universal character.

Vedic gods have high moral values, which explains why they are adored as the principal entities responsible for the welfare of the universe. The praises and oblations to them are possibly symbolic. In mathematics, there is a concept of the complex variable, which refers to the combination of two parts, the real variable and the imaginary component. The addition of the imaginary component makes up for the unknown quantity, which when added to the real value makes the actual value of a variable. If X is the quantity of ozone required for the proper balance of the atmosphere and the actual value, and for whatever reason it has eroded to x, then the addition of an imaginary value '*iy*' could restore x to X ($X = x+iy$, i being the imaginary component, x and y being real values). The yajna process could be considered as a means of enriching y (through oblations, sound energy, etc.)

---

[7] *Vedic Mythology*, A. A. Macdonnel, trans. by R.K. Rai, Chaukhamba Vidya Bhavan, Varanasi, 1963

to reach the value X, thus resetting the dynamic equilibrium. This analogy points to the possibility of viewing the prayers and oblation processes from a different angle, which may appeal to intellectual reasoning. It is said that Vedic devatas receive their share of food through *bhautic* (external) yajna. Due to the oblations offered in dravya yajna, the 'iy' component in the equation (X=x+iy) is adjusted, and the devatas are pleased because they get their food.

According to *Brihad Devata*, Vedic gods are of many types. Some of the important classifications are *divya devata* (celestial entities like the Sun), *antariksha devata* (Indra, for example), *parthiv devata* (related to the earth, rivers, for example), *amurta devata* (formless, conceptual ones like Aditi), etc.

A good understanding of the concept, form and character of the devatas helps one to appreciate the concept of yajna karma, the relevance of the prayers to devatas, and the offerings made to them through the medium of Agni. Supplementary parts of Vedic literature like *Brihad Devata*, *Sarvanukramani*, etc. provide an adequate understanding of the basics of the concept of devata.

In addition to Vedic and Puranic devatas, there are other types such as 'protective' devatas and tantric devatas. Protective devatas are invoked at the beginning of any Brahma karma to protect the venue and participants from all evils. Ganapati (the chief of the Ganas), Vastoshpati (the deity of the house), and dhvaja devata are examples of protective devatas. Tantric devatas are significant in the rituals of tantra shastra.

Dravya

A physical or external yajna is not complete without offering oblations to the yajna devata. Some articles like *ajya* (clarified cow's butter), milk (from cows and sheep) and curd made from cow's milk are common to all yajnas. In addition, herbs, leaves, small sticks from the dried branches of special trees *(samidha)*, rice cakes *(purodasha)* and special grains (*vrihi*, *yava*, etc.) are also used as items of oblation. The type of samidha and herbs used depends on the type of yajna. The details of these herbs and plants are generally found in the Brahmana Granthas and Kalpa Sutras.

IN CONCLUSION

We have taken a broad overview of the parts of Vedic literature that have a bearing on the concept of yajna, the origin of physical yajna and yajnic procedures. The encyclopaedia Vedica would include parts of Vedic literature such as Smriti, Darshan, Itihasa, Upaveda, etc. These are important in their own respect, but as they do not have a direct bearing on the concept of yajna, they are not covered here. Interested readers may refer to the original texts or commentaries. It also devolves from the above exposition that yajna is at the centre of the Vedas, the Veda Samhitas are formulated for yajna, and yajna is a means of remaining on the right path to lead a purposeful life. To sum up:

- Yajna is a concept from the Vedas. Its foundation consists of the beliefs, culture, code of conduct and philosophy of Vedic society, which can be understood through the Vedic literature.
- We have taken an overview of the parts of Vedic literature that have a bearing on the concept of yajna.
- Vedic literature consists mainly of four Vedas, six Vedangas, two Upavedas, two Upangas (Smriti, Puranas, etc.) and six Darshans.
- The structure of the four Vedas is the same: Samhita, Brahmana, Aranyaka and Upanishad.
- Vedangas were developed to understand the contents of the Vedas and to chant the mantras properly.
- In a yajna,
  - mantras from the *Rig Veda* are used to invoke the devata(s) of yajna.
  - yajus mantras from the *Yajur Veda* are used during actions relating to oblationary work.

    - procedures and prescriptions are taken from the Brahmana Granthas (for smarta yajnas Smritis are used).
    - sama mantras from the *Sama Veda* are sung in praise of the devatas during a yajna.
- Mantra, oblation and devata form the three parts of a yajna.
- Yajna is at the centre of the Vedas, and the Veda Samhitas were compiled to facilitate the proper conduct of yajnas.
- Yajna is a ritualistic karma. It is a means of remaining on the righteous path in order to lead a purposeful life.

4

Devata – the Luminary in a Yajna

We have taken a bird's eye view of the Vedic literature that formed the base on which the palatial building of yajna has been raised. This palace is for the devata of yajna. Just as a king is a unique figure in his kingdom, the devata too is unique to yajna. All the other constituents of a yajna, such as items of oblation, mantras, priests, etc., can have alternatives, but not the devata. There can be no worship without the object of worship, so in yajna the devata is indispensable and an understanding of its role is of paramount importance. Below we will delve into the details of devatas, in particular Vedic devatas, focusing on their definition, description, classification and importance.

The concept of devata

Today, most believers would perceive God as an omnipresent, omnipotent and omniscient superhuman power. Words such as 'divine', 'heavenly', 'holy' are associated with this power. The concept of 'devata' in the Vedas is slightly different. The origin of the concept dates back to a period when there were no external aids such as scientific instruments to analyze and interpret the various natural phenomena. Therefore, forms of energy responsible for the creation and sustenance of the universe and displaying 'shininess' were treated as superhuman powers. Rishis visualized them in advanced states of mind, and gave expression to their experiences in coded forms. These codes are the hymns of the *Rig Veda*, and the objects of the hymns are known as 'Vedic devatas'.

Vedic devatas are defined and described in the supplementary text *Brihad Devata*, written by Rishi Shaunaka. In another text, *Nirukta*, written by Yaskacharya, the etymological meanings of devatas are discussed. The *Brihadaranyaka Upanishad* explains the concept of multiple devatas differently. According to it, the Vedas consider that behind every perceivable object in the universe, manifest or unmanifest, there is a single primal energy, known as Narayana. To begin with, there was no universe. Only Narayana existed. Then came that point in time when he felt that he was single, and desired to multiply. So he created Brahma. Brahma is also known as Prajapati, and was the first devata to be created. He in turn, created 33 more devatas, which were perceived by seer rishis in multiple forms. The rishis named their objects of vision, and so we have many devatas in the *Rig Veda*. The definition of rishi and devata is provided in the following sloka:

यस्य वाक्यं स ऋषिः या तेनोच्यते सा देवता।

Yasya vaakyam sa rishih, yaa tenochyate saa devataa.

One whose experience is recorded is a rishi and the object of his experience is devata.

The object of the vision of a rishi could be both sentient and non-sentient. The *Rig Veda* is a collection of prayers to such devatas – objects from the sky, heaven and earth. During the yajna process, these devatas are worshipped and offered oblations. Such processes result in the fulfilment of the desires of the host and also help in sustenance of the universe.

Etymology of the term 'devata'

In Sanskrit, the word used to denote 'god' or 'deity' is *deva*. Devata is also an alternate word for god. Both are derived from the root verb *div* – that which glows. The sun has a glowing property. Fire (Agni) blazes. Therefore, sun and fire are devatas, called Surya devata and Agni devata respectively.

In the *Nirukta*, Yaskacharya explains that three more meanings of the verb 'div' make an object worthy of being addressed as deva or devata: (i) the quality of being munificent in nature, (ii) the quality of shininess, and (iii) that it is a body from the sky (dyu loka). The moon and planets do not blaze, but they shine and are from dyu loka. Therefore, they are termed devata. Nature is a donor of the highest rank. Therefore, all natural powers are embodied and given names such as Vayu, Indra, Rudra, etc. and are devatas.

Characteristics of devatas[1]

- A devata is omnipresent but invisible; it can be approached through Agni.
- If the worshipper can raise his faith and devotion to the zenith, the devata can manifest in a visible form. (Ramakrishna Paramahamsa was said to talk to the Divine Mother just as he would with anybody else.)
- A devata mercifully accepts the offerings made by a devotee and, being pleased, reciprocates by fulfilling the desires of the worshipper.
- A devata clears stumbling blocks from the devotee's path and makes his life free from fear and problems.
- A devata constantly stays with the devotee in an invisible form and protects him.
- A devata is delighted by the worship and becomes angry if not worshipped.
- A devata befriends the five elements of the universe for a devotee.

Some of these qualities are directly attributable to the personified form of the devata. It may be difficult to imagine or accept that, like mortal beings, devatas too are pleased and hence grant the desired results in reciprocation. Also, if

---

[1] As recorded in *Encyclopaedia of Indian Culture (Bharatiya Samskriti Kosha)*, Pt Mahadev Shastri Joshi, Bharatiya Samskriti Kosha Mandal, Pune

devatas are kind-hearted and merciful, it is difficult to understand why they can become angry and inflict penalties upon the worshipper if they are not worshipped.

However, rather than ridiculing such expressions, a little faith in the wisdom of the learned ones can lead to meaningful inferences. Very often, Vedic literature has deeper meanings for words/sentences/phrases, which are overshadowed by the external meaning. One has to make an effort to remove the veil.

The idea that devatas are ever ready to shower boons is not correct. They are like a mother who is always caring and loving towards her children, but whose love sometimes takes the form of anger and even punishment. The objective is not to teach her children a lesson, but to firmly ingrain in their minds the importance of staying within limits. Thus, the ultimate objective is everlasting welfare.

Devatas are natural powers. They are ready to shower grace, but only as long as we are righteous. Pure air is essential for the biosphere and is available in plenty, but if excesses are created whereby the cycle is broken or the balanced proportion of gases in the atmosphere is disturbed, we are punished. In metaphoric language, it means that the devata is satisfied by praise and angry if not worshipped.

Importance of devata dhyanam

The Vedic hymns are composed and sung mainly: (i) to highlight the qualities of devatas, (ii) to express gratitude for their kindness in showering abundance in living conditions on earth, and (iii) to request further well-being. Such hymns are used to invoke the assigned devata in the yajnic process.

Before the chanting of suktas/richas (hymns/verses), it is customary to pronounce the name of the rishi, the concerned devata and the metre before dispensation of the sukta/richa. There is a reason for this tradition which can be explained by drawing an analogy.

To draw electric current from a source (battery, generator or powerhouse) to a point, the two need to be connected through a medium. Similarly, in the yajnic process when the host or yajamana desires to establish a one-to-one relationship with the devata (with a view to drawing power), he needs to form a connection with it. A medium for this (virtual) connection is formed by 'calling aloud' the name of the rishi, the metre and the devata of the sukta. The chanting of mantras and the rituals that follow work as a switch to enable the flow of power from the source – the devata.

When a deity is remembered with full faith, the yajamana successfully establishes a connection with it. He is then in a position to send the essence of the oblations to the yajna devata, who becomes favourably disposed. Through the same medium, the yajamana receives the aspired for fruits.

It is also extremely important to have a one-pointed focus on the devata, *devata dhyanam* (meditation on devata) throughout the process of oblation. The *Aitareya Brahmana* explains how this should be done. Before an article of oblation is offered to Agni, the *adhvaryu* (the priest in charge of the act of oblation) calls upon the *hota* (the priest who chants the mantras) to commence the chanting. The call is termed 'praisha'. The hota now needs to focus his mind one-pointedly on the devata, and maintain the focus throughout the chanting of the mantras. At the end of the chanting, he has to say aloud: "Vaushat." This is known as *vashatkara*, and is an indication to the adhvaryu to drop the articles of oblation into the *agni kunda* (in the middle of the glowing flames). The yajamana also needs to maintain his attention on the devata throughout the process, and at the vashatkara, say, *Idam na mama* – "This (the articles being offered) is not mine." The call of the hota, the oblation by the adhvaryu and renouncing the right to the articles by the yajamana must all synchronize. When there are multiple devatas to whom oblations are offered, the entire process must be performed for each devata, maintaining full concentration on the form of the devata.

According to Sayanacharya, by so doing the hota develops actual affection for that devata. The devata then becomes delighted and favourably disposed. In addition, even though the devata is invisible to the human eye, it becomes actually visible on the mental screen of the hota due to his one-pointed focus, concentration and deep contemplation. The connection is thus total and results in a successful two-way virtual transmission.

The importance of devata dhyanam is also underlined by Rishi Shaunaka in *Brihad Devata*. He says that it is absolutely essential to have the right knowledge of the yajna devata. This knowledge must be earned through conscious effort. Those who know the devata in a mantra also understand the secret and deeper meaning of the mantra. In the absence of such knowledge, any karma (yajna-related action) or samskara will not bear the desired fruit. Shaunaka also says that such persons are held in high esteem, as they are considered to have participated in the sacred yajna being performed in the heavens. It is very emphatically stated that devatas accept havi only from such knowledgeable priests/yajamana. They do not accept havi from the ignorant. In the absence of acceptance of havi, how can one expect the desired fruits? Other important treatises such as *Sarvanukramani* and *Rigvidhan* also express similar views.

An important corollary is that the priests and participants in large-scale yajnas like ahina, kratu, samvatsara, etc. must necessarily have experience-based subtle knowledge of the devata tattwa. In its absence, the offering of havi in the yajna fire is equivalent to throwing food in a garbage can; it is totally fruitless. Only one who realizes the object of worship and also the abstract form of the principle in one's own self can maintain full awareness of the richas and their compound words while chanting. Such a person is said to enter the immortal and eternal Brahma tattwa.

Yoga and devata dhyanam

As assured by Rishi Shaunaka, knowledge of devatas promises convergence of the individual identity (of the self) into the totality to attain Brahman. Interestingly, the prerequisite for this appears to be mastery in yoga. Words like 'conscious effort' can assume meaning only within the framework of asana, pranayama, dharana and dhyana. Devata tattwa is a very subtle principle. Its real knowledge is not possible without attaining a state of mind that is super-sensitive and makes one a dispassionate observer. This is precisely the point made by Sage Patanjali in the *Yoga Sutras* (YS 1:14). He says that such a state can be achieved through protracted and faithful efforts in dhyana.

स तु दीर्घकालनैरन्तर्यसत्कारासेवितो दृढभूमिः ॥

Sa tu deerghakaala nairantaryasatkaaraasevito dridhabhoomih.

There is no practice other than yoga that can develop the dispassionate attitude *(sakshi bhava)* of an observer. Projection of the image of the devata cannot occur without mastering the techniques of yoga. Merging into the ishta devata is the principal sadhana of yoga in general and bhakti yoga in particular.

Having mastered the yoga techniques, the host couple and the priests should meditate on the yajna devata. The *Rig Veda* declares that beneath every word of every richa lies sacred knowledge. One who does not understand the devata cannot reach it. The effort to attain the end result without such knowledge is a futile exercise.

Therefore, the devatas should be properly and fully understood. One way to start is to know about their total number, classification, functions, characteristics and qualities as described in the *Rig Veda*, *Yajur Veda*, etc., and then ponder over their significance and deeper meanings.

Number of devatas

The Vedas contain descriptions of a large number of devatas. Before listing them, it is interesting to note the total number mentioned in the Vedas. In the *Rig Veda*, there are at least four richas giving this number, and no two richas give the same number, varying not by tens or hundreds, but by thousands! The maximum number mentioned is 3339 and the minimum the cardinal one. But before we hasten to conclude that the Vedas are irrational on this topic, let us try to find the rationale behind it.

Once Yajnavalkya, a bright scholar and authority on the subject of Brahman, arrived at a meeting of learned brahmins who were discussing subjects from the scriptures in the presence of King Janaka. Some were delighted at his appearance and others resented it. One such boastful brahmin who did not like Yajnavalkya's presence was Uddalaka, who began questioning Yajnavalkya randomly on various topics. Although Yajnavalkya did not approve of the method of questioning and sensed the ulterior motive behind it, he answered every poser with a cool demeanour.

After some time, the questioning turned to devatas. Uddalaka repeatedly asked only one question. This is how the dialogue progressed.

Uddalaka: Tell me, Yajnavalkya, how many devatas are there?
Yajnavalkya: 3339.

U: Tell me the names.
Y: They are the large forms of god based on qualities, performance, etc.

U: Tell me how many devatas there are?
Y: 333.

U: Tell me how many devatas there are?
Y: 33.

U: What are they?
Y: 8 Vasus, 11 Rudras, 12 Samvatsaras, and Indra and Prajapati.

U: Tell me how many devatas there are?
Y: 6.

U: Name them.
Y: Agni, Vayu, Sun, Earth, Sky and Heaven.

U: Tell me how many devatas there are?
Y: 3.

U: Tell me how many devatas there are?
Y: Prithivi, Antariksha, Dyu.

U: Tell me how many devatas there are?
Y: Two, Prana and Anna.

U: Tell me how many devatas there are?
Y: One and a half (Vayu).

U: Tell me how many devatas there are?
Y: One, Prana.

Prana is Brahman and is also called 'tyat', which means indirect *(paroksha)* knowledge of Brahman. The story illustrates the notion of Brahman in Indian philosophy. Brahman assumes multiple forms and shapes, and individual souls are also a reflection of Brahman. This reflecting material is present in all parts of the universe. Yajnavalkya's 'numbers' come from the assumption that in the three-tiered structure of the universe represented by Earth, Sky and Heaven, Brahman is present as Agni, Vayu and Sun, respectively. The representatives together with the represented three levels take the number up to six. With 11 subdivisions in each tier, the number goes up to 33, and so on. The number 3339 probably signifies that the forms of Brahman, and devatas, can be as many as the stretch of one's imagination!

Devatas in Vedic verses

The way in which a multiple number of devatas is addressed in the suktas of the *Rig Veda* is explained by Yaskacharya in the *Nirukta*. In fact, one full chapter of the *Nirukta* is an exposition on devatas. In his characteristically deductive way, Yaskacharya explains how the word 'devata' is used. He calls the collection of all nouns that describe forms of devata as *daivat sangraha*. These nouns appear in mantras.

The description could be: (i) direct, like Karpurgaura, meaning fair-complexioned, Lambodara, meaning pot-bellied, or (ii) implied, like Umapati, meaning the husband of Uma – goddess Parvati, Vighnaharta, meaning the one who alleviates obstacles.

The mantra is said to be dedicated to a devata when the composer rishi, having a desire in mind, adores the devata. Such richas or mantras employ three ways of addressing a devata: (i) indirect reference, (ii) direct reference, and (iii) a statement by the devata itself. In the first type, the reference is through usage of the proper noun of the devata, like "Sing the samas for Indra" (R 8.98,1). Here, although the name of the devata (Indra) appears, the main focus of the richa is on asking the priests to sing his praise. In the second type, the devata is referred to in the second person, like "O Indra, (you please) destroy our enemy" (R 10.152,4). In the third case, the devata makes an assuring statement. Hence, the form of the noun is Uttama Purusha; for example, Lord Krishna says in the *Bhagavad Gita*, "Leave all paths and take shelter in me. I shall rid you of all sins. Do not worry or brood" (BG 18.66).

In the Veda Samhitas, most richas are of the first two types. Richas of the third type are very few. Generally, a richa contains sufficient information to enable a conclusion about the devata being praised. In some exceptional cases, however, there is no reference, direct or otherwise, to any devata. The accepted practice is to consider such a richa, mantra or sukta to be in honour of the devata for whom the yajna is being performed.

Sometimes a question arises as to why an entity like a horse or a herb should be treated as a devata. For an explanation, Yaskacharya points to the *advaita* (non-dual) principle. According to him, such entities in non-human forms are, in fact, different manifestations of Brahman. They differ only superficially in the outer form, the inner content being the same Brahman.

Forms of devatas

This universe is divided into three parts called *lokas*. They are: *prithivi loka*, the region covered by earth, *dyu loka*, the region covered by space in the sky, and *antariksha loka*, the space between the two. All devatas adored in the *Rig Veda* belong to one of the three lokas. The *Nirukta* (3.7.2) opines that there are only three cardinal devatas – Agni, Vayu and Surya, each representing a layer of the universe. Agni dwells in prithivi loka, Vayu in antariksha loka and Surya in dyu loka. However, their jurisdiction is not watertight. They are described as taking forms that span lokas other than their normal abode. Thus, Agni takes forms that operate in antariksha and dyu lokas, Vayu in prithivi loka, and Surya in prithivi and antariksha lokas. In fact, Vayu and Surya are said to be specific forms of Agni.

Devatas are considered to have human-like, non-human and dual forms. Although examples of non-human forms can be readily given (such as earth, sea, etc.), Yaskacharya feels that all devatas have a human form. Any non-human form that is visible, whether earth, sea, etc., is just a different manifestation of the basic devata with a human form. Such manifestations are the outcome of the karmas of the basic devatas or their functions. Just as a yajamana is related to yajna through his resolve and participation (less at the physical, more at the mental level), so also non-human forms of devatas are related to the basic devata of the respective groups that have human forms.

The Puranas take a more direct approach to explain this, and personify the devata. In the Puranas, earth takes the form of a lady and approaches Brahma pleading against the increasing burden inflicted upon her by sinful people. The ocean presents himself in a human form to Lord Rama who is furious that it did not accede to his request to give way to Lanka. Agni emerges out of the sacred yajna fire to present himself to King Dasharatha in the *Ramayana* or King Drupada in the *Mahabharata*.

Functions of devatas from the three lokas

Devatas from all three lokas are embodiments. This was done possibly for an easy understanding of their characteristics and overall role with respect to phenomena in nature. They are given a name and qualities. Thus, Brahma is the creator and his main attribute is creation. Vishnu is the saviour and Mahesh the destroyer.

Agni is a devata from prithivi loka. Its main function is to act as a medium of communication between the yajamana and the devata(s) in a yajna. Agni receives the items offered by the yajamana on behalf of the yajna devata, and takes them to the devata in essence form (the items are burnt and only the essence remains, which can reach different lokas). It also acts as a representative of the yajamana to bring the yajna devata to the yajna venue.

Indra, as a devata from antariksha loka, is embodied as a natural power that controls clouds, rain, etc. Surya, as a devata from dyu loka, works to extract the essence from substances and to bear the essence in its rays. Also known as Aditya, he knows everything due to his reach. Nothing can remain a secret from him, but it is his function to keep such secrets.

Description of devatas

So far we have seen the etymology, characteristics and forms of Vedic devatas. The following section describes some of these devatas. Devatas worshipped in smarta yajna, and those referred to in the Puranas and tantra shastra are also covered.

1. Prithivi-based devatas

Devatas with earth as the prominent element fall in this category. Among this class, Agni is the chief devata. It takes different forms such as Jatavedas, Matarishva, Vaishvanara, Dravinoda, etc. The other two groups of prithivi-based devatas are 12 apri devatas and 36 prithivi sattwa devatas. Apri devatas are related to yajna and prithivi sattwa devatas include articles used in yajna (horse, grinding stones to crush soma, grain for rice cakes, etc.).

Agni: Agni holds a prime position in Vedic religion. Hardly any other devata has been ascribed equal importance or prominence. He also has the closest link with and relevance to an individual, family, society, nation, even the world. This importance stems from his association with all these bodies on a daily basis. At the physical level, he is 'fire', without which our daily life would come to a standstill. Even with the sheer number of richas dedicated to a devata, he ranks only next to Indra.

In a sense, Agni stands for the principle of aspiration. Aspire not, you will work not. Work not, you will also progress not. Progress not, no power will manifest in you. And without the power of the mind, you will cease to be a human being. To aspire is one thing, and to work for it is another. In this context, one may understand the meaning of the saying "There is no fire in his stomach."

Agni is equally dear to other devatas. In any yajna intended for any devata, one comes in direct contact only with Agni. It is Agni who accepts the oblations and is said to extend them to the yajna devatas. No dravya yajna is possible without Agni, and therefore one cannot do any sadhana or worship God by excluding Agni.

Since he extends the havi to the devatas, Agni is also called *havya vahana* (the vehicle of havi). As he is closely associated with the human household, he is known as *grihapati* (*griha* means home, and *pati* means major family member). Thus, Agni is the link between man and the gods. Agni is the only devata who has come down from the heavenly abode to the mortal world, and firmly stays here. The *Rig Veda* praises him through various richas and suktas. The description of his birth, form, figure and functions is summarized below.

Agni is naturally born as well as artificially created. He was born of the sky, and again devatas created him (R 10.45,8, 3.2,3). He is the son of Dyu, Prithivi, Vanaspati, etc. He was born of water. He takes birth from wood, the friction of stones, and so on (R 2.1.1).

In his natural form, Agni shines like the sun. Flames are his flowing hair (R 3.17.1), wood is his food (R 2.7.6). He can consume even a large forest (R 1.127.4). His luminous outer form looks like a silver robe. Agni is flamboyant, and his hair is like stormy, rain-bearing clouds and lightning. He crushes big stones using his sharp tongue and breaks even big mountains to pieces.

In his human form, Agni has a beautiful body (R 1.94.7). He can look in all directions (R 1.97.6). He has three tongues and four eyes (R 3.20.2, 1.31.13). In another place in the *Rig Veda*, it is said that he has four horns, three legs, two heads and seven hands (R 4.58.3). His glow is powerful and scorching. He is very well built due to constant consumption of the essence of butter (ghrita), etc.

He resides in the intestines of waters. He lives in the forest. He spans all three lokas. He is present in wood. He is in the air, beneath the seas, on the earth, everywhere. In short, there is no place in the universe where he does not reside. In that sense he is omnipresent.

He is man's crusader. He is the ruler of yajna. He carries food to the gods, brings them to the yajna venue and is the leader of humankind. He is the god of the learned. He is very kind to human beings. He is called *Jatavedas* or 'the one who knows everything'. Knowledge is equated with the Vedas. Therefore, it can be said that the Vedas were created from him.

He is our father, mother, brother, friend and son. He is our leader and the representative of God. He rides a golden chariot with a single wheel pulled by blood-red horses. One who worships Agni and offers oblations to him acquires immense wealth in this world, lives for a hundred years and becomes immortal. Agni has two distinct roles. As ordinary fire, it is used in the kitchen and other daily chores. As sacred fire, in yajna it has the role of leading the ordinary person in performing kratvartha and accepts oblations for ancestors and yajna devata(s).

So much for the ubiquitous description of Agni in the Vedas. The esoteric form of Agni is the unique power from which everything has taken form. Indra, Vayu, Surya, Soma, etc. are just different forms of this devata. Agni also resides in living beings. A person is alive because there is fire in him, called prana. Once it leaves, the body becomes cold and decomposes. Agni is the essence of everything. Matter has its existence and individuality due to the presence of this energy. The Vedics called it pranic energy and the modern world knows it as nuclear energy. This energy is at the root of all dynamism in the universe. Agni is a unique devata and all other Vedic devatas seem to be just its various forms manifested for a specific purpose/function.

Vedic dharma prescribes that a person worship Agni throughout their lives. The association with Agni starts even before taking birth and ends with death. The 42 samskaras done for the soul[2] have Agni as the witness. It is Agni in whose presence a Vedic takes an oath to perform purusharthas throughout life to the best of his capacity, neither falling short in his duties nor indulging excessively in the pursuit of artha, kama and even dharma. Finally, on departure from this world, the prana (which itself is a form of Agni) merges with the universal consciousness, and the mortal body merges with the flames of Agni. The Agni that accepts the mortal body is called *kravyad*, and the form that accepts the soul is Brahman. According to Vedic belief, a person comes into this world as a guest, and is sent here to undertake specific functions. Agni is their companion at every stage – from the time the soul separates from Brahman (birth) until its re-convergence. This function of Agni is very aptly embedded in the *Brihad Devata* (2:24).

Apri devatas: The 12 apri devatas comprise: (i) the yajna implements, (ii) instruments, and (iii) the performer of the yajna. They are to be remembered at the commencement of the yajna and also at the end. The first invocation is called *prayaja*, and the invocation at the conclusion of a yajna is known as *anuyaja*. In every shrauta yajna, five

---

[2] See Chapter 8

oblations are offered at the beginning and five at the end. Mantras such as "O Agne, this yajna is solely for you. The people residing in all lokas bow to thee" (R 10.51.9) are chanted while offering prayaja and anuyaja ahutis. They are called apri mantras and were composed by Bhargava rishis (members of the Bhrigu family).

Prithivi sattwa devatas: *Prithivi sattwa* means essence of the earth element, so prithivi sattwa devatas are sentient beings like the horse, bull, etc. and non-living objects like the river, crushing stones, grinders, etc. associated with yajna. The *Rig Veda* praises all such articles. The horse, bull, rivers, king, sun, wind – all exert a great influence on civil and agricultural life. In the Vedas, every karma is respected as having great value. Therefore, all those who help in furthering the cause of karmas like transportation, maintenance, agriculture, etc. find praise from the grateful Vedic people.

2. Antariksha-based devatas

Antariksha is the middle layer of the universe. Devatas active in this region are called antariksha-based devatas. In the famous Gayatri mantra, this is known as *bhuvah loka*. In modern terminology, it is called the sky. The space occupied by the sky above the sphere of earth is filled with air, wind or vayu. Therefore, Vayu is the prime devata of this loka. It is also equated with Indra.

For the inhabitants of earth, the main use of antariksha comes from its two constituents – wind and clouds. Air and water are the basic requirements of living beings. They come from Vayu and Megha (rain-bearing clouds). Forces such as air, rain, storms and lightning are probably praised for this reason in the Vedas. Further, these devatas work in union for their benevolent activity. Therefore, they are worshipped in pairs like Mitra+Varuna, Indra+Pusha, Agni+Pusha, Vayu+rain, etc. Oblations are also offered to such pairs of devatas in yajnas.

Vayu: Just as Agni is the prime devata of the *Rig Veda*, Vayu is the principal devata of the *Yajur Veda*. He is invoked by saying, "O Vayu, here is soma that is pure and worthy of exhibition. Do drink it and listen to our invocation" (R1.2,1). Vayu is also connected with prana. One form of prana is the vital force of living beings. The word is indicative of non-stop actions like the ticking of a clock or the beating of the heart. Since the original prana is present in antariksha loka in a subtle form, this devata is praised as being present in the mid-region, capable of spanning all three lokas, kind-hearted, helping living beings to progress. Incidentally, the word 'vayu' is a modified form of the original word 'aayu', but since Vayu is a proper noun, this should not cause any ripples except among grammarians.

Varuna: According to the *Brihad Devata*, the moisture-laden air that engulfs the antariksha in the form of rain-bearing clouds is Varuna (BD 2.33). As one of the meanings of 'varuna' is also asura (demon), this devata was wrongly associated with asuras initially. Vritrasura, the principal enemy of Indra, is a progeny of Varuna. Varuna is described as the eldest child of Aditi, senior to Surya (Vivasvana), Indra, etc. He is respected by the devas too. Unlike asuras, there are no mantras in which Varuna has been criticized or looked down upon. One of the epithets of Varuna is 'Pracheta', the lawgiver, because he is said to be a strict law enforcer. Therefore, the respect that he commands contains an element of fear too. In one of the Rig mantras, it is said that Varuna, whose face looks downwards, has created Megha. The earth and sky are formed from him (R 5.85,3).

Rudra: Rudra has a roaring quality. All devatas are soft-hearted with gentle facial expressions, but not Rudra. He has a ferocious look and a frightful attitude, but this extreme exhibition of anger is only against enemies. In the invocations to him, he is appeased first, requested to calm down, praised, and then many demands made of him. The sukta devoted to Rudra, *Rudra Sukta*, prays to him through various descriptions and requests for benevolence. The sukta is a classic example of what should be requested of a mighty and generous person, and for what purpose. It is a good reflection of the mindset of the Vedics.

Sometimes, before coming down in droplets, rain-bearing clouds make a great, even frightening, show of thunder and lightning. Vayu in this form is called Rudra. In the *Rig Veda*, Rudra is requested to vent all his anger on enemies, so that it does not affect the yajamana and the priests.

Indra: Agni and Vayu were both called Indra in pre-Rig Vedic times. Indra was supposed to be the principal devata of antariksha loka. This devata is related to water, as the principal nourisher. *Ira* in Sanskrit means food or water. He who pierces the storage or beholds it or bestows and donates this essence of life is called Indra. Yaskacharya has another etymology for Indra: Indu Indha, Idam Idanti, then Indra.

Indra is a mighty devata. He has fought with Vritra and many other asuras. One interpretation of Indra based on intellectual analysis is that Vritra represents the wicked forces, and created blockades to stop the water flowing from the Himalayas. Indra represents righteous power and the might to combat this wicked force. He fought with the demon, destroyed him and demolished the blockades. He gained control over water storage in antariksha loka (rain-bearing clouds) and released the flow, thus channelling the (rain) water for the benefit of all.

Soma: In Vedic literature (Vedas, Brahmana Granthas, Kalpa Sutras), the word soma is used to denote: (i) a deity (Soma devata), (ii) the vitality principle (soma tattwa), and (iii) a herb (soma valli).

Soma is an important devata of antariksha loka. It has multiple characteristics. Like Indra and Varuna, it too represents valour. Together with Agni, it represents the vital force. It is munificent and blesses its worshippers with intellect and wisdom. It is the most ferocious among warriors and has not known defeat in battle. It is uniquely honoured with the title *Rakshohan*, meaning one who has slain demons (or demonic attitudes). Soma is customarily addressed in union with other devatas such as Indra-Soma, Varuna-Soma,

Agni-Soma, etc. He is believed to have a reddish-brown complexion.

According to the *Rig Veda Samhita*, Soma is at the base of all creation – organic and intellectual. It works with the principle of Agni for all creativity. It gives the quality of radiation to the sun, enhances Indra's strength so he can overpower demons like Vritra, and it was he who made the oceans bear the life-embryo thus becoming the source of the creation of life.

Modern science also explains the phenomenon of the constant and never-diminishing ability of the sun to emit heat and light due to the presence of the chromosphere, which can be equated with soma.

The soma principle is also associated with healing, soothing and cooling effects. Therefore, the moon (which represents these qualities) is also called Soma devata.

Soma assumed the form of a herb, *soma valli*, and became the physical source of vitality for Indra and other devatas. Garuda, the vehicle of Lord Vishnu, brought it to earth from dyu loka. Soma and its juice are very important items of oblation in a group of yajnas called soma yajna.

The *Rig Veda* has devoted a full chapter (9) to describing the qualities and importance of soma. It calls soma the mind of rishis, the 'rishiness' of rishis (the quality that makes a person a rishi), Brahma among devas and the soul of yajnas.

3. Dyu loka-based devatas

Devatas who are active in dyu loka are called dyu loka devatas. There are 31 major devatas in dyu loka. Ashvinau, Usha, Vajina, Varuna, etc. are some of the important ones often referred to in the yajus and mantras of shrauta yajnas.

Sun: Sun, with its various forms and figures, resides in dyu loka. Sun gives the basic energy required by the devatas of antariksha loka to bestow all that aids the living conditions in prithivi loka. Sun is found everywhere in the *Rig Veda*. He is held in high reverence and praised accordingly. Usha is described as possessing poetic qualities.

Prajapati: The meaning of the word *prajapati* is 'master of creation'. It is said that in creating the universe, Prajapati devata expanded himself and 33 devatas were created from him. The *Shatapatha Brahmana* puts this event metaphorically: "Prajapati is the father of devatas." In the *Rig Veda*, the same event is described as 'the sacrifice of Prajapati'. It says that Prajapati performed the first-ever yajna of the universe wherein he offered himself as the havi (oblation material). This sacrifice became an 'example' for all man-made yajnas. Due to his importance as the master of creation, he is offered havi in all man-made yajnas.

4. Vishvedeva

There is no single entity called Vishvedeva. Equivalent words such as Sarve Deva, Nana Deva, etc. indicate that it refers to many devatas. During the yajna process, whenever more than one devata is present in a mantra or sukta and it is not possible to mention them separately, 'Vishvedeva' is used to jointly address all devatas. Therefore, the devata of a mantra or sukta that adores multiple devatas is said to be Vishedeva. For example, one mantra may refer to nine devatas – Indra, Vayu, Brihaspati, Mitra, Agni, Pushan, Bhaga, Aditya and Maruta (R 1.14,3). Instead of calling out all nine names, the term Vishvedeva is chanted to address them all together. In another context, Agni, for example, is one devata, but is addressed by many names – hence it is Vishvedeva too. Sun is a single entity, but has infinite rays going in all directions – it is Vishvedeva too. In fact, theoretically, all devatas and objects in the universe are Vishvedeva.

The *Yajur Veda* makes mandatory the offering of havi to multiple devatas referred to as Vishvedeva. From the point of view of yajna, a question can arise – how many devatas are jointly addressed as Vishvedeva? According to Nighantu, there are 52 devatas of prithivi loka, 68 devatas of antariksha loka and 31 devatas of dyu loka. Thus, the maximum number of devatas that can be addressed as Vishvedeva becomes 151. However, it is customary to assume there are 11 devatas in each loka, thus the number totals 33. Sometimes Prajapati is added to this list and the number becomes 34. Interestingly, although multiple devatas are invoked through chanting 'Vishvedeva', only one oblation is offered.

5. Devatas in smarta yajna

Smarta yajna differs from shrauta yajna in form, style, complexity, etc. There are two main differences: (i) the rituals in smarta yajna are based on details taken from smriti granthas, and (ii) they use a single fire which is called *aupasana agni* or *grihyagni*.

Devatas of smarta yajna mostly have a human form. Their origin, form, abode, characteristics, preference for specific flowers and colours, etc. are described in the Puranas. For example, Ganesha, the prime devata invoked at the beginning of any smarta ritual, is the son of Lord Shiva and Parvati. Shiva or Shankara has three eyes, a blue neck and prefers to remain in seclusion. Lord Vishnu is the most popular devata, with benevolence being his chief attribute. He has four hands holding weapons and a lotus, and prefers to stay amid his bhaktas. Almost all devatas are perceived in the form of couples like Vishnu and Lakshmi, Shiva and Parvati, Rama and Sita, etc.

6. Tantra and tantric devatas

The word tantra comes from the root word *tan*, meaning 'to expand' or 'spread'. Here knowledge is assumed as the object of expansion. Therefore, tantra is defined as processes that help knowledge to expand in manifold ways. A similar explanation comes from breaking the word tantra into tan+tra. Tan stands for *tanotu* – 'to stretch', and tra stands for *trayate* – 'to liberate' or 'take beyond'.

Human beings have four basic instincts – hunger, sleep, fear and sex. In Tantra Shastra they are treated as *vikaras,* passions. It is a well known fact that animals of the lower world live by instinct and faithfully follow the laws of Nature; they do not cross the limits. Due to superior faculties, man has a choice of staying with the passions or rising above them to expand his individual consciousness and touch super-consciousness. However, very often he chooses to indulge only in passions and emotions, and does so quite indiscriminately, causing imbalances in physique, mind and consciousness. Tantra is a spiritual practice to gain control over and regulate the passions so as to regain the lost balance. It is an accepted belief that this science has originated from Lord Shiva.

The devatas found in tantra shastra are different from the devatas described earlier. In some cases, the names are the same but the similarity ends there. The forms, features, characteristics, functions and descriptions differ widely from Vedic devatas. However, in spite of such deviation, the root of tantra lies in the Vedas.

The following description is based on an exposition contained in *Bharatiya Samskriti Kosha*.

Shaiva tantra: In Shaiva tantra, Shiva is the principal devata. He is called Adinath Mahakala, is fair-complexioned, has five faces, three eyes, four hands and two legs. The five faces are called *ishana,* representing *chita shakti* or chetana, *tat purusha* (related to the experience of bliss), *sadyo jyoti* (related to knowledge), *vamadeva* (related to desires) and *aghora* (related to action). He holds a hatchet *(parashu)* and a deer in his upper two hands. His lower arms are raised in the pose of blessing *(varada mudra)* and reassurance *(abhaya mudra)* respectively. He wears a crescent moon on his head and is seated on a lotus with his army (Shiva *gana*) surrounding him.

In Shaiva tantra, Adinath Mahakala is assumed to be the first god and the seed of the universe. All forms of Adideva Shiva are equally worshipped. Among them, two forms, Kshetrapala and Bhairava, are assigned special importance. In tantric worship, it is mandatory to worship Kshetrapala before the main ritual. In some tantras, rice balls and sacrifices of flesh are recommended as oblations to Kshetrapala. He is a folk devata. In Bengal, women fast while worshipping Kshetrapala.

Bhairavas are eight in number. They are said to be equivalent to Shiva in form and similar in quality. Bhairava is worshipped using a five- or six-letter mantra. In some places he is worshipped along with Goddess Kali. The form of Bhairava called 'Batuk Bhairava' is very popular in Bengal.

Ganapatya tantra: Here the devata is Ganapati. Some forms of this devata are used in incantations (black magic). In some other forms, he is found with respective wives, lost in ecstasy. Ganapati's vehicle is the rat, but the vehicle of his Heramba form is the lion. Maha Ganapati holds a bowl of gems in one of his hands, which he showers on his disciples. Viriganapathy holds a skull filled with wine.

Saura tantra: Here the devata does not have a large number of different forms. Sun or Surya is the prime devata. Moon, Bhairava and Agni are associated with it. Moon has blue locks of hair. Martand, another form of Surya, is four-faced, three-eyed and has eight arms. He holds a skull in his hand, and his wife forms half of his body. Agni has eight arms and three eyes. Surya also has four arms. He is seated on a lotus studded with gems and holds a lotus in one of his hands.

Vaishnava tantra: In this tantra, the chief devata is Vishnu. His incarnations and many other forms are considered independent devatas. The details of these devatas are given in books like *Sharada Tilaka* and *Tantrasara*. The main forms of Vishnu are Lakshmi-Vasudeva or Lakshmi-Narayana. Harisvaroopa is next in sequence. Of the ten incarnations of Vishnu, Narasimha, Rama and Krishna are the most popular. In addition, the following forms are also worshipped.

Dadhi Vamana: He holds two golden jars, one containing pure water and the other rice mixed with curd.

Hayagriva: This form has a human body and a horse's head. It has four arms. The upper two hands hold the reins of a chariot, and the other two rest on the knees.

Gopala Krishna: Here Krishna is standing amidst a band of gopis with Vrindavan in the background. One gopi has embraced Krishna. On the background of Dwaraka, the same Krishna is perceived with eight wives.

Shakta tantra: In this tantra, Vidya and Nitya are the two prime devatas. Vidya devata has ten forms according to *Munda Mala Tantra*, and each is called a maha devata. They are: Kali, Tara, Shodashi, Bhuvaneshvari, Bhairavi, Chinnamasta, Dhumavati, Bagala, Matangi and Kamala. In another place, the number of forms is given as 27.

Nitya Devata has 16 forms, described in *Nitya Shodash Karnava*. They are: Bhaga Malini, Klinna, Bherunda, Vanhi Vasini, Maha Vajreshvari, Dooti, Twarita, Kulasundari, Nityanitya, Neel Pataka, Vijaya, Sarva Mangala, Jvala Malini, Chitra and Adya.

Maha Tripura Sundari represents the different forms of Nitya Devata. In this tantra, Kali has forms different from the other tantras. They are: Dakshina Kali, Bhadra Kali, Shmashan Kam Kala Kali, Dhana Kali, Siddha Chandi Kali, etc.

Tripura is the major Vidya devata. Its forms are: Bala, Panchadashi, Shodashi, Shatsambhava, Parameshwari, etc.

In Shakta tantra, the ritual of *kumari poojan* has been accorded high importance. Here, the kumari or virgin is the embodiment of all the Shakti devatas taken together. Her worship grants welfare to the worshipper. Indirectly, it is said that if one does not worship Kumarika, the pooja does not bring the desired fruits. *Prana Toshini Tantra* says that there is no doubt that a virgin is an incarnation of all vidyas together and hence a devotee should worship a virgin by installing one's intellect in the form of the devi.

The Shakti forms of devata are worshipped with a view to acquiring the powers required in this material and physical world, and also for spiritual powers. In fact, all such forms and variations of Shakti are manifestations of Adi Shakti (the primal power). The different forms ensure the dynamic equilibrium of the universe through the process of creation-sustenance-destruction or contain the upsurge of demonic powers that tends to disturb the tranquillity (the steady state which is an outcome of dynamic equilibrium) from time to time.

7. Other devatas

In smarta yajnas, a few ancillary functions relating to the conduct of yajna are associated with devatas. These include protection of the yajna venue, purification of the atmosphere (physical and mental) of the yajna venue, etc.

Stambha devatas: The yajna pavilion is raised according to the directions in the scriptures. Sixteen pillars support the roof. This number can rise to 64, depending on the type of pavilion and yajna. At each pillar, a devata is installed so as to be protected from all sides. According to Siddhanta Shekar, the 16 devatas installed on the pillars are: Brahma, Vishnu, Rudra, Indra, Surya, Ganesha, Yama, Sarpa (Nag), Skanda, Prushdashva (Vayu), Chandrama, Pracheta, Ashta Vasu, Dhanada (Kubera), Brihaspati and Tvashtunandana (Vishvakarma).

Dhvaja devatas: The asuras consider any holy place without a flag as a mere winery and invade it. To keep them at bay, the place of worship must have a flag on top. According to *Agni Purana*, the following devatas are installed in the flag at the yajna site : Kumuda, Kumudaksha, Pundarika, Vamana, Shanku Karna Sarva Netra, Sumukha and Supratishthita.

Pancha gavya devatas: Yajnas use *pancha gavya*, a mixture of five items (outputs of the cow), to purify the venue and the minds of participants. The five devatas are: Varuna (in gomutra), Agni (in gobar), Chandra (in milk), Vayu (in dadhi), Surya (in ghrita), Brahmadi (in kusha), Vishnu (in water)[3].

---

[3] *Yajna Mimamsa,* Pt. Veniram Sharma Gaud, Chaukhamba Vidya Bhavan, Varanasi, 1999

IN CONCLUSION

- Devatas are an inseparable part of yajna. They represent the manifest form of the primal energy that is behind the existence of each and everything in the universe.
- Devata dhyanam is essential for acquiring the full benefit of yajna, and yoga is helpful in achieving this state.
- There are a number of devatas, but Brahman is the only reality.
- Devatas are classified under three lokas, but their jurisdiction is not watertight.
- Some important devatas are Agni, Surya, Soma and Varuna.
- Smarta and tantric yajnas have several other devatas.

5

Tri-polar Interpretations of Yajna

Etymologically speaking, the meaning of yajna has three connotations, each of which has three polarities. In addition, the Vedas indicate that a person inherits three liabilities at birth, and suggests yajna as the means of liquidating them. So there seems to be some connection between yajna and the number 'three'. The following diagram illustrates the point.

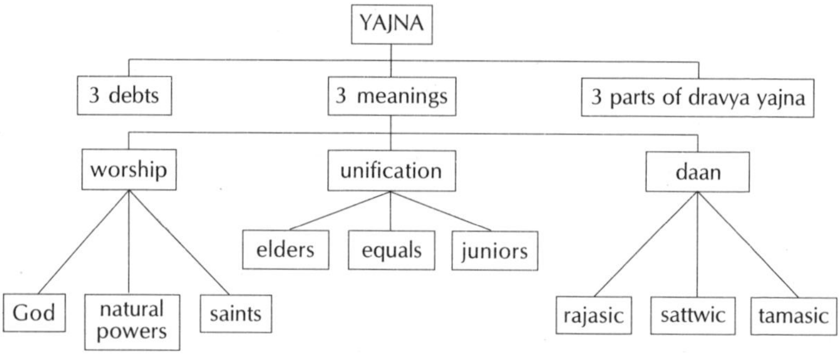

Fig. 3

Three debts

We owe our appearance in this world to the Almighty. Our progress here is based on the inheritance of samskaras. From time immemorial, the human race has tried to develop an understanding of the cause of the universe, the purpose of human life and the means of achieving salvation. In the horizontal line representing infinite time, our life is a tiny dot. There was something before our appearance and there will be something after we leave. We use the joint contribution of our ancestors, add to it our own (positive or negative) contribution, and pass it on to the next generation. This is reflected in the Vedic belief that every human being is born with three kinds of debts, *rin*. We are indebted to:

- The Almighty for everything – *deva rin*
- The learned who have given us a heritage to reckon with – *rishi rin*
- Our ancestors and society for nurturing us until our maturity – *pitri rin*.

How is this concept of debt related to yajna? We have to return what we owe to all three in this life. To discharge the three liabilities, the *Taittiriya Samhita* of the *Yajur Veda* recommends yajna in the following forms:

- Worshipping the Almighty through dravya or external yajna
- Pursuing knowledge and studying the literary works of rishis, which is called brahma yajna
- Having good progeny, and raising them to be an asset to society.

By performing yajna and other methods of worship we carry forward the tradition of our ancestors. The resulting advantages are: (i) exhaustion of the liability, and (ii) progress in self-evolution. A by-product is that the objectives of life are automatically defined, i.e. creation of an appropriate lifestyle and pursuit of corresponding goals throughout our lifespan.

So, the shastras recommend yajna as a means of repaying in reciprocation what one has inherited. For this purpose, one has to grasp the technique of performing external or physical yajna, transcend the mechanics, and inculcate the meaning and principles for the two processes that must go on in life simultaneously: (i) being fully involved at the physical level in material pleasure and pain, and (ii) continually working inwardly for self-evolution, maintaining detachment from worldly acts.

Three meanings of yajna

We have seen that the Sanskrit word 'yajna' is derived from the root verb 'yaj', which means 'to worship', 'to unite/congregate' and 'to give'. From the root verb 'yaj', the word yajna can be formed to mean: (i) *yaga,* i.e. a sacrificial rite, and (ii) a sacrifice-based act or karma. The first meaning leads to the definition and development of the ritualistic process called dravya yajna. In the literature on the Vedas, dravya yajna is also termed 'bhautic yajna', 'artificial yajna', 'pratyaksha yajna', 'external yajna' and 'physical yajna'[1]. The karma-based form of yajna suggests three alternative meanings:

- worship of the Lord, *devapooja*
- unification or congregation of people, *sangatikaran*, and
- giving, *daan*.

Normally, all the three meanings implied by 'yajna' are relevant concurrently in our lives. Each meaning is like a pole, and taken together the three give a solid and stable tripodal stand on which the plate of yajna is placed as the theme of life. Any of these poles taken either singly or in a pair will not support the plate adequately.

Each pole, in turn, has three qualities. There are three objects of worship: God, godlike figures (saints) and devata(s) representing natural principles. The people of a society who are to be united have three attitudes – sattwic, rajasic and tamasic. Giving is also of three kinds. These three poles are explained in detail below.

Worship: Worship means offering our sentiments, regards and respects. The purpose of worship displays the quality of mind of the worshipper. If we seek personal and material prosperity or assistance to manage our routine problems, it displays a lower quality of mind. In such a case

---

[1] See Chapter 8

worship is only a glorified term for begging. When we say that yajna means worship, it implies that the worshipper has a higher level or state of mind. Yajna is intended for self-evolution and the welfare of society. Therefore, yajna as worship means a prayer from one who possesses superior qualities. The idea is: (i) to express gratitude for benevolence, and (ii) to express the desire to raise the quality and potential of the mind to be like the object of worship. Benevolence comes from munificent and altruistic personalities. Therefore, through yajna one pays respect to God – the Almighty, devatas – the representation of godly qualities, saintly personalities and the elders of society who represent wisdom ripened by experience. Worship of this type or practising yajna in this form makes us grateful. It also reminds us that there are people who are superior to us in many respects. Together, the two attitudes help us to keep a tab on the ego. They also help to develop an attitude where we want to be like the ones we worship. Slowly we are led towards being positive in our approach and selfless (sattwic) in our interactions with the world.

Congregation: This meaning of yajna is related more to the social than the personal environment. A society is strong only if its members are united and ready to sacrifice personal interests to the larger interest of society, as and when called upon to do so. There will always be some members of society who are: (i) our elders and to be respected, (ii) our equals or peers, and (iii) our juniors and those who are less equipped than us in terms of physical, material or even emotional strength. To be united, we have to maintain continued and cordial relationships with members of all three groups. Yajna gives us the secret of maintaining such relationships.

Love is the thread that binds people together and hatred is the separator. Sacrifice is the basis of love and greed the basis of hatred. Rita is the path of unification, and anrita leads to separation. Love does not 'demand' or 'expect'. Greed knows nothing else. It is very clear which path one should follow. Thus, sacrifice or yajna is the desirable principle of life. A prayer from the *Rig Veda* used in soma yajna to adore Soma devata says, *Krinvanto vishvam aryam* – "O Soma, help me to make all people wise and loveable." The daily prayer drawn from the Vedas also says, *Asato ma sat gamaya, tamaso ma jyotir gamaya* – "O Lord, take me away from anrita to rita, take me away from darkness and ignorance to the light of love."

Therefore, love is the mantra for congregation. To maintain a relationship with our elders, love should take the form of faith *(shraddha)*, which amounts to following the principles of worship. We should respect our elders, serve and obey them and seek their guidance with humility on all important issues. This helps us to practise sacrifice of the ego.

To maintain relations with our peers, love should take the form of affection and friendship. There should be proper coordination, respect for the views of co-workers and concern for their well-being. In this way, we learn to practise sacrifice of self-interest for the benefit of others.

To maintain relations with our juniors, the weak and the underprivileged, love should take the form of empathy and oneness *(atmabhava)*. We should extend all the help we are capable of and continue giving until the need is fulfilled. Shortfalls should be made good by giving all that we possess – money, matter, compassion. We should come forward spontaneously rather than waiting to be called upon for assistance. In this way, we learn to sacrifice the material goods we have acquired for ourselves and our family, thus extending our family's boundaries and enlarging the definition of 'near and dear ones' *(vasudhaiva kutumbakam)*.

By uniting, the strength of a society increases. If every capable member of society were to sacrifice a few personal items, the combined effect would make society strong. Even the weaker members would be able to derive enthusiasm and power from this combined strength to achieve progress and attain the ultimate human goal – moksha.

According to the 'universal mind' theory put forward by Swami Sivananda and taught through practice by Swami

Satyananda, the minds of individuals (souls) are connected with the universal mind (Brahman) through a subtle medium. If individuals were to give expression to love in the three forms explained above, the pollution in our *manomaya kosha* (the layer of personality dealing with the mind) would be progressively reduced by constant practice of the sacrificial principle of yajna, and there would come a point where it would reduce to near extinction. Manomaya kosha has an additive property. Therefore, the universal manomaya kosha of society would also become purified. Peace and serenity would then dwell everywhere. This process can be compared with an observation from physics wherein repeated unidirectional friction on an iron rod organizes the dissipated magnetic forces present in the rod, thereby becoming the cause of its transformation into a magnet – a strength to reckon with.

Daan: This meaning of daan is very important, as it forms the basis of the principle of sacrifice. Daan means offering one's possessions (money or other useful items) to others unconditionally. An important point is that we should give only those items we have earned. Further, giving should be in the name of God, as if it is His grace *(prasad)* and the giver is only a medium for delivering it to the end-beneficiary.

Daan has different shades of meaning depending on the purpose and mode of 'giving'. In a yajna, the host makes three kinds of offerings. The priest offers oblations into the sacrificial fire on behalf of the host. The host gives an honorarium to the priests and also to other participants in the yajna. When the host (or anybody for that matter) decides to make an offering, their state of mind and objective determines the quality of the giving in the following ways.

Sattwic giving: When the giver considers the act of giving to be a pious duty, selects the end-beneficiary who has never obliged him in any way, chooses the most appropriate place and time for the gift, and gives, not indiscriminately, but to meet a specific need of the end-beneficiary, it is sattwic giving.

Rajasic giving: When giving is done with expectation, to improve our image, to spread our name and fame, or when inwardly the giver feels the pain of parting with the item being given, it is rajasic giving.

Tamasic giving: Giving at an inappropriate time, indiscriminately, to an unworthy end-beneficiary, or by insulting or ridiculing the end-beneficiary, is tamasic giving.

It is obvious that anything other than sattwic giving is not really daan, but a self-deceiving activity that does more harm than good. This point should be borne in mind while hosting a yajna or participating in one (by contributing to any service physically, materially or even emotionally). Swami Satyananda has been performing Sat Chandi Yajna at Rikhia since 1995. It is an ideal example of a sacrifice done selflessly for the benefit of the neighbourhood, which in this case consists of the underprivileged section of society. It is the experience of the participants that their contributory service (seva) is rewarded by long-lasting and deep satisfaction and peace of mind. They possibly earn good spiritual mileage too.

This meaning of daan and the behaviour recommended to maintain a relationship with the underprivileged members of society are interrelated. Those who are continually denied their rightful share of health, wealth, education and social status, and those who are weak in any of these respects, are the rightful end-beneficiaries of sacrificial giving. So also are the helpless, the physically-challenged, and the entire animal world, which has an equal right over all earthly resources but is denied them. The giver must bear in mind that it is an opportunity to undo some of the wrongs done by society, knowingly or unknowingly. Swami Satyananda says that unless the prana of a sadhaka becomes soft, he is unlikely to make any spiritual progress. Unconditional giving enlarges the mind, thereby making the prana soft.

Someone who spent his entire life making such offerings – Swami Sivananda – has a ready recipe for us in his thoughts on giving. He says: "Give to the poor, the sick, the helpless and the forlorn. Give to the orphans, the decrepit, the blind, and the helpless widows. If you give your whole wealth, the world will be yours. This is the secret of abundance and divine life. Therefore, give, give, give. You make a living by what you get, but you make a life by what you give. Give in plenty, you will enjoy peace and prosperity. You will attain purity of heart. You can experience an indescribable thrill of divine ecstasy and spiritual bliss. This will give you tremendous inner strength. Radiate thoughts of goodwill and share what you have with others. Disseminate spiritual knowledge to one and all. Use the material wealth, knowledge and spiritual wisdom that you possess as a divine trust for the benefit of His children. Prayer takes you halfway to God. Fasting takes you to the door of His supreme abode and charity procures your admission."

Three parts of dravya yajna

The ritualistic process of yajna requires three components – dravya, devata and tyaga. Dravya refers to the special articles that are sacrificed in the sacred fire to the chanting of mantras. Devata is the object of worship. Tyaga is the offering of oblations with an attitude of non-possessiveness towards that which is being offered.

Spiritual aspect of yajna

In order to understand the spiritual aspect of yajna, we need to understand two things: the process of external, physical yajna and the 'induction effect'. First, let us recapitulate the yajna process.

In physical yajna one invokes the fire god. The sacrificial fire is created by churning an instrument called *arani*. The middle rod of the arani is churned and through friction, fire is created. It is then taken into the sacrificial pit or altar, called the *kunda*. The fire is kindled using sticks from specified trees. Into the well-lit fire, articles of oblation are dropped amid the chanting of mantras and the singing of songs in adoration of the yajna devata. Fire converts the items of oblation into essence – fragrance spreads when the items come into contact with fire. The essence rises high, and is said to reach dyu loka, the abode of devatas, who receive and accept the oblations.

After the yajna essence comes into contact with the yajna devata, something that was not present prior to this event – *apoorva* – is created. It descends to the yajna venue via the path created by mention of the names of the rishi, chanda and devata (this precedes the chanting of the mantra). The apoorva, together with the fruit of the yajna, is received by the priest adhvaryu on behalf of the yajamana (host). The adhvaryu symbolically returns it to the host in a ritual called *shreyodanam* at the culmination of the yajna. The host is said to derive mental satisfaction, inward peace and greater purification of actions from the process, which indicates spiritual advancement.

The induced effect of yajna is a phenomenon that can be explained through modern science. It is associated with the flow of energy, such as electrical energy or magnetic energy. Suppose a high current is passing through a wire held in an east-west direction. When another piece of wire is held near it, either parallel to it or in a ring form around it, then, although the second wire is not connected to any source of electricity, the electric current is induced in it due to its proximity to a live wire. Similarly, if a strong magnet is brought near a tiny pin, the pin becomes magnetized merely by the magnet's presence.

The source is said to induce energy in both the wire and the pin. However, there will be no induced effect if a wooden stick is brought near the high-voltage wire or the magnet, because wood is not a conductor of electrical or magnetic energy, and its internal structure is not altered by proximity to the source. The power of the induced effect and the duration of this effect depend on the power of the input source and the time it is kept near the object of induction. Using these two pieces of information, we can attempt to understand internal yajna and the importance of external, physical yajna in inducing internal yajna in the yajamana.

Process of spiritualization: The supreme consciousness or Brahman descends into the human body in the form of a 'soul'. In Shakta philosophy, it is called the *jiva* or individual spirit. Brahman is called Shiva or the universal spirit. Shiva is the inert power, which needs a driving force. This force is Adi Shakti, which is responsible for bringing Shiva into the body (as jiva). The abode of Shiva is sahasrara, situated in the human body at the crown of the head. Just as Shiva in the body is known as jiva, Adi Shakti in the human body is known as the mother principle, *matri tattwa*, possibly because the mother is the seat of creation and the means for the manifestation of jiva. This female principle is given various names like Tripura Sundari, Bhuvaneshvari, etc. In raja yoga, it is called kundalini shakti.

After creating the body and fetching Shiva, this shakti contracts. Therefore, it descends to the lowest point in the body, mooladhara plexus, where it remains dormant. It is said that since becoming inactive, Shiva as jiva loses awareness of the supreme truth. His awareness becomes confined to the physical world as the sole reality. In the absence of the power of kundalini shakti, prana shakti controls the bodily functions of jiva, which is established in body consciousness alone. This phenomenon is described as impurity of the soul, and requires samskaras (sacrificial rites) to be purified[2].

Yogic understanding: The aim of yoga is to awaken the kundalini from its dormant state and direct its rise upwards to unite with Shiva, so that awareness of the transcendental truth is regained and brought to the normal level of consciousness. The jiva thus becomes enlightened. This is also the transformation of the jiva, the individual soul, into Shiva, the supreme soul.

Raja yoga is all about arousing the kundalini power and establishing its ascent up through the chakras to unite with Shiva in sahasrara. The recommended practices for this purpose are asana, pranayama, kriya yoga and

---

[2] See Chapter 8

meditation[3]. When the kundalini awakens and its ascent begins, it passes through and ignites six major power centres which open up different domains of subtle knowledge to the practitioner. These centres are known as mooladhara, swadhisthana, manipura, anahata, vishuddhi and ajna chakras.

In a satsang in 2005, Swami Satyananda described the manifestation of the spiritual ascent of jiva as a major life event. Quoting from *Saundarya Lahari* (a hymn to the Divine Mother by Adi Shankaracharya), he explained that when the kundalini meets Shiva in sahasrara, it explodes the nectar. It remains in sahasrara for some time, and when it descends once again to mooladhara, it nectarizes the chakras and the five organs of knowledge on its way (*Sudha dhara sarai* . . ." Verse 10, *Saundarya Lahari*). Sri Swamiji also explained the importance of physical yajna, which he called 'external yajna'. Efforts to arouse the kundalini are equivalent to performing yajna internally.

Yajna as the first step in spirituality: The yajna fire is ignited using the arani. A well-kindled fire evokes flames that visibly rise upwards. The greatness of external yajna lies in the fact that it induces internal yajna. The effect depends on the strength, potential and quantum of energy in the source. So the extent of the ignition in internal yajna depends on the power and purity of the external yajna. But in theory, external yajna sets internal yajna in motion.

To achieve internal yajna, the yajamana (host) uses his spinal cord to ignite the symbolic fire. In external yajna, the fire is ignited at the bottom of the arani. In internal yajna, since the spinal cord acts as the rod of the arani, the fire is ignited at its root, i.e. in the mooladhara plexus. Therefore, this chakra can be equated with the fire-pit of physical yajna. This fireplace is called a 'kunda'. The mooladhara plexus can then be called *chit agni kunda*, the bowl where *chit*

[3] For details, refer to publications of the Yoga Publications Trust, Munger, Bihar, India

or awareness is concentrated. The energy which is in a dormant form in that kunda is called kundalini ('that which comes from the kunda'). Mooladhara is the seat of awareness. The energy that emerges from the chit agni kunda is known as *chit agni kunda sambhuta* (*sambhuta* means 'that which originates', feminine gender). It is no coincidence that one of the thousand names of the Goddess in *Lalita Sahasra Nama Stotra* is Chit Agni Kunda Sambhuta.

In external yajna, the flames rise from the fire-pit, accept the oblations, convert them into essence, take it to the yajna devata, and return, bringing with them the fruits of the yajna. The yajamana (host) receives contentment and peace. In internal yajna, the yajamana arouses the kundalini. The chit agni kunda sambhuta power reaches sahasrara, opens the pot of nectar, and on its way back showers nectar on the host, purifying his body and enlightening his soul. He experiences the bliss of *anandamaya kosha,* the abode of supreme consciousness. In fact, at this point in time, he achieves moksha, salvation.

Individual effort: If the yajamana has not purified himself completely or is not able to generate sufficient induction power through external yajna, he will either not be able to ignite the kundalini or will do so in a weak manner. The end result may not provide sufficient force to push the kundalini up to sahasrara. Also, if the host is not truly purified through samskaras, or has not heightened the powers of his body, mind and soul, he may not be able to act as a conductor of energy. He will be like a stick of wood, totally inhibiting the flow of energy. His external yajna will not induce internal yajna at all. So the mechanics of physical yajna, the internalization of the meaning of yajna by the host, and the samskaras and sadhana all become very important in making the proper impact on the personality. The internalization of external yajna spiritualizes the aspirant[4].

---

[4] See Chapter 9 on internal yajna

We have seen that when sacrifice takes the form of action, based on ritualistic processes, it is external or dravya yajna. It has three parts: the sacrificial fire, articles of oblation, and devata(s) for adoration. Dravya yajna is done for personal gain like discharging one's duties with respect to the three debts inherited at birth, for satiating personal desires such as earning peace, prosperity, a ticket to heaven, etc. They are also performed for their overall benefits to society. An important advantage of dravya yajna is its induced effect to create the yajnic process in oneself, which leads to spiritual upliftment. Although an individual's spiritual development is not dependent solely on the performance of dravya yajna, it definitely works as a catalytic agent.

The second form of sacrifice is karma or actions to discharge one's duties and to interact in the world. It does not involve physical oblations in the sacrificial fire, but implies application of the sacrificial principle in one's interactions with the world. It is an intermediate position, above the gross state in which ritualistic yajna is performed and below the spiritual attainment wherein a constant internal yajna takes place in oneself and every action becomes an oblation in karma yajna.

Yajna in the universe

Ritualistic and karma-oriented yajna are man-made. The first is called dravya yajna, and the latter may be called karma yajna. In yogic parlance, it is called karma yoga. The foundation of sacrifice is derived from the principle of give and take found in Nature that sustains the universe. When rishis had the revelation of this principle, they probably used the word sacrifice because give and take between different entities in the universe is cyclical, and not in the form of mutual exchange. One gives to the second entity, but takes from the third, and so on. This cyclic phenomenon is the basis of the concept of yajna in the universe (yajna in Nature).

The *Rig Veda* speaks at length about the universe – its creation, expansion, sustenance, etc. The rishis' vision of the universe, as brought out through various mantras and suktas, can be understood as follows.

- The universe has been created by the will of God, who took the form of Prajapati or Brahma for its creation.
- The universe is expanding and sustaining on the basis of a give and take process that is occurring continuously in Nature. God took the form of Vishnu for sustenance and growth.
- All that is created has an end and all that has ended is reborn. God takes the form of Rudra or Shiva for destruction.
- All entities in the universe are made up of five basic elements. The different objects are the forms created due to a combination of these elements. After destruction of the form, its elements disintegrate and return to the storehouse of the five elements.

Principle of sacrifice in universal yajna: Every creation in the universe is based on sacrifice by an already created entity. Since creation in the universe is eternal, yajna is continuously going on in Nature.

All parts of the universe are interdependent for their sustenance and growth. For example, the sun gives energy to all elements of the solar system. Its energy is replenished by Soma. Trees receive the essence required for their growth from the earth and atmosphere, but give their fruits to the sentient world. Since such an act of giving is not for oneself, and is also not in return for what has been received, it is worthy of being called sacrifice. Thus, earth can be said to have sacrificed for the trees, and the trees for the sentient beings. In other words, every entity is both a giver and taker. In Vedic parlance, every part of the universe is food for someone, and it is also the recipient of food from some other part. In Sanskrit, food is known as *anna* and its recipient *annad*. The anna-annad principle is universal and similar to the sacrificial principle.

The universe is the creation of Prajapati. It is said that he created it out of himself, and after creation it became his part in the new form. Therefore, while describing the process of sacrifice at the universal level, the Vedas describe it as, "Prajapati sacrificed himself for himself through the process of yajna." Rishis call this process yajna in Nature. It is a non-stop and continual process occurring everywhere in the universe. However, it is beyond human vision, so it is called paroksha yajna. *Para* means 'beyond' and *aksha* means 'eye'. Hence the term *paroksha* for that which happens beyond the human eye.

Metaphoric expressions of rishis: Rishis understood the principle of give and take and the sacrificial principle behind creation and sustenance, so they emulated it to create wealth of all kinds. Since they clearly saw the divine force behind all creation, the element of adoration of devatas entered the man-made yajna processes. This is evident from the fact that all the Vedas, Brahmana texts like the *Shatapatha Brahmana*, *Taittiriya Brahmana*, *Tandya Brahmana*, etc. have described yajna as a process to be equated with god. So it is that we see varied expressions for the single term yajna in the Vedas, such as:

- Yajna is at the centre of the universe
- Yajna is a karma of superlative order
- The anna-annad principle is yajna
- Prajapati is yajna
- Agni is yajna
- Vishnu is yajna, and so on.

Yajna then is defined in various ways. Yajna in Nature can be understood through symbolic events from the physical world. Such symbols are many. However, there is no equivalence between them. The symbolic forms of yajna (as representations of natural yajna) are not alternatives to each other for the definition of yajna. They are, in fact, partial representations of larger than life phenomena. At one place, we find that yajna is defined as Agni. At another place, yajna is called Vishnu. At yet another place, yajna is said to be Brahma. This creates a dilemma and we are at a loss to decide whether Agni is yajna, Vishnu is yajna or Agni is Vishnu!

Mathematically, if A=B and A=C, then it follows that B=C. But here the mathematical equivalence is not intended. If we still want to use mathematical language, we can, at best, say that if B is a subset of A, and C is also a subset of A, then A is a superset of both B and C. It does not lead to the conclusion that B and C are similar or equivalent sets.

If yajna is Agni, and yajna is Vishnu, it should follow that Agni is Vishnu. But Agni is not Vishnu, as they both represent two different qualities. Therefore, when we say that yajna is Agni and yajna is Vishnu too, it should mean that Agni represents one quality of yajna and Vishnu represents another. Yajna is Agni from a particular angle and Vishnu from another. Yajna is partially equal to Agni and also partially equal to Vishnu. Yajna is Agni as also Vishnu as also Prajapati and so on. From the point of view of the principle of origin, yajna is Agni, and from the point of view of expanse, yajna is Vishnu. So there is actually no need for confusion. However, if this point is not taken into account and partial representations are wrongly taken as the total representation, it could lead not only to confusion, but also to wrong interpretations of yajna.

The multiple definitions indicate the sway of yajna. However, there are partial overlaps in interpreting the concept of yajna. Dr. Urmila Devi Sharma[5] discusses their relevance in great detail. The gist of her exposition based on the *Rig Veda* and *Shatapatha Brahmana* is that yajna is at the centre of Vedic science. It is a means of gaining control over the mortal world and heaven, the visible and the invisible, sentient and other beings. This universe is divided into three distinct parts: prithivi (earth), antariksha (sky) and dyu (the space beyond) lokas. Yajna is the visible, manifest form of the events and reactions continually taking place in all three lokas. Sage Yajnavalkya has defined yajna as the navel of the universe. Our universe is action-bound and dynamic, not static. Yajna, which represents the directive process of events in the three lokas, is the best

---

[5] *Veda Navaneetam*, Dr. Urmila Devi Sharma, Astha Prakasham, Ram Kutir, Jaipur, 2000

display of the action-bound universe. Therefore, the *Shatapatha Brahmana* defines it as the most superior karma – *Yajno vai shrestham karma* (SB 1.7.1.5, TB 3.2.1.4).

Thus we see that sacrifice in three forms can lead to either dravya yajna, karma yajna or yajna in Nature. Therefore, the principle of sacrifice has to be internalized to be successful in life. It is said that knowledge has to be earned by investing in every second, and building wealth by collecting every penny. If a second is wasted or a penny lost, one cannot expect to expand wisdom or build wealth. It is imperative then that to build the wealth of broadminded generosity, one has to continually and consciously make an effort.

The *Rig Veda* assures that yajna can be the best means for this. Yajna is equated with a boat that will steer the traveller through stormy waters and strong currents, and lead him surely and safely to the destination. In *Vishvedeva Sukta* (R 10.63.10), the composer rishi says, "We board the 'yajna karma' boat equipped with a spade or an oar with a view to achieving prosperity and godliness." What is the speciality of this boat? It is our saviour and best protector; it is expansive and huge, flawless, cosy, blissful, and above all without even the smallest hole.

IN CONCLUSION

- The term 'yajna' has tripolarity in many different ways.
- Yajna has three forms – dravya yajna, karma yajna and yajna in the universe. The first two are man-made yajnas, and the third was created by God.
- External (dravya) yajna can (and should) induce internal yajna. This is the spiritual aspect of yajna at the physical level.
- Yajna is a universal phenomenon, even though not perceivable by the human eye.
- There are multiple definitions of yajna that explain its universality. Taken together, they indicate the vastness of yajna. Each definition is only a partial representation of the universal phenomenon.

6

Classifications of Yajna

Yajna has many attributes. Using some of the important, commonly used ones, we can group yajnas into classes. Such a classification facilitates easy reference, as it helps in visualizing the broad structure of a yajna. If the type of oblationary material is a classified characteristic, for example, then a reference to soma yajna would immediately reflect a yajna in which the principal item of oblation is soma juice. Since the attributes are not mutually exclusive, a yajna may fall in more than one class. Thus, rajasooya yajna may fall in the shrauta class since its procedures are based on the Shrutis, and it could also be grouped under soma yajna since soma juice is its main item of oblation.

Role of agni in dravya yajna

Before going into the details of this division, we need to know more about agni, as the sacrificial fire is the basic component of external or dravya yajna. Agni and dravya (ingredients) are the two prime requirements of a dravya yajna, and no dravya yajna is possible without them. Agni is an important devata from the *Rig Veda*, and is considered as the Lord in manifest form. Agni means the one who:

- Was the first among the creations of the Creator
- Is offered the first oblation in any karma kanda
- Gives upward direction to the worshipper
- Gives his own form to anything that touches him

• Brings the yajna devata(s) to the yajnashala and also accepts the oblations on their behalf.

Agni has two distinct forms as far as utility is concerned.
1. **Laukikagni**: The fire routinely used in daily household work and other everyday activities. It is not to be used in yajnic rituals.
2. **Yajnagni**: Agni used in rituals is commonly known as yajnagni. It has two forms – smartagni and shrautagni.

(i) **Smartagni**: All grihya samskaras, smarta karmas and smarta yajnas are performed on smartagni. These may include samskaras such as the children's thread ceremony, routine samskaras *(nitya karma)*, incidental karmas *(naimittic karma)*, or purpose-specific karmas *(kamya karma)*. It has many alternative names – aupasana agni, grihya, grihapati, grihyagni, shalagni, and avasathya agni. This form of agni is installed at the time of marriage for *upasana* (ritualistic karmas) in life, hence the term 'aupasana' agni. It is worshipped and kept alive in the house at least in the form of a spark throughout life. Unless a person is a smartagni holder, they cannot take and install shrautagni. This underlines the importance of smartagni.

(ii) **Shrautagni**: The form of agni used to perform yajnas prescribed and recommended by the Shrutis (Vedas) is known as shrautagni. Since the yajamana can expand his desire to transcend prithivi loka and reach dyu or swarga loka, it is also called 'expansive agni', *vaitanikagni*. It is used in the agnihotra ritual and other shrauta yajnas. It has five different forms, each of which has a specific role to play in shrauta karmas. Collectively called 'panchagni', their names are garhapatya, dakshina, ahavaniya, sabhya and avasathya. The Vedas assign a major role to the first three forms in most of the shrauta yajna karmas. Collectively, they are called 'tretagni'.

Garhapatya: According to Panini, since this form of agni is related to a householder, the *grihapati*, it is known as garhapatya. It is said that the oblation offered to the devata through this form of agni helps the yajamana to conquer earth. The earth being spherical, it is symbolically represented by building a circular fire-pit (kunda) in which the garhapatya agni is installed (TB 1.1.8).

Dakshinagni: The kunda used for this agni is situated to the south of the mahavedi, and hence it is called dakshinagni (*dakshin* means south). The oblations offered in dakshinagni help in conquering the second (antariksha) loka, the region of the sky. The sky being bow-shaped, the shape of the dakshinagni kunda is semicircular.

Ahavaniya agni: All oblations to invoke the devatas are offered in this agni, hence the name ahavaniya (*ahavan* means to invoke). The oblations offered here help in conquering dyu loka or swarga (heaven). Hence its shape is square or rectangular (swarga is perceived as possessing such a shape).

Classification by type of sacrifice

Yajna is sacrifice. This sacrifice occurs in Nature and elsewhere too. The type of sacrifice leads to the first classification of yajna.

- If the sacrifice is at the level of Nature, it is universal yajna *(paroksha yajna)*. It is at the base of the dynamic equilibrium in Nature.
- If the sacrifice is at the mental, emotional or spiritual level, it is internal yajna *(antaryama yajna)*. It is at the base of our mental set-up.
- If the sacrifice is at the physical level, it is *(pratyaksha yajna)* a model of paroksha yajna.

Classification of dravya yajna

The Mimamsa texts and Shrauta sutras interpret yajna as sacrifice of articles *(dravya)* done with the purpose of offering them to the yajna devata. The oblation made to the devata in this type of yajna is called *havi*. Therefore, external or physical yajna is also known as man-made, artificial, bhautic (material), havi or dravya yajna. We shall use the term dravya or external yajna to denote pratyaksha yajna.

Dravya yajnas are many in number, and are characterized by purpose, procedure, type of dravya, duration, etc. They differ in procedural complexity, duration and dravya. There is no specific rule for classifying dravya yajnas. However, the type of Vedic texts in which they are described, their purpose, the 'institution', dravya used, etc. can be used as characteristics for classifying them.

Classification by Vedic text

Depending on the Vedic texts in which they are described, yajnas are classified as shrauta, smarta and tantric yajnas.

Shrauta yajna: *Shrutyuktam yajna shrauta yajna* – "Yajnas defined by the Shrutis are shrauta yajna." Yajnas having a base in the Samhita and Brahmana texts are known as shrauta yajna. Their mantras are taken from the Vedas, and procedural details, ritualistic statements and rules of conduct from the Brahmana texts. Initially, shrauta yajnas were based on the trio of the Vedas – *Rig, Yajur* and *Sama*. Later, however, the *Atharva Veda* was also included. The shrauta yajnas performed today have mantras drawn from all four Vedas. They are 21 in number[1]. Examples of shrauta yajnas are agnihotra, darshapoorna, chaturmasya, pashubandha, soma yaga, etc.

Smarta yajna: *Smrityuktam yajna jasmarta yajna* – "Yajnas defined by the Smritis are smarta yajna." This type of yajna is based on the Smriti granthas. It is mentioned in the *Rigvidhan Grantha* that smarta yajnas are performed using Vedic, Puranic and Tantric mantras. Procedural details are given in the *Grihya Sutras*. Each Veda has its own independent and separate *Grihya Sutra*. The 21 samskaras, 23 smarta yajnas and the pancha maha yajnas fall in this category[2].

Tantric yajna: This type of yajna is based on procedures and mantras taken from the tantra shastra and *Atharva Veda*. Rig mantras are also employed. It is said that tantric yajnas are part of smarta yajnas, and are performed on laukikagni.

---

[1] See Chapter 8

[2] See Chapters 8 and 11

Classification by purpose

Some yajnas are to be done routinely (nitya yajna), others at the occurrence of specific events (naimittic), and yet others are prescribed for accomplishing a cherished desire (kamya).

Nitya yajna: The Smritis and Brahmanas have recommended that everyone should perform five yajnas daily, known as nitya (perpetual) yajna. Normally, the outcome of a yajna is called *punya*. However, unlike other yajnas, nitya yajnas do not result in accumulation of punya. Interestingly, however, if the above mandate is violated and they are not performed daily, it results in the accumulation of sin or *papa* on the part of the doer (or non-doer!). Although it sounds strange, the message refers to the value of righteousness and the ill effects of its absence. (If you do righteous work, you are said to have done your duty, so you are not rewarded, but if you do not do righteous work, you disturb the harmonious cycle of society, which is your moral downfall, so you earn a penalty[3].)

According to Advaita Vedanta, a system of Indian philosophy, regular practice of nitya yajna results in the purging of ills accumulated through past births. Such purification has to be a continuous process, otherwise it is easy to fall back into the old patterns of mind and action. Naturally then, if nitya yajna is not performed regularly, no purging will take place and the accumulated ills (known as samskaras in yogic parlance) will be carried forward to the next birth as liabilities. Further, the damages of the current birth will be added too. In Vedic society, each family head performed nitya yajnas himself, not through hired priests or others.

Naimittic yajna: Yajnas have been recommended for special events like the birth of a child, a baby's first haircut, excessive and/or heavy rains, earthquakes, etc. Such yajnas could also be performed by a priest.

Kamya yajna: This type of yajna serves to satiate cherished, unfulfilled desires. The desires could be for

---

[3] Refer to the description of pancha maha yajnas in Chapter 9

oneself or society, the nation, the monarch, etc. The desire for a son *(putra kameshti)*, good rainfall *(kariri ishti)*, good health *(jyotishtoma)*, etc. are examples. According to the Upanishads, this type of yajna emerged and became popular in society during Treta yuga (MuU 1.2.1). A detailed study of these yajnas will in fact reflect the beliefs of Vedic society.

Classification by havi dravya

This classification applies only to shrauta yajnas. The item of oblation or havi used in a yajna decides the classification as ishti, pashu yaga and soma yaga.

1. **Ishti**: Uses the essence of butter *(ajya)* and a cake made from special flour *(purodasha)* as the dravya for oblation.
2. **Pashu yaga**: In addition to the dravya used in ishti, this yajna also uses a sacrificial animal.
3. **Soma yaga**: Uses the dravya used in ishti and pashu yaga, plus the juice of a special creeper called soma valli.

Classification by yajna samstha

Another way of classifying yajnas is according to *samstha* or institution. In Vedic parlance, the term 'institution' has a specific meaning. Before grouping yajnas by institution, we will look at this concept.

Being the symbolic representation of sacrifice occurring in Nature, yajna must be performed properly to reflect the natural processes. Nature has immaculate and exhaustive ways of giving and taking, but each one is done perfectly. Therefore, yajna as a process should also be carried out systematically from beginning to end according to the prescription of the Vedic texts. Successful culmination of a yajna depends on meticulous preparation of all sub-processes. Preparation of the yajna vedi, fabricating and assembling the implements, organization of the dravya, appointing the priests, raising the yajnashala or yajna mandap are some of the important aspects that must be looked into carefully by the host. In the process of yajna, the host must have exact procedural and sequential knowledge. Alternatively, he should have recourse to a knowledgeable person so that from start to finish things go exactly according to the prescriptions of the Smritis, Shrutis and Brahmanas.

The activities leading to the preparatory processes, the way of going about them, details of the materials to be used, etc. were standardized over a period of time and became the necessary prerequisite for any yajna. All that needs to be done to accomplish the logistic work, gathering the implements and materials, directions on creating the right state of mind in the host and other participants, assembling knowledgeable priests, etc. is jointly known as yajna samstha (institution).

Yajna samstha is an arrangement of all the activities required to perform a particular yajna. It is an institution without a constitution *(asamsthaka samstha)*, i.e. it is not a body of people working for a cause according to a code (like a medical or sports institution). Exhaustive information about instituting the whole yajna conglomeration is contained in systematic compilations of the Kalpa Sutras. Now let us look at the classification of yajna by yajna samstha.

Sapta paka samstha: Yajnas that use havi dravya prepared from food items consumable by human beings, like grain *(yava)*, rice *(vrihi)*, milk, curd, etc., fall in this category. There are seven paka yajnas: (i) prathah homa, (ii) sayam homa, (iii) sthali paka, (iv) bali vaishvadeva, (v) pitri yajna, (vi) ashtaka, and (vii) pashu. Paka yajna samstha falls in the smarta category and uses ekagni, one fire.

Sapta havi samstha: In these yajnas, the oblation material is cooked using raw material called havi dravya[4], hence the term havi samstha. Havi is a cooked item made from rice, flour from grains like yava, etc. The seven yajnas are: (i) agnyadheya, (ii) agnihotra, (iii) darsha, (iv) poornamasa, (v) navasyeshti, (vi) chaturmasya, and (vii) pashubandha.

Sapta soma samstha: In this type of samstha, soma juice is offered to the gods as havi. The sapta soma samstha are:

---

[4] See Chapter 7

(i) agnishtoma, (ii) atyagnishtoma, (iii) ukthya, (iv) shodashi, (v) vajapeya, (vi) atiratra, and (vii) aptoryama. Both sapta havi and sapta soma samsthas fall under the shrauta category and use tretagni, three fires.

Classification by procedure

A yajna can also be characterized by its procedures. In some cases, a group of yajnas follows the same or similar procedures by and large, and differs in only a few details. Thus, the procedure adopted in a yajna can indicate its class, or a procedure can be a classificatory characteristic. The types of procedures are listed below.

Prakriti yajna: Some yajnas are called prakriti yaga. A prakriti yaga is the role model for other yajnas. They define the main procedures for a group of yajnas. For example, darshapoornamasa is the prakriti yaga, or model, for all yajnas falling in the ishti category. All ishtis are performed along the lines of darshapoornamasa.

Vikriti yajna: A yajna whose major procedure is more or less along the lines of its prakriti yaga, but which has certain special additional/deviational procedures, for example, about the principal devata, main havi or karma, is termed vikriti yajna. Kamya yajnas like putra kameshti and kariri are some examples of these yajnas.

Ubhaya swaroopa yajna: Such yajnas are of both types – prakriti and vikriti. This means that they have some procedures from prakriti yajnas, but a few others are different, for example, agnishomiya pashu yaga.

Unubhaya swaroopa yajna: Some yajnas are of neither the prakriti nor the vikriti type, and are known as novel (apoorva) karmas. One ishti called *grihamedhiya*, which is a part of chaturmasya yajna, is an example of this type of yajna.

Other yajnas: A few yajnas do not fall into any of the above classifications. They are large in every dimension – duration, procedure and scope. In a way, they are vikriti yajnas. They include many ishtis, soma yaga, etc. Vajapeya, ashvamedha, and rajasooya are some examples of such yajnas.

7

Mechanics of Yajna

To perform a yajna, a large pavilion-like structure called a yajnashala or yajna mandap is constructed at the yajna venue. Normally, it is surrounded by an outer pavilion intended for spectators. When a layperson visits a yajna venue, the gross objects that catch the attention could be the neatly raised yajnashala, its decoration, the fire-pits, large and somewhat peculiar wooden spoons, spatulas and vessels, articles of oblation, and so on.

As a general rule, when everything appears orderly, spic and span, it implies that several systems and precision methods have been at work to produce that effect of 'normality'. So it is possible that our friend visiting the neatly laid-out yajna site misses the point that no structure or dimension at a yajna site is randomly created or chosen at the whim of the host or priest. It is a result of the substantial engineering work done by the Vedic sciences to create a perfect yajnashala. The mechanics of yajnas are very precise indeed, and detailed in specific Vedic texts. Topics such as dimensions of the mandap, how to locate east exactly, placement details of kundas, dhishnyas, vedis, etc. and other structural aspects are covered in the supplementary part of Vedic literature, the Kalpa Sutras.

To reap the benefits of a yajna, the mechanics must be as strictly adhered to as the sequence of oblations or the chanting of mantras. We will take a broad overview of the science of raising a yajna venue, casting a brief look at the principal structures and delving into a few dimensional details to get an inkling of the exactitude that must be practised in its creation.

Shulba Sutras

The adhvaryu priest has to ensure that the construction of various structures within the yajnashala such as the kundas, vedi, chiti, etc. required for ritualistic operations and the directional and dimensional details of the mandap are according to the injunctions of the shastras. The Brahmana Granthas explain the need for different fire altars and give details of the procedures for using them. They also give dimensional specifications, directional details for the mandap, etc., but do not cover construction. This is where two Vedangas, Kalpa and Jyotish, come in.

The Kalpa Sutras are comprised of four parts: Shrauta, Shulba, Grihya and Dharma Sutras[1] . Details of the mechanics necessary for constructing the kunda, chiti, vedi and erecting the mandap are covered by the Shulba Sutras. Agni kunda, chiti, etc. are required only in dravya yajnas. Their procedures are covered in the *Yajur Veda*, and the Shulba Sutras give the engineering details. Therefore, only the Kalpas of the *Yajur Veda* contain Shulba Sutras. Incidentally, there are seven major Shulba Sutras of the *Krishna Yajur Veda* and only one Shulba Sutra of the *Shukla Yajur Veda*.

The Shulba Sutras are not treatises on Vedic geometry, but contain information about theorems required for drawing figures and structures used in yajna. This information is in the form of sutras. *Shulba* means 'thread'. It also means 'to measure'. *Sutra* means a 'thin thread'. It also means a rule expressed in cryptic yet unambiguous words to convey the essence (an aphorism). So, *shulba sutra* can be interpreted as a set of rules for drawing structures and geometrical figures using a piece of thread (and a peg). It contains methods of calculating values of mathematical parameters like pi, the

---

[1] See Chapter 2 and Annexure 1

square root of 2, etc., required in deciding the areas of geometrical figures. It also gives methods to decide the length of the hypotenuse of a right-angled triangle using the areas constructed on the other two sides (a theorem popularly associated with the Greek mathematician Pythagoras). It employs ingenious methods to make even or odd numbers of equal parts of length of a straight line and so on.

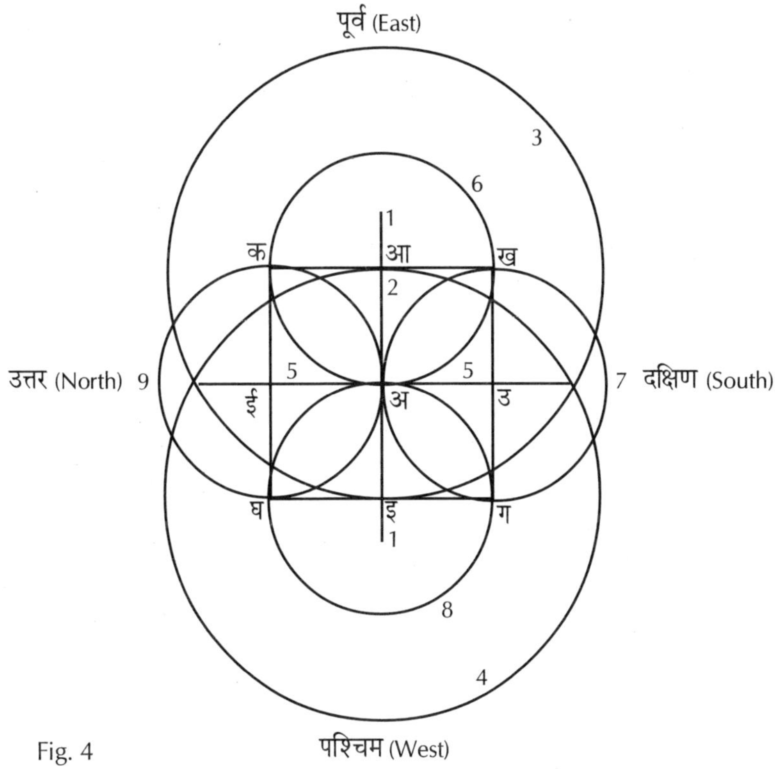

Fig. 4

Diagram from the Shulba Sutras showing how to draw squares using circles

To draw a geometrical figure, one needs a unit of measure and tools of measurement. The Vedic standard unit of measurement is an *angula*, which means the breadth of the forefinger of the yajamana, i.e. a finger-length.

The Shulba Sutras use tools called *dori* (a cord or thin rope), *kalaka* (thread without elasticity) and *shanku* (peg). A dori is a thin rope made out of grass (*shun, balva, kusha* or *munja*)[2].

The geometry used in the Shulba Sutras is quite mind-boggling. The positions of the sun and solar planets, and the time of the year, *nakshatra,* is used in an ingenious way to decide the directions. The rules to be followed for placing bricks in construction of the chitis are meticulous.

The Shulba Sutras use various units of measurement. The following table gives a list of measures used in *Baudhayana Shulba Sutra*.

Table 2: Vedic units of measurement

Unit	In terms of standard unit	Approx. value in cm
1 angula (finger-length)	14 grains of anu or 34 grains of sesame	1.9 cm
1 kshudrapada	10 angula	19 cm
1 pradesha	12 angula	22.8 cm
1 prithottar yuga	13 angula	24.7 cm
1 pada	15 angula	28.5 cm
1 esha	188 angula	357.2 cm
1 aksha	104 angula	197.6 cm
1 yuga	86 angula	163.4 cm
1 janu	32 angula	60.8 cm
1 shamya = 1 bahu	36 angula	68.4 cm
1 prakrama = 2 pada	30 angula	57 cm
1 aratni = 2 pradesha	24 angula	45.6 cm
1 purusha = 5 aratni	120 angula	228 cm
1 vyama = 5 aratni	120 angula	228 cm
1 vyayama = 4 aratni	96 angula	182.4 cm
1 virata = 10 pada	150 angula	285 cm

Principal structures at a yajnashala

An important aspect of any dravya yajna is the process of offering *havi* (articles of oblation) to Agni. The *kunda* (fire altars), *vedi* (flat space between altars), *mandapa* (small canopy

[2] We have used *Baudhayana Shulba Sutra* and its Marathi translation published by the Govt. of Maharashtra as the main source to understand the application of Vedic geometry in drawings, figures and structures used in a yajna.

Pavilion (havirdhana mandap) of a yajnashala

for special functions) are the principal structures around which a yajna process is centred. Let us take a brief look at them.

In a shrauta yajna, fire (agni) is established in three pits. Smarta yajnas use a single fireplace. These fireplaces are the platforms for the main process of offering oblations, and are known as kunda(s). Apart from the main process, a few other processes (especially in shrauta yajnas) require the priests to perform rituals with separate, small fireplaces known as dhishnyas. Normally, a *dhishnya* is a small, circular platform raised on the ground.

Near the kunda an area is earmarked for specific activities by the yajamana and the priest in charge of oblational activities (adhvaryu). Normally, its location is between two kundas. It is known as a vedi.

Shrauta yajnas need one more type of fireplace over and above the agni kunda and dhishnya. It is known as *agni chiti*, and constructed using specially-made bricks. The process is known as *agnichayana*.

Lastly, a pavilion or shade-like structure needs to be raised to cover all the fireplaces and the work area used by the priests and the yajamana couple. It is the yajnashala or the main mandap. Depending on the type of yajna, the main mandap has one to five sub-mandaps.

Yajna Mandap

(Fig. 5)

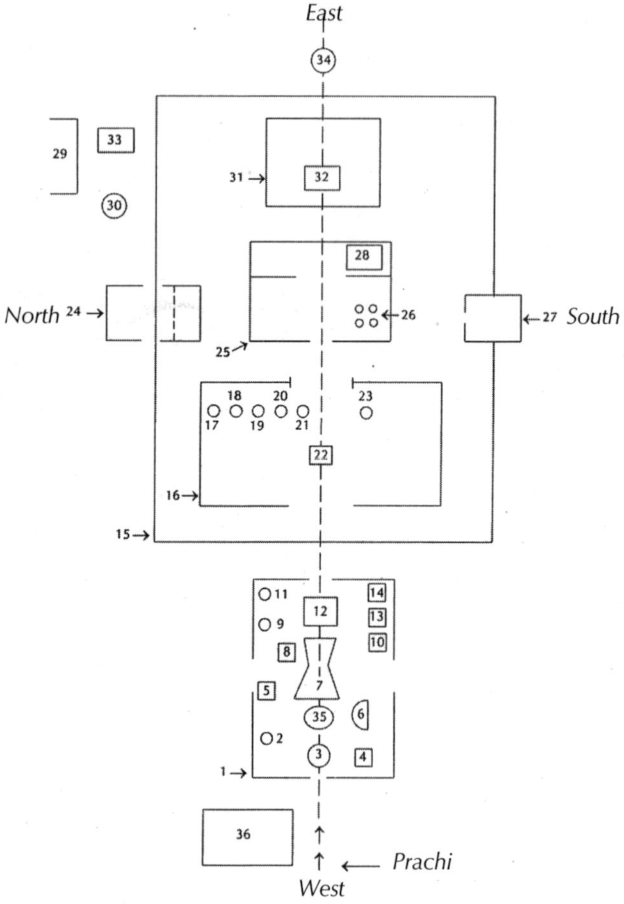

1	Pragvansha	13	Brahma	25	Haviradhana mandap
2	Pravargya khara	14	Sadasya	26	Uparava
3	Garhapatya agni	15	Mahavedi	27	Marjaliya mandap
4	Seat of yajamana patni	16	Sadomandap	28	Graha khara
5	Hota	17	Acchavaka dhishnya	29	Shamitra mandap
6	Dakshinagni	18	Neshtha dhishnya	30	Utkara-2
7	Yajamana vedi	19	Pota dhishnya	31	Uttaravedi
8	Place of agnidhra	20	Brahmanacchansin	32	Chiti
9	Utkara-1	21	Hota dhishnya	33	Chatvala
10	Seat of yajamana	22	Udumbari	34	Yupa
11	Praneta	23	Maitravaruna dhishnya	35	Antarlayama
12	Ahavaniya agni	24	Agnidhriya mandap	36	Patnishala

Significance of functional areas of a yajnashala

The priests use the agni kunda, vedi and agni chiti to complete the oblationary processes. Their location in the yajna mandap together with the position of the yajamana, priests and others is fixed.

Fig. 5 shows a typical yajnashala used in shrauta yajnas, in particular, soma yajnas. The structures, sub-mandaps, people working in a yajnashala have been assigned numbers. There are 36 entities in all. Table 3 gives the names of the corresponding structures, people, etc. For example, 10 indicates the position where the yajamana sits during the yajna proceedings, 16 shows the sub-mandap, called a sadomandap. The 36 entities are regrouped according to function in Table 4, under six headings. Column 3 gives the name as it appears in Fig. 5. So the yajamana who was shown as the 10th entity in Fig. 5, appears in row 6, column 3 of the table below.

Table 3: Details of yajna mandap of a shrauta yajna

Group No.	Group Name	Names of entities *(Numbers in bracket indicate the location of the entity in Fig 5)*
1	Agni kunda	*Types*: Garhapatya (3), Dakshinagni (6), Ahavaniya (12), Pravargya Khara (2)
2	Vedi	*Types*: Yajamana Vedi (7), Uttaravedi (31), Mahavedi (15), Shamitra (29)
3	Dhishnya	*Used by*: Acchavaka (17), Neshta (18), Pota (19), Brahma (20), Hota (21), Maitravaruna (23)
4	Chiti	Uttaravedi (32)
5	Sub-mandap	*Types*: Pragvansha (1), Sadomandap (16), Agnidhriya (24), Havirdhana (25), Marjaliya (27)
6	Other	*Used for*: Yajamana Patni (4), Hota (5), Agnidhra (8), Utkara (9), Pranita (11), Yajamana (10), Brahma (13), Sadasya (14), Udumbari (22), Uparava (26), Graha/Chamasa Khara (28), Utkara 2 (30), Chatvala (33), Yupa (34), Antarlayama (35)

IMPORTANT ENTITIES OF A YAJNASHALA

There are many architectural details that must be carefully considered in erecting a yajnashala. The most important constructional entities are given below.

Agni kundas

The havi is poured into agni through oblations. In shrauta yajnas, there are a minimum of three agni kundas.

Garhapatya agni kunda: Generally, it is a circular pit with a diameter of 96 finger-lengths (approx. 182.4 cm). Its position is near the western entrance of the pragvansha mandap. This kunda is constructed by using either rectangular or square bricks. The procedure for making the circular shape is given in a specific sutra (B 2.62–72).

Ahavaniya agni kunda: This kunda is square in shape and located towards the eastern entrance of the pragvansha mandap. Its sides are 96 finger-lengths. There is no specific mention in *Baudhayana Shulba Sutra* about the types of bricks used. It is likely to be along the lines of construction of the square garhapatya agni kunda.

Dakshinagni kunda: This kunda is located towards the southern entrance of the pragvansha mandap. It is semicircular in shape with a radius of 77.82 finger-lengths (147.86 cm).

The area of all three kundas is the same, irrespective of shape. The distance between the garhapatya and ahavaniya agni kundas depends on the varna of the yajamana. If the yajamana is a brahmin, the distance is 240 finger-lengths (456 cm), for a kshatriya 300 finger-lengths (570 cm) and for a vaishya it is 360 finger-lengths. Dakshinagni kunda is between the two, but the three kundas are not in a single straight line, nor is dakshinagni kunda placed equidistant from both. It is nearer to garhapatya agni kunda (B 1.66–70). *Baudhayana Shulba Sutra* gives four different ways of drawing figures to place the three agnis at the vertices of geometrical figures.

Utkara (9 & 30)

Yajna karma generates a few disposable items (used grass, flowers, etc.), which are not disposed of like ordinary garbage. All waste is consigned to the fire at the end of the yajna. The waste is collected at a place called an utkara (9), located near the northern entrance of the pragvansha. The utkara (30) is on the northern side of the mahavedi. It is a circular pit with a diameter of 6 finger-lengths (11.4 cm) and a depth of one finger length (1.9 cm).

The utkara and dakshinagni kunda are on opposite sides of the line joining the garhapatya and ahavaniya agni kundas. To find the exact placement of the utkara, the procedure followed for dakshinagni kunda with respect to garhapatya and ahavaniya agni kundas is reversed.

Dhishnya (17–21 & 23)

The number of dhishnyas in a yajna ranges from 6 to 16, depending on the type of yajna. They are formed using a single layer of bricks. The arrangement of the bricks is explained in a sutra (B 2.74–77). Dhishnyas are placed in the sadomandap near the eastern side parallel to it and are separated from each other by a distance of 24 finger-lengths. Their diameter is also 24 finger-lengths.

Vedi

There are four vedis: yajamana vedi, uttaravedi, mahavedi and shamitra. The yajamana vedi (7) is in the pragvansha. Its dimensions differ according to the yajna. In darsha-poornamasa yajna, the length of the east-west perpendicular line (called *prachi*) of the yajamana vedi is 96-finger lengths, that of the westerly line is 64 finger-lengths and the easterly line 48 finger-lengths (B 1.72). Semi-circular arcs connect the east-west lines. The yajamana vedi in pashubandha and pitrimedha yajnas differs in size and shape from the vedi of darshapoornamasa yajna. The lines on the eastern and western sides are joined by arcs instead of straight lines, thus giving it a shape resembling the female body.

Uttaravedi (31): This is square in shape. There are six types of uttaravedi, which differ only in size. The most commonly used uttaravedi has a dimension of 32 x 32 finger-lengths (60.8cm x 60.8cm). It is located on the eastern line of the mahavedi.

Mahavedi (15): The area between the ahavaniya kunda and the yupa is the mahavedi. It is rectangular in shape. The line on the east is smaller in length than the line on the west. The east-west perpendicular distance or prachi is 36 pada (1026 cm), the western side is 30 pada (855 cm) and the eastern side is 24 pada (684 cm). The distance of the mahavedi from ahavaniya agni kunda (on the western side) is 6 prakrama (180 finger-lengths or 342 cm) and from the yupa (on the eastern side) is one pada (15 finger-lengths).

The prachi (east-west central perpendicular line) of the pragvansha, the line joining the centres of the garhapatya and ahavaniya agni kundas, and prachi of the mahavedi are co-linear.

Shamitra vedi (29): The boucher (yajna functionary) uses this vedi – his agni is kept here. It is towards the north of the mahavedi at a distance of one prakrama (57 cm). It is square in shape with each side as long as one bahu (42 finger-lengths or 79.8 cm).

Agni chiti (32): This is the principal vedi of shrauta yajnas. It is used for offering the main oblations. The process and oblations, *havyakavya,* differ depending on the desire with which the yajamana takes the sankalpa. Agni chitis are made in the form of a falcon – *shyena*, *kanka*, *alaja*, etc. or a tortoise. Other chitis are triangular, equilateral, quadrilateral, circular (like the wheel of a chariot), or conical.

Shyena chiti is a very important chiti, but rather difficult to construct. It uses five layers of bricks. There are two ways of constructing it – one results in a structure that resembles a flying falcon and the other in the form of the shadow of a flying bird (B 3.2–6, 3.9). The time spent on constructing this type of chiti depends on the duration of the process called *upasad*. There are other rules to be observed, details of which are found in the relevant parts of Vedic literature.

The first layer of the chiti has an area of 7.5 sq. purusha. Subsequent layers are created proportionately, each layer augmenting the area by 1 sq. purusha. The final area of the three-dimensional structure is 101.5 sq. purusha (B 2.1–7).

Construction of the shyena or such forms of chiti for agni chayana in shrauta yajnas is optional, but it is mandatory for ashvamedha and other large scale yajnas. The dimensions of the layers are generally three times those of a normal shyena chiti (B 10.21).

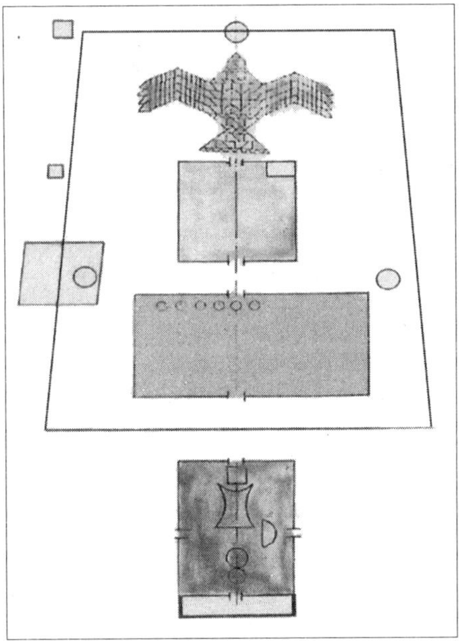

Saumiki Vihar – map of a shrauta yajnashala with falcon shaped fire-pit at the top

8

Ingredients and Implements of Yajna

YAJNA INGREDIENTS

All shrauta and smarta yajnas require the yajamana (host) to invoke the sacred fire and offer oblations in it. The act of giving in a yajna – oblation – is a special process, for such 'giving' results in automatically 'receiving' something. The simultaneous action of two opposite processes is aptly expressed by the Sanskrit word *havan*, since it stems from the root *hu*, which means both give and take, *danadanyoh*. In the daily ritual of agnihotra, one offers ghrita, rice grains (consecrated by ghrita) and/or milk to the devatas through the medium of Agni. If the oblations are offered to Vayu, for example, he returns the offerings by bestowing upon us a cleansed atmosphere – *vayu shuddhi, vrishti shuddhi, vatavaran shuddhi.* The offerings in smarta and shrauta yajnas, however, are not so simple but require processing of the articles of oblation. Therefore, knowledge of those processes is also required.

Since yajna includes the process of havan, the material used as an offering to the devatas via the medium of Agni becomes extremely important. A generic term – *yajna samagri* – is used to refer to all types of materials and articles required in dravya yajnas. It covers:

- *Havi dravya* – items of oblation
- *Arhaniya dravya* – material used to honour elders

- *Dakshina dravya* – material used to adore gods and priests performing yajna (god-like figures)
- *Yajnyaudha* – the ten special vessels used in shrauta yajnas, known as weapons of the host
- *Yajna sadhana* – the implements generally used in all yajnas.

The first three can be called yajna dravya, or ingredients, and the last two yajna implements.

Havi dravya

Items offered to Agni through the havan process are called *havi*. The word also stems from the root 'hu' (meaning give and take). It is the finished product poured into Agni; for example, a cake of rice or boiled milk, essence of butter, etc. Its raw material is called *havi dravya*. This raw material is converted into havi by consecrating it. The methods of consecration used in Vedic times were cooking, heating, sprinkling of sacred water, etc.

The Brahmana Granthas and Shrauta Sutras give elaborate descriptions of havi dravya and havi. They indicate the type of havi to be used as an oblation to honour different devatas. The type of havi also depends on the class of yajna. For example, soma juice is used as the oblation only in sapta soma yajnas, purodasha in sapta havi yajnas, and charu in sapta paka yajnas. However, there are a few havi items such as ghrita, rice, milk, etc. which are used in all yajnas.

Classification of havi dravya: Havi dravya can be broadly classified under:

- Items obtainable from the earth (agricultural produce, forest trees, etc.)
- Items produced by insects (honey) and animals (milk, curd, etc.)
- Parts of dead animals (flesh, blood, etc.)
- Articles from nature (water)
- Items obtainable from metals (gold).

Baudhayana Shrauta Sutra categorizes seven types of agricultural produce, *gramya dhanya,* and seven types of forest produce, *aranya,* obtainable from plants and trees.

Table 4: Havi dravya from plants and trees

From plants *(Gramya)*	Til (sesame)	Mash (black gram)	Vrihi (coarse rice)	Yava (barley-like grain)	Pryangu	Anu	Godhuma
From trees *(Aranya)*	Shyamaka	Neevara (jungle rice)	Jartila	Gavidhuka	Garmuta	Vastva	Venuyava or kuruvinda

In addition, there are creepers such as *somalata* and grasses such as *barhi*. Havi is prepared from a single item or a combination. The following is a partial list of the havi commonly used in shrauta as well as smarta yajnas.

Table 5: Havi used in shrauta and smarta yajnas

Havi dravya	Name of havi
From earth (20)	Apupa, barhi, charu, dhana, karambha, karir, kharjura, krishnala, laja, mantha, oil, parivap, phalikrut dravya – barn, prithuka, purodasha, saktu, somarasa, samidha, sura, yavagu
From living animals (11)	Milk, curd, ghrita, sannayya, ajya, prushadajya, tanunaptrajya, amiksha, payasa, vajina, honey
From dead animals (4)	Flesh, blood, intestine, fat
From nature (1)	Water
From metals (1)	Pieces of gold

Preparing the havi: In smarta yajnas, a mixture of items like sesame, rice, jaggery, guggul, etc. is used as havi. Below are some details about preparing such havi.

Shakalya havi: Articles of oblation such as til (sesame), unbroken grains of rice, yava (a barley-like grain), jaggery, ghrita, etc. used together are called shakalya havi. The following proportions need to be observed when mixing these items together.

Ingredients:

- Til: 1 part
- Rice: ½ part of quantum of til
- Yava (jau): ½ part of quantum of rice

- Jaggery: ½ part of quantum of yava
- Ghrita: ½ part of quantum of jaggery
- Guggul and other materials used as scent – equivalent to the quantity of yava.

Pratinidhi dravya: If the designated havi dravya is not available, the daily havan can be completed using alternate dravya known as *pratinidhi* (*Katyayana Sutra* 1.4.2) as below.

- Milk should be used if curd is not available.
- Jaggery should be used if honey is not available.
- Milk or curd should be used if ghrita is not available.
- If cow's ghrita is not available, the following alternatives are recommended (in order of preference):
  - ✧ Ghrita from buffalo or sheep's butter
  - ✧ Purified sesame oil
  - ✧ Mustard oil
  - ✧ Gum obtained from trees.
- Wheat should be used if yava is not available.
- Sathi rice should be used if dhana is not available.

Samidha: This is the havi for Agni devata, also used to keep the fire alive. Small sticks from the branches of yajniya trees make up the samidha. The following points need to be observed while making samidha.

- The samidha should be about 6 to 8 inches in length (the distance between the tips of the thumb and forefinger of the yajamana's hand is the ideal length).
- Bare wood should not be used as samidha, i.e. the sticks should be covered with skin.
- Very thin branches should not be used; the recommended thickness is the size of the yajamana's little finger.
- Stems with branches and leaves should not be used.
- The samidha should not be infested with maggots, larva, etc.
- Trees selected for the samidha should not contain birds' nests.
- Samidha sticks should not be crooked or cracked.
- The most preferred tree for making samidha is palasha. In its absence, ashvattha, khadira or udumbara trees could be used.

- The samidha should be brought (not bought) by the yajamana/ritvijs themselves. If that is not possible, samidha obtained from other sources should be consecrated by chanting *Pavamana Sukta* and sprinkling sacred water on it.

Arhaniya dravya

These articles are used to honour the learned, the elders and the VIPs of society. They include *vishtara* (also known as *darbhasana*) offered as a seat, water offered to wash the hands and feet, *madhuparka* – items of food mixed with milk, curd, honey, etc.

Dakshina dravya

In yajna parlance, the priests performing the yajna are called *bhudeva*, and are like living gods or semi-gods. Gods are offered articles through oblations and semi-gods are offered items of wealth such as money, bullion, cows, bulls, horses, chariots, clothing, etc. as a token of gratitude and honour. This is called dakshina, and is neither an honorarium nor a fee. In the olden days, to offer cows as dakshina was a common practice.

In major shrauta yajnas, there is a team of 16 priests. Customarily, the four major priests are offered the same quantum of dakshina each. The second group of four is offered half each of what is offered to the major group, the third group of four is paid one-third each of what is offered to the major group, and the juniormost group is offered a quarter each.

YAJNA IMPLEMENTS

Yajna in Nature, i.e. paroksha yajna, does not depend on us. However, its prototype, the physical or pratyaksha yajna being our creation, depends totally on us. Here, the host of the yajna has to arrange everything, starting from the location of the yajna site to the preparation of the havi to be used in oblations. We have discussed the process required to erect the yajna pavilion and the ingredients that must be gathered to conduct the rituals. Now we come to another precise science of the system of yajna – the implements and utensils with which the process of yajna is carried out. These form a major part of the yajna infrastructure, with each implement having a specific purpose.

Yajna trees

Most yajna implements are made from wood although some are made from metal and a few from rock/stone/soil. The Brahmana Granthas list the trees, called yajna trees *(yajnavriksha)*, that can be used to make such implements and vessels. Table 6 includes the major yajna trees.

The table gives the names of trees that are acceptable for making samidha and yajna implements. However, according to Puranas like the *Brahma Purana* and *Vayu Purana*, a few trees such as tamarind, jackfruit and babul are forbidden to be used in a yajna. Even acceptable trees covered with creepers or infested with maggots, larva, etc. or containing birds' nests are omitted.

There are very specific rules for making the vessels and other implements. The type of tree from which the wood must be drawn, where such a tree should be planted and when it should be cut are some of the details mentioned in the Brahmana texts. Even the kind of person eligible to make the implements and when should they undertake the task have been given due thought and recorded. It is mandatory for all associated with a yajna to follow these guidelines. Detailed knowledge of these aspects is absolutely necessary for a yajna to be successful in terms of the desired outcome.

The description of yajna patras, their form and figure, intended use, classification, etc. given here are taken from the *Shatapatha Brahmana*. There could be marginal variations between this and other texts like the *Aitareya* or *Taittiriya Brahmana*. However, they may be of relevance only to an in-depth researcher. For a beginner who just wants to get a feel for the subject, it may not matter as such variations are not 180 degrees apart.

Table 6: Yajna trees (yajnavrikshas)

Name of tree	Botanical name	Reference in Brahmanas	Implements
Ashvattha	Ficus religiosa	11.5.1.13	Arani, sruka, chamasa, upabhruta, pranitah patra, shurpa (phalikarana patra)
Bent (Vansha)		10.6.5.9	Dhavitra
Bilva	Aegle marmelos	13.4.4.8	Yupa
Khadira	Acacia catechu	1.3.3.20, 13.4.4.9	Sruva, sphya, ulukhala, prashitra, haran
Nyagrodha	Ficus bengalensis	13.2.7.3–4, 5.3.5.13	Pranitah
Palasha	Butea monosperma	5.3.5.11	Samidha, diksha danda, sruka, shanku, juhu, ulukhala
Plaksha	Ficus lacor	3.8.3.10	Uttara barhi
Shami	Ekeciasuma	9.2.3.37	Sruka, juju, upabhruta, dhruva, pracharani, sruva, arani
Udumbar	Ficus glomerata	6.7.1.13, 9.2.2.3	Rohina havani, sruva, ulukhala, upayamani, chamasa
Varana	Creteva roxbarhi	Ath 10.3.16	Shanku, paridhi, sruva, pranitah, ulukhala, pishtapatri, prokshana, patra, chamasa, dronakalasha, ida patra
Vikankatha	Flecortia cepida	2.2.4.10	Agnihotra havani, pranitah, prokshana patra, drona kalasha, dhruva, ida patra
Soma (pootika)	Sacrostema acidum	14.1.2.12	
Grass – darbha (kusha)	Imperata, cylendrica	5.3.2.7	Pavitraka, diksha vastra
Grass – maunji	Saccharum munga	4.3.3.16, 6.6.1.23, 12.8.3.6	Abhidhani, threads, ropes, brooms, etc.

Implements and utensils

Yajnas are varied in Nature and many in number. Each is unique, with its own end results, and so different ingredients, procedures and implements are used. Some implements, however, are common to all yajnas. Broadly, yajna implements can be grouped as follows.

1. *Ajya patra* – vessels used to store the essence of butter, *ajya*: ajyadhani, prishadajyadhani, agnihotra havani, rauhina havani, pracharani, juhu, upabhruta, dhruva, darvi, vasordhara.
2. *Manthana upakarana* – churning implements: agni manthana shakala, uttararani, adhararani.
3. *Yajnyayudha* – 'weapons' for the person doing the yajna: sphya, abhri, parshu, shamya, shurpa, ulukhala, musala, drishad, upala, krishnajina.
4. *Dohana upakarana* – storage vessels for milk: palasha, shami branches, shakha pavitra, ukha, kumbhi, nidana, dogdhra.
5. *Havi patra* – vessels and related items used in cooking and storing rice cakes to be offered in the fire: 12 kinds of kapala, upavesha, madanti patra, samachana patri, mekshan, charu-sthali, purodasha patra, pishta patri, sharava, mahavira, anvaharya-sthali, upayama, upayamani, parigraha, pranitah, pishtodvapani.
6. *Upayojana patra* – sacred broom, fan for sacrificial fire, etc.: ved, dhavitra, vidhruti, prastara, asandi, kurcha, shakata.

Implements used in shrauta yajna

7. *Pratisvik upakarana* – materials like sacred sticks, firewood, water jug and glass, etc., which are essential and uncompromisable parts: samidha, prokshana patra, idhma, paridhi, barhi, pushkara parna, sambhara, shulba.
8. *Chamasa and graha patra* – wooden cups for soma juice and other materials: 10 kinds of chamasa, 19 kinds of graha patra, savaniya, drona kalasha, dasha pavitra.
9. *Diksha upakarana* – items used during initiation: mekhala, danda, yoktra, krishna vishana, kshauma vastra, trayi kakubha anjana, navanita, darbha, vrata-sthali, ushniva.
10. *Bhakshana patra* – vessels for offering havi to yajnic priests: prashitra harana, yajamana patra, patni patra, ida patra.
11. *Astarana* – mats and spreads used by the priests and host: kashtha charma, asana, krishnajina.

Important yajna implements

Sruka is a commonly used ladle in yajna. It is one bahu (36 angulas or finger-lengths) long and made of wood from shami, ashvattha, palasha or vikankata trees. It has an elegant form, and holds mystical symbolism and ritualistic significance. The priests use it to pour the sacred, saturated butter into the yajna fire at appropriate times during the mantra chanting. It has a depression *(pushkara)* on the top end with a beak (shaped like an elephant's lips or a swan's beak) for pouring the liquid *(prasechana)*. The handle is in the form of a crow's tail *(vayasa-puchha)*. When carving the sruka, the front part of the ladle should be from the top part of the piece of wood, while the rear part should be from the bottom part (i.e. the part facing the root of the tree).

Variations of the sruka are **juhu** supported by **upabhruta**, and used along with **dhruva** and **pracharani** in soma yaga. The *Apastamba Sutra* recommends the alternative use of gold if sami trees are not available.

Agnihotra havani is a sacrificial ladle used in agnihotra yajna and is a variation of the sruka. It is prescribed that it be made of vikankata wood (*Flacourta sapida*). Its length is one bahu (36 angulas or finger-lengths).

Rauhina havani is also a sruka. It is made from udumbara wood and is one bahu in length. It has a small bowl carved out at one end, and is used in a pair at the pravargya ritual to offer the rauhina purodasha where special cakes called purodasha are used as havi.

Sruva is a dipping spoon used for scooping out liquids in rituals like garhapatya, anvaharya-pachana, darsha-poornamasa and also agnihotra. It is one aratni (24 finger-lengths) long, with a small bowl not greater in diameter than the tip of the yajamana's thumb. It is usually made of khadira or parna wood, but for the pravargya ritual, udumbara wood is prescribed.

The **arani** is especially important. The fire used in the sacrifice must be produced at the yajna site. It is invoked and created through the use of wooden plates called arani.

To ignite the fire, dry sticks from ashvattha trees which have been grown in close proximity to shami trees are used. The shami tree is regarded as the 'mother of fire' *(agni-garbha)*, hence this requirement. Another acceptable tree is aranika (*Premna spinosa*). The expression 'arani' suggests the process of producing fire by 'turning around' (or by fitting one stick into another using the stick-and-groove method). Fire is produced by friction or contrition, by

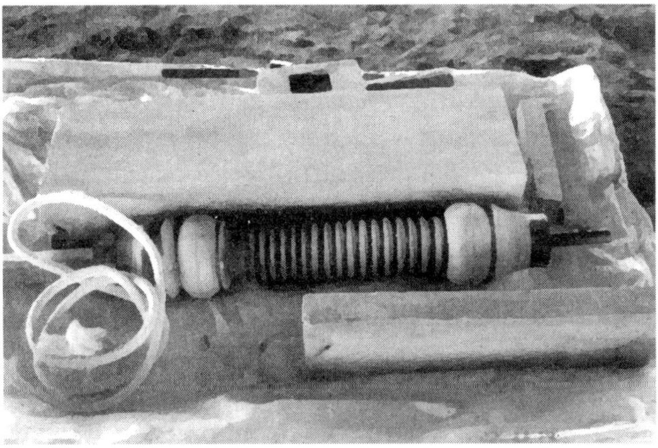

Arani, a device for creating the sacrificial fire

rubbing one stick over the other. Aranis are said to be the two mothers of Agni. (Agni is said to have two mothers, *dvi matri* – R 1.31.2). It symbolizes the two births of Agni who is said to have been born twice *(dvi janma)*, once in the heavens and then again on earth. Two arani sticks represent this (R 5,11.3 7,3.9 and 8,60.15); the lower is called *adhararani* and the upper *uttararani*. The priest who ritualistically establishes the fire is called the *ahitagni*. Once the fire is produced, it is maintained by pouring butter and adding dry medicinal twigs *(oshadhi)* and fuel sticks *(samidha)*.

Sphya is the sword-shaped knife used for cutting the darbha grass to the required size for marking lines on the sacrificial ground. It is also used to stir the boiling oblationary substance during cooking. Its length is one aratni or 24 finger-lengths, and it is made of khadira *(Acacia catechu)* wood. In rajasooya yajna where a separate altar is not constructed, it is used to remove the surface soil, *uddharana*, to dig the earth, *khanana,* and to mark the area of the altar, *parilekhana* (*Apastamba Shrauta Sutra* 2.2).

Shurpa is a flat wicker basket, squarish in shape with two corners rounded off so it can hold and fan the grain to remove the husk. It is made of reeds, mango leaves, *Arundo tibialis*, long-stalked grass *(kusha)* or cane. Its size is 24x20 or 18 finger-lengths.

Krishnajina is the black antelope's hide used in sacrificial rituals for the sacrificer to sit on, and for the mortar *(ulukhala)* and pestle *(musala)* to be placed on. It is also used in soma yaga during consecration *(diksha)* of the yajamana.

Samaya is a wooden peg or pin, stick or staff, shaped like a mace, and used as a measuring device. It is one bahu long, and made from khadira or varana wood.

Ulukhala is a wooden mortar used for pounding the grains or crushing soma shoots prior to the oblations. It is cylindrical in shape with a bowl-like depression at the top and is narrow in the middle. Generally, it is knee-high but the specification for height is not mentioned. Usually, it is made of khadira, varana or udumbara wood, but any other sacred tree is also acceptable. In agni chayana, it is four-cornered. It goes with the musala.

Musala is the pestle used for pounding the grains or soma shoots placed in the ulukhala (mortar). It has an iron plate at its base. It is three aratnis long and one *mushti* (fist) broad.

Drishad is a large stone slab on which are placed the soma creepers to be crushed or ground with the help of an upala. It is also called grava. Upala is a smaller mull-stone resting on the drishad, used for crushing or grinding the soma creeper placed on the drishad. It is also called adri. Drishad and upala are normally used only in soma yaga.

Kumbhi, shakha pavitra, abhidhani and **dohana patra** are vessels called **sannayya patras**. They are associated with milk, and are used to store milk and curd *(dadhi-payo-rupa-sannayya)*.

Kapala is a group of earthen fry pans, round in shape and small in size, used for baking rice flour from which cakes called purodasha are made to be offered as havi.

Pranitah is a wooden vessel made of nyagrodha, rauhitaka, varana or vikankata wood in which consecrated water is stored. This water is used to mix the rice powder used to make purodasha. The pranitah is also used to store the soma juice. It is square in shape, eight finger-lengths each in length and breadth, four finger-lengths high and three finger-lengths deep. It holds about half a prastha of water.

Pishta patri is a container for storing rice flour (used in preparing purodasha). It is made of varana wood.

Pishtodvapani is a rectangular container made of wood or clay. Its dimensions are 20 x 24 finger-lengths, and it has a circular depression for the dough. If made of wood, it has a handle.

Purodasha patra is a vessel to keep the baked purodasha cakes in. Square in shape, it is 12 finger-lengths each in length and breadth, and six finger-lengths deep at the depression in the middle.

Sthalis are several kinds of earthen bowls or dishes used for various purposes. **Agnihotra-sthali** is for fresh cow's milk *(go dohana)*, and it is prescribed that the sacrificer or one of the officiating priests should prepare it. **Ajya-sthali** is for storing the sacred, saturated butter required for oblations. Similarly, there are other sthalis like **prasad-ajya-sthali, charu-sthali, dhruva-sthali, madanti** and **agrayana-sthali** used for specific purposes.

Mahavira is described as 'the head of a yajna' *(makhasya shirah)*. It is used in the pravargya ritual. It is a curious vessel, which looks like three pots placed one above the other. The three pot-like elevations are symbolic of the three worlds, represented by the three Vedic metres: Gayatri, Trishtubh and Jagati. The three worlds are: earth, the mid region and the heavens *(bhuh, bhuvah and suvah)*. Its prescribed height is a span *(pradesha-matra)*. It is like a cauldron or boiler, made of baked clay, and is used for boiling milk for oblation purposes.

Upayamani and **shapha** are the two tongs used to handle the mahavira (since it is a boiler, it cannot be handled with bare hands). Shapha is a tong and upayamani is a long ladle (36 finger-lengths long) with a fairly large depression so it can hold the base of the mahavira. It is made of udumbara wood.

Graha are wooden vessels of diverse shapes. Generally, they resemble the ulukhala, and are meant to contain soma juice.

Graha patras that hold the soma juice for graha devatas

Upavesha is a wooden stick used to stoke the fire. It is one pradesha (12 finger-lengths) or one aratni (24 finger-lengths) long, and its head is shaped like an extended palm *(hastakriti)*.

Dhavitra is used to fan the sacred fire, and each of the three priests making the gharma oblation use it. It is a stick of bamboo *(venu)* or udumbara to which is fastened a piece of black antelope's hide *(krishnajinani dhavitrani)*.

Prokshana patra is a vessel made of varana or vikankata wood with a long handle. It is 12 finger-lengths long, and has a depression shaped like a lotus leaf *(padma-patrakrti)* or lotus bud *(kamala mukulakrti)*. It holds the holy water used for consecrating (*prokshana* or ceremonial sprinkling) the articles of oblation. Into the water are dropped darbha blades *(Saccharum cylindricum)* to make the water holy.

Chamasa is a cup in which the ten priests are offered soma by the priest in charge of the soma pot *(chamasadhvaryu)*. The chamasas differ in shape so that the cups meant for the priests are easily identified. The cups are made of udambara, nyagrodha, rauhitaka or varana wood, and are generally square in shape with handles.

Drona kalasha is a large vessel made of a strong and hard wood like varana or vikankata for storing the soma juice. It is a trough *(drona)*, square or circular in shape with a handle *(danda-yuta)*. Alternately, it may be shaped like a boat *(naukakara)*.

Dasha pavitra is a device used to strain the soma juice. This fringed strainer is made from a piece of cotton cloth in the centre of which is attached (or woven) a round piece of woollen cloth.

Pariplu (or udanchana) is a small wooden bowl *(laghu patra)* shaped like a sruka, but without a handle *(yatha sruka adanda)*, used to take the soma juice out of the drona kalasha for oblation.

Grahas are mortar-like vessels which span high, but are narrow in the middle, used for storing sacred food for the fire and priests.

Ida patra is a vessel similar in shape to a graha, used for storing the oblation materials. According to the *Taittiriya Samhita*, it has an oblong shape with the corners rounded off, and is narrow in the middle. It is made of varana wood.

IN CONCLUSION

To summarize, a man-made yajna requires: (i) havi dravya, (ii) fire, (iii) prayers of invocation, and (iv) instruments or implements. There are many instruments. The Brahmana texts and Kalpa Sutras give details of the procedures to be performed when the mantras are being chanted and give details of the type of instruments that must be used during the yajna process.

It is said that the performer of a yajna (yajamana) uses these implements to invoke the Yajna Purusha, who in turn invokes the Supreme to bestow the choicest blessings – material prosperity and serenity. In a way, the instruments are the weapons of the Yajna Purusha, because it is through them that the yajna is performed and the Supreme or *Virata* invoked. Yajna is, therefore, a creative process.

Creation is a process of generation *(srijan)*. In this context, it is interesting to note that the yajna procedure requires the ten instruments (weapons) to be arranged in pairs and kept near the yajna vedi at the beginning of the yajna. A pair or couple is the symbol of creation. By placing the five pairs, the priest (adhvaryu) of the yajna indicates that he is performing an act of creation.

The Brahmana texts, Kalpa Sutras, etc. use many anecdotes and metaphors to convey the essence of the subjects under consideration. An interesting anecdote is found in the *Aitareya Brahmana* (34.1) which explains why the instruments used in yajna are called its weapons.

Prajapati created Yajna, and then he created Brahma (priestly functions) and Kshatra (princely functions). For some reason, Yajna fled from them both, and so they ran after him to persuade him to return. Kshatra ran with his weapons of war and, watching him, the priest also ran with what he had – the yajna instruments.

Seeing that Kshatra was chasing him, Yajna became frightened and ran faster, thus making it impossible for Kshatra to catch him. Dejected, Kshatra returned. The priest tried harder, somehow came level with Yajna and prevented him from going any further. Yajna looked at Brahma's 'weapons', recognized them as his own and agreed to return. Thus, Yajna stayed with the priests, and the 'weapons' came to be known as Yajna's weapons. Of course, later the princely function also befriended Yajna and he agreed to be with Kshatra also!

The moral of the story is that, just as horses, chariots and weapons are necessary for a warrior to fight and win a war, so also the instruments are uniquely important and essential for a priest to successfully complete a yajna.

9

External Yajna – Procedures and Performance

By now we are familiar with the fact that external or physical yajna is man-made, that it is also known as dravya yajna, and that it involves the sacrifice of items in a fire to honour the devata(s). Elaborate processes have been designed to offer oblations to the devatas amid the chanting of mantras. The articles of oblation, the deployment of mantras and even the devatas that are invoked differ according to the purpose of the dravya yajna. For example, for good rainfall, the principal yajna devata is Indra, whereas for overall peace, prosperity and welfare, the goddess in the form of Chandi, Lakshmi, etc. is invoked. Although the underlying fabric of all yajnas is by and large the same (self-evolution and social advantage), the Vedas prescribe yajnas for almost every conceivable desire. Added to this list is a set of yajnas recommended by the Smriti texts, Puranas and tantra shastras. A large number of other sacrificial rites, large and small, have also been recommended by supplementary texts such as the Shrauta Sutras and Grihya Sutras. These sacrificial rites are called *samskaras*, and their purpose is to purify the soul so as to accelerate the journey towards salvation.

Workbooks are prepared so that practising priests can correctly perform all the rituals that go into the yajna processes using the Brahmanas, Kalpa Sutras and other texts. This chapter describes the processes and procedures of major shrauta yajnas and other popularly conducted yajnas.

Yajnic terminology

Reference to a some terms and techniques not discussed earlier is essential before we can fully understand external or physical yajna. Terms like karma, samskara, etc. assume meanings that may seem to be at variance with the conventional meaning implied in yogic and other texts, and need to be explained with reference to the Vedic context.

Karma and Vedic karma: In terms of the cause and effect theory, karma as action is an outcome of thought. It is an action to fulfil a desire that is the cause of the thought. Thus, walking towards a refrigerator to fetch a glass of cold water is an action to fulfil the desire to quench our thirst – a bodily requirement. This action does not make any significant or lasting impression on our mind or any level of consciousness. But there are other actions that do. Sometimes the imprint is made in the conscious part of the mind, but more often than not it affects the subconscious and unconscious levels, influencing our personality. Each such action takes us a step forward or backward on the road to spiritual progress. Normally, these actions are signified by the word 'karma'. Thus, to help a needy person is karma. To earn wealth by legal means is karma. To earn money by employing unscrupulous methods is also karma.

The Vedas expect an individual to follow the righteous (rita) path: Due to this boundary, the third karma in the above example automatically becomes avoidable. We have seen that man-made yajnas – dravya yajna and karma yajna – are action-based[1]. Therefore, in Vedic parlance karma means yajna. Sometimes yajna-related activity or oblationary and other acts in the process of yajna are also known as karma.

Yajna is a Vedic karma. Therefore, yajna based on the Shrutis (an epithet for the Vedas) is called *shrauta yajna* and that based on the Smriti texts (Puranas, etc.) is *smarta yajna*[2].

---

[1] See Chapter 4

[2] Refer to the third classification of yajna in Chapter 5

Vedic karma is further classified as shrauta karma or smarta karma. Shrauta yajnas use three forms of fire, so they are sometimes also called tretagni karma (*tri agni* means three fires). Smarta yajna is performed using only one form of fire and hence smarta karma is sometimes called ekagni karma (*eka agni* means one fire).

Words such as yaga, homa, havan, ishti and kratu are used to refer to different types of yajna. There is a technical difference between each one[3]. However, in loose terms they are used as synonyms for yajna. Popularly, havan and homa are used to refer to small yajnas. *Havan* denotes a small-scale smarta karma, and needs no priest – the host can perform it himself. The term *homa* is used to refer to regular agnihotra karma – it does not require a priest either. An *ishti* may need one to four priests. The words *yaga* and *yajna* are used to indicate medium to large yajnas needing a team of three to sixteen priests. *Kratu* indicates a yajna of a much larger dimension in terms of duration, complexity and scale of procedures.

Yogic and Vedic samskara: In yogic parlance, this term means an imprint made in the deeper layers of consciousness. It is also equated with a seed sown there which fructifies over a period of time. In Vedic terminology, 'samskara' indicates many rituals (or small yajnas) performed from the birth to death of an individual to purify the soul. Even the disposal of the mortal remains after physical death, called *anteyshti* (last rite), is intended to liberate the soul from the binding passions, lust, greed, etc. which were harboured by the jiva (individual soul) in the state of ignorance when it occupied the body. It can be readily seen that the meaning of the term samskara drawn from the yoga shastras is not really different. It is a conscious imprinting in the Vedic context, and an act of the mind beyond awareness in the yogic context. If the ritual is performed according to the instructions of the Grihya Sutras[4], it is called a grihya

---

[3] Refer to Glossary
[4] Refer to Chapter 2

samskara. Similarly, samskaras done according to the Shrauta Sutras are called shrauta samskaras.

Samskaras under Vedic karma are many, and recommended at various stages of life. Each has a specific purpose, and when performed with complete understanding and awareness, helps in the process of evolution.

Vedic karma and the journey of the soul

The Vedas expect a person to follow the virtuous path throughout life. One is expected to remember the sacrificial principle at every step and for every act. Life itself then is yajna. It is an avenue for the achievement of spiritual objectives, and every action should amount to hard work done sincerely. Vedic karma is of two types: samskara-oriented, based on the Grihya Sutras, and yajna-oriented, based on the Shrutis and Smritis. There are many samskaras and yajnas. We shall consider the principal ones. These samskaras and yajnas have a great bearing on an individual's progress on their spiritual path. Therefore, their connection with the journey of the soul needs to be first established to understand their significance.

We have seen that when Brahman arrives in the human body, it is called jiva (soul). As its awareness is now confined to the physical world as the sole reality, it loses awareness of the universal truth. This illusion is sometimes referred to as a 'veil' or *maya*. The Vedas call it 'impurity of the soul'. According to Vedic philosophy, the soul has to take repeated births until it is purified and merges with Brahman. Thus, it starts marching on the spiritual path from the time it is born until its eventual merger. In other words, the soul's journey starts with the separation from super-consciousness and ends when it meets it once again. The original station and the terminus are the same. The journey is therefore circular. This phenomenon can be explained as follows.

Fig. 6

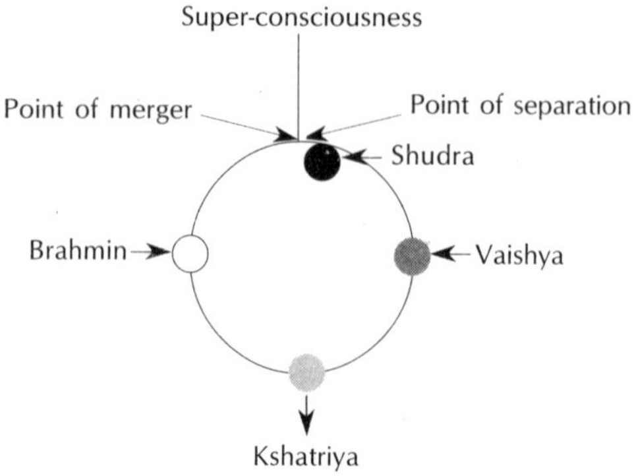

In this diagram, the path is circular and clockwise. When the soul separates, it is shrouded with the impurities of this material world (maya). This impure state is shudra-ness. *Manu Smriti* says that at the time of birth, everyone is a shudra – *Janmana jayate shudrah*. Therefore, to merge back into super-consciousness, it has to become pure. As the journey of the soul proceeds, it sheds impurities and evolves on the way. Conversely, evolution is a measure of the path traversed. There are four milestones along this journey: the states of shudra, vaishya, kshatriya and brahmin.

- 1st milestone – underdeveloped state – shudra state
- 2nd milestone – developed state – vaishya state
- 3rd milestone – fully developed state – kshatriya state
- 4th milestone – highly developed state – brahmin state.

These are the states of purity (or impurity) of the soul, and should not be confused with the four varnas. The first milestone is reached by birth. The other three are to be reached through deliberate effort – they are the outcome of purushartha. And purushartha, as we have seen, can be best achieved by following the kratvartha path (performing ritualistic actions for yajna at the external level).

Samskara is the fuel of the vehicle used by the soul for its journey. The speed, acceleration, occasional retardation and even reversal all depend on the gear chosen by the driver of the vehicle (mind). With better samskaras, there is less adulteration in the fuel, fewer jerks and improved speed and mileage. Samskaras make the vehicle move forward smoothly and steadily. They are so important that Manu, the author of *Manu Smriti*, says that to purify an individual through samskaras amounts to giving him a second birth.

Understanding samskaras

How does one define samskara? Samskara is a purifying process that cleanses the soul of its attitudes, likes and dislikes, attachments and detachments, passions and emotions. Samskaras act on the soul to slowly remove impurities *(dosha marjana)*, expand purity *(gunadhana)* and make good the shortfall wherever required *(heenanga poorti)*. It is said:

दोष अपनयनपूर्वकं गुणाधानः संस्कारः।

Dosha apanayanpoorvakam gunaadhaanah samskaarah.

All processes performed on the jiva to remove impurities and to instil total purity are samskaras.

Swami Niranjanananda Saraswati has explained samskara as follows: "Samskara means impressions in the mind leading to creative performance. Educating the total mind and creating these impressions is a continuous, life-long process. The entire pattern of our personality, mind, behaviour and attitudes is being educated not only by the academic form of education, but also by the education we derive from our culture, family and environment. This samskara, this inner education, begins at the time of conception. These samskaras or basic impressions determine the quality and future direction of our life."

Samskaras are of three types: (i) purifying samskaras, *shodhaka samskara*, which remove impurities from the soul, (ii) cultivating samskaras, *gunadhana samskara*, which help to expand the good qualities already present, and (iii) augmenting samskaras, *bhavaka samskara*, which make up for any shortfalls, qualitatively and quantitatively.

One can see that the process of samskaras is complete in scope and scientific in approach. It removes unwanted impurities, cultivates the pure quality and, if the form is not pure enough, it also augments the purity. Taking into account these scientific principles, the Vedas professed a method to achieve the merging of the soul with the superconsciousness. The method is yajna. Put mathematically, yajna = the process of performing samskaras on the soul.

The yoga shastras postulate five layers of human existence: *annamaya* (matter), *pranamaya* (energy), *manomaya* (mind), *vijnanamaya* (psyche) and *anandamaya* (bliss) *koshas*. A samskara taken individually touches one or more of these layers, but in totality they exert a positive influence on all layers. The samskaras/yajnas that purify the first three koshas are known as *brahma samskaras* and those that additionally help in expanding the remaining two koshas are known as *daiva samskaras*.

The interrelation of samskara and yajna would imply that Vedic karma can be samskara-oriented or yajna-oriented. Samskara-oriented karmas are, in fact, small yajnas (havan or homa type) and find their base in the Grihya Sutras. Therefore, they are also known as *grihya karmas*. They are performed using only one form of fire. Yajna-oriented karmas are of two types: shrauta yajnas and smarta yajnas. Shrauta yajnas are performed using three forms of fire, and smarta yajnas use only one form. Grihya karmas are simple in terms of ritualistic needs, so to differentiate them from yajna they are simply called samskaras. Naturally then, yajna-oriented karmas can be interchangeably (and simply) called yajna.

VEDIC KARMAS: AN OVERVIEW

There are 21 major grihya karmas and 52 yajna karmas, making a total of 73 Vedic karmas. Some karmas are a one-time activity and others periodic. Some can be repeated on a need-to-do basis. Together, the Vedic samskaras cover a person's entire life. Every event, every day has a ritual associated with it, but when performed with proper methodology and focus, each one is a step forward in evolution – simply because every event in life has a spiritual significance. Take the event of marriage and the subsequent life, for example. Marriage is considered a solemn event, marking the beginning of household life, which is filled with many duties. It cannot be completed by one person alone. Married life is a partnership, a bond of trust, duty, compromise and adjustment. The joy of life is never denied, whether in terms of sex or material happiness, but duty is considered the first and foremost principle. Therefore, the samskara of marriage is performed as an oath of partnership with the fire god as a friend, guide, philosopher and guru. The same is true of all other events in life.

The diagram on the following page (Fig. 7) explains the distribution of the 73 Vedic karmas.

VEDIC KARMA: SAMSKARA-ORIENTED (TOTAL 21)

The three types of samskara-oriented Vedic karmas are enumerated and explained below.

Purifying samskaras

There are eight purifying samskaras. Some are covered in the eighth chapter of the *Atharva Veda*.

- *Garbhadhana*: This rite is performed on the fourth day of marriage, but before the commencement of sexual life. It is also called *chaturthi karman* or *ritu shanti*. The samskara is intended to purify the uterus.
- *Punsavana*: A rite wishing for the birth of a male child. According to M.M. Kane, in *History of Dharmashastra*, it is actually a rite to ensure the healthy growth of the embryo.
- *Simantonnayana*: This rite is purificatory in nature for the pregnant woman, and to a certain extent it is a social function to declare the new arrival in the family.
- *Jata karma*: This is performed immediately after the birth of a child, but before the umbilical cord is severed. The

Fig. 7

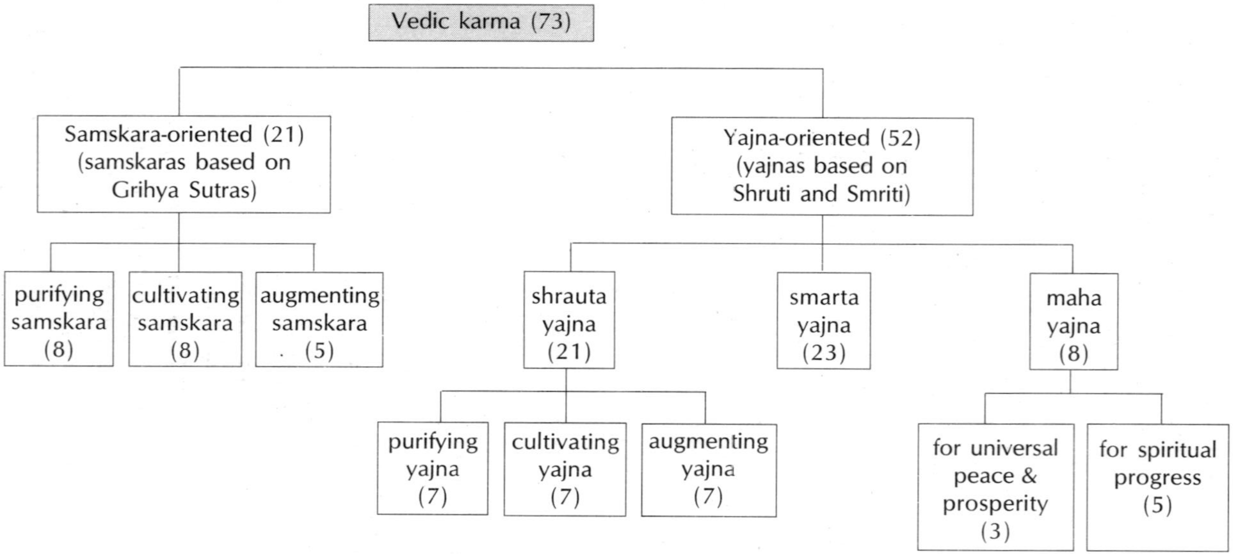
Vedic karma (73)
Samskara-oriented (21) (samskaras based on Grihya Sutras)
Yajna-oriented (52) (yajnas based on Shruti and Smriti)
purifying samskara (8)
cultivating samskara (8)
augmenting samskara (5)
shrauta yajna (21)
smarta yajna (23)
maha yajna (8)
purifying yajna (7)
cultivating yajna (7)
augmenting yajna (7)
for universal peace & prosperity (3)
for spiritual progress (5)

father draws 'aum' on the tongue of the newborn using honey and a golden spatula.

- *Namkarana*: This is performed on the eleventh day of the baby's birth. The baby is ceremonially given a name according to the position of the stars, etc. at the time of its birth by consulting an expert in reading the Indian almanac.
- *Nishkramana*: The baby is taken out of the house for the first time – traditionally, to the city temple to seek the blessings of the gods. Then a visit is paid to a dignified relation. Mantras are chanted to invoke various devatas to bestow blessings and protection on the child.
- *Anna prashana*: Rite of first solid, cooked food given to a baby.
- *Chaula karma* (or *chudakarana*): Rite of a child's first haircut.

Cultivating samskaras

There are eight cultivating samskaras.

- *Karnavedha*: Rite of piercing the ear lobes, which has medicinal importance and is normally performed by a medical expert.
- *Upanayana*: This is the famous thread ceremony, which is an important ritual for a young boy, as it prepares him to face life. Now he undertakes work to free himself from rishi rin[5]. In pre-Vedic times, this ritual was performed for both boys and girls. It is said that the father, who has already raised his potential through ascent of the kundalini, transmits his power to the child using the famous Gayatri mantra. The ascent of the boy's kundalini starts with this ritual[6].
- *Vratadesha*: Rite enabling a pupil to study the Vedas under the guidance of an able guru. He has to stay with the guru, follow the guru's method of teaching with humility and observe certain holy practices *(vratas)*.

---

[5] Refer to Chapter 4

[6] More details in Chapter 11

- *Veda swadhyaya*: Studying the Vedas and other useful literature.
- *Keshanta*: On attaining the age of 16 (the age differs for different varnas), a ritual is performed in which a boy's head is shaved totally leaving only a tuft *(shikha)*. A cow is offered to the priest as a token for having performed the ritual (Ath 8.2.17).
- *Snanam*: The rite marking the end of student life and the return home from the gurukul after education is completed. The pupil takes a ceremonial bath which turns him into a *snataka*. He is now fit to enter the next stage of life, *grihastha ashrama* or married life.
- *Vivaha* or *panigrahana*: This is the wedding ceremony and the most important samskara in the life of a member of Vedic society. The bridegroom holds the hand of his life partner and takes an oath that they will march forward together. By being married, he enters grihastha ashrama, and his dharma now includes helping to support society and working to liquidate the debts of his forefathers and the Almighty[7].
- *Agni parigraha*: The married couple undertake to keep the fire alive (not necessarily in the form of a flame but possibly in a mellowed form) throughout their joint life. This fire is used for cooking as well as Vedic karmas.

Augmenting samskaras

There are five augmenting samskaras.

- Purification of the body, *sharira shuddhi*: This is a holy bath which helps to bring additional energy to set right mental and physical deformities, if any, making good the lack of wisdom and warmth.
- Purification of materials, *dravya shuddhi*: This refers to consecration of all the materials a person uses. Any incoming wealth, for example, is to be used only after a portion has

[7] Refer to Chapter 4

been earmarked for sattwic donation. The ritual is intended to eliminate non-harmonious vibrations in the materials.

- Purification required due to participation in last rites, *agha shuddhi*: Participation in a funeral can leave marks on the mind and also affect the physical health. This samskara helps to restore balance in body and mind.
- Purification required due to new arrivals and departures to/from family, *enah shuddhi*: The significance is the same as above.
- Rituals for maintaining purity at mental and spiritual levels, *bhava shuddhi*: Interaction of the extroverted mind with the world results in depletion of physical and spiritual energy. This samskara helps in the rebuilding process.

VEDIC KARMA: YAJNA-ORIENTED (TOTAL 52)

Yajna-oriented Vedic karma means performance of yajnas. There are 21 shrauta yajnas, 23 smarta yajnas and 8 maha yajnas. Maha yajnas are further divided into two subgroups: three soma yajnas of large dimensions and five pancha maha yajnas. Like samskaras, shrauta yajnas are classified into purifying, cultivating and augmenting yajnas. Smarta yajnas are simplified forms of shrauta yajnas. Perhaps for this reason the above classification is not strictly adhered to. Maha soma yajnas are performed with the main objective of universal peace and prosperity. Pancha maha yajnas are daily rituals that ought to be performed to imbibe sacrificial principles and accelerate spiritual growth.

SHRAUTA YAJNA: GENERAL INFORMATION

Shrauta yajnas are dravya yajnas, and are based on the injunctions of the Vedas. The procedure employed is complex in its operational aspects, and based on the Brahmana texts and Shrauta Sutras. Clarified cow's milk butter, rice, other grains, juice extracted from the soma creeper, and a few other oblationary articles are used. To perform a shrauta yajna, the host needs a team of priests. The yajna uses three to five types of fire, and the area it affects is said therefore to extend to the three lokas. Shrauta yajnas are more expansive than other types of yajna, and also more expensive.

Shrauta yajnas were very popular in the Vedic era. Under the auspices of the *yajna samstha*, yajna institution, a large number of shrauta yajnas were performed. Those intended for fulfilling aspirations at personal as well as social and national levels were generally of medium to large size. Among shrauta yajnas, soma yajnas (which use soma juice as the main item of oblation) were the most important for self-development and social reasons. The popularity of shrauta yajnas continued almost until the time of the famous Mahabharata war, and then started waning. Slowly, the expert priestly community also became fewer in number. Today, a shrauta yajna is a rare phenomenon.

Some shrauta yajnas have been described step-by-step below. However, in order to develop an understanding of the process, it is a good idea to study an introductory text (such as this book), and then progressively go deeper into the subject through a chain of events like reading→ witnessing→analyzing→next reading→witnessing. Keeping this in mind, the explanation of the steps below has been kept at a general level. Broadly, the main elements of a shrauta yajna include:

- The host, *yajamana*
- Priests, *ritvij,* and their role in yajna
- Resolve of the host, *sankalpa*
- Sacred fire, *shrautagni*
- Sacred piece of land, *yajna bhoomi*
- Yajna venue, *yajnashala*
- Articles of oblation, *havi dravya*
- Yajna implements, *yajnayudha*
- Auspicious time for yajna, *yajna muhurta*
- Helper group for miscellaneous activities, *parikarmi.*

The main process

Ishtis and other homas make up the main process of shrauta yajnas. Oblations are offered almost throughout. The participants in a shrauta yajna fall into three groups: basic, priests and non-priests. The basic group consists of the host, his wife and a stand-by for the host (in case of contingencies only) called *purodha*. The priestly group consists of those knowledgeable in yajna mantras and procedures, and experienced in conducting shrauta yajnas. They perform the yajna for the host. The non-priestly group consists of people called *sadasya*, *soma pravaka* and *parikarmis*. In addition, there are a host of other people such as masons, carpenters, smiths, helpers, etc. who attend to miscellaneous work for the ritualistic part. Some yajnas, however, need no work force, and can be performed by the yajamana alone.

The role of each and everyone associated with a yajna is defined explicitly, and described in the Brahmana Granthas. The following description is based mainly on the exposition in the *Shatapatha Brahmana* and *Katyayana Sutras*.

The shrauta sutras discuss in detail the items required for a yajna and the steps to be followed in conducting it. The major items discussed are: identification of a suitable place and time for the yajna ceremony, details of austerities and initiation of the couple hosting the yajna, the team of priests possessing the authority and experience to conduct the yajna, various implements and dravya, details of havi, selection of mantras to be used, and expiation or atonement procedures.

The host (yajamana)

All shrauta yajnas need a host, whose life partner accompanies him in all the yajna processes – physically, emotionally and mentally. In a yajna, the wife is a very important personality. In fact, a person becomes eligible for any shrauta karma only when (and as long as) he has a wife. Marriage is a solemn function in which a man and woman agree in the presence of Agni (sacred fire) to accept each other as life partners: (i) to be the cause of good progeny, (ii) to make a joint contribution to society and the nation, and (iii) to achieve personal evolution with mutual help. The couple is expected to carry part of the sacred fire home and worship it every day throughout their joint life.

To be eligible to host a shrauta yajna, a person has to undertake austerities and satisfy certain minimum requirements. While prescribing this eligibility, the Vedas specify, among other things, four requirements: (i) knowledge should have been earned through contemplative study, (ii) smartagni should have been installed ceremoniously after marriage, (iii) *agnyadhana* should have been undertaken (a ritual wherein the person establishes three forms of agni and undertakes to worship them throughout life), and (iv) sound health and the financial capacity to undertake the yajna should exist.

For most shrauta yajnas, the host can generally be from any of the three varnas – brahmin, kshatriya or vaishya. There is a difference of opinion over the eligibility of the fourth varna, shudra, but that is outside the current context. Only a kshatriya can perform yajnas such as ashvamedha and rajasooya.

The public performance of a shrauta yajna is a costly proposition. It is the responsibility of the host to bear the entire expenditure of the yajna. All the advantages, including the *punya* (the fruit of righteous activities) emanating from the yajna go to him. His wife, being his life partner, automatically participates in the yajna anushthana and becomes a natural claimant to the yajna's advantages. It is believed that on completion of the yajna according to the prescriptions of the Vedic texts and without faults and flaws, something unprecedented or novel *(apoorva),* not present at the yajna's commencement, emerges to fulfil the host's wish.

The host has the yajna performed through priests, but a few actions are also expected of him. If, for unavoidable reasons, the yajamana has to abstain from the yajna, a stand-by (purodha) takes on this role. Like the other priests, the purodha is also offered an honorarium but is not considered a ritvij since he is not required when the yajamana is present.

The priests (ritvij)

The rituals of a shrauta yajna are called shrauta karma. A brahmin who performs shrauta karma according to the resolve of the host is called a *ritvij* (Manu 2.143). Shrauta karmas are to be performed according to the injunctions and prescriptions of the Brahmana Granthas and Shrauta Sutras. Therefore, it is imperative that a ritvij has studied the Vedas fully and mastered the processes of the Brahmana Granthas. Traditionally, a ritvij would specialize in one branch of the Vedas. He would be educated at an appropriate 'Veda gurukul' or receive training from his father. Since brahmins pursued learning of the Vedas in this manner, they were known as *rigvedi* (an expert on the *Rig Veda* with a deep knowledge of the *Rig Veda Samhita* and its related granthas), *yajurvedi* (an expert on the *Yajur Veda*) and so on.

It is obligatory for a ritvij to have thoroughly studied the branch of the Veda to which he belongs. His knowledge of the respective Samhita, Brahmana Grantha and Aranyaka should be based on contemplative study. He should also have studied the Vedangas, in particular the Shrauta Sutras of his branch.

Shrauta karma is a combined and cooperative activity. Many ritvijs have to work together, each carrying out a designated work. The Shrauta Sutras have laid down many restrictions in selecting a person to act as a ritvij in a yajna, which are over and above the basic qualification (deep Vedic knowledge). The person should come from a learned family, which has ancestral links with acknowledged rishis. He should have in-depth ritualistic knowledge, high morals and be of righteous behaviour. He should be without any physical deformity and should not have a profession incommensurate with Veda vidya. In short, all ritvijs should be authorities in their respective fields and have sound health.

Over and above these basic qualifications, some ritvijs need to be from specific family cults *(gotra)*. It is desirable to have the adhvaryu from Angiras gotra, the brahma from Vashishtha gotra, the hota from Vishvamaitri gotra and the udgata from Aysaya gotra. The sadasya should be from Kaushitaki gotra. The other ritvijs should be from Bhrigu or Angiras gotra.

Such high standards of family background and personal qualifications are expected of the yajamana also. He should be well versed in the Vedas, faultless, have a high moral character, be prosperous enough to bear the cost of the yajna, including the fees of the priests. The host should respect the ritvijs and receive them with regard and humility. The ritvijs on their part are also expected to be courteous and helpful.

The Brahmana Granthas say that a ritvij should not work for a fee. Whatever is paid to him should be accepted as an honorarium, as a token of a gift from the Lord, not as compensation for the efforts he has made. Even if a host is not too well-to-do, they should not refuse to work in his yajna if his desire to perform it is intense and pure. However, when it comes to the code of conduct of the host, it is emphasized that he must be generous in paying the fees. Further, he should not have an owner-labourer feeling while offering the fees. The mantras to be chanted while paying the fees imply that the host does not view it from the angle of a rich person giving away alms. He should not think that he is giving away money and articles to the brahmins, but offering his own limbs and parts. This is a classic example of the effort of the Vedas to develop and maintain harmony and cordial relations among the different elements of society.

Strained relations between the yajamana and ritvijs can cause harm to the host because a disgruntled priest can perform rites which are not in the interest of the yajamana. In fact, the host-priest relationship is a major part of yajnic social conduct.

Role and responsibility of priests

Shrauta yajnas, in particular soma yajnas, are very large productions. Unlike the agnihotra ritual, they require many ritvijs. Their objective transcends desires for the self or family. Only an ahitagni is eligible to be the host of a soma yajna. He resolves to perform it for the general welfare of society (or similar). He needs a team of 16 ritvijs who are grouped into four categories, one each for yajna functions based on the four Vedas. The group leaders are called *maharitvijs*. Their individual names are hota, adhvaryu, udgata and brahma, respectively.

- *Hota* is the leader of the group that chants the Rig mantras.
- *Adhvaryu* is the leader who follows the procedures detailed in the *Yajur Veda*. The mantras he chants are known as yajus.

Hota priest (standing) with one leg touching the vedi, and adhvaryu (sitting) arranging oblation materials

- *Udgata* is the leader of the team that sings the samas from the *Sama Veda* in praise of yajna devatas at various stages during the yajna proceedings.
- *Brahma* is the leader of the group that oversees the proper conduct of the yajna.

The tables below depict the designations of the assistants of the four leaders and the number of ritvijs required for different shrauta yajnas.

Table 7: Ritvij groups at a shrauta yajna

Maharitvij	Names of assistants	Relating to Veda
Brahma	Brahmanacchansin, Agnidhra, Pota	Atharva Veda
Hota	Maitravaruna, Acchavaka, Gravastut	Rig Veda
Adhvaryu	Pratiprasthata, Neshta, Unneta	Yajur Veda
Udgata	Prastota, Pratiharta, Subrahmaniya	Sama Veda

Table 8: Yajna-ritvij ratio

Yajna	Numbers of ritvijs
Agnihotra	Nil
Darshapoornamaseshti	4
Chaturmasya yajna	5
Pashu yaga	6
Soma yaga	16

Agnihotra is to be performed by the host himself, and as such there is no ritvij for it. But if the host belongs to the kshatriya or vaishya varna, it is necessary for him to have one ritvij as assistant. The roles of the 16 ritvijs are briefly described below.

Hotri group: In this group, the maharitvij is the hota, who leads the team that chants mantras from the *Rig Veda*. He has to chant the Rig mantras to invoke the devatas of the yajna indicated by the adhvaryu. In addition, when the adhvaryu starts picking up havi dravya to offer it to the main yajna devatas, he has to chant mantras called *puronuvakya*. When the adhvaryu pours them into the agni kunda, he must recite mantras called *yajya*. At the end of yajya, the hota says in a loud voice, "Vaushat!" Exactly at that time, the adhvaryu makes the oblation. In addition to these principal items of chanting, in a yajna like the agnishtoma, the hota has to chant specific groups of mantras called *shastra* in praise of the main devata. Others assist him in this chanting. The mantras used by the hota and the actions he performs are derived from the *Rig Samhita*, Brahmana Granthas like the *Aitareya Brahmana*, and Shrauta Sutras like *Ashvalayana* or *Apastamba Sutra*. Thus, the hota's main role is to chant mantras from the *Rig Veda*. The other ritvijs from the hotri group are as follows.

Maitravaruna (prashasta): He is the chief support of the hota. He holds the staff *(danda)*, stands on the vedi and passes orders *(praisha)* at appropriate times to the hotri group ritvijs to chant yajya. He also chants the puronuvakya mantras and shastra along with the hota, and has to partially perform a few action-oriented movements and minor havans. Just as in a court of law a crier announces, "The proceedings are now over," at which everyone vacates the court, the Maitravaruna, too, orders all the ritvijs to leave their seats and vacate the sadomandap at the right time. For this he calls out, "Sarpat!"

Acchavaka: He is the third hotri ritvij in order of functional importance, and participates in the chanting of yajya and shastra.

Gravastut: This ritvij has a special job during the crushing of the soma sticks to extract their juice in soma yajna. During the crushing process, he has to chant suktas in a standing pose. At that time he covers his eyes with a piece of cloth. It is said that he blindfolds himself because he cannot bear the harsh sight of soma, the king of medicinal plants, being crushed, and does not have the courage to witness its destruction. Among the suktas that the gravastut chants are included suktas in praise of the stone used in the crushing process *(grava)*. Since he praises *(stuta)* the grava, he is called gravastut. Before the soma sticks are crushed, they are kept on a special throne-like seat and covered with a turban, which the gravastut is given as a special gift by the yajamana or adhvaryu.

Adhvaryu group: Almost all actions in the rites are the responsibility of the maharitvij of the adhvaryu group. The adhvaryu is to the yajamana like a prime minister to a king. He issues various orders *(praisha)* to the ritvijs at different times to initiate appropriate rites. For this purpose, he seeks the consent only of the yajamana or the overseeing maharitvij, brahma. Just as in a democratic set-up, the head of state first appoints the prime minister and then the cabinet ministers in consultation with the prime minister, it is the same in soma samsthaka yajna. First, the yajamana hunts out a suitable brahmin to act as his adhvaryu. Thereafter, the adhvaryu recommends the names of other ritvijs-to-be, decides on the yajna devatas, the organization of havi as per the shastras, etc. The movements from one agni kunda to another and other (hand) actions performed during the yajna process is the sole responsibility of the adhvaryu. He chants various yajus (prose mantras) during such movements and actions. The yajus are drawn from the *Yajur Veda Samhita* and the actions are based on the injunctions of the related Brahmana Grantha. Other ritvijs of the adhvaryu group include:

Pratiprasthata: This numero uno assistant of the adhvaryu has to be with him during the entire yajna process. According to the orders of the adhvaryu, he has to carry out many actions either jointly with the adhvaryu or singly. In terms of the number of actions and movements, he is next only to the adhvaryu. He has to partially work at issuing orders to other priests. The responsibility of offering oblations to some main devatas also falls upon him.

Neshta: This assistant of the adhvaryu helps him in the process of crushing the soma. On orders from the adhvaryu, he has to usher the *yajamana patni* (hostess) from her temporary residence called a *patnishala*, to the place of austerity. He also joins the hotri group to chant some parts of yajya mantras for some devatas.

Unneta: This ritvij renders special assistance in the sadomandap where soma juice extraction and dispensation is carried out in soma yajna. Crushing the soma, filtering the juice in designated pots, placing these containers in appropriate places, filling the pots used to offer the soma oblation, etc. are his functions. In addition, two important yajna karmas of soma yajna – *atigrahya* and *hariyojana* are performed by the unneta.

Udgitha group: This team sings sama verses from the *Sama Veda* and is led by the udgata. This maharitvij transforms the solemn atmosphere created through the rig and yajus chanting into a delightful and enchanting one with his musical notes. The yajna mandap reverberates with the sama tunes, which are prayers to the yajna devatas. The udgata, however, sings only selectively at the time of important activities during the yajna process, for example, agnyadhana, pre- and post-gharma invocations, Subrahmanyam stuti, etc. On other occasions, he deploys his assistants for the sama chanting. He does not partake of the prasad of purodasha, pashuangas, etc., but only consumes soma juice. He does not participate in other action-oriented rites either. His responsibility is simply to sing the praises of the devatas with the help of the richas. He and his team enjoy special treatment compared to other ritvijs. In soma yaga in particular, the somayaja songs of the udgata have a special importance. The honour of offering song-based praises to the principal devata goes to the udgata, ahead of even the hota. The order of offering praises to the principal devata is first the singing by the udgata, then the praises by the hota followed by the oblation of soma juice by the adhvaryu. Importance-wise, a yajna with sama singing weighs high compared to one without it. Other ritvijs of the udgitha group are:

Prastota: He is the special assistant to the udgata. His job is to sing the samas in praise of the devatas during various ishtis like dikshaniya, etc. Also, during the gharma rite, when the adhvaryu carries out various actions, the prastota sings the samas associated with the respective actions. The prastota sings the introductory songs in the main praises of the principal devata of soma yaga. This singing is a repetitive process. The prastota uses udumbara sticks to keep count of the repetitions and arranges them on a piece of cloth spread out in front of him. He follows a sequence, placing the sticks to progressively form a beautiful geometrical figure.

Pratiharta: This ritvij of the udgitha group is a member of the team of three that sings samas for the main devatas. He sings the last part of these songs individually. This part of the sama is called *pratihara*, and as he sings the pratihara, he is called pratiharta. Like others of this group, he does not participate in the actions and movements of the yajna.

Subrahmanya: He has the most important function of steering the chariot loaded with soma creeper (after it is purchased) to the pragvansha mandap at the yajnashala. His job is also to request the main devata of soma yajna, Indra, to arrive at the yajna venue by praising him. This is done only through the singing of samas. In fact, this is one of the most melodious pieces of sama singing and creates a beautiful atmosphere in the yajna mandap.

Brahma group: This is headed by the brahma. Although he is not the chief authority at the yajna, he almost holds that degree. He has to keep a vigil over the actions, movements and chanting of all the ritvijs, and ensure that all rites are performed without faults or flaws. On some important occasions, the adhvaryu has to seek the consent of the brahma. If any difference of opinion arises about an action/rite, it is the responsibility of the brahma to resolve the differences and give his considered ruling. To offer oblations of expiation is also his job, next to the adhvaryu's. He is the watchdog of the yajna, and therefore has almost no responsibility for chanting or performing rites. He is always at the helm of the yajna-ship, watching that it progresses in the right direction and with stability. The details of his role clearly underline the prerequisites of who can be the brahma. He has to be well-versed in all three Vedas, particularly the *Atharva Veda*. He must have practical knowledge of minute details of the procedures and rites required in a soma yajna. If he has all these attributes and belongs to the Vashishtha gotra, he is respected as an authority of superlative order in soma yajna. Other ritvijs of the brahma group are:

Brahmanacchansin: Although he is an assistant to the brahma, he has very little work in the brahma group. Instead, he has to join the hota's assistants to sing a few yajyas and shastra mantras. Sometimes the brahma appoints him to work in his place.

Pota: He is also an assistant to the brahma but helps the hota, if needed. His only duty is to chant yajyas according to the order (praisha) of the maitravaruna.

Agnidhra: Even though this ritvij is from the brahma group, in practice he helps the adhvaryu. Miscellaneous work such as igniting the fire, bringing the wood sticks and special grass called barhi from the store and arranging them in the designated place in the yajna mandap, and consecrating the wooden spoons, are his responsibility, conducted according to the orders of the adhvaryu. He stands by the vedi at the time of all yagas, holding a weapon called a *sphya* (representing a thunderbolt) in his right hand and resting it on his right shoulder. Sometimes, under the orders of the adhvaryu, the agnidhra has to cook the rice and make purodasha in soma yaga. In pashu yaga, he has to lead the team that carries the pashu to the shamitrashala, holding agni in his right hand. The list of duties and type of weapon used by the agnidhra would indicate that he is an armed guard specially appointed to ensure proper defence arrangements for the yajna. In addition to helping the adhvaryu, the agnidhra joins the hotri group and chants yajyas.

Sadasya: Over and above these 16 ritvijs, one important senior ritvij is the sadasya. Although he has precious little work like *chamasa prashana* (drinking the soma juice using the specially-made wooden cups called chamasa) and upasthana, he needs to have a complete and in-depth procedural knowledge and practical experience in performing a yajna. Normally, the brahma is supposed to take care of the correctness of the proceedings. However, as a yajna is a complex process, having multifarious activities by several groups of people, it is likely that he may miss some omissions or commissions. The sadasya has to catch them and suggest remedial atonement. Similarly, in the case of a difference of opinion over ritualistic details, he has the authority to step in and give a ruling. Generally, his suggestions cannot be by-passed or his decision overruled. Clearly, the sadasya is a high-ranking ritvij.

Lastly, 10 to 11 ritvijs called *chamasadhvaryu* are required in soma yajna. When the adhvaryu offers soma to the fire using a special wooden jar called a *graha*, the chamasadhvaryus also have to do the same using wooden bowls called chamasa. Thereafter, they have to carry the chamasas with the balance of the juice to the hota and other ritvijs for them to take as prasad.

Honorarium – dakshina

The honorarium of the ritvijs, called *dakshina*, is an important part of shrauta yajna. Without it, the yajna cannot be completed. The word dakshina has possibly been derived from a cow being given away to honour the ritvijs. In olden times, cows were the main honorarium, not money. In soma yajna, these cows would enter the yajna pavilion (sadomandap) from the south (called *dakshin* in Sanskrit) of the garhapatya agni and sadasya. They would be taken out of the pavilion through the place dividing the seats of the sadasya and agnidhra, passing through a passage near the chatvala and utkara. A cow entering the pavilion from the south, dakshin, would be called 'dakshina'. An offering to a priest while honouring him for his important contribution to a yajna is thus dakshina. Money as an honorarium is also called dakshina. It is the compensation paid to the ritvijs for their work and effort. The Shrauta Sutras and Brahmana Granthas say that no yajna should be conducted without dakshina. It is like lubricating a wheel. The yajna becomes fruitless in the absence of dakshina, like a cart without bullocks.

When the representative of the host, called *soma pravaka*, goes to a brahmin to propose his selection for the said yajna, the would-be ritvij asks some questions. One is, "Is any honorarium likely to be paid in the proposed yajna?" Even if such a question is asked to elicit general information, the decision of the brahmin to accept or decline the proposal of the soma pravaka should not be based on it. There is an injunction in the *Shatapatha Brahmana* saying that the ritvijs should not bargain for dakshina.

The quantum of the honorarium is said to depend on the type of yajna. As a general rule it is fixed, but there can be exceptions to the rule. Such exceptions are acceptable to the Brahmana Granthas, which say, "A yajna without dakshina does not bear fruits. Therefore, dakshina must be paid, even if it is less than the prescribed quantity." In agnishtoma yajna, the dakshina is ordained as 112 cows. If one does not have 112 cows, 21 will suffice. In fact, an agnishtoma can be completed even if the host has only seven cows ("One for the purchase of soma, one for welcoming king Soma, one for anubadhya yaga and four for the main dakshina." *(Baudhayana Shrauta Sutra* 25.4). It is also said that dakshina should not be offered to a brahmin who begs for it. Similarly, dakshina should not be paid to a priest under duress.

The quantum of dakshina varies with the yajna. The least could be the gift of leftover milk to the performer of agnihotra homa, or a *charu* (rice cake) given to the four ritvijs (to be shared by them) in darshapoornamaseshti. However, some yajnas like ashvamedha and rajasooya shower abundant wealth on the ritvijs. There is no upper limit for dakshina in such yajnas.

Expiation (prayashchitta)

All yajnas have to be conducted exactly according to the injunctions of the Brahmana Granthas. However, due to human folly or circumstantial difficulties, sometimes the rules are violated. Such a yajna does not yield the desired results. The Brahmana Granthas suggest alternatives for unavoidable situations and expiation methods for mistakes. In this way, the lost fruits can be recovered. The brahma is the watchdog who points out mistakes, procedural deviations, commissions and omissions. The yajamana and priests perform expiation rituals in such cases.

Resolve (sankalpa) of host

A yajna process, in fact, starts from that point in time when a person feels a desire to perform yajna. When he converts this desire into a resolve, the thought about yajna translates into action, and he is transformed into a yajamana, and physical yajna becomes the outcome. This is the general or colloquial definition of sankalpa.

In shrauta yajna parlance, sankalpa is also a ritual. In this process, the priest chants mantras indicating the type of desire of the host with which the yajna is to be performed, the purpose of the desire (for prosperity and welfare at personal, social, national, universal level, etc.), and the yajamana takes a spoonful of water in his right palm to symbolically declare that he promises to stand by the declaration of the priest, and requests the Almighty to help him in his resolution. The sankalpa is a mandatory ritual.

Sacred fire

Fire or agni is the most important aspect of all yajnas. For shrauta karma, three forms of fire – garhapatya, dakshinagni and ahavaniya agni – are essential. An individual desiring to perform shrauta karma goes through the process of agnyadhana (described under 'sapta havi samstha' below). The host of a yajna brings his garhapatya agni to the yajna venue, and installs it ceremoniously.

Agni kunda: Shrautagni is always installed in specially constructed geometrical figures. The construction is known as a kunda. It is not normally invoked in floor-based pots. Garhapatya kunda, dakshinagni kunda and ahavaniya agni kunda are specially constructed in the yajna mandap for installing shrautagni. The garhapatya kunda is circular in shape, the dakshinagni kunda is semi-circular and the ahavaniya kunda is square[8]. Irrespective of shape, their measurements are such that their area is the same. The construction of the kundas is based on pure mathematics.

Three sacrificial fire-pits and vedi used in shrauta yajna. The agnidhra priest is in action.

Garhapatya agni is invoked using the agni manthan ritual. The agni has to be constantly protected. The ahavaniya and dakshinagni are taken from this agni. Ahavaniya agni is very important because all havi dravya such as samidha, ajya, milk, curd, etc. is offered to the devatas through this agni. Not many rituals are performed on dakshinagni, but all rituals for ancestors are carried out on it.

Agni manthan: At the commencement of the yajna process, when the host arrives at the yajna venue, agni has to be

---

[8] See Chapter 6

invoked. The process followed is called *agni manthan*, which literally means producing fire by churning. A pair of plates is carved out of wood from the holy fig tree *(Ficus religiosa or pipal)*. It is desirable that this tree comes from the stem of the shami tree *(Ekeciasuma)*. A small slit is dug into each one. A wooden rod in held between the two plates. The upper plate is known as *uttararani*, the lower one as *adhararani*, and the rod is known as *mantha*. A small metal grip is fixed on the lower part of the mantha. This pointed end of the rod is called *devayoni* – the point where the sacred fire arrives during the churning process. Using a string wound around it, the rod is churned with force. Simultaneously, invocation mantras are chanted for agni to appear at the root of the churning rod. The rotation of mantha on the adhararani causes friction, and fire is produced.

Creating the sacrificial fire using arani

The yajamana couple arrives at the yajna venue along with their arani. They hold their shrautagni in a hibernating state. The transfer of agni into the arani is done symbolically by the couple before leaving the house for the yajna venue through a rite called *agni samaropana*. Normally, after the daily rituals, shrautagni is preserved in the form of a spark in the garhapatya kunda. It is symbolically transferred into the arani through a simple ritual, and then the garhapatya agni is extinguished. At the yajna venue, agni is invoked through another ritual and installed in the kunda prepared at the yajnashala. All other kundas are ignited using this agni. On completion of all the yajna rituals, a last ritual is performed for the transfer of agni from the garhapatya kunda of the yajnashala into the arani to be taken home by the couple. There the agni is once again transferred into the garhapatya kunda for regular daily rituals.

Sacred piece of land (yajna bhoomi)

The Shrauta Sutras give norms for selecting the venue for the intended yajna and the method of consecrating it. Sage Yajnavalkya has also written about it in *Shukla Yajur Veda Samhita*. Selecting a proper place to construct the yajna kundas, to raise the yajna mandaps, etc. is very important because the vibrations of the place create a complementary and compounding (or otherwise) effect on the fruit of the yajna.

The yajamana and his chief priest set out on an auspicious day or time to select a suitable place for the yajna. They conduct preliminary tests from the point of view of the vibrations of the place followed by a soil test for similar purposes. After selecting the venue, the purification process is carried out following the guidelines of the sutras. Kundas are then dug and a canopy raised.

In simple terms, the yajna venue should be flat and smooth without deep tilts, free from bad smells, rodents, insects, excessive dampness, and have a tillable soil. It should be away from crowded activity, preferably in the vicinity of an old temple site.

Yajna venue (yajnashala)

The venue chosen for the yajna is called a *yajnashala* or *yajnavihara*. At the selected place, a canopy or small pavilion is erected following a special process. Under the pavilion, an area is earmarked for the actual yajna process to be performed. This place is called the *devayajana*. The area is called the yajna *mandap*. Built facing the east, its measurement and form differ according to the type of yajna. Broadly, however, the mandap at a shrauta yajna has six functional divisions – pragvansha, sadomandap, havirdhana mandap, agnidhra mandap, marjaliya and shamitrashala.

At the extreme west of the yajna mandap is the *pragvansha*. It has three entrances, one each on the east, west and south. The havi dravya to be offered to agni for the yajna devata is kept in a designated place in the pragvansha, called the *antarlayama*. All ishtis are performed in the pragvansha. The place between the garhapatya and ahavaniya agni kundas is called the *vedi*. Its length is approximately equal to the height of the yajamana. By drawing a line of bricks, the boundaries of the vedi are marked out. This vedi is always covered with a special grass called darbha. It is believed that when the devata arrives at the yajna mandap to accept the oblation, he takes his seat here. Avahaniya agni kunda is constructed on the eastern side of the vedi, garhapatya on the western side and dakshinagni kunda on the southern side. The bamboo poles supporting the roof of the pragvansha are so arranged that the ends tied together point towards the east. Perhaps because of this the mandap is called *pragvansha* ('bamboo pointing east').

Beyond the pragvansha and towards its east is the *sadomandap*, also called the *udagvanshashala*. The sadomandap is used for intellectual discussions by the ritvijs, and also to relax in during free periods. It has entrances from the east and west. The rest of the boundary is covered using bamboo and sheets. The sadomandap also contains a pillar, which represents the yajamana and is made to his height from the stems of udumbara trees.

Beyond the sadomandap and towards its east is the havirdhana mandap, which acts as a storehouse for all the articles used in a yajna. The carts that carry the purchased soma valli are also stationed here. To the south of the cart four ditches called *uparava* are dug and covered with two wooden sheets. The ritual of crushing the soma valli to extract the juice is carried out here. Beyond the havirdhana mandap and towards the east is the uttaravedi. Ahavaniya agni is brought here from the pragvansha.

The entire yajna mandap is divided (north-south) into two parts. The first contains the pragvansha and the second, called the *mahavedi*, contains the other three mandaps. The oblation of soma juice and animal sacrifice is carried out here. On the south of the mahavedi is the *marjaliya*, a place to wash and clean the yajniya implements and vessels. The waste generated at the time of preparing the vedi is collected in a pit called *utkara*. On the north of the mahavedi is a mandap called *agnidhra*, half of which is in the mahavedi and half outside. The ritvij agnidhra stands here at the time of soma oblations and gives the praisha and vaushat calls. It is also used to install the dhishnya in. To its right is a pit to collect waste called *chatvala*. The yajnashala is prepared at least a day in advance of the yajna.

The yajna mandap is artistically personified as Yajna Purusha (*Shatapatha Brahmana* 3.5.1–6). "This yajna mandap is verily the Yajna Purusha. Havirdhana is its head, the ahavaniya on the uttaravedi its mouth, agnidhra and marjaliya its two arms, sado its abdomen, the two front uparava its nostrils and the rear ones its ears, the sheets covering uparava its jaws, the red bull's skin its tongue, the crushers its teeth, the old ahavaniya and garhapatya (from pragvansha) its feet, and the udumbari pole its navel."

Articles of oblation (havi dravya)

The articles mainly used as havi dravya in a shrauta yajna are ajya, ghrita, milk, curd, yava, vrihi, purodasha, various types of samidha, etc. An important havi dravya is soma juice. Today, knowledge about the creeper has been lost and it is difficult to find it using the available description. The adhvaryu uses a special wooden pot or chamasa to offer the soma oblation. The ritvijs have the right to consume the balance of the dravya left after the oblation process has been completed. It is said that the devatas assemble near the yajna fire-pit to receive the havi offered to Agni (for them). Soma juice is believed to be Indra's most preferred havi dravya.

Yajna implements (yajnayudha)

Special kinds of wooden pots, spatulas, spoons, cups, and earthen pots and plates[9] are used to prepare the purodasha, offer ghrita and hold the hot pots. The agnidhra uses a special wooden, symbolic war weapon and other instruments. Stone crushers and other such implements are also used during the crushing of soma and a few other rituals.

Yupa: In pashu yaga, parts of a cow (pashu) are offered as oblation. A pole, called *yupa,* is used to tie the pashu near the yajna vedi. The killing of an animal for the sacrifice is not considered 'killing', says *Manu Smriti* (5.3). Authors of other smritis express similar views. There are passionate arguments for and against this ritual. At many places, a symbolic pashu is made out of grain flour.

Auspicious time (yajna muhurta)

Great emphasis is laid on the time of day the yajna is to commence, taking into account the position of various planets and stars, the season, the phase of the moon, position of the sun, etc. These details are contained in the Jyotish part of Vedic literature. It is said that a yajna which takes into account such auspicious moments will have a good result. For example, Agni is a prithivi devata, but spans other lokas too. If Agni devata is not active on earth at a particular time, it can affect the end-result of the yajna.

Helpers for miscellaneous activities (parikarmi)

A shrauta yajna is a social event of a sizeable dimension. Like any other large social event, a yajna also needs managers specializing in logistics, construction, media management,

---

[9] See Chapter 7

finance, etc. Their coordinated efforts go a long way to making the yajna event a useful and memorable one, besides achieving the main objective of the overall welfare of the participants and society. They are called the parikarmi and include smiths, carpenters, etc.

SHRAUTA YAJNAS: DESCRIPTION (TOTAL: 21)

Shrauta purifying yajnas

These number seven and are known as *sapta paka samsthaka yajnas*. After the wedding samskara, the householder (from the three varnas) qualifies to establish the smartagni. This activity is totally optional, but once he installs the smartagni, he can undertake the austerity and rituals based on smartagni. He has to worship the agni through the rituals that fall under sapta paka samstha. These are:

Aupasana homa: The oblation made daily through a havan is called aupasana homa. The havan is to be done at sunrise and sunset. In the morning, oblations are made to Surya devata, and in the evening to Agni devata. At both times, an offering is also made to Prajapati. The havan must be performed jointly by the husband and wife throughout their life. This agni is also known as smartagni and the ritual as smarta agnihotra.

A part of the aupasana agni is taken to the kitchen for cooking food. The daily meals are to be treated by the couple as prasad. After the cooking is over, the agni has to be brought back in smartagni. The *Atharva Veda* recommends this homa for eliminating a large number of maladies. However, the material used in oblations differs according to the malady. Varying the oblation material on the basis of the *Atharva Veda*, this yajna can be used for removing pollution and getting rid of diseases like tuberculosis.

Vaishvadeva: This yajna was first performed by Vaishvadeva. It is done before lunch. *Odan* (rice) is cooked on smartagni and offered to all the devas and *pitras* (ancestors). The offering for pitras is called *swadhakara*.

Parvan: The full-moon and no-moon days are called *parva*, and the rite performed on no-moon days is called *parvan*. It is a type of *shraaddha* yajna, i.e. it is performed for the preceding three generations – *pitri* (father), *pitamaha* (grandfather) and *pra-pitamaha* (great-grandfather).

Ashtaka: This is also a shraaddha ritual. It is done on the eighth day *(ashtami)* following the full-moon in the winter months according to the Indian calendar *(Hemanta* and *Shishira)*. Normally, there are four such days. Special sweetened bread *(apupa)* is prepared and offered to Indra, Vishvedeva, Prajapati and ancestors.

Masi shraaddha: The rite performed every month for ancestors.

Shravana karma: Bali is offered to snakes daily in the evening, starting from the full-moon days of Shravana and continuing up to the full-moon days of Margashirsha. The ritual is also sometimes called *sarpa bali* ('offering for snake').

Shulagava: This is the havan for Rudra devata, so it is also called *Ishanabali* (Ishana being one of the names of Rudra). Offering a cow used to be part of shulagava. Since slaughtering of cows has been forbidden in Kali yuga, it is not included in *Paraskara* or *Katyayana Grihya Sutras*, and its followers (Madhyandina Shakha) do not perform this ritual. Others perform it using alternate offerings such as the sthali paka preparation.

Evidently, havans (homas) under the sapta paka samstha are daily and periodic undertaking of religious rites (anushthanas). They keep the ahitagni busy through the year and are his nitya karmas.

Shrauta cultivating yajnas

These number seven and are known as sapta havi samsthaka yajnas. Rishi Gautama has prescribed seven *(sapta)* havi yajnas (GS 8.20–21), which are: (i) agnyadheya, (ii) agnihotra, (iii) darsha, (iv) paurnamasa, (v) navasyeshti, (vi) chaturmasya, and (vii) pashubandha. Their complete details can be found in the Shrauta Sutras. Below we broadly define their procedures and rituals.

1. Agnyadheya or agnyadhana

This is the basic and the most important karma under havi samstha. With reference to this ritual, *adhana* means to establish, with the chanting of mantras, the agni that rises out of the arani-manthan into the designated kunda. To establish agni at one's place according to the precepts of the shastras is known as 'adhana of agni'. Adhana is of three types according to the resolve while establishing the fire.

Homa purvaka adhana is where the resolve is, "Hereafter I shall perform the agnihotra ritual till the end of my life." A person making this resolve for agnyadhana is called an *agnihotri*. He must perform the agnihotra ritual every morning and evening from now on.

Ishti purvaka adhana is where the resolve is, "Hereafter I shall perform the darshapoornamasa ritual till the end of my life." A person making this resolve is called a *darshayaji*. He must perform the agnihotra ritual every day, as well as undertake poornamasa ishti on every full-moon day and darsheshti on no-moon days.

Soma purvaka adhana is where the resolve is, "Hereafter I shall perform the soma yaga ritual till the end of my life." A person making this resolve for agnyadhana is called a *somayaji*. He has to perform the agnihotra ritual every day, undertake the darshapoornamasa ishti every full-moon day and on no moon days. In addition, in *Vasanta ritu* (spring), he has to undertake soma yaga.

If an agnihotri desires to perform soma yaga, for example, it becomes kamya karma for him. But for a somayaji, it is a mandatory karma. If an agnihotri does not perform soma yaga, he does not attract any penalty, but if a somayaji misses a soma yaga in a given year, he is considered a defaulter worthy of being penalized.

To take adhana for smarta karmas is *smartadhana* and to take it for shrauta karmas is *shrautadhana*. A person who takes possession of agni in either way has to maintain and worship it for the rest of their lives. Agni has to be kept alive and oblations offered in it daily. This is the fire worship *(agni upasana)*. Worship under smartadhana and shrautadhana are done differently. A person who is a shrauta fire worshipper *(shrautagni upasaka)* is called an *ahitagni*.

Smartadhana is a prerequisite for shrautadhana. Only an ahitagni can perform shrauta yajnas like soma yaga. Therefore, the ritual of agnyadhana is very important. In Vedic times, every second person was probably an agnihotri, or even an ahitagni. Every city had agnihotris. However, their count has significantly dwindled now, and today there are barely 200 agnihotris in the whole of India[10]. Let us now go through the process of taking shrautadhana. There are five types of agnyadhana.

1. *Apurvadhana*: The first initiation of a person who is not an ahitagni.
2. *Anvadhana*: The first samidha to be offered in any yajna or ishti to ignite the fire for that yajna or ishti.
3. *Punaradhana*: If within one year from the date of agnyadhana, the fire worship breaks for unavoidable reasons like a long illness, etc., the person has to once again take agnyadhana. The time for this ritual would be a no-moon day when the Punarvasu star appears. This is called punaradhana. The old agni must be immersed after a year and three days from the second agnyadhana. At this time, the fire ignition should be done with kusha (grass) instead of samidha. The rainy season is the proper time for this ritual. Dakshina in the form of ornaments is recommended.
4. *Tritiyadhana*: If, during the period of the second agnyadhana, a financial calamity forces the agni worship to break within a year, the agnyadhana has to be repeated for the third time.
5. *Vicchhinnagnyadhana*: If all three agnis are extinguished, agnyadhana becomes necessary. Such an agnyadhana is called vicchhinnagnyadhana.

---

[10] Ahitagni Nana Kale has published interesting statistics together with details of agnihotris with the assistance of Sankara Matham, Mumbai. All ahitagnis in the compilation have performed shrautadhana as the prerequisite ritual.

Anyone is eligible to host a shrauta yajna after taking any of the above five adhanas. They should neither be too young nor too old, and have at least one child. People from all three varnas (brahmin, kshatriya, and vaishya) have an equal right to perform shrauta karma, but the specifications of time, seasons and stars are different as per the following table.

Table 9: Varnas and shrauta karma

Varna	Season for performance	Star
Brahmin	Vasant ritu (spring)	Hasta
Kshatriya	Grishma ritu (summer)	Chitra
Vaishya	Varsha ritu (the rains)	Not specific

Agnyadhana process: Agnyadhana is an independent karma, and not part of any other act, i.e. it is the first yajna of this samstha. Using the given guidelines, an auspicious day and time is chosen for agnyadhana. It is a two-day ritual – day one is for preliminary preparations, and day two for the main karma. Agnyadhana is done with the help of four ritvijs: brahma, hota, adhvaryu and agnidhra.

Day 1: The first day is called *upavasatha*. On this day, the implements are organized and the yajnashala raised. Three pits are prepared for the three agnis. The following preliminary rituals and acts are performed.

- Sankalpa and appointment of ritvijs.
- Establishment of agni in garhapatya kunda. This agni is either created through agni manthan or taken from the *aupasana agni* (smartagni of the host).
- Brahmaudana havan.
- Cooking the rice or yava grains (in four vessels) on the established agni using water or mik. (This cooked material is called *brahmaudana,* and hence the agni on which it is cooked is called *brahmaudanic agni.*)
- Offering a part of the cooked rice as oblation in brahmaudanic agni.

- Offering a major portion of the rice to the ritvijs.
- Dipping samidhas in the remaining part and offering them to agni.
- Donating three calves each to the ritvijs.
- Expiation homa for all sinful acts that may have been committed by the host in the past.
- Kushmanda homa and abhyudaya shraaddha.
- After being purified in this manner, the couple observe celibacy in thought and action, keep silence *(mouna)* and one-pointedly concentrate on the resolve to be taken.
- During the night, the host ties a goat with black spots near the garhapatya agni, periodically offers samidha in the agni, and maintains a vigil to keep the agni alive throughout the night. If the host owns the goat, it is donated to the agnidhra the next day.
- The couple observes a fast during the night, as it is believed that the yajna devatas assemble at the venue, and to take food without offering anything to the guests would not be appropriate. (Since the host observes a fast on upavasatha day, fasting has generally come to be known as *upavasa*.)
- The adhvaryu gives the arani to the host. The couple keep it in their lap throughout the night like holding a child in their arms.

Day 2: On this day the actual establishment of shrautagni takes place. The following rites and actions are performed.

- In the early morning before sunrise, the adhvaryu heats up the arani on the brahmaudanic agni, and then extinguishes it (the action symbolizes that agni enters and hibernates there – to be invoked at a later time).
- The garhapatya kunda is consecrated and pancha sambhara done.
- The agnidhra draws three west-east lines in the kunda using a wooden weapon called a *sphya*. He takes a pinch of soil from there and sprinkles water on the lines. Then he places a small piece of gold on the lines and pours salted soil and a particular soil (dug by rodents and

collected specially for the purpose) over it. Now he arranges 50 calcium crystals over it. The ahavaniya and dakshinagni kundas are also prepared in this manner using 73 and 22 calcium crystals respectively.

- After sunrise, agni is established in the garhapatya kunda. Sitting behind the garhapatya kunda, the yajamana churns the arani to produce fire. While the churning is in progress, mantras are chanted to invoke the hibernating agni. A white-brown horse with black spots on its front knees is made to stand on the eastern side of the garhapatya kunda, but facing it. After the agni is ignited in the arani, it is kept on an earthen plate and kindled using small samidha and powdered dung. The kindled agni is installed in the garhapatya kunda by chanting *"Bhuhu Bhuvah . . . "* As soon as the fire is established in the garhapatya kunda, the brahma sings the *Rathantara* sama.
- Now the *agni uddharana* process is completed (establishment of ahavaniya and dakshinagni). A part of garhapatya agni is taken ceremoniously on an earthen plate to the ahavaniya kunda. The horse is taken towards the ahavaniya kunda too, and the yajamana follows. The adhvaryu carries the plate, and makes the horse put its right hoof in the ahavaniya kunda. After the impression of its step is obtained in the kunda, the horse is taken four steps ahead and made to stand facing the ahavaniya kunda (the Vedics believed that the horse represented a protector who destroys demons and evil spirits). The brahma sings the sama called *Brihatsam*. The adhvaryu picks up the burning samidhas from the plate, and with the chant *"Bhur bhuvah swaha swadhaur riva . . . "*, installs the agni in the ahavaniya kunda. The yajamana chants the three mantras and does the 'upasthana' of agni.
- Dakshinagni is established using the *aupasana agni* (smartagni of the host) or through manthan.
- Sabhya and avasathya agnis are also established in the same manner.

- At the end, after all agnis have been ceremoniously installed and established, the yajamana offers the poornahuti, and then honours the ritvijs by offering them dakshina according to his capacity.

The agnyadhana process culminates here. After the ritual, the yajamana has to observe certain rules for twelve, six or three nights. It includes three ishtis (pavamana, havishka, etc.), which are described in the *Katyayana Sutra* (KS 4.10.16) as well as other sutras like *Baudhayana*, albeit with minor differences. A grihastha who completes agnyadhana in this manner is worthy of being addressed as 'ahitagni'.

2. Agnihotra

This is the second yajna in the series of sapta havi samstha. It is a daily ritual. From the evening of the day of agnyadhana, the grihastha undertakes the agnihotra homa until his death or until he takes sannyasa.

Agnihotra is a havan ritual wherein articles such as milk, ghrita, etc. are offered as oblations (*Shatapatha Brahmana* 12.4.1.1, 12.4.1–7). According to the *Aitareya Brahmana* (Ai 32.8), even an unmarried person is eligible to perform agnihotra.

The main devatas of agnihotra are Agni and Surya. Agni is the devata of night and Surya of day. Oblation is made

Table 10: Agnihotra processes and their mantras

Type of agnihotra process	Ahuti time	Mantra
Shrauta	morning	सूर्यो ज्योतिर्ज्योतिः सूर्यः स्वाहा। *Suryo jyoti jyotih suryah swaha*
	evening	अग्नि ज्र्योतिर्ज्योतिः अग्निः स्वाहा। *Agni jyoti jyotih agnih swaha*
Smarta	morning	सुर्याय स्वाहा सुर्याय इदं न मम। *Suryaya swaha suryaya idam na mama*
	evening	अग्नये स्वाहा, अग्नये इदं न मम। *Agnaye swaha agnaye idam na mama*

every day to Surya in the morning and to Agni in the evening. The morning homa process should start after sunrise, and the evening process just before sunset (ApS 6.4.7–9). The shrauta agnihotra process differs from the smarta agnihotra in terms of mantras and actions. The mantras to be used are as shown in Table 10 (SYaju 3.9).

The havi dravya to be used for the oblation depends on the purpose of the agnihotra homa. For example, if the objective is to accomplish a sacred duty or general welfare, cow's milk is used. The agnihotra process is simple in form. Smarta agnihotra, in particular, is very easy to follow, and takes less than five minutes to complete. However, its effect and the vibrations created are inversely exponential to the time taken. The shrauta process has about 20 steps, and takes less than half an hour to complete. There is no poornahuti in agnihotra[11]. In both types of agnihotra, the second oblation is offered to Prajapati in the morning as well as in the evening.

3 & 4. Darshapoornamaseshti

This is the combination of two yajnas – darsha and paurnamasa – done at two specific times *(parvakala)* – no-moon day *(Amavasya)* and full-moon day *(Poornima)*. It is an ishti in that it is performed by the yajamana with the help of four ritvijs. It is the role model for all ishti-type yajnas.

The main devatas of darshapoornamaseshti are Agni, Agnishoma, Indra and Indragni. Prajapati and Vishnu are the secondary *(upanshu)* devatas. The duration is two days, i.e. darsha ishti starts on Amavasya and ends on *Shukla Pratipada* (the first day of the waxing fortnight) and paurnamaseshti starts on Poornima and ends on *Krishna Pratipada* (the first day of the waning fortnight). The first day is known as *upavasatha* and the principal day as *yajaniya* day.

---

[11] Interested readers may refer to Katyayana or other shrauta sutras for details.

Darshapoornamaseshti is completed through 70 steps, actions and rituals, but we will go over them only cursorily[12]. A day prior to Poornima, the yajamana shaves off all his hair except for the tuft at the top of the head and genital hair. The wife clips her nails only.

Day 1: On the upavasatha day the yajamana has to perform:

- *Pancha bhu sambhara* (consecration of agni kundas) as in agnyadhana.
- *Sankalpa*: Holding six samit in the right hand and sitting to the west of the garhapatya, the yajamana makes the sankalpa, "Tomorrow I will do a yajna in which I will offer specially prepared purodasha for Agni, ajya for Agnishoma upanshu, purodasha for Agnishoma upanshu . . ." Then he offers two samit oblations in the garhapatya agni. The first is with the mantra and the second without (called *tushnim ahuti*). Similar offerings are made in the other two agnis.
- *Anvadhana* (explained earlier in agnyadhana).
- *Paristarana vidhi* (the ritual of spreading darbha grass around the agni).
- *Vrata dharana* (acceptance of austerity until the end of the yajna). After a light breakfast of items approved for upavasa, the yajamana walks through a space between the garhapatya and dakshinagni and stands to the west of the ahavaniya kunda, facing east. He dips his forefinger in sacred water and applies the droplets to his eyes as a token of having accepted the mantra being chanted at that time.
- The couple spends the night in the vicinity of garhapatya agni, observing a fast and celibacy. They have to avoid

---

[12] It must be remembered that any attempt to explain the performance of yajnas, in particular shrauta yajnas, in writing or verbally is really a futile exercise. To understand its real meaning, the process has to be witnessed. For a deeper insight, only repeated participation (bearing in mind that no step in a yajna process is without reason and no ritual without significance) will achieve the result.

eating urad dal, meat, salt and the ingredients of the purodasha to be made the next day as havi for the devata. A darbhasana is used instead of a mattress for reclining. Vrata dharana makes the couple eligible to perform the yajna.

The ahitagni performing the darshapoornamaseshti for the first time has to perform another ishti called *anvarambhaniya* ishti. Here, he first makes two offerings to goddess Saraswati, and then purodasha roasted on 11 earthen plates, called *kapala*, are offered to Agni and Vishnu. There are other oblations too. Anvarambhaniya ishti is to be performed only once.

Day 2: On the yajaniya day, the main yaga is performed. Rituals start after sunrise. Prior to that, the yajamana completes his routine ritual of agnihotra. Some of the important steps/rituals performed on the second day are as follows.

- *Ritvij varana*: Appointment of the ritvijs.
- *Patra sadan*: Arranging all the implements near the vedi.
- *Apa-pranayana*: The adhvaryu takes water in a vessel called pranitah patra and performs some rituals.
- *Vrihi nirvapa*: Examining the grains brought in a cart for cooking purodasha (sacrificial cakes).
- *Patni sannahana*: Tying a rope *(yoktra)* made of grass around the wife's waist like a belt.
- *Samidheni*: Singing 15 special richas at the time of kindling the agni and offering samidhas in it.
- *Kandana, peshana, adhishrayana,* etc.: Rituals for purifying the vessels, pounding the flour, cooking purodasha on the kapala, etc.
- *Paridhi paridhapana, juva sadana, agni samindhana, aghar,* etc.: Bringing agni to life in the kunda before commencing the oblationary processes.
- *Prayaja*: Offering five ajya ahutis for the five seasons to the devatas called Samidha, Tanunapat, Ida, Barhi and Swaha.
- *Ajyabhaga*: Offering oblations to Agni and Soma.

- *The main yaga*: The adhvaryu gives praisha to the hota for agni, and the hota sings anuvakya mantras. Simultaneously, the adhvaryu performs many actions relating to arrangements for the purodasha. When the hota chants *"Bhuvo yajnyasya"*, sings yajyas of Agni and calls out "Vaushat" loudly, the adhvaryu offers purodasha to the ahavaniya agni with a spoon-like instrument called a *juhu*. Other purodasha oblations are also made in a similar manner.
- *Agni swishtakrit homa*: There is a ruling that if any sacrificial food is offered to any deity, Swishtakrit Agni should invariably have a share. Accordingly, the oblation is made.
- *Anuyajya, patni sanyaja,* etc.: After bringing agni to life again, oblations are offered to devatas called Barhi, Narashansa and Agniswishtakrit. Some oblations are offered from where the wife is seated to devatas and their wives.
- *Samishta yajus*: This is the last ritual of the ishti. The devatas are offered oblations to bid them farewell. Thereafter, a few rituals are completed before the yajamana does *vrata visarjana*, the completion rite.

The rituals in darsha ishti are more or less similar. The difference lies in the devata and havi dravya. Here, the main devatas are Indra and Indragni as against Agni and Agnishoma of paurnamaseshti. One more important difference is that the oblation material for Indra is not ajya but a liquid called *sannayya*.

5. Navasyeshti (navannyeshti or agrayaneshti)

The name of this havi yajna or ishti is derived from the fact that the havi dravya (such as purodasha and charu) is prepared using the newly-harvested grains. This is, in fact, the first use of the new harvest. The ishti is performed in autumn and spring. According to *Shatapatha Brahmana* (2, 4, 3.1), the new crop is the essence of Dyava Prithivi. An ahitagni should perform this ishti and only then use the new crop for personal consumption. But Yajnavalkya has argued that the ishti is done to ensure that the black magic powers of the asuras do not contaminate the medicinal essence of food.

Purodasha ahuti (12 kapalas) is made in honour of Indra and Agni, and charu is offered to Dyava Prithivi (one kapala). New vrihi and yava are the main ingredients of the purodasha and charu. A calf (first issue) is the dakshina of this yajna.

6. Chaturmasya

This yajna is performed every four months (*chaturmas* means four months). Each period is called a parva. An ahitagni has to perfrom it either once or periodically every year. The first is called *utsarga paksha* and the second *yavajjiva paksha*. In the *utsarga paksha,* the yajamana performs the chaturmasya only once, and then does pashu yaga and soma yaga. One does not perform chaturmasya ever again. In the second type, his annual worship is done only through chaturmasya yajna. One who desires to do such chaturmasya has to follow certain procedures for repetition of yajna through the four periods (parvakala). The four parvakalas are vaishvadeva, varunapraghasa, sakmedha and shunasiriya parvas.

7. Pashubandha

This yajna is performed every year in the rains. It is done on two days, once when the sun turns northwards from the tropic of Capricorn, and then again when it turns southwards. Animal parts like intestines, heart, etc. are offered as oblations. The devatas are Indragni, Surya and Prajapati. This yajna requires six ritvijs: hota, adhvaryu, agnidhra, brahma, pratiprastha and maitravaruna. It is the model of agnishomiya yajnas of the jyotishtoma group. In this yajna, 11 prayaja and anuyaja yajyas are to be chanted. A bull or cow is given as dakshina.

Shrauta augmenting yajnas

These also number seven and are known as sapta soma samsthaka yajnas. All yajnas in this category are called soma yajnas because they use soma juice as the main havi. One-day soma yagas are known as *ekaha*, and two-day soma yagas as *dviratra* (in fact the term used is 'night', but it means a period of 24 hours). The third type is *ahina*, lasting from three to 12 days, and the fourth is a *satra*, held for more than 12 days.

Soma samsthaka yajnas yield a qualitative and quantitative improvement in the psyche of the yajamana. There are seven: (i) agnishtoma, (ii) ukthya, (iii) shodashi, (iv) atiratra, (v) atyagnishtoma, (vii) aptoryama and (vii) vajapeya. The main havi dravya is soma juice. Other important dravyas are milk, essence of butter, curd, charu, purodasha and a specially-made item called sannayya.

1. Agnishtoma: This is the model of ekaha yagas. In ekaha yajnas, three mantra groups are chanted and soma is offered as oblation. They are known as (i) *pratah savana*, (ii) *madhyandina savana*, and (iii) *sayam savana*. In each, four shastras are chanted. Thus, 12 stotras are sung in all. At the end, a sama called *Agni Stoma* is sung in praise of yajnagni, which is why this yajna is known as agnishtoma. Here an animal (actual or symbolic) is also offered. To gain full charge of all yajnas is the objective of this yajna. It is believed to have been first conducted by the devas, which is how they gained control over all the events in the universe.

2. Ukthya: This yajna ends on the note from a stotra called *Ukthya*, hence its name. All the 12 stotras chanted in agnishtoma are chanted here too. In addition, three more stotras (ukthyas) are sung. During ukthya, soma creepers are crushed and the juice extracted. An animal is offered to Indra and Agni.

3. Shodashi: In this yajna, a sixteenth *(shodasha)* stotra is used over and above the 15 stotras of ukthya. This is not an independent yajna like agnishtoma; rather it is part of atiratra, the next in the series.

4. Atiratra: Along with the rituals of shodashi yajna, one additional anushthana is done here. It is performed overnight, and hence is called *atiratra* (through the night) yajna. In the night ritual, three repetitions of a group of stotras are done, and at the end of each cycle an oblation of soma offered. The ritual is completed before dawn. In all, 29 stotras are chanted in atiratra yajna.

5. Atyagnishtoma: The sequence is slightly changed here. After agnishtoma (the first in the series), ukthya is skipped so that the number of stotras chanted works out to be thirteen.

6. Aptoryama: This yajna is an extended form of atiratra. Aptoryama and vajapeya yajnas are variations of the main model of jyotishtoma yajnas. It employs all shodashi stotras, and four additional shastras such as the *Ashvina Shastra*. In a major soma yajna called *sarvamedha,* which lasts for ten days, aptoryama is the principal function of the seventh day.

7. Vajapeya: This major soma yajna is closer to shodashi than atiratra or aptoryama. In addition to the 16 stotras of shodashi, it employs one more shastra. Normally performed in autumn, if done as part of the sarvamedha yajna, vajapeya is performed on the sixth day. A vajapeya yajna can continue for even one year. In addition to the three sacrifices of shodashi, one more sacrifice is offered to Goddess Saraswati. The number 17 has a special place in the vajapeya yajna (17 stotras, 17 shastras, 17 pashu, 17 articles of dakshina, the length of the yupa is 17 aratni, duration is 17 days, 17 dikshas, 17 elixir chamasas, 17 soma chamasas, 17 chariots, etc.). An interesting feature of this yajna is the chariot race. The yajamana is made to win the race, and the victory celebrated by playing 17 drums. In another important ritual, the yajamana, accompanied by his wife, climbs the tall yupa using a ladder. This is the couple's symbolic walk to heaven.

Broadly, the day-by-day coverage of functions during sapta soma yajnas is:

Day 1: Selection of ritvijs, madhuparka, dikshaniya ishti, diksha to yajamana.

Day 2: Prayaniya (the commencing) ishti, purchasc of soma valli, atitheya ishti (in honour of the arrival of King Soma), pravargya, upasada ishti (twice, at dawn and dusk).

Day 3: Two repetitions of pravargya vidhi (pre- and post-lunch).

Day 4: Agni pranayana, havirdhana pranayana, pashu yajna.

Day 5: (Known as sutya or savaniya sutya) Crushing soma valli, extracting and filtering soma juice, soma havan and prashana during dawn, noon and dusk, *udaniya* ('the last one') ishti, *avabhrutha snanam* (a purificatory bathing ritual on the bank of a sacred river or lake to mark the end of the process. The poornahuti of smarta yajnas is equivalent to this rite.).

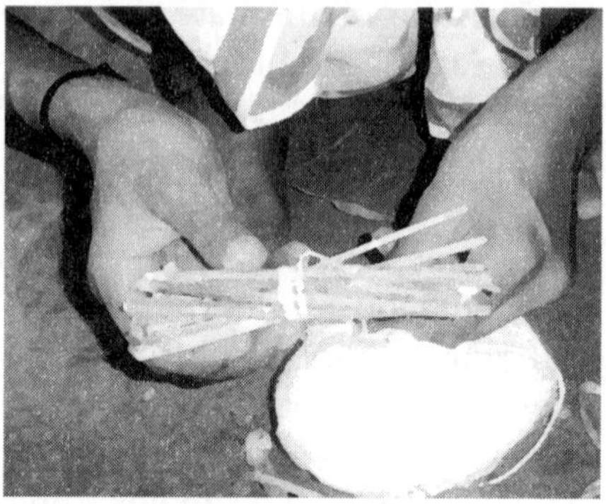

Sticks of the soma creeper. The juice is extracted to offer as oblations in soma yajna

Note that the processes of days one to three are the same for all yajnas in this series. They differ from one another due to variations in the suktas chanted on the fourth and fifth days.

Soma yajnas are the crowning glory of the entire shrauta yajna series. They have very complex steps. The stotras and shastras chanted and the sama songs sung during this group of yajnas excel in procedural neatness, internal meaning and objective.

One important vidhi called *pravargya* and the gharma homa that follows it takes one very close to the objectives and achievements of kundalini yoga. (The initial rites are equivalent to yogic practices to cleanse the body, the nadis and awaken the chakras. The flame that erupts when the oblation is made emits a very powerful glow, rising with a zoom to a height of 20–25 feet for a split second. This is equivalent to the awakening of kundalini in mooladhara and its ascent through sushumna nadi.) The three savanas take one through the three phases of life and make one feel elevated, as if being purified to the core of one's personality. During the poornahuti ritual, a sense of oneness with the universe can be felt, so one is ready to devote oneself to serving the whole uiverse. Incidentally, poornahuti is a laukika vidhi, and not a part of shrauta vidhis.

The pravargya flame rises high in the air

SMARTA YAJNAS (TOTAL: 23) GENERAL INFORMATION

So far we have looked at 21 grihya samskaras and 21 yajna-oriented karmas, i.e. shrauta yajnas. Yajnas rccommended by the Smritis (Smriti texts, Puranas, etc.) are called smarta yajnas. There are 23 major smarta yajnas. They may be performed for personal benefit and to acquire a place in heaven, but their main purpose is social welfare and overall peace. According to the *Aitareya Brahmana* (1/2/3), yajna is performed for the welfare of people in a village, city, or a larger section of society. Since social welfare is the main purpose, they are relevant in all times and ages. An apt example is the Sat Chandi Mahayajna which has been performed at Rikhia by Swami Satyananda since 1995 for the benefit of his neighbourhood. Not only has the entire area around the Rikhia ashram benefited, but the thousands of devotees and disciples who participate receive a major boost to their spiritual efforts.

Compared to shrauta yajnas, smarta yajnas are simpler as far as procedures and rigidity (observing rules and restrictions) are concerned. Most Indians are better acquainted with the devatas of smarta yajnas too. The names of the yajnas generally indicate the devata and purpose. The following table lists the 23 most popular smarta yajnas.

General structure of smarta yajnas

Smarta yajnas comprise a large number of rituals to be followed in an orderly manner. These rituals are described in the Grihya Sutras and/or Puranas (mainly *Matsya Purana*). The operational procedures for performing these rituals are bound in a sequence of events and actions.

There are two main technical workbooks governing the conduct of smarta yajnas: (i) *Sthalipaka Tantra*, and (ii) *Vaishvadeva Tantra*. The first is predominantly based on procedures from the appendices of the Grihya Sutras. As such, yajnas following *Sthalipaka Tantra* are known as *parishishtokta* yajnas ('found in the appendix of a text'). Normally, all yajnas performed before a grihya samskara fall in this category. The second is based mainly on procedures from *Matsya Purana*, and hence yajnas following *Vaishvadeva Tantra* are known as matsyokta yajnas. Rudra yaga, Chandi yaga, Vastu Shanti, Janana Shanti, etc. fall in this category. The main structure of both techniques is broadly the same. The

Table 11: List of smarta yajnas

Sr. No.	Name of yajna	Principal devata
1	Amba Yajna	Jagadamba
2	Chandi Yajna	Chandi
3	Durga Yajna	Durga
4	Ganesha Yajna	Ganesha
5	Gayatri Yajna	Veda Mata Gayatri
6	Go Yajna	Cow
7	Koti Homa Maha Yajna[13]	
8	Lakshmi Yajna	Lakshmi
9	Lakshmi Narayana Yajna	Lakshmi and Narayana
10	Maha Shanti Yajna	Mahadeva – Shiva
11	Maha Mrityunjaya Yajna	Mahadeva – Shiva
12	Nava Graha Yajna	Sun, Mercury, Venus, Saturn, Moon, Mars, Jupiter, Rahu, Ketu
13	Parjanya Yaga	Indra, Agni
14	Prajapati Yajna	Prajapati
15	Santan Yaga	
16	Rama Yajna	Rama
17	Rudra Yajna	Rudra – Shiva
18	Shri Krishna Yajna	Vasudeva Krishna
19	Sudarshana Yajna	Vishnu, Sudarshana
20	Surya Yaga	Sun
21	Vasudeva Yajna	Vasudeva
22	Vishnu Yajna	Vishnu
23	Vishva Shanti Maha Yajna	

difference lies in minor variations in the sequence of rituals, use of mantras, havi dravya and some procedural aspects.

Smarta yajnas are based on procedures taken from the Shrutis, Smritis, Puranas and Tantras. Therefore, they

[13] Koti homa yajna is characterized by 10 million (one crore) mantra repetitions. If Vishnu yaga mantra is repeated 10 million times, it becomes Koti Vishnu Yajna. If Chandi path is repeated 10 million times, it becomes Koti Chandi Yajna.

contain Rig mantras and methods of worship from the Vedic tradition, procedures such as installation of idols or photos of devatas, poornahuti, etc. from the Puranic tradition, and rituals such as smearing sacred ash over parts of the body from the tantric practices. All the 23 popular yajnas mentioned in the preceding table follow these practices. They are performed following the same or similar procedures as described below.

Graha yajna is the prototype of all smarta yajnas. Graha yajnas are of three types – *nitya* (routine), *naimittic* (incidental or occasional) and *kamya* (for personal desires). Nitya graha yajnas are routine yajnas that are performed regularly. Yajna on the date of birth (by the Indian almanac), the new year, or during an eclipse are examples of nitya graha yajnas.

Naimittic graha yajnas are performed before any smarta samskara, at the time of installation of a deity, before occupying a new house, etc. Kamya graha yajnas are performed for the removal or elimination of suffering, for prosperity, long life, etc.

Rituals of smarta yajna (based on graha yajna)

By and large, the following rituals are performed in a smarta yajna.

Nitya karma: This includes shaving the head, a holy bath, wearing a tilaka on the forehead, prostration to guru and the Almighty, japa, sandhya and surya namaskara. It prepares the sadhaka for the day's proceedings by raising his spiritual energy.

Expiation: As explained earlier, one commits wrongs either knowingly or inadvertently, calling for corrective action at both mental and spiritual levels. Sometimes even actions at the physical level are involved, such as donations. Additionally, the expiation process also includes offering oblations on behalf of the forefathers. Expiation rituals purify the body, mind and soul.

Sankalpa: This is the same as in shrauta yajna. The resolution one makes to undertake a particular job is very

Table 12: Rituals of a smarta yajna

1. Nitya karma	9. Mandap pravesha	17. Poorna patra daan
2. Expiation karma	10. Dig rakshanam	18. Go daan
3. Desh kal sankirtan	11. Mandap poojan	19. Shreyah sampadanam
4. Ganesha poojan	12. Graha sthapana	20. Mandap, etc. daan
5. Swasti vachana	13. Devata homa	21. Abhisheka visarjan
6. Matrika poojan	14. Swishta pooja	22. Vipra dakshina
7. Nandi shraddha	15. Bali pooja	23. Brahmin bhojan
8. Acharya varana	16. Poornahuti	24. Blessings

important from the point of view of the end result. Swami Satyananda has explained the significance of the process as follows: "Whenever you want to go somewhere, there is always an aim, an objective, in the absence of which you will never be able to reach the desired place." The resolution is the pivot of focused action. Without it, the action will be half-hearted, the attention dissipated, the mind very likely wavering, and half the energy lost. Therefore, the gain will also be truncated. A resolve ensures that every mini-action is performed with full awareness and one-pointedness. As yajna is a selfless activity, everyone participating should make a resolution, irrespective of their role. It is also customary to declare the venue where the resolution is to be made – a necessary act to establish a link with the yajna devata.

Invocation, installation and worship of 56 devatas through a yantra called *sarvato bhadra mandal* precede any pooja, path or yajna. During the havan, oblations are made to these devatas too, so they help in the successful completion of the yajna according to the sankalpa of the yajamana.

Ganesha poojan: Lord Ganesha represents the power that keeps all hurdles at bay and enables a pious act to proceed smoothly. Ganesha poojan is done to invoke this power at the commencement of the yajna.

Swasti vachana: This ritual is performed to create a positive and peaceful atmosphere so that the mind expands.

Matrika poojan: The Devi tattwa is present in water and on ground. This is the basic energy that holds everything together; it is the root support of creation. The Devi is invoked through prayers and an offering of sacrifice so that the yajna karma is completed successfully.

Nandi shraaddha: On all auspicious occasions, the forefathers are always remembered and offered oblations as a token of gratitude. This ritual is also intended to express the desire to grow.

Acharya varana: A person wanting to perform a smarta yajna normally approaches a knowledgeable person (a priest) who has the necessary experience and authority to perform the yajna, and requests him to act on his behalf. As a symbol of his request, he hands over a betel nut to the priest – this is called *acharya varana*. The priest, after accepting the yajamana's request, conducts the yajna with the help of a group of assistants with sincerity and to the best of his capacity. Since he performs the yajna, he is said to earn its fruit too. Therefore, at the end of the yajnic process, he undergoes a ritual called *shreyah sampadanam* wherein he passes on the earned fruit (punya) of the yajna to the yajamana. As a symbol, he returns the nut given by the yajamana at the commencement of the yajna.

The main part of the yajna is the *path* (the chanting of mantras in praise of the yajna devata). Normally, the priests do the path, but spectators can also opt to join in. The duration of smarta yajnas can range from one to 15 days. The path is done every day, and havan is performed on the last day. The following rituals precede the path.

Pashubali: Pashubali is a type of oblation to propitiate demonic powers. In some large-scale yajnas, offering an animal is considered an important part of the yajna. As flesh is the food of demonic powers, parts of a sheep or goat are offered as oblation in the yajna. (A yajna is intended to please everyone and as these powers are part of creation, they should also be pleased.)

Sacrificing an animal is not the same as slaughter, and is not to be equated with an act of violence. There are fixed rules for making an animal sacrifice. If the animal brought for sacrificial purposes refuses to go to the yajna vedi, it is set free. It is only when an animal comes willingly to the vedi that it is used for the sacrifice. Also, the animal is not killed by a violent act, but made lifeless through the chanting of mantras, and then its parts offered as oblation. According to the scriptures, the animal attains salvation through the process.

In Chandi yajna, four types of bali are offered:

1. *Payasa balidan*: An offering of rice cooked in milk. Rice represents human life and milk represents devotional love towards the goddess. The objective of this oblation is for life to be filled with innocent love and bhakti for the Mother.

The rice in milk is offered with the right hand in a specific way so that it falls in a flat, circular metal (silver or copper) platter. The naam-mantras are chanted while the offering is made. It is a kind of completion ritual. Later, the offering is distributed to participants as prasad.

2. *Kushmanda balidan*: A white pumpkin is worshipped with the chanting of mantras. It is then cut into six pieces, which are offered to the Goddess. At the end, the pieces are removed from the yajna venue and placed at the nearest crossroad to be consumed by animals.

A host, like any other human being, has six *vikaras* or impurities: *kama* (lust), *krodha* (anger), *lobha* (greed), *mada* (arrogance), *moha* (attachment) and *matsarya* (jealousy). With the performance of yajna, these are eliminated to some extent. This offering represents this fact symbolically.

3. *Masha-pishta pashu balidan*: A goat-like form is made from the flour of urad dal (in composition urad dal is equivalent to animal flesh). After worship, it is cut into three pieces and offered to the Goddess. At the end, the pieces are disposed of in the same manner as in kushmanda balidan.

The bali is a symbolic representation of the removal of the host's conceit *(ahamkara)*, ignorance *(ajnana)* and illusion *(avidya)* through the yajna.

4. *Graha balidan*: The form of a human face is made out of cooked rice and placed in a small, round basket. A

vertically cut lemon, some money, etc. are also placed with it and black gram sprinkled over them. After the worship, the basket is carried to the nearest crossroad by the host. While worshipping during this bali, the host requests the nine planets *(navagraha)*, the eight chiefs managing the eight directions *(ashtalokapala)* and others to protect him and his family from all evil powers.

Poornahuti: This is offered at the end of the havan. The yajamana stands in front of the kunda, facing east. He makes a poornahuti sankalpa. A big *sruva* (large wooden spoon) or a vessel called *prokshani patra* is held in his right hand. The acharya or another designated ritvij pours the essence of butter – 4 or 12 measures – in the sruva. Other pooja items, coconut and a piece of silk cloth are placed on it. The sruva is decorated with flowers. The priests chant the poornahuti mantra, and at the end the yajamana neatly places the items held in the prokshani patra into the well-kindled fire. Thereafter, a few more rituals such as *vasordhara homa*, *agni pradakshina*, *poornapatra daanam*, *shreyo daanam* and *dakshina sankalpa* are completed. Optionally, the yajamana makes a resolve to feed *bhojan* to eligible brahmins, and perform a ritual called *chaya patra daanam* wherein he views himself in a large plate containing clarified butter and donates it afterwards.

Expiation and blessings: The last ritual is the blessing of the yajamana couple by the priests. The yajamana prays to be pardoned for all mistakes committed inadvertently during the proceedings. Thereafter, the priests chant (in a high tone) Puranic mantras and bless the yajamana couple, their family, other participants in the yajna and all present at the pavilion. *Uttara pooja* (culminating worship) is done, and farewell bid to the devatas (principal yajna devata and all supporting ones).

This completes the brief description of the major rituals that go into a smarta yajna. Rituals like sankalpa, devata dhyanam, ahuti dhyanam, poornahuti and dakshina are very important, which is evident from the mantras chanted during the respective rituals. The sankalpa indicates the resolution to undertake a good cause for overall welfare, and poornahuti indicates the mental state in which all that is held in one's possession is offered up. The shanti mantras express the desire for peace and friendliness to dwell everywhere and at all times.

Smarta yajnas have several common features like devata, purpose, yajna mandap, dravya kunda, etc. They differ only in details of their characteristics[14].

Planning a smarta yajna

It may be seen that there are many similarities between smarta and shrauta yajnas. Many steps and procedures are the same, but the difference is in the details. Shrauta procedures are more rigid and complex. Smarta processes, on the other hand, are simple to follow and easy to understand. Therefore, in spite of their apparent similarity with shrauta yajna, they are described here. To perform a smarta yajna, the following points have to be planned: (i) selection of the venue, (ii) raising the structure for the yajna (iii) yajnyagni and agni kunda (iv) selection of the team of priests (v) yajna samagri and other logistics (vi) selection of an auspicious time and (vii) the daily program.

Selecting the venue: The shastras take into account minute details such as the physical structure of the site, the quality of the soil, directional considerations, etc. to select a yajna venue. It is recommended that the yajamana should select, in consultation with the guru, a place that is on the bank of a river, in front of the city temple or in the vicinity of a spot that has good vibrations. After selecting the team of priests, the yajamana should have the proposed site examined by the chief priest. The chief priest generally knows about the type of fruit that the soil will extend to the yajamana in terms of peace, prosperity and health. Participants in Sat Chandi Mahayajna at Rikhia will recollect that the yajna

---

[14] Details of major smarta yajnas are given in the Appendix

mandap or pavilion is raised at a specific place outside the ashram premises, taking into account the directions and other details. A picture of the yajnashala is shown below.

Raising the structure: At the selected venue, a structure with a thatched roof supported by pillars is to be raised. Normally, there should be two rounds of pillars, the inner layer having four pillars and the outer layer 12 or more pillars. The structure is called the yajna mandap. The purpose of the specified number of pillars is to match them with the devatas invoked in them at the commencement of the yajna. The pillar devatas are requested to guard the venue from their place of installation. The structure is supposed to be a representation of the sky holding the stars and planets.

Smarta yajna pavilion with 16 pillars at the yajna venue in Rikhia

Puranas (*Agni*, *Matsya*, etc.) give details of yajna mandaps. There are 27 different types of mandaps recommended for smarta yajnas. The number of pillars varies between 12 and 64. The magnitude of a yajna in terms of the number of participating priests, number of mantra repetitions, the principal devata, etc. generally decide the size of the mandap to be constructed. Each type of mandap has a specific name; for example, a 16 pillar mandap is called *kama bhadra*.

The mandap is also named after the devata of the proposed yajna. For example, a Shiva yajna mandap is called *ishvara* and a mandap for Devi yajnas is called *shakti vardhan mandap*. The mandap should have four entrances, one each at the east, south, west and north. Their recommended dimension is 3 x 2.5 (full) hand-lengths. Each is embellished with a strip of cloth used as a lining called a *torana*. The wood for these doors should be from the holy fig tree (peepal) for the eastern and western doors, udumbara for the southern, and baniyan for the northern door. The liner should be yellow, black, white and yellow respectively for the east, south, west and north doors.

The size and shape of the pillars and also the distance between every pair of pillars is fixed. They are also given specific names.

Table 13: Details of pillars in a yajna mandap

Name	Devata	Colour of Liner
Shubhad	Brahma	Red
Vijay	Vishnu	White
Krishna	Rudra	Black
Shriman	Indra	Yellow
Mangal	Surya	Red
Guru	Ganesha	White
Jay	Yama	Black
Dhanad	Sarpa (Nag)	White
Kalyani	Skanda	White
Shubha	Vayu (Prishdashva)	Smokey
Shanta	Chandrama (Soma)	White
Manohar	Pracheta (Varuna)	White
Ridhi	Ashta Vasu	White
Siddhi	Dhanad (Kuber)	Yellow
Vichitra	Brihaspati	Yellow
Divya	Twashtunandan (Vishvakarma)	Red

Around the mandap, 18 pots *(kalasha)* holding consecrated water are kept. This could be to catch the vibrations of the yajna. Ten pots are intended for protective devatas at 10 directions: (i) at major directions: E, S,W, N, (ii) at cross directions: E-S, S-W, W-N, N-E, (iii) at the centre of East and E-S (for Brahma), (iv) at the centre of West and S-W (for Ananta). Eight pots are kept for the guards at the entrance (two each near the four entrances of the mandap).

Flags are raised on the top of the mandap and protective devatas installed in them to protect the venue from negative elements and vibrations. There are 11 flags, the main flag *(mahadhvaja)* and 10 others as directional guards. The flags should be mounted on a pole with a height equal to 10 hand-lengths (of the yajamana). They should be triangular in shape (dimensions: 2 x 5 hand-lengths). The pataka is rectangular (dimensions: 7 x 1 hand-lengths) and mounted on a pole 10 hand-lengths high. The main flag should be 10 x 5 or 7 x 3.5 or 5 x 3 in size, have five or multiple colours,

Table 14: Details of flags in a yajna mandap[15]

Direction	Devata of flag	Colour	Vehicle	Pataka with Weapon
East	Indra	Yellow	White elephant	Vajra
South-East	Agni	Red	White sheep	Sword
South	Yama	Black	Male buffalo	Staff
South-West	Nirutika	Blue	White lion	Khadaga
West	Varuna	White	Silver fish	Pasha
North-West	Vayu	Smokey green	Black deer	Ankusha
North	Soma	White or green	Golden horse	Gada
North-East	Ishvara	White	Red bull	Trident
Between N-E & East	Brahma	White or red	White swan	Kamandalu
Between S-W & West	Anant	White or black	Garuda	Chakra

[15] Source: *Yajna Rahasya,* K.M. Bapat Shastri, Joshi Bros, Pune, 1982

and raised on a pole that is 32, 31 or 16 hand-lengths high. It should be erected either in the centre of the mandap or in the N-E direction. These specifications are aimed at representing the events in the sky above the venue.

Yajnyagni and agni kunda: Smarta karmas are done on smartagni[16]. In Vedic times, grihyagni used to be carried to the smarta yajna venue by symbolically transferring it into the instrument called arani. At the yajna site, it would be invoked by churning the arani. Since the tradition of maintaining agni at home has almost died out, nowadays agni is created through the arani carried by the priest. The agni in this form is also, in fact, laukikagni and in effect no different from the fire produced for domestic purposes. However (for yajna purposes), it is still desirable to invoke laukikagni through an arani rather than use matches or a lighter. The wood used for the arani has a special quality, and it is said that the point of friction of the mantha and adhararani – devayoni – is the seat of the sacred fire.

Traditionally, the yajamana couple churns the arani while priests chant mantras to invoke the agni. The yajamana holds the upper plate of the arani *(uttararani)* and his wife churns the mantha. If her force is not sufficient, the priest helps her. The manthan could also be done by a representative of the yajamana for whose sankalpa the yajna is being performed.

For smarta yajnas, the agni kunda is made by digging a pit for the fire, and constructing a three-layered wall around it. The agni invoked through arani at the yajna site is established in the specially-made agni kunda. It is the symbolic representation of the form (body) of the creative universe. As described in the Puranas, if eight lines are drawn in a square pit connecting the four corners and bisecting the four sides, the line towards the east indicates its head. N-E and S-E are its arms, N-W and S-W its groin. Its origin is the yoni of the kunda, and the hollow volume of the pit its abdomen. The

---

[16] Refer to Chapter 5

main parts of the kunda are the navel, throat, a cord joining the navel and throat, point of origin (yoni) and the abdomen. Details of the dimensions, i.e. the length, breadth, height, depth, etc. of the kunda, are given in the Shulba Sutras and Puranas. A kunda has a chain garlanding the waist called a *mekhala*, which is a small wall with three layers of bricks constructed around the pit. The lowest layer is black, the middle one red and the upper white. The form, shape and dimensions of the mekhala differ with the kunda. A gap of about two inches is left between the border of the pit and the mekhala. It is called the *kantha* (throat) of the kunda.

Normally, the agni kunda is placed at the centre of the yajna mandap between the four inner pillars. It is called *acharya kunda*. The yajamana and the chief priest offer oblations here. Kundas are of eight shapes – square or rectangular, triangular, semi-circular, circular, hexagonal, octagonal, lotus-shaped and yoni kunda. The type of kunda to be used in a yajna depends on the sankalpa, the devata, and the varna of the yajamana. The square-shaped kunda is the most commonly used form. It is also called *chaturastra kunda* (a figure with four equal sides). The reason for a square kunda may be traced to the fact that it represents the ahavaniya kunda of shrauta yajnas.

In smarta yajnas, the kunda is also alternatively called a vedi. In shrauta yajnas, however, the vedi designates the place between the garhapatya kunda and ahavaniya kunda.

In some yajnas like Rudra yaga, Vishnu yaga, etc. multiple kundas are used. Such yajnas are performed with the help of several priests, as the number of oblations are many. To enable simultaneous oblations, multiple kundas are used. So the number of kundas to be used in a yajna depends on the type of yajna, the number of oblations and the number of priests making simultaneous oblations. Placement of the kundas and their shapes are predetermined. In a yajna with multiple kundas, the central kunda is within the four inner pillars. It is either square or lotus-shaped, and used by the chief priest.

If, for whatever reason, it is not possible to construct a kunda, an alternative is recommended in the form of a temporary altar using soil and sand, called a *sthandila*.

The size of the kunda is decided by the number of oblations to be offered. The table below shows the number and size of kundas for different numbers of oblations.

Table 15: Details of oblations and numbers of kundas[17]

No. of oblations	No. of kundas	Dimensions of kunda
< 50	Nil (Sthandila)	
51–99	1	½ the hand-length of yajamana
Up to 1000	1	1 hand-length
Up to 10,000	1	2 hand-lengths
Up to 100,000	1	4 hand-lengths
Up to 1 million	1	6 hand-lengths
Up to 10 million	1	8 hand-lengths

The shastras have laid great emphasis on the exact proportion (and shape and size) of the yajna kunda, its placement, direction, mekhala, the parts of the kunda like yoni, nabhi, kantha, etc. It is said that any violation can lead to truncation of the fruit of the yajna, and even result in negative effects. It is recommended that the yajamana as well as the chief priest are careful about precisely following the prescriptions of the shastras for the construction of a kunda.

Priests: Smarta yajnas are larger in dimension than personal smarta karmas. They need a team of priests to attend to various functions requiring specialized expertise. The yajamana selects the chief priest and on his recommendation chooses other members of the team. A brief description of the qualities of the priests and their area of expertise is given below.

---

[17] Source: *Yajna Mimamsa,* Pt. Veniram Sharma Gaud, Chaukhamba Vidya Bhavan, Varanasi, 1999

Chief priest (acharya): To have the yajna performed by all the participating priests (ritvij) for all the rites according to the injunctions of the shastras and to minutely observe their work are the major functions of the chief priest. Among many personal qualifications and characteristics, he has to be well-versed in Vedic mantras, Puranas, etc. He must also have prior experience in conducting yajnas. He should have a pleasing personality, be able to spread serenity and command the respect of other priests and spectators alike.

Brahma: His main functions are to oversee the work of the priests and the yajamana, and to give advice on expiation procedures, if required.

Sadasya: His main function is to remove doubts and solve problems in procedures and performance. He also keeps a defensive vigil to protect the yajna and its participants.

Upadrashta: He sees to the overall arrangements in the mandap and keeps a close watch on the work of the priests.

Ganapatya: He undertakes japa and such rituals with a view to ensuring the desired result of the yajna, and the safe and sound completion of the whole process.

Dwarapala: These are a group of four ritvijs, each expert in one of the Vedas. They occupy seats near the four entrances of the yajnashala, their main functions being to recite mantras from their respective Vedas and guard the entrances.

Japaka: He is supposed to chant mantras with due attention to their meaning. He concentrates his chitta on the mantras and observes silence during the chanting, maintaining the same posture throughout.

Hota: To invite yajniya devatas with adoration and to offer oblations with appropriate actions and rites is the principal work of this ritvij.

Yajna samagri (items of oblation, implements and other articles): Articles such as cow's milk, curd, essence of butter and samidha are commonly used items of oblation in all yajnas. Items such as sesame, unbroken grains of rice, yava (a special type of grain), and a host of medicinal plants are also used, depending on the type of yajna[18].

In addition to articles of oblation, other items normally used in daily worship such as holy water, flowers, garlands, etc. are also required in adequate measure. It is necessary to assemble all the yajna implements and pooja articles at least a day ahead of the ceremony. Items such as milk, water, flowers, etc. need to be organized on a daily basis if the yajna lasts for more than a day. The implements used in smarta yajnas include sruva, pranitah, prokshani, sphya, sruchi and arani.

Selecting an auspicious time: In all physical or dravya yajnas, Agni brings the yajna devata(s) to the yajna venue, accepts the oblations on their behalf and extends the essence to them. Therefore, Agni is invoked at the commencement of a yajna. Although Agni is a prithivi-based devata, it travels to other lokas also. So, when a yajna is performed, it is imperative that Agni is positioned in prithivi loka (earth), otherwise the oblations will not reach the devatas and the yajna will not bear fruit.

To decide the position of Agni, the location of the planets with respect to the earth's orbit and the position of the sun is essential. This is estimated using mathematical calculations. If Agni is not on earth at the commencement of the yajna, it needs to be ensured that it is there for poornahuti (the culmination ceremony) at least.

The Indian almanac also indicates certain days, constellations, position of the sun, etc. as advisable for starting a yajna. It is said that a yajna performed at such times bears good fruit. Conducive days of the week are Monday, Wednesday, Thursday and Friday. The yajamana has to take into account these factors and consult the chief priest to decide the most favourable day and time for the yajna. The chief priest is expected to be knowledgeable in jyotish shastra.

---

[18] See Chapter 7

The daily program: There are two main rituals at a smarta yajna – path and havan. The others are pre- and post-rituals, respectively known as *poorva tantra* and *uttara tantra*.

Day 1: On this day, all the preparatory work such as erection of the yajna mandap, organization of the implements and yajna samagri, and identification of the priests is completed.

The rituals begin with the yajamana performing an expiation ritual according to his capacity. In the course of the day's activities, one may deviate from the expected behaviour and duties. To seek pardon for such errors, the ritual is required. Thereafter, he and his wife take a holy bath and apply sandalwood paste or other tilaka on the forehead. The yajamana should tie the tuft on his tonsure (if he has maintained one) and the woman should tie back her hair securely.

Having completed this simple ritual, the couple takes a seat facing east, on a woollen shawl or neatly washed cotton cloth. A lamp is lit, and the priest and other brahmins begin chanting the shanti mantras. The priest chants mantras of adoration to various devatas, and the yajamana pays salutations to the devatas.

Thereafter, rituals of poorva tantra up to acharya varana (explained above) are completed. The chief priest together with his team is honoured and requested to assume responsibility for performing the yajna according to the injunctions of the shastras. He accepts the responsibility and immediately sets to work.

Day 2 (onwards): The day starts with a ceremonial entry into the yajna mandap by the yajamana couple and priests (there are rules as to who should enter from which entrance). The yajna venue is worshipped; mandap devatas, stambha devatas and dhvaja devatas invoked and installed at designated places. The yajna kunda is consecrated.

The yajamana occupies a seat of darbha grass to the west of the central kunda. Thereafter, rituals such as *graha sthapana*, *sarvato bhadra pooja*, installation of the seat for the yajna devata, etc. are completed and the main part of the yajna – *devata homa* – starts.

The yajamana meditates on the devata and performs a ritual called *anga nyasa* to invoke multiple devatas and request them to position themselves on various parts of his body. All who participate in the path chant in chorus the suktas and/ or swahakara mantras in praise of the devatas. The sukta is repeated a predetermined number of times.

Last day: During the daily path, oblations are made only through a mental process. An actual offering into the sacred fire is made during the havan. On the last day, agni is kindled in the kunda. Some yajnas use multiple kundas in whch agni is taken to all the kundas from the acharya kunda. It is kept well-kindled throughout the havan. The havan is done with the chanting of swahakara mantras and offering oblations of havi dravya with every mantra. The havi dravya is held in the right hand during the mantra chanting. At the end of each mantra, priests chant 'swaha'. Exactly at that time, the priests sitting around the kunda drop the havi into the kunda with the left hand touching the heart. If the essence of butter or milk or other liquid is offered, a wooden spoon called a sruva is used. Havi dravya is held in the right hand fingers, using one of three mudras – *hamsi*, *mrigi* or *sukari*. The palm is held upwards. To hold the sruva, however, the palm is held downwards. The number of repetitions of the swahakara mantra is one-tenth of the mantras chanted in the path. The number of repetitions of the tarpan mantra is one-tenth of the mantras chanted in swahakara. The number of repetitions of the marjana mantra is one-tenth of the mantras chanted in tarpan. For santarpan (sankalpa to feed brahmins), the number of brahmins is one-tenth of the mantras chanted in marjana.

Rituals of uttara tantra from swishta pooja onwards follow the havan. The mandap and its surroundings reverberate with pious and serene vibrations. Amid this cheerful atmosphere, a prayer is offered to the Almighty to shower grace on the entire universe. The yajna is completed with a prayer for peace at all times and places.

Sometimes, due to lack of time, the whole process – from expiation, sankalpa to havan and prayer – are completed in just one day. Nevertheless, it needs to be ensured that all the sub-processes are carried out properly, and that no compromise is made on the number of oblations during the havan in particular.

MAHA YAJNAS (TOTAL: 8)

Maha soma yajna

The suffix 'maha' is used for these yajnas to indicate their large size. Rajasooya, ashvamedha and vishvajit yajnas are known as maha soma yajnas. They are performed on a very large scale and magnitude. Only a selected class of people are eligible to perform them.

Rajasooya yajna: This is basically a soma yajna with modified procedures. The main differences lie in the type of ishtis (small homas performed by ritvijs), items of oblation like purodasha, selection of mantras, devata, etc. It includes many ishtis, pashu yaga and soma yaga. The main procedure includes several other events such as races, equestrian sports, coronation, musical concerts, etc. in addition to mantra chanting and related rituals. In this yajna, a large number of different substances are used in a ritual called *abhisheka* (pouring holy liquid on the object of worship).

A rajasooya yajna can be performed only by a kshatriya, preferably a king. It commences on the first day of the waxing period of Phalguna (twelfth month of the Indian almanac). Between this time and the year's end, the yajamana has to complete chaturmasya yajna. Performance of 12 ishtis named *ratninam havinshi* is the speciality of and unique to this yajna. The host gives out donations of different kinds such as clothing, grains, utensils, ornaments, etc. This continues in an orderly manner over a long period (sometime spanning even 12 years). Normally, in a soma yajna, the host consumes the soma juice during the oblation processes.

After completion of the main part of the yajna ritual, the ritvij brahma holds the hand of the host and loudly iterates the name of the host along with the names of his forefathers (up to the great-grandfather). Thereafter, he proclaims to the subjects of the kingdom, "So and so is your king." Holy water brought from famous pilgrimage spots is sprinkled on the king and a stotra called *Mahendra Shastra* is chanted. This stotra is in honour of Indra who is the acknowledged 'super king' (emperor of the devas), and its chanting implies that the host is being equated with Indra.

The host is presented with many special clothes and ornaments. He is also given the choicest items to eat. As *Mahendra Shastra* is underway, he is made to wear a bow and arrow, presented with a tiger skin, and once again declared king. Now the anointed king boards the chariot and symbolically points his arrow at some kshatriyas, implying his victory over them. A golden chain and a pair of shoes made of boar-skin are presented to him. The king ascends the throne. The hota takes his seat on a golden chair, and signals to the adhvaryu to tell the story of Shunahshep[19]. At the end of the storytelling, one ishti is performed and donations made to all and sundry. This marks the culmination of the rajasooya ceremony.

Rajasooya yajna, ashvamedha yajna and vishva shanti yajna are generally performed for the prosperity and peace of a kingdom or even the universe. We have covered the broad details; however, it must be remembered that there are variations in the interpretations of the shastras for performing them.

---

[19] See Annexure 1

Pancha maha yajna

These yajnas are included as daily rituals in the routine of a householder. They are aimed at spiritual evolution, and should be performed with complete awareness of their purpose to gain the full benefits[20].

IN CONCLUSION

- External or physical yajna means sacrifice of dravya (articles of oblation) for devatas.
- Vedic karma means rites, rituals and yajna performed to purify the soul.
- Vedic karma falls under two categories – samskara-oriented karma and yajna-oriented karma.
- Samskara is a ritual to purify thc soul. Samskaras are of three types – purifying, cultivating and augmenting.
- Samskaras are 21 in number (8 purifying, 8 cultivating and 5 augmenting). They are recorded in the *Grihya Sutras*.
- Yajna-oriented Vedic karma means shrauta and smarta yajnas. They are 52 (21 shrauta, 23 smarta and 8 maha yajnas).
- Shrauta yajnas are performed as per the Brahmana Granthas. Smarta yajnas are based on Smriti texts.
- Large-scale shrauta yajnas and some smarta yajnas like Vishnu yajna and Chandi yajna are performed for universal peace and prosperity.
- Other yajnas are performed for personal, material and social gain.
- External yajna induces internal yajna.

---

[20] Details in Chapter 11

10

Internal Yajna

So far we have analyzed three forms of yajna – paroksha yajna (yajna in Nature), dravya yajna (man-made yajna) and karma yajna, all of which follow the universal law of give and take (GnT). Dravya yajna has an additional, important quality – it exerts a positive influence on the soul as well as the surroundings. In the preceding chapter, we saw that 21 samskara-oriented Vedic karmas and 52 yajnas help to purify the soul, thus speeding up its spiritual journey. Essentially, they are physical activities or external aspects of yajna. However, they also modify the different layers of the mind – conscious, subconscious and unconscious – in a subtle way. To understand this process, we have to go beyond the mere mechanics of the physical processes, and understand the internal aspects of yajna.

Understanding internal aspects is an experience of the consciousness achieved through meditation. Before reaching this stage, however, all the components and processes of yajna must be understood in a clear and unambiguous manner, so that physical acts are performed diligently and the mind absorbs the principle of yajna well enough to ponder over it constantly.

In the Vedic period, external or physical yajna was developed and perfected in the Brahmana texts. Its internal aspects were considered in the Aranyaka texts, which were the result of the introspections of the vanaprasthis or forest dwellers. In Vedic society, elderly householders would retire to a secluded life after their duties to family and society were over, spending their time in meditation and introspection. When they attempted to unearth the deeper significance of the various processes in physical yajna through their meditation, they realized its importance in individual spiritual upliftment. The Aranyakas therefore stress that external yajna should induce internal yajna in the yajamana. Possibly this led to the development of the concept of internal yajna. The Upanishads carried the notion forward and regarded yajna as a philosophy of life.

We shall study the internal aspects of paroksha yajna through *Purusha Sukta* from the *Rig Veda*, pratyaksha yajna through *Trisuparnam Sukta* from the *Pranagnihotra Upanishad*, karma yajna through the *Bhagavad Gita*, and jivan or life yajna through the *Chandogya Upanishad*.

Purusha Sukta and yajna

Physical yajna is based on the principle of sacrifice. According to the *Rig Veda*, the creation and existence of the universe is also based on the same principle. In its characteristically philosophical way, the most important sukta of the *Rig Veda* (R 10.90), known as *Purusha Sukta*, links the dynamism of creation-sustenance-destruction to the principle of sacrifice. In this sukta, the principle of yajna is established through the mythical story of the creation of the universe, by describing the Almighty as Purusha. It is a poetic rendition of the concept of yajna in Nature, and a very lucid and original one.

The sukta introduces three concepts: (i) Purusha at three levels, (ii) sacrifice as the cause of creation of the universe, and (iii) sacrificing the created elements. It also views the universe as Purusha having four major limbs, which represent the four basic functions – knowledge *(gyana)*, strength *(bala)*, trade *(vyapara)*, and physical work *(parishrama)*, for sustenance and development. This can be easily seen as a representation of the structure of human society.

Purusha at three levels:

1. *Adi Purusha*: The primal energy or *parabrahma shakti* is eternal, infinite and immortal. Some call it the Almighty, others the supreme soul. This sukta describes it as Purusha. *Pur* means the body, the one who resides in the body is called the purusha *(puri shete iti purushah)*. Thus, in this sukta it is assumed that the primal energy (also known as Brahman) resides in one body encompassing the whole of existence, and that body is called Adi Purusha. The sukta describes Adi Purusha as the one with thousands of eyes, heads and legs. This means that Adi Purusha is the sole factor *(vishvasya mooladhara)* behind the whole universe, encompassing the past, present and future as also the manifest (known or unknown) and the unmanifest.

2. *Virata Purusha*: A part of the Adi Purusha transformed into the perceivable form. It is said that one quarter of the Adi Purusha is transformable *(vyakta)* whereas three-quarters is not *(avyakta)*. The transformable part is known as Virata Purusha. This is the *brahmanda*, including our galaxy, other multiple galaxies, if any, and all that is perceivable.

3. *Adhi Purusha*: A part of the Virata Purusha (its size is not mentioned) transformed into earth, and the sentient and non-sentient beings on it. This part of Virata Purusha (in turn, part of Adi Purusha) is called Adhi Purusha. It is undergoing a continuous process of creation, sustenance and destruction, and the cycle is called *srishti chakra*. *Purusha Sukta* says that this process is the outcome of the yajna in the universe, which was initiated by God. Thus, Adhi Purusha covers the earth and our solar system.

Sacrifice as the cause of creation of the universe: When Adhi Purusha was born, the sadhya devas and rishis placed him on darbha grass, consecrated him by sprinkling sacred water and offered him as havi to Adi Purusha with the chanting of mantras, in the first-ever yajna performed by them. This marked the beginning of yajna in Nature. Spring (being conducive to cultivation) became the ghee, summer (being heat-producing) became the burning wood or samidha, and winter (being conducive to production) became the article of oblation or havi. Thus Adhi Purusha became the havi of the yajna in the universe.

Re-sacrifice of the created elements: *Purusha Sukta* states that Adhi Purusha is constantly undergoing creation-sustenance-destruction. It means that when Adhi Purusha was first born, an unending chain of destruction and creation also began exactly at that point of time. Therefore, it is logical to conclude that the universe, srishti, brahmanda or whatever term one may choose to name the totality that formed through Adhi Purusha, started to move immediately after being created. In the absence of such an assumption, one cannot explain the transition of Adhi Purusha from the state of creation to the state of destruction. Thus, after each cyclic sacrifice of the created srishti, there is a rebirth of the srishti.

Further, during this journey from one point to another, Adhi Purusha managed to keep all its constituents together. There was obviously a balancing force at play to sustain the conglomeration called Adhi Purusha, in general, and every element, in particular. The conclusion is that Adhi Purusha passes through three states – creation, sustenance and destruction, before its rebirth, and is endlessly following the cycle. Having been born of cyclic destruction, Adhi Purusha is the creation of self-sacrifice and hence is *yajna swaroopa* (like yajna).

Cause of re-creation: What causes re-creation and how? It is the secret of Nature, the manager of the universe. We know that the seed of a mango tree makes way for a mango tree (creation). Over a period of time, the offshoot grows, develops into a full-grown tree, bears flowers, fruits, etc. (sustenance), and eventually perishes (destruction) – but not before making new seed available. Thus, in a way, through its destruction the mango tree paves the way for its own re-creation. The seed once again creates the mango tree. We cannot imagine that it would create anything else. Each species destroys itself only to create its own progeny, and thus maintain the continuity of existence. This is Nature's secret for re-creation, and also its economic principle for the reuse of matter. This establishes that the chain of events through which Adhi Purusha passes loops back, creating an endless, repetitive cycle of self-creation through self-destruction (self-sacrifice) via self-maintenance.

Purusha Sukta says that in the first-ever yajna performed by Adi Purusha, he offered a part of himself – Adhi Purusha, as havi in his yajna (yajna in the universe), and then it became a premier law (dharma) of Nature, which is responsible for holding the creation together.

So yajna in Nature originated through the desire of the Lord to become many from one (*ekoham bahusyamah*). It was the sankalpa of his yajna in which sadhya devas and rishis were the ritvijs, Adhi Purusha the havi, and so on. The apoorva (unique and unprecedented effect) that emerged from this yajna was our universe (srishti). This is called paroksha yajna.

To make a transition from external yajna to internal yajna, it is necessary to develop a clear understanding *(yajnasya antarangah)* of paroksha yajna, which in essence means that self-sacrifice results in self-creation, and such creation should be for the benefit of others in tune with the desire of the Lord.

Trisuparnam Sukta and yajna

An important sukta, *Trisuparnam Sukta* is part of the *Pranagnihotra Upanishad*. It establishes the equivalence between parts of the human body and parts of physical yajna. Knowledge dawns after constant meditation, and wisdom flourishes after its dispensation. The life of a wise person is yajna, a process continuing until death. In this yajna:

- the soul (atman) is the yajamana (host)
- faith (shraddha) is the patni (yajamana's wife)
- the body is the fuel (samidha)
- the chest cavity is the yajna vedi
- the body-hair is the barhi (special grass spread in the yajna mandap for the devatas to sit on)

- the tuft is *darbha mushti* (another type of grass)
- the heart is the yajna pillar
- the desires are ghrita (the essence offered in agni).
- anger *(krodha)* is the yajniya pashu *(bali)*
- austerity *(tapa)* is *dama,* restraining the mind
- the ability to control passions *(shama)* is dakshina, the priests' honorarium
- speech *(vani)* is the hota (the priest who chants the Rig hymns)
- prana, the vital force, is the udgata (the priest who chants the Sama mantras)
- the eyes are the adhvaryu
- the mind is the brahma
- the ears are the agnidhra
- the whole of life is yajniya initiation *(diksha)*
- food is havi
- drink is soma paan
- enjoyment is upasada ishti
- movements such as sitting down, getting up and wandering are pravargya
- the mouth is ahavaniya agni
- the chant of vyahriti is oblation
- awareness of the meaning of the chants is homa
- regular intake (lunch and dinner) is the samidha offered to Agni
- breakfast, afternoon and evening snacks are the three savanas (morning, afternoon, evening)
- day is pournamasa and night is darshamasa
- fortnights and months are chaturmasya yajna
- the seasons are pashu yaga
- the years are adhvara yajna and samsvatsara yajna
- wealth (material, physical, mental, spiritual) is long-lasting yajna
- death is avabhritha.

It would seem then that a person is initiated at birth into soma purvaka adhana. Throughout life, he performs the daily rituals of agnihotra and the annual ritual of soma yajna. At death, he is given a holy bath *(avabhritha snana)*. The period in between these two events is the agnihotra period. We have seen that no dravya yajna can be successful without the yajamana and his wife making a joint resolve before the yajna starts. The soul (yajamana) and shraddha or faith (the yajamana's wife) must work together for a yajna to be fruitful. An anecdote from the *Kathopanishad* illustrates this principle.

Vajashrava, father of a bright young boy called Nachiketa, once performed a yajna with a view to securing a place in heaven. But he did not do it faithfully, offering aged, non-milking and unproductive cows to the priests as the honorarium. Thus he did not obtain the cherished seat for which he performed the yajna. He even offered Nachiketa to Yama, annoyed by the boy's questions. However, Nachiketa accepted this with great faith, and on that strength alone he could elicit the great knowledge of the yajna principle from no less a personality than Yama, the lord of death. Not only that, due to Yama's grace, he returned alive from Yama's court, a feat never achieved before or after!

Chandogya Upanishad and life as yajna

Every part of the body is a constituent of yajna; indeed our whole life is yajna. In Sanskrit, life is called *jivan yajna*, which means that life is nothing but a big yajna. Every action of an individual, each of their karmas is to be considered as an oblation in this yajna. Salvation is then effortless.

It is a proven fact that the body becomes active when the soul enters it. In the *Chandogya Upanishad*, the journey of the soul is called yajna. The soul is the yajamana in this yajna. All the sense organs are assembled in the body to help the yajamana perform yajna. Therefore, they are the priests (ritvijs) of the yajna. The soul can never be inactive when it is in the mortal body. Actions emanate from the mind, sense organs and body. Therefore, yajna means the totality of actions performed by a human being throughout life.

Chandogya Upanishad (3.16) describes jivan yajna mathematically. It considers the span of human life as 116 years, divided into three parts, which are equivalent to the three savanas of shrauta yajna. According to the *Yajur Veda, savana* is offering the soma elixir as oblation to the devatas through the medium of Agni devata. There are three important offerings of soma wherein oblations are made at the end of the chanting of long suktas. The first is called *pratah savana*, intended for eight Vasu devatas, the second is *madhyandina savana* for 11 Rudra devatas, and the third is *sayam savana* for 12 Aditya devatas.

Chandogya Upanishad divides life, which assumes meaning due to the existence of the soul in the body, into three parts. In each part a person is expected to pursue specific objectives. All actions are supposed to be in pursuit of these objectives. Since life is equated with yajna, its three parts are naturally equated with the three parts of soma yajna – the three savanas in soma offering. The duration of each savana of jivan yajna is also defined.

The first savana of jivan yajna, pratah savana, has a duration of 24 years. The devata is Vasu. The oblation offered uses mantras of the Gayatri metre, which has 24 alphabets. This probably explains why the savana is given a length of 24 years. A person is supposed to worship Brahma under the direction of a guru and earn knowledge in this period.

The second part, madhyandina savana, has a duration of 44 years. Rudra devata is worshipped through suktas in the Trishtubh metre, which has 44 alphabets. In the madhyandina savana of a soma yajna, Rudra, the devata known to wield the power required for hard work, is worshipped. The hard work required by a person in the second phase of life – married life (efforts to earn name, fame and money) – demands a resolute state of mind. This is defined as the madhyandina savana of his life yajna.

The third part, sayam savana, has a duration of 48 years. Aditya devata is worshipped in this savana through suktas in

Jagati metre, which has 48 alphabets. This savana, at the end of one's life, is characterized by contemplation. At the end of this period, one is supposed to take *avabhritha snana* (death).

Chandogya Upanishad expects a person to live for 116 years, during which time austerities are undertaken with service to others as the basis of all actions. However, service to others requires good health and vigour. Therefore, in each savana the respective devatas are prayed to for health, and a request made to enable a person to reach the next savana so he can accomplish all that is expected of him. The order, limits and duties of a person's life are predefined, and purushartha, or the effort required to achieve one's goals, has a framework.

The Upanishads are philosophical treatises, so their sponsors and supporters say that knowledge is superior to karma. However, we have seen that knowledge loses its superiority in the absence of a proper dispensation technique. Therefore, our knowledge of yajna should be total (including theory and practice). It is said that if it is not possible for a person to actually do yajna karma as prescribed by the Vedas, one can reap the fruit of the yajna karma by faithfully (with due meditation on the principles) chanting the part of the Vedas related to yajna. In this connection, the *Taittiriya Aranyaka* (2.15) says:

यं यं क्रतुमधीते तेन तेनास्येष्टं भवति।

Yam yam kratumadheete tena tenaasyeshtam bhavati.

He who recites the richas connected with various yajnas earns the benefits of the respective yajnas, as if he has actually performed them.

Bhagavad Gita and yajna

No discussion on actions related to the mind is complete without reference to the *Bhagavad Gita* in which the complex relationship between the mind and action, cause and effect, etc. are discussed, and the remedy for problems – often created by wrong applications – offered authoritatively. So when we discuss internal yajna, which is the process beyond the physical act at the mental and spiritual levels, we must necessarily fall back upon this famous discourse.

Yajna under kratvartha (ritualistic action to move towards righteousness) means *dravyam devata tyagah*. Here, the meaning of dravya is articles of oblation, which are restricted to such items as clarified butter from cow's milk (ajya), rice cake (purodasha), sticks from small branches of yajniya trees (samidha), etc. The meaning of yajna changes when the definition of dravya is expanded, and yajna does not remain confined to activity at the physical level, like homa/havan (where oblations are offered into the sacred fire). It is heightened to mental, emotional and spiritual levels. The *Bhagavad Gita* envisages this broader base to the act and manner of performing yajna.

What is dravya in this broader sense? In Sanskrit, *dravya* means wealth. Wealth has an associated power. Money as wealth has purchasing power. Health as wealth is physical power. Knowledge as wealth is the power of comprehension. To use any type of wealth in one's possession for the benefit of others, especially the needy, is an act that leads to: (i) respecting and felicitating those who have godly qualities as defined in the sixteenth chapter of the Gita, (ii) being with such people and being like those who possess godly qualities (and who therefore are worthy of being addressed as the 'elders' of a society), or (iii) the desire to donate all that one possesses *(atmasarvasva danah)*.

All actions based on such thinking are a kind of yajna. Therefore, the Gita categorizes yajna as *dravya yajna*, *indriya sanyam yajna*, *tapo yajna*, *yoga yajna*, *prana yajna*, *swadhyaya yajna* and *jnana yajna*. It can be said that the *Bhagavad Gita* is all about knowing the attitudes of the mind, analysing these attitudes so that a distinction is made between the right attitude for oneself and others, choosing the appropriate attitude, and resolutely springing to action to use them for self-evolution.

The *Bhagavad Gita* recommends *anasakta karma yoga* as the principle for every action, and donating the outcome of one's actions for the benefit of others – *nishakama karma yoga* – as the principal way of life. One who leads life in this way can be said to be performing yajna at every moment. Indeed, our whole life should become the joyful display of such a yajna.

Yajna in Nature revisited: Let us discuss the concepts of yajna in Nature and dravya yajna (or physical yajna) in the light of the teachings of the *Bhagavad Gita*. Yajna means 'to offer', 'to give', 'to sacrifice' or 'to donate'. The different elements of the universe are bound together in an interdependent manner through the principle of sacrifice. In this infinite universe, such a yajna is a constant process. As explained in the *Purusha Sukta*, the universe is not static, stagnant or invariant. A portion is constantly being created, sustained and destroyed, and this happens in a cyclic manner. That which is sustained or manifest today is destroyed tomorrow, and the same is re-created the day after.

Thus, even if creation, sustenance and destruction appear as three separate principles, they are not independent of each other. Sacrifice or yajna is the thread that holds them together. This is yajna in Nature. Sustenance without creation has no significance. Similarly, destruction is meaningless in the absence of creation and sustenance. In fact, the process of destruction starts with sustenance. Every living being that takes birth is destined to die. The period between these two events is their life – the period of sustenance. One who dies takes birth again *(punarapi jananam punarapi maranam, punarapi janani jathare shayanam)*. A person who joins a company as a manager, officer, clerk or labourer is sure to retire from service at a predetermined time (the age of superannuation), but the moment he joins the organization, he starts to work for it and ascend in status. It means he is in a state of motion while being in a 'state of sustenance'.

This principle holds good in the plant and animal kingdoms, among human beings, in fact, everywhere in the universe. There is no creation without sacrifice; what is created has an end and again out of the destruction comes rebirth. This mechanism of Nature is in itself a great yajna. The whole universe is sustained by this sacrificial principle. Trees, rocks, animals, amphibians, reptiles, mammals, in spite of being different are all completely bound to each other and have the same underlying principle of life. The Gita says that to evolve, it is necessary to understand the principle of life and be in tune with Him while performing all the worldly actions (BG 3.30).

The Gita also says that human beings did not create the yajnic process – Prajapati, the Creator, did so along with the universe (BG 3.10). What then is its relevance to us? We only have to understand this principle of yajna, the sacrificial base of existence and dynamism, in order to adopt it for all our actions. In this way, we should consciously and deliberately (but without self-interest) help the cause of the Lord, and thus become a true karma yajnic. This is how we will be able to fulfil all our worldly desires and also meet the two basic objectives of yajna – self-evolution and building a healthy society.

How should we perform the yajna of life? Krishna tells Arjuna that we should start with *indriya sanyam yajna* (BG 4.26). This is the first stage of yajna, which amounts to making efforts to control our passions for sensual pleasures, and doing the duty that devolves upon us due to birth or profession. We have seen that the Vedas have grouped individuals into four varnas (brahmin, kshatriya, vaishya and shudra) based on functions and aptitude. If our inborn qualities or adopted profession are related to knowledge, we should consider our mission in life as the pursuit of knowledge. If our nature is adventurous, we should dedicate our life to the duties designated for the kshatriya varna, and so on. No karma is superior to the designated karma or the one that is in harmony with our inner nature. We cannot skip yajna karma – Krishna said that the Creator created yajna along with human beings, and advised them to use yajna to fulfil all desires.

Therefore, those who base their karma on the yajnic principle in tune with His will cruise through the ocean of life effortlessly. The Lord promises that acts done for yajna will not lead to bondage, whereas acts done otherwise will bind a person to worldly suffering.

Yajna, human beings and other living and non-living beings are co-products of Prajapati's creation. All the lower species follow the rules of Nature and hence are performing yajna, but they are neither aware of this nor are they doing it deliberately. Therefore, they do not obtain the fruits of yajna. However, that is not the case with human beings, who have the capacity to think, choose and act after deliberation. What will we achieve if, after having been born as human beings, we live like the lower species and merely become involved in selfish activities? What use have we made of our life if we merely succumb to sensual desires, act indiscriminately, or remain in a state of indolence? Even if we choose to accede to worldly desires within the framework permitted by dharma, we can at best be said to be working for our own evolution. But we can instead choose to perform every action according to the sacrificial principle. If consciously, we work to control the senses, modulate their activities and perform all our designated duties without attachment but with passion, we will be said to have lived like a human being in the true sense of the term.

If a tiger kills a cow, neither does the cow receive credit for self-sacrifice *(atma yajna)* nor is the tiger blamed for committing a sinful act. But if we kill a cow for self-consumption, or slaughter any animal for that matter, not only do we not receive the benefit of gomedha, but also attract the penalty for a violent act. If a weak person is robbed, he cannot claim to have done sarvamedha yajna. A penniless person cannot donate, a weak person cannot extend protection, and an idiot cannot educate. Only a person with something in their possession is eligible to make a donation. Therefore, we have to work to earn wealth through purushartha, deliberately choose to utilize our earnings for a good cause, and consciously work at distributing it to the needy without attachment. This is the simplest way to evolve.

Indriya sanyam yajna is the first extension of kratvartha-based dravya yajna as envisaged by the *Bhagavad Gita*. One has to supplement it with *anasakta nishkama* karma yoga (karma performed without any attachment to the results). This extension is equally important. The sacrifice of oblationary articles in the fire spreads fragrance throughout the yajna area and all the participants enjoy it. In an ideal situation, the participants should not concern themselves with who has spread the fragrance, and the yajamana should not worry about the number of people he has thus made happy. The donor should not know the receiver, or the receiver the donor. The yajamana should have no expectation of any reciprocation from the participants in the yajna. If the donor does not desire anything (even gratitude or a word of thanks) in return for his donation, such a donation rates high in quality. The extension of dravya yajna from agni-based sacrifice to action-based sacrifice as stated in the *Bhagavad Gita* is *tapoyajna* (working for austerity) and *jnana yajna* (working to spread one's acquired skills and knowledge).

Lastly, Krishna asserts that if one performs dravya yajnas in this state of mind, it will lead to worldly prosperity. All living beings are supported by food, which is grown with the help of rain, which is caused by yajna (or sacrifice-based action), and actions are the outcome of the deployment of right knowledge. Knowledge is the presence of the Lord himself. Therefore, Brahman is the axis on which the wheel moves in a cyclic manner, and righteous action or Vedic karma is the driving force moving the wheel forward. One who helps to move the wheel through virtuous behaviour remains in tune with universal principles, and can be said to be performing constant internal yajna. For any yajna to take place, it is the action that is most important. This action has to be the outcome of a deliberate resolve of sacrifice, and a conscious effort to translate the resolution into an act. The cycle of yajna can be shown diagrammatically (view the cycle clockwise from the top of the circle).

Fig. 8

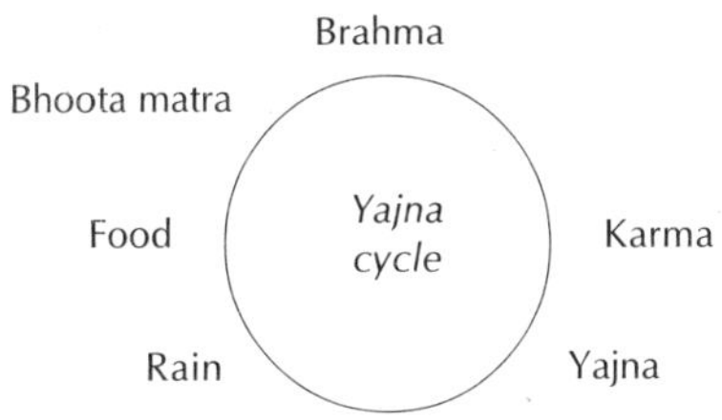

This cyclical path is how one should understand yajna in Nature, appreciate the result of havi yajna, and ponder over its extension for the purpose of developing wisdom. There are about a dozen internal yajnas described in the *Bhagavad Gita*. We could choose one or many depending on our personality, and put in wholehearted efforts to live them throughout our life.

11

The Environment and Yajna

We have seen yajna from the perspective of personal evolution, spiritual development and social advantages. Now we come to a different and very relevant aspect of yajna – its direct and proven impact on ecology. Given the alarming proportions that the harm caused by our indiscriminate use of natural resources has assumed, the significance of yajna becomes proportionately high. This Vedic science can effectively reverse the man-made imbalances that have become a global concern. However, to understand the relationship between yajna and ecology, we must understand ecology first. Most of us possess a basic awareness of the subject, but to understand the impact of yajna on ecology, we must understand ecology and hone our scientific awareness to appreciate the scientific impact of yajna. So we will delve into ecology as defined by modern science, look at the approach of the Vedic sciences, understand the causes and effects of an unbalanced ecology – and finally see how yajna can repair the damage already done and pre-empt future imbalance.

Ecology according to modern science

Ecology is essentially the study of the workings of the earth. It is the scientific study of the distribution and abundance of living organisms and how these properties are affected by interactions between organisms and their environment. The environment of an organism includes physical properties, which can be described as the sum of local abiotic factors like climate and geology, as well as other organisms that share its habitat. The term *oekologie* was coined in 1866 by the German biologist Ernst Haeckel; the word is derived from the Greek *oikos* ('household') and *logos* ('study') – therefore, 'ecology' means the 'study of the household of Nature'.

The ecology of a region consists of two factors – environment and atmosphere.

Atmosphere: The atmosphere is the mass of air that envelops the earth from all sides, containing many gases and particles of various materials. Nitrogen and oxygen constitute the major part (99 percent). The atmosphere also contains water vapour, sand particles, smoke, salt, volcanic ash particles, meteoric dust, pollen and gases like methane, nitrous oxide, carbon monoxide, hydrogen, ozone, helium, krypton, xenon, etc. in minor proportions.

It is estimated that the atmosphere extends up to a height of 1000 km above the earth's surface. The pressure, density and temperature of the atmosphere varies with height. It is dense near the earth's surface and rarefies with height. The atmosphere around the earth's surface is in five different layers, which help to protect living beings from the dangerous radiations of the sun, meteors, etc. The bio-kingdom dwells in the first layer called the troposphere, which extends up to a height of 17 km. Rain, clouds, storms and snow form in this part. The second layer, the stratosphere, extends up to 50 km and contains ozone in its upper portion. The other three layers are the mesosphere, the ionosphere and the exosphere.

As the atmosphere protects us from dangers such as exposure to radiation, climatic extremes, etc., any harm to this protective layer can prove self-destructive not only for the human race, but also for the entire living kingdom.

Environment: The environment is the totality of surrounding conditions, the area in which something exists or lives, the interrelationships between living things and their environment, or the study of these interrelationships.

It could be said to comprise the 'natural environment' and 'developed environment'.

The natural environment includes all the living and non-living things that occur naturally on earth, in contrast to a developed environment, which is the result of human activity or intervention. Some would argue about the usage of the term 'natural environment', in that most natural environments have been directly or indirectly influenced by human beings. In order to address this concern, some level of human influence is thus allowable without the status of a habitat ceasing to be 'natural'. The meaning of the term, however, is usually dependent more on the context than a specific definition. Many natural environments are the product of interaction between Nature and human beings. For this reason, the term ecosystem has been used to describe an environment that contains nature and also includes people. It follows then that environmental problems are human or social problems.

Vedic view of ecology

According to Vedic philosophy, the entire universe is made up of five basic elements – soil, water, fire, air and sky. It is divided into two parts – sentient and non-sentient. Substances are of two types – visible and non-visible. Prana shakti, the subtle form of energy, drives the sentient portion of the visible part. The non-sentient entities contain energy in an inert form.

The fourth basic element, air, surrounds the earth. But its reach is not restricted to earth – it spans the entire universe (dyu, prithivi and antariksha lokas). The enveloping substance is called *vatavaran*. Together with the other four basic elements (which extend to the whole universe), it is called *paryavaran*. The related science is called *paryavaran shastra*, which can be translated as ecology. Thus, according to Vedic theory, the components of ecology are: (i) visible substances like rivers, mountains, trees, shrubs, creepers together with planets, stars, the sun, etc., cohabitants of human beings like birds, animals, reptiles, amphibians, etc., and (ii) the non-visible part like space in which are found celestial bodies, air (charged with the fragrance of flowers and fruits), the fragrance-laden essence of yajna, the essence of all other substances, and energy in all forms.

Dynamic equilibrium in the universe

The universe is vast, and its managing agent is Nature. Nature has amazing methods of maintaining balance among the constituents of the universe, which consists not only of the earth, the sun, the solar system or other stars and galaxies, but also of limitless objects, known and unknown. These are hanging in space, but Nature manages to balance them through the tremendous energy, speed, gravitational forces, heat, radiation and so on that it has provided them with. It has given us the sun, the source of energy, and also layers of atmosphere to create a conducive living environment and protect us from harmful radiations and meteoric objects.

GnT law: The basic formula of Nature is the law of give and take (GnT). A continuous process of give and take among the constituents maintains the balance. Since these processes are occurring in nature continuously, the universe is in a state of dynamic equilibrium. In the man-made environment too, the same process must take place. When electricity is consumed in homes and factories, for example, it has to be replenished continuously at the source, which is the powerhouse. The powerhouse in turn takes from a generating station, and the generating station takes its energy from hydraulic or thermal sources, and so on.

The main source of such 'giving' in Nature is the sun. It is what gives us energy. According to the Vedic interpretation, the soma principle replenishes the energy of the sun, and since the sun continuously receives strength, its energy is not depleted. The *Shatapatha Brahmana* describes the world as a combination of give and take between Agni and Soma. This can be understood in another way. The sun has two parts, photoshpere and chromosphere. It gives light and heat through the photosphere, and the chromosphere gives energy to the photosphere. Thus, the sun gives through the photosphere but takes from the chromosphere. The loss occurring due to 'giving' is made good by the equivalent and simultaneous 'taking'. The give and take principle generates a circular or cyclic phenomenon. The processes recur, and nothing new is generated – what is created is through different combinations of the old. Physics also states that matter is neither created nor destroyed – it only changes form. So the process of dynamic equilibrium in Nature includes various cycles such as the nitrogen cycle, carbon cycle, weather cycle, and so on.

Mechanism of Nature: As part of its dynamic equilibrium, Nature has its own mechanism for using the waste of one entity as nourishment for another. For example, flesh and blood are the food of carnivorous animals, and the leftover rotten flesh and bones are items of feast for scavenger birds. This helps to keep the forests clean and pollution-free. In this way, Nature maintains an equilibrium. However, if the limit of Nature's self-sustaining measures is crossed, the result is the catastrophic situation we face today. Snakes, for example, are useful for keeping the rat population in check, but by eliminating them (out of human fear) we create problems, and then need to spread pesticides and anti-rodent poisons. Nature's measures are thus disturbed. To avert the calamities that may follow from such interference, something substantial has to be done. We shall shortly see that yajna holds great promise in this regard.

The mechanism of dynamic equilibrium through GnT becomes necessary because natural energy sources keep changing form. When energy is in a dormant, unused state, it is not consumed, but when it manifests, work gets done. In terms of the laws of physics, when work is done, energy is released. Through their observations and meditation, the rishis had understood two principles: (i) to get work done, energy has to be invoked (made to manifest), and (ii) the resulting depletion in energy has to be replenished through the process of giving 'food' in its essence. This probably gave rise to the principle of 'dravyam devata tyagah'. Thus, to replenish the depleted energy 'dravya' is offered to these energies (devatas) in the form of oblations. The oblations turn into essence through the sacrificial fire and become the food for the energies.

Imbalance among components – pollution

Pollution is the release of harmful environmental contaminants, or the release of substances in the atmosphere that generate contaminants when they come in contact with atmospheric elements. When not in accordance with natural principles, such releases cannot be accommodated by natural corrective processes, which creates an imbalance. This imbalance is, in effect, pollution.

Generally, for a process to be regarded as pollution, it needs to result from human activity. Even relatively benign products of human activity are liable to be regarded as pollution if they precipitate negative effects later on. For example, nitrogen oxides produced by industries are often referred to as pollution because, although the substances themselves are not harmful, sunlight converts them into smog. Thus, the precipitative process also becomes important while defining pollution.

Pollution can take two major forms: local pollution (e.g. smoke produced by burning coal) and global pollution (e.g. nuclear testing). In the past only local pollution was thought to be a problem, but now awareness is rising that some forms of pollution can also pose a global problem. Indeed, it is the awareness of both kinds of pollution (among other things) that has led to the environmentalist movement, which seeks to limit the human impact on the environment.

Whether something is pollution or not depends almost entirely on the context. Blooms of algae and the resulting eutrophication of lakes and coastal ocean is considered pollution when it is fuelled by nutrients from industrial, agricultural or residential runoff. Heavy metals such as lead and mercury have a role in geochemical cycles (i.e. they occur as within 'Nature'). These metals may also be mined and, depending on the processing, may thus be released in large concentrations into an environment previously not playing host to them, and considered to be 'polluting'. Such pollution could also occur due to natural geochemical activity.

One of the most common forms of pollution is smoke. Smoke is produced due to incomplete combustion of fuels. Most fuels contain carbon, hydrogen, oxygen, nitrogen and small quantities of sulphur. For complete combustion, a large quantity of oxygen is required. Smoke consists mainly of carbon dioxide, water vapour and carbon particles. It is the biggest air pollutant and very harmful for the heart and lungs.

Causes of imbalance

The mushrooming of industries, the lacklustre attitude towards the disposal of industrial waste, the growth of cities, motor vehicles, and the tendency to use rivers and oceans to dispose of domestic and industrial waste are the main causes of pollution. They damage plant and animal life, and interfere with many of Nature's cycles such as the food chain, carbon cycle, nitrogen cycle, oxygen cycle, etc.

Air pollution: The burning of fuels in factories, houses and motor vehicles causes air pollution. The release of harmful gases such as carbon monoxide, nitrogen dioxide, sulphur dioxide and smoke causes the healthy atmospheric proportion of gases to go haywire, affecting every creature breathing in that air.

Water pollution: Factories, farms and homes cause most of the water pollution. Sewage, industrial discharge, human and animal wastes flow into rivers and pollute the waters, giving rise to bacterial growth. Many insecticides used to preserve grains eventually flow into and poison the water. We drink such polluted water and consume larger than acceptable proportions of insecticides.

Land pollution: Pesticides and other chemicals used in an attempt to grow better crops cause much of the land pollution. Often a pesticide poisons many more organisms than originally intended. Solid wastes are another major cause of land pollution.

In addition to these three major types of pollution, modern life has created another set of polluting agents such as nuclear radiation, out-of-proportion noise levels, television and computer screen radiations, etc.

Effects of imbalance

Scientists believe that four billion years ago, planet Venus had seas, but due to the extreme increase in its surface temperature, all the water evaporated, and now it is so hot that even lead will melt there. Satellite photographs of Venus support this view. If the temperature of the earth's atmosphere keeps increaing and the environment continues to be polluted at the current alarming rate, one wonders if the earth won't meet the same fate one day. Already the effects of the imbalances are showing up in various ways.

Hole in ozone layer: As explained earlier, the top of the stratosphere contains a layer of ozone gas (24 to 48 km above ground level). This has two major functions with respect to living beings. It stops harmful radioactive waves and ultraviolet radiations of the sun. It also reflects back the infrared waves that try to rise from the earth. In this way, it protects living beings. In 1985, scientists observed that a hole has been created in the ozone layer above the South Pole, with the quantity of ozone having been reduced by as much as 20 percent.

Scientists believe that certain chemical processes and air pollution, in particular the use of chlorofluoro carbon (CFC), are the main causes of the hole. CFC is used in refrigerators, air-conditioning equipment, cosmetics, and even equipment for keeping fast food fresh. If the situation continues, it will become difficult to stop the ultraviolet radiations from reaching earth. The results could be an increase in cancer, eye tumours, etc. Trees and vegetation would also be affected.

Weather map of earth

Diseases induced by polluted air: The industrial use of coal increases the carbon dioxide content in the atmosphere. According to a Survey of India report, the content of carbon dioxide has increased by 16 percent. The use of petrol as a vehicle fuel generates white smoke which contains lead in excess quantities. Inhalation of such air causes many lung diseases. A traffic policeman standing at a traffic square for four hours inhales gastric poison equivalent to that produced by 100 cigarettes. Motor vehicles also consume oxygen during fuel combustion. The oxygen consumed by a vehicle to travel a distance of 960 km is sufficient for a human being to breathe for one whole year. So, while on the one hand the increased number of vehicles has been consuming more oxygen than ever before, on the other speedy deforestation to accommodate the ever-increasing population is reducing the generation of oxygen. The overall result? Thick smog in city areas and a rise in the earth's temperature.

Unhealthy minds: Polluted and negative mental attitudes also affect the environment. Emotions like envy, hate, greed, anger, etc. and acts of terrorism and violence exert a combined negative effect on ecology. The negative vibrations so created result in stress, stress-induced diseases as well as unhealthy interactions with the rest of the world.

Having seen the causes of pollution and their frightening effects, it can be definitely said that the Vedic advice to follow the righteous path *(ritasya panthah)* and the Vedic lifestyle based on ritualistic action *(kratvartha purushartha)* can provide a lasting solution.

Yajna as corrective action

Vedic philosophy interprets the entire creation or universe as the outcome of the first-ever yajna performed by the lord of creation, Prajapati. In this yajna, seasons (spring, summer, autumn) supported the sun (in the form of agni) by supplying food in the form of energy to replenish it. Thus, the source of energy is in a position to continuously supply energy to the constituents of the universe.

In addition to being the root cause of creation, yajna, as the GnT principle, is also responsible for ecological balance in the created universe. This yajna is going on in Nature without human intervention or support. It helps to keep the five elements pure and in perfect balance with each other. The quality of these elements is very important from the human point of view, because we are not only surrounded by them (in the form of the environment and atmosphere) but also made up of them. Therefore, they affect us in more ways than one. If the environment is pure, it leads to peace, prosperity and harmony, but if it is not, negativity prevails.

If we were to live in accordance with the principles of Nature, and lead an eco-friendly life vis-a-vis the basic five elements, we would have no need to worry about ecological imbalance, depletion of resources, etc. It is estimated that the age of the earth is about 4.6 billion years. If Nature has been able to maintain the balance over so many years without external aid, there is no reason to believe that it will not continue to do so in the future as well. No species is known to aid Nature externally in maintaining the balance, but no species is found to cross the limits of Nature either. Only human beings, through their ignorance and arrogance, indulge in activities that violate the rules of Nature.

Given that human beings are different from other species due to the quality of our intellect, and given that we are likely to continue analyzing the workings of Nature, let the excesses that occur in the process be inadvertent only, restricted to a section of the human race, and not the defining quality of humankind. Let society, by and large, be occupied in taking corrective action.

In the effort to provide an antidote to human excesses, yajna should be considered one of the best solutions, if not the only one. External or physical yajna is a proven method, tested over millennia, to correct the disturbed ecological balance. It can be and should be employed by society, if necessary with appropriate alterations to suit modern life: (i) to purify the atmosphere, (ii) to bring good rainfall, and (iii) to develop positive and healthy minds. The first effort is required for good living conditions, the second for abundance, and the third for peace, harmony and spiritual evolution.

Purifying the atmosphere through yajna: Clean air is a gift of Nature. The Vedas attach high importance to a clean environment. The *Rig Veda* says, "Air in its pure form is the best medicine, leading to peace of mind, good health and long life. If a house is without the treasure of pure air, it is not worth living in. O Vayu, by bestowing a small part of your nectar-like wealth, give us long life." (RV 10.186.1–3).

The treasure referred to is oxygen. Yajna purifies the air (*vayu shodhaka*) and makes it sacred (YV 1.2). Purification of the air is achieved through oblations. According to the *Yajur Veda*, yajna is developed so it becomes: (i) a purifying process to clean the environment based on a scientific approach, and (ii) a destroyer of disease-spreading germs and viruses from the point of view of medical science.

A physical yajna (smarta or shrauta) like agnihotra or soma yaga is performed with simultaneous actions at two levels. Mantras are chanted and oblations offered to Agni devata. The mantras generate a desirable anti-polluting effect through the appropriate sound waves. Havi dravya such as ajya and other fragrant materials with air purifying, anti-disease and nourishing qualities are poured into the well-lit fire, kindled by sticks from trees with special medicinal qualities. The oblations are consumed by the fire to produce their essence. The yajna agni spreads the essence in all directions through the medium of air (YV 8.62). According to the *Atharva Veda*, havi dravya works like medicine to provide a soothing effect for maladies (Ath 6.52.1). According to the *Rig Veda*, organization of yajna in this manner makes it possible to remove every atmospheric impurity (R 1.11). The proposition that air is purified by yajna and such purified air helps to bestow physical health is also supported by richas in the *Sama Veda* and *Atharva Veda*, which pray for the proper application of dravya (SV 1.7.1) and destruction of the enemies of health (Ath 3.11.1).

Science of oblation: The oblations are offered when the adhvaryu says 'swaha'. The sound wave created by the word and the conversion of havi dravya into essence makes the fire rise high in the air (YV 6.16). The repetition of 'swaha' and the pouring of oblations creates a cyclic action, giving rise to a wave pattern. Therefore, to strengthen the wave pattern it is recommended that everyone present in the yajna mandap utters 'swaha' along with the adhvaryu.

In agnihotra homa, oblations are offered at sunrise and sunset. The same havi dravya is used on both occasions, but the mantras are different. The morning offering generates air-purifying vapours that progressively rise in the air as it becomes hot with the ascending sun. They keep cleaning and filtering the air, thus nullifying the polluting agents. The essence of the evening offerings does not rise high due to the comparatively higher percentage of smoke in the air and the lower atmospheric temperature. They barely rise to one-fourth of the morning essence or half a kilometre high. However, they help to stop the polluting agents (which would have risen in the air during the day) from descending to the lower strata of atmosphere near the ground. In other words, they produce a kind of protective umbrella. It is observed that the area affected (positively) by one agnihotra homa can extend up to an area of even 20 sq. km.

The energy released from the yajna kunda through the medium of air replenishes the oxygen content of the atmosphere and purifies it. So it can be used in developing our physical and mental powers. The *Rig Veda* acknowledges this and says, "Let my progeny be free from unknown diseases as also (the known ones like) tuberculosis through the healing power of the devatas (Indra, Agni, etc.)" (RV 10.161,1). It further advises, "O my son, you can be healthy and happy only due to a purified atmosphere. Therefore, for this to happen undertake to do havan of dravya in yajna, satiate the devatas by so doing, and receive the boon of good health from the favourably disposed devatas."

Concept of good rain (suvrishti): Yajna helps to balance Nature, harmonizing the seasons and regularizing natural cycles. A given state of Nature and its related forces may be altered and redirected through the power of yajna, but not by transgressing natural laws. The process of yajna requires the fullest use of human potential to achieve an end-result,

Parjanya yajna in progress.
Young initiates offering sticks from a special creeper as oblation

but this is attempted by working with Nature, not against it. This is possibly the major difference between modern science and Vedic science too. Vedic rain induction technology is one example, though a very important one, of how natural forces can be turned to our advantage through yajna, instead of trying to bring them under our control.

The Vedas have developed special packages for bringing about good and timely rainfall. Rain is necessary for domestic and agricultural purposes. Rishi Devapi was an expert in Vedic rain induction technology, and is said to have brought rains to end the decade-long drought in the kingdom of Shantanu.

The Vedas define good rain *(suvrishti)* as rains received at proper times, in adequate measure and spaced out over the full season in accordance with the requirements of the crops and soil absorption. Behind the rain induction technology is the hypothesis that the water embryo is installed in space. Nature exhibits five symptoms to indicate the formation of this embryo. If the moon is positioned in specific constellations, the wind has a specific direction and speed, white clouds are formed, lightning and thunder are observed, then the formation of the rain embryo is confirmed. The health of the embryo is reflected by the simultaneous occurrence of these indicators. For example, if all five symptoms are noticed, the embryo is healthiest. The embryo is nurtured by Nature in the womb of space for 195 days (approximately 6.5 months). Thereafter, the rain child appears on earth! Just as a medical professional helps a pregnant mother to properly nourish the baby in the womb (prescribing diet, exercises and medicines), yajna helps to nurture the rain baby properly.

That rain is the outcome of yajna (*Yajnat bhavati parjanah*) is as much a truism as 'rain comes from rain-bearing clouds'. If it does not rain irrespective of the sky being overcast, no one concludes that 'rains are due to clouds' is a wrong hypothesis. Similarly, even if the cloud formation does not take place after a yajna, it does not disprove the hypothesis. Possibly, the yajna did not extend its effect into space sufficiently to induce the formation of clouds. Rain-bearing clouds are formed through the weather cycle. This cycle is based on the GnT law, and therefore is termed by the Vedics as paroksha yajna – yajna in Nature. Similarly, if a prototype of paroksha yajna, i.e. physical yajna or pratyaksha yajna, is performed exactly according to the injunctions and prescriptions of the scriptures, it is also bound to result in the formation of clouds, and one does get rains from these clouds. This is why the *Yajur Veda* calls yajna a rain augmenting process – *Yajna varshavriddhamasi*, and says:

वृष्टिश्च मे यज्ञेन कल्पताम्

Vrishtishcha me yajnen kalpataam

Let my process of inducing rain through yajna be possible and let it rain after that.

Vedic theory of cloud formation: The *Yajur Veda* explains that when a yajna is performed, its essence reaches the sky and results in rain at the yajna venue. In another place it explains that the essence of the oblations travels by air, crosses the antariksha loka and reaches dyu loka. From there, it brings rain to prithivi loka. According to the *Yajur Veda*, this is how yajna induces rain at the venue – by reaching the clouds. Where there are no clouds, it reaches dyu loka, and becomes the cause of rain. So there is a positive correlation between the process of yajna and the process of rain. And the mantra *Nikame nikame nah parjanyo varshatu* – "Whenever we desire rain, the clouds should give rain" – can be proved to be true.

It is interesting to note that Shri N.R. Kale, an ahitagni (one who has undertaken to perfom shrauta agnihotra every day) has successfully used the Vedic rain induction technology to bring rain to the area of his residence in Maharashtra, India. During 2005, he conducted parjanya yajna at 12 places on the monsoon trough-line. The rain embryo was formed, and it rained exactly after 195 days (October 17, 2005) at the yajna venue[1].

Recorded impact of yajna

Many experiments have been conducted in India and abroad to study the yajnic process and its effects. These experiments have tested the effects from various perspectives and parameters. Some recorded instances of the positive effects of yajna are described below.

✧ A few years ago, banana plantations in Peru were severely affected by a deadly fungus, *Plastica fungs toka venegue*. The crop was as good as destroyed, and it was apparent that acres of farmland would yield nothing. Then it was suggested that yajna be performed on the plants. As all other efforts had failed, no one objected to this rather strange suggestion. Mahamrityunjaya havan was performed every day in the banana fields for four hours. On full-moon and no-moon days, the havan was performed for 24 hours. Smarta agnihotra was also performed in the morning as well as evening every day at the same place. And the results? The fungus was eliminated to almost zero level, the vigour of the plants improved substantially, the harvest showed an improved yield, outstanding bank loans came down, the farmers experienced a perceptible calming effect, and sickness among the farming community was reduced. It is understood that the results of the experiment have had the banks and the government of Peru so enthused that they are now enlarging the scope of the experiment[2].

✧ In a research study by Gurukul Kangdi University, Haridwar, India, an exercise was conducted specifically to measure the effect of smarta agnihotra yajna on the surrounding atmosphere. The parameters under observation were physical (temperature, odour, respiratory suspended

---

[1] The results of this research are at *www.yogirajashram.org*.

[2] Details of the results can be seen at *www.terapiahoma.com*.

particulate matter, suspended particulate matter), chemical (nitrogen oxide, nitrogen dioxide, other nitrogen oxides, sulphur dioxide, carbon dioxide, ozone content) and microbiological (bacteria count). It was found that after the yajna, the atmosphere was almost totally free of all chemical parameters considered to be harmful. Physical parameters also showed a distinct reduction and the bacteria count came down from 860 to 70!

The research also pointed out that yajna consumes minimal oxygen. Yajniya wood has a fast-burning property, i.e. it creates very little combustion resulting in ash. So the intake of oxygen from the atmosphere and the release of carbon dioxide are proportionately low too. This is one reason why the essence that emanates from a yajna does not induce discomfort (unlike normal smoke) but is extremely refreshing.

✧ Agnihotra homa was performed in German hospitals. Terminal patients and those suffering from heart disease both showed good to marked improvement.

✧ In his book *Nature,* Dr. Shirovich from Russia has recorded the qualities of cow's milk, which he says has miraculous powers to protect one from nuclear radiations. A place smeared with cow-dung remains totally protected from radioactive effects. (Cow's milk is a principal havi and smearing the yajnashala with cow-dung is a prerequisite for yajna.)

✧ Prof. Trillbert from France has found that the smoke created by burning sugar has a healing effect. It kills the germs of deadly diseases like tuberculosis, typhoid, diarrhoea, etc. (Sugar is one of the havi dravyas or ingredients for smarta agnihotra.) In fact, different diseases can be combated using different oblation materials in a smarta agnihotra, as recommended in the *Atharva Veda*[3].

✧ In New Jersey, USA, a society is spreading the use of agnihotra to contain and combat pollution.

---

[3] See Chapter 9

✧ During British rule in India, Dr. K. King, a commissioner, had advised students to use ghrita, saffron and rice as oblation in yajnas to protect themselves from plague. In more recent times, during the plague epidemic in Surat, Gujarat, in 1994, doctors used yajna to purify the atmosphere and kill germs. Hundreds of thousands of packets containing havi (ghrita with dhoop, turmeric, camphor, etc.) were distributed.

✧ An American scientist, Dr. Havard, has observed that chanting of the Gayatri mantra with proper pronunciation generates 110,000 waves which calm negative emotions and feelings.

Clearly, yajna is a healthy and long-lasting solution for the ill effects of modern behaviour and processes. It is recommended that agnihotra or other yajnas are regularly conducted around factories, plants and workshops where the incidence of pollution is highest. The area to be covered by one yajna site (in sq. km) should be decided, and multiple yajna sites permanently maintained where yajna is conducted on a regular basis. Yajnas could also be conducted in schools, colleges and market areas. Regular yajna could also be performed on farms, in dairy plants, etc. to improve yield. Individuals/industry owners/social bodies should make efforts to set up projects towards this end, and the results should be properly evaluated. Such an analytical approach would gainfully employ the yajnic process in combating ecological and other imbalances that are posing a substantial danger to the peace and prosperity of society.

12

Yajna for the Enhancement of Life

By now it should be clear that yajna is not just a term, but an expansive phrase. It is as large as one's life. Yajna does not only mean external, physical or dravya yajna where articles of oblation are offered in a sacred fire with the simultaneous chanting of mantras to worship the yajna devata(s). It means a philosophy of life, a way to evolve, a code of conduct based on the principle of give (with humility and love) and take (as if receiving prasad).

On the hypothesis that yajna is a code of conduct, we shall examine the principles that governed life in Vedic society, the recommended code of conduct for daily practice and some details of this code. However, what is significant is that all these codes are equally relevant in modern life, in fact more so. If we had certain basic precepts on which to base our life as the Vedics did, the dissipations and stresses that result from our modern way of living would invariably decrease, and we would be far more creative in our interactions with the world. Of course, we may not practise the codes in the way the Vedic people did, for the structure of life then and now is very different. However, it is not difficult to interpret the codes so that they apply to us and we work them into the existing structure of our life. Keeping this in mind, we will first understand the significance of the 'pancha maha yajnas' or five essential daily rituals that formed the basis of daily yajna for the Vedics, and thereafter see how they can be interpreted in modern life. It is also interesting to note that these practices can be considered as prerequisites for adopting yoga as a way of life.

Pancha maha yajnas

So that there was a proper environment for people to evolve in and develop, Vedic society had daily rituals, known as *pancha maha yajnas,* that would act on a person's psychology in five different ways. These five ritualistic actions were a must for everyone. Such a mandate was in vogue even in pre-Vedic times. The *Shatapatha Brahmana* mentions them (11.5.6.1), the *Taittiriya Aranyaka* also describes them (2.10) as daily actions of great value, and the *Apastamba Sutras* (1.4.12.13–1.4.13.1) use metaphoric language to call them yajna. As may be expected, there was a deeper philosophy behind the practice.

The individual soul interacts with the world through the sense organs when the mind is extroverted, which is much of the time. This interaction is through action. Throughout life, we are busy performing actions at the physical, mental and emotional levels. In the *Bhagavad Gita,* Lord Krishna said to Arjuna that one cannot remain without action even for a second. Therefore, one must understand what actions are and know which actions one should choose for oneself. However, the irony of life is that by the time we come to the stage of making a choice, we are already conditioned or regimented by the environment in which we have grown up. As children we are independent in thought, but due to our upbringing we often lose our originality. This is where the pancha maha yajnas come in.

The word *maha,* meaning great, is prefixed to indicate that these yajnas were obligatory acts that had to be performed daily. 'Greatness' here is implied to praise the attitude of mind that considers them to be obligatory. The pancha maha yajnas were deployed to enable a person to maintain an appropriate relationship with the rest of the world, and allow them to evolve through the *dana daana yoho* (GnT) principle. The five great yajnas are:

1. *Brahma yajna*: Incessant study of the scriptures that held the Vedic society together. (Practice period: from childhood onwards.)
2. *Deva yajna*: Performing dravya yajna to satiate the devatas (principles of Nature). (Practice period: after marriage through agnihotra.)
3. *Pitri yajna*: Remembering the ancestors (for their knowledge, to express gratitude, etc.). (Practice period: on becoming a responsible progeny.)
4. *Bhoota yajna*: Offering all lower species a share in the food that one consumes. (Practice period: on assuming family responsibility.)
5. *Manushya yajna*: Helping the needy members of society to enable them to achieve a livelihood in an honourable manner. (Practice period: progressively on gaining prosperity.)

The application of these yajnas essentially enables one to maintain the appropriate relationship with other members of the sentient world. However, Pt. Satavalekar, a great scholar of the Vedas and Vedic literature, interprets the pancha maha yajnas as the medium through which one:

- establishes a channel with the Almighty (brahma yajna)
- is linked with the principal powers represented by devatas like Agni, Vayu, Surya, etc. (deva yajna)
- remains grateful to ancestors and elders (in respect to age as well as knowledge) through worship (pitri yajna)
- becomes a friend to those younger (in respect of age as well as knowledge), other ranks like lower species, people who lack good health, etc. (bhoota yajna)
- establishes links with the society through seva or service (manushya yajna or atithi yajna).

In each of the above five types of action, there is an embedded element of sacrifice (oblation) on the part of the doer. Hence they are called yajnas. However, except in a limited way in deva yajna, there is no real oblation offered in a fire. Therefore, they differ from shrauta or smarta yajnas described earlier. The differences chiefly lie in that:

- The pancha maha yajnas can be performed by householders, and do not need specialized priests, unlike shrauta and smarta yajnas.
- Their objective is not the fructification of personal desires like a seat in heaven, wealth, health, prosperity, progeny, etc. Instead, the objective is to do one's duty towards the Creator, ancient rishis, ancestors and the entire sentient world (other members of one's society, other societies, the animal world, plant kingdom, etc.). In other words, ecology is at the base of these yajnas. Due to their magnanimous intent, the pancha maha yajnas are treated as actions which are superior to shrauta yajnas. They inevitably raise one's state of mind, and are considered the base for internal yajna.

The social scientists of Vedic society were possibly prompted to make the pancha maha yajnas mandatory daily rituals because of the desirable qualities such as devotion (bhakti), gratitude, respect, compassion, tolerance, etc. associated with them. Later, other (good) motives were also attached to them. Manu, in his famous work *Manu Smriti*, has said that householders inadvertently but inevitably become the cause of the death of cohabitant non-human species at five places – the cooking range, flour grinder, water storage tank, pounding equipment, etc. or harm them through acts like sweeping, mopping, etc. The 'sin' so committed can be balanced by good, counter acts like the pancha maha yajnas.

Having understood the broad import of the pancha maha yajnas, let us now take a look at them individually. While brahma yajna makes for a separate regiment, the other four yajnas are often treated together as 'Vaishvadeva'.

Brahma yajna

Vedic interpretation: Brahma means supreme knowledge (or knowledge of the supreme), and yajna (here) means effort. So brahma yajna is pursuit of knowledge. Knowledge, the enemy of ignorance, *tamas,* or darkness, is regarded as the highest power. It is knowledge alone that has given man supremacy; there is nothing that cannot be achieved if one has the right knowledge. Indeed, knowledge as an art of life is of paramount importance. The *Bhagavad Gita* says that nothing is as sacred as knowledge.

The pursuit of knowledge has been a continuous process through the ages. However, the basic process of acquiring knowledge used to be 'initiate children into learning and allow them to graduate'. The modern process is no different. A child is admitted to a school and allowed to progress there until graduation. Further learning, which is optional (a Masters or PhD), can lead to specialization in branches of knowledge.

In Vedic times, a pupil was to pursue learning on a daily basis by undertaking recitation of all the scriptures (in progressive parts). He was normally sent to a boarding school called a gurukul. However, over a period of time the process of daily practice slowly dwindled away. In modern times, brahma yajna is hardly ever done daily. Instead it is performed as an annual ritual. By definition, a brahmin is a person devoted to the pursuit of knowledge throughout life, and different branches of brahmins are to study different Vedas. Therefore, the annual ritual became the symbol of the Vedic literature that was to have been studied by the branch of brahmins (rigvedis, yajurvedis, etc.) performing it. Brahmins from southern India perform this ritual in the month of Savana (July–August). Given below are details of the ritual followed by rigvedis[1].

- Chanting of vyahritis (*Om bhu bhuvah swaha*, etc.) and Gayatri japa thereafter.
- Chanting of the first nine richas of the *Rig Veda.*
- Reciting the first sentence of the *Aitareya Brahmana.*
- Reciting the first five sentences of each of the five parts of the *Aitareya Aranyaka.*

---

[1] From: *Dharma Shastra Itahasa*, M.M. Kane, Bhandarkar Oriental Research Institute, Pune, 1990

- Chanting the first richas of the *Krishna Yajur Veda*, *Shukla Yajur Veda*, *Sama Veda* and *Atharva Veda*.
- Reciting the first sentence each of Nighantu and six Vedangas (*Ashvalayana Shrauta Sutra*, *Nirukta*, *Chandas*, *Jyotish*, *Shiksha*, *Vyakarana* of Panini).
- Chanting the first pada of the *Yajur Veda* and the first sutra each of the *Mahabharata*, *Nyaya*, *Poorva* and *Uttara Mimamsa*.
- Reciting the shanti mantra: *"Tachchamyoravrnimahe . . . "*
- Chanting three times the mantra: *"Namo brahmane . . . "*

The above steps are followed by special rites called *tarpan* to commemorate the learned ones (rishis, forefathers, etc.).

Modern adaptation: The essence of brahma yajna is inculcation of the desire for and the habit of pursuing the process of learning, remaining grateful for the knowledge received from the ancestors, adding to it the fruits of our own contemplative meditation, and passing the whole treasure on to the next generation. The process of development inevitably follows this pattern. From the pre-Newton era to Einstein to Hoyle-Narlikar, etc., each developed a theory based on the knowledge honed by their predecessors. In a way, therefore, brahma yajna is always being performed. However, the practice needs to become a conscious effort on the part of everyone so that all of us can develop this art of life. An agriculturist should pursue learning to improve harvest yields, engineering professionals should acquire new skills even in post-college days, social scientists should undertake similar exercises in their respective fields – with all efforts aimed at making life a richer and more purposeful event.

In Vedic times, concentrating on the object of learning with one-pointed focus on the end-objective (the dharana stage of Patanjali yoga), total concentration on the subject and loss of other awareness (dhyana), and merging into the object of learning (samadhi) were considered as the highest achievements in brahma yajna. The last stage is total surrender, *vaiyaktika sarvamedha*. This should be the method in any learning exercise undertaken even today.

Brahma yajna is an internal process. External, physical yajna only helps us to internalize the awareness. A person who has mastered internal yajna does not need to observe any physical yajnic processes. A sannyasin is always in the state of *antara yajna* (the process of yajna is continuously going on internally). Therefore, a true sannyasin who is constantly doing brahma yajna is free from the external yajnic processes.

Vaishvadeva yajna

Deva, pitri, bhoota and manushya yajna, the other four maha yajnas, are together known as Vaishvadeva yajna. The basic thought behind each one is (individually) a supreme quality of an evolved mind, which sees itself as the whole universe and the whole universe in itself. The underlying spirit of each of these yajnas needs to be properly understood so we can bring them into our lives.

Vedic interpretation: In Vedic times, every householder maintained the sacred fire from the time of marriage. All yajnas were performed with this fire. Oblations were made in honour of various devatas as well as ancestors and lower species.

The food that we eat is not the result of our isolated efforts. Contributions come from God (favourable agricultural conditions), other fellow human beings, animals, birds and even the inanimate (land, water, etc.). Since we get so much from others for our nourishment, it becomes our moral responsibility to offer a due share to each contributor. The idea of Vaishvadeva yajna is based on this premise.

In this context, the *Bhagavad Gita* says that a person must take only the remnants of the yajna material as their share – *yajna avashishta*. Those who do not follow the practice of offering a share to others and instead consume the entire produce by themselves are thieves. This concept has given birth to the idea of including deva yajna (for the devatas), bhoota yajna (for the bio-kingdom), pitri yajna (to express gratitude to ancestors) and atithi yajna (for fellow citizens) into a set of daily rituals.

Vishva means 'universe' (the inclusion of everybody). The sacrifice of a part of one's food, or earning, for the benefit of others, is called Vaishvadeva yajna. Every householder (head of the family) was expected to perform it. When a family divided into two or more parts, each sub-family was expected to perform independent Vaishvadevas. Initially, the ritual was undertaken twice a day (morning and evening). Later, just once a day (before lunch) became the accepted practice.

Vaishvadeva is performed in some brahmin families even today. Normally, it is done at a sacred place in the house by installing the yajna agni in a kunda and offering oblations to devatas, ancestors, etc. The material used for oblation is cooked rice purified by sprinkling ajya on it. The rice cake is divided into three parts. The first part is offered to the devatas in the yajna agni. The second is for animals, and is offered on the ground beside the yajna kunda. The third part is offered to the ancestors by placing it outside the house on a banana or palasha leaf (for crows to eat on behalf of the ancestors).

The fourth yajna (atithi yajna) was done in an interesting manner. After the three offerings had been made to devatas, animals and forefathers, the yajamana would stand in front of the house waiting for a passer-by. Such an unknown, unsolicited guest would be requested to honour the yajamana by accepting his food. The guest would be ushered into the house, and after felicitations, a sumptuous meal would be offered with great humility. This would be an everyday affair.

Modern adaptation: The performance of all four yajnas is actually symbolic. As mentioned earlier, the concept of Vedic devatas has a close link with natural powers and energy sources. Depletion of energy due to the distribution of power is replenished by Nature through auto processes. They are a reminder to us to do our own duty – to see that we supplement and support the equilibrium of Nature. Thus, in principle deva yajna is intended to strengthen ecology.

The process of evolution is aided by the development of pious habits. This is how a person learns to tread the righteous path. Being compassionate to the needy and protective of the defenceless are two virtues that take one away from the selfish principle of 'live by leaving (others)', supports the principle 'live and let live', and leads them to its superlative degree of 'live to help others live'. The spirit of bhoota yajna is precisely this – be grateful to all who help you and to all others too. It reminds the performer daily of the need for restraint and helpfulness (at times at the cost of one's own comfort). The lives of great saints like Gyaneshwar, Tukaram, Nanak, Sivananda, St Francis of Assisi and Mother Teresa, and leaders with a spiritual base like Mahatma Gandhi, Abraham Lincoln, Martin Luther King and Nelson Mandela are embodiments of such principles of compassion, protection and helpfulness.

In modern times, the practice of such restraint is diminishing. Recklessness, extravagance and selfishness are assuming alarming proportions possibly due to the lack of a method for the inculcation of such practices. There is a pressing need for social reformists, educationalists and bodies responsible for social governance to come together and do some collective thinking to reintroduce these time-tested values. A restructuring of the social code is overdue.

The principle of atithi yajna is to develop respect for the act of feeding the needy ahead of oneself. The following cryptic explanation of culture (humanity, samskriti, etc.) drives the point home. Shri Vinoba Bhave, a saintly Indian social worker, once said, "Two persons come together during lunchtime, open their respective lunch boxes and eat. It is *prakriti* (a natural thing). Two persons come together, but the stronger of them takes away a part or whole of the other's lunch. It is *vikriti* (abnormality). Two persons come together, one knows that the other has a bigger appetite so he parts with a portion of his lunch and gives it to the other – it is samskriti." It takes restraint and courage to bear personal loss (of food, fame, fidelity) and develop a helpful attitude. This can be the result of self-education or a conducive social environment. If such qualities are deliberately and consciously developed, the society as a whole will reflect compassion of the highest order. As the classical texts say:

सर्वेऽ पि सुखिनः सन्तु, सर्वे सन्तु निरामयः ।
सर्वे भद्राणि पश्यंतु मा कश्चित् दुःख माप्नुयात् ॥

Sarve pi sukhinah santu, sarve santu niraamyah
Sarve bhadraani pashyantu, maa kashchit dukha maapnuyaat.

Let everyone be happy, healthy and see the good things. Let no sorrow and pain come to anyone.

Atithi yajna was intended to develop such an attitude of compassion. And it can be easily adapted in modern times too. Today, it may not be possible (or necessary) to hunt out a hungry person every day. After all, who can manage to slip out of the office during the just adequate lunchtime! But once the principle is understood, it is possible to earmark an amount that we would like to share with the needy (say, on the pay day of each or certain months). Now we could identify a genuine social organization that helps the needy and hand over the sum to it. This would be the modern version of atithi yajna, but in the real sense of the term (the desire needs to be genuine, the methodology can always be invented).

Clearly, all four maha yajnas – deva yajna, pitri yajna, bhoota yajna and atithi yajna – are very relevant and necessary in modern times. In fact, they may be the best antidotes for all the wrongs being committed, and they can be easily adopted to enrich our daily life and improve our surroundings.

Prerequisites for pancha maha yajna

Three rituals – sandhya vidhi, Gayatri japa and surya namaskara – supplement the rituals of pancha maha yajna. An important samskara, upanayana, is a prerequisite for all. It is not out of place to discuss the relevance and ritualistic details of these rituals.

We have seen that devata dhyanam is a very important aspect of yajna to obtain the desired result. Now we can interpret such dhyanam as a process to concentrate on the spirit, or an important internal aspect of yajna without which the process would become a mere mechanical exercise. The major support to devata dhyanam is the process by which the dormant, semi-asleep and inactive prana shakti, which is the representation of paramatma shakti, is awakened. The ascent of this energy is used to meditate in a dispassionate manner *(sakshi bhava)* on the principle of the devata.

There are many types of austerity (asana, pranayama, hatha yoga, raja yoga, bhakti yoga, laya yoga, etc.), which can ignite the dormant energy in the human body, known as kundalini shakti. Although they are elaborated in the Vedic scriptures, awakening the kundalini shakti by oneself is not without danger. The prana shakti of a disciple can be awakened only through the grace of guru, and the spiritual journey starts from that point. Among Vedic samskaras, upanayana is very important, for it ignites the prana shakti (and the dormant kundalini shakti) in the consecrated young disciple *(batu)* through application of the Gayatri mantra. It is only after such an awakening that the batu becomes eligible to undertake the study of the Vedas and to perform the subsequent rite *agni karya* (various personal-level yajnas).

Upanayana samskara: This was an important and mandatory samskara for every child in Vedic times[2]. In fact, it was the step that signalled the end of the merry days of infancy. It was an entrance point to studentship; now the child had to start learning about life. The literal meaning of *upanayana* is also to take the child to a teacher with a view to admitting him into studenthood.

The teacher is responsible for developing the pupil in all respects and building the capacity to lead life in a successful manner. Brahma vidya being the mother of all branches of knowledge, the teacher has to generate the capacity in the

---

[2] See 'cultivating samskaras' in Chapter 8

pupil to absorb it. Through his research on the subject, sage Yajnavalkya establishes the pupil's relationship with the Gayatri mantra. The teacher has to use the method of *shaktipat* to transmit his own power and capacity to the pupil. Needless to say, the teacher must himself be an authority in the field. Shaktipat initiation is done in three ways – transmission of energy through touch, through eye contact and through sound. In upanayana, the teacher uses all three methods.

Before establishing a heart-to-heart relationship with the pupil, the teacher prays to the pancha (five) devatas – Agni, Vayu, Surya (Sun), Chandra (Moon) and Indra – for the new relationship to flow smoothly. Then the maha vyahritis are used to consecrate the child at an auspicious time. A special type of grass, deer skin, and special cloth and thread (called *kaupin* and *upavita* respectively) are used during the process. The best age for upanayana initiation is around eight. It differs depending on the varna of the child. Details are in the following table.

Table 16: Upanayana samskara

Varna	Age	Auspicious Season	Mekhala	Ajina	Upavita	Length of danda
Brahmin	8–16	Vasant (spring)	Munja	Krishna mriga	White coloured	Up to skull
Kshatriya	11–22	Grishma (summer)	Arc of a bow	Spotted deer	Red coloured	Up to forehead
Vaisya	12–24	Sharad (autumn)	String of a bow	Sheep/ goat	Yellow coloured	Up to nose tip

The batu has to wear the sacred thread after the upanayana. The length of the thread is proportionate to his height measured in terms of the breadth of his forefinger. The measure is in multiples of four fingers. The number four here represents the four stages of consciousness – *jagriti* (conscious mind), *swapna* (subconscious mind) *sushupti* (unconscious mind) and *turiya* (super-consciousness).

The thread has three strings, and each string has three strands. In these nine strands, nine devatas – Aum, Agni, Naga, Soma, Pitri, Prajapati, Vayu, Surya and Vishvan, are installed. The three strings bear the three Vedas – the *Yajur Veda* in the first, the *Rig Veda* in the second and the *Sama Veda* in the third. The *Atharva Veda* is installed in the knot. All these devatas are meant to protect the student through life. The initiation process is as follows:

- A day prior to the initiation day, the aspirant batu is required to observe silence (mouna).
- The child's head is shaved amid the chanting of mantras, leaving a tuft. The batu prepares for the ceremony by asking for the blessings of family elders.
- The teacher accepts the lifetime responsibility for the pupil, and a sankalpa is made by the batu who then expresses the desire to learn brahma vidya by uttering *Brahmacharyamagama*. The teacher accepts his prayer-cum-request and says to him, "O child, Guru Brihaspati had performed a samskara on Indra using special clothing and processes. I do the same for you by using the same articles. Let them make you strong and healthy, give you a long life and the supreme level in knowledge of Brahman."
- The batu is then given the sacred thread *(yajnopavita)*. The mantras chanted during this ritual make a prayer that the batu may earn strength, power and long life. Thereafter he wears a *mekhala* (a cloak made of special grass), deerskin, and bears a staff.
- Next comes the important ritual of shaktipat to awaken the pupil's prana shakti. The teacher goes into a trance and takes the pupil to an isolated area or covers them both with a shawl or bedspread. He whispers the Gayatri mantra in the pupil's right ear and asks him to repeat it thrice. Chanting the mantra *"Om tam dhiraso kavaya unnyamti swadhyaya manasa devayantaha,"* he touches the chest and transmits his power to the pupil. Then he makes the pupil sit on his lap, and gazes at his face,

looking deep into his eyes. Thereafter, cupping water in his palms, he looks towards the sun, the devata of the Gayatri mantra, collects the power of the sun into his eyes, looks into the pupil's eyes and transmits the power through eye contact. In this manner, he invokes the power in the pupil's consciousness. He pours the water from his palms into the palms of the batu, and makes him look at the sun, the protector, pronouncing that Vratapati Surya is hereafter with the batu.

- One more important symbolic ritual is to ask for alms. The student is not supposed to earn his livelihood, nor is he expected to use the resources of his parents. He is required to ask for food (just adequate for the day) from pious families. He starts with his own mother, seeking her help, saying, *Bhavati bhiksham dehi*. Now he is instructed in undertaking to learn brahma vidya.
- The teacher (who now becomes the guru also) has the consecrated pupil *(upanita batu)* do the upanayana homa. Agni is installed on the *sthandila* (sacred seat for fire) and is called *samudbhava agni*.

In this way, the initiation process is completed. The batu is transformed from a child (who was like a raw mould without any shape or size) to a new personality, possessing a new glow (after all, his dormant energy has been ignited, so he has a different look and feel). He is said to have taken birth a second time – *Janmana jayate shudrah, samskarat dvija uchyate*. With the backing of the guru, he becomes busy with his studies for which he lives in the guru's ashram.

The upanayana samskara is still performed in all parts of India, and for all three varnas, more or less on traditional lines. However, in many cases, as the significance of the process has been lost sight of, its effect has become diluted.

Sandhya: The batu becomes a dvija (twice-born) after the upanayana samskara. On attaining this status, he is expected to perform a series of recommended daily rituals. In fact, his day starts with a sankalpa for righteous acts in the name of and solely for the Almighty. Then commences his process of learning Veda vidya – *brahmopasana*, which starts with *sandhya vidhi*.

The *Devi Bhagavatam* describes the sandhya vidhi and Gayatri japa in great detail. It assumes that a dvija becomes converted into a luminous tree through the pursuit of knowledge *(brahmopasana)*. Its glow emanates from the branches (the four Vedas) – dharma being its leaves, karma its fruit, and sandhya the root. Being the most important part of a tree, conscious effort should be made to protect the root so as to ensure proper maintenance and sustenance of this sacred tree. Sandhya vidhi provides this caring treatment.

This important ritual, which a dvija performs from the day of upanayana, is based on the injunctions of the Smriti granthas, and uses richas dedicated to Surya and Prajapati. The shastras recommend that a dvija perform sandhya vidhi three times a day, every day, at the transition periods between the three parts of the day (i.e. at dawn, dusk and mid-noon).

The ritual comprises: (i) pranava (Aum) chanting and pranayama (for tattwa shuddhi), (ii) achamana (for atma shuddhi), iii) arghya to Surya and Gayatri japa (for merging with the cosmos). It has many similarities with the yogic practices of tattwa shuddhi, kriya yoga and kundalini yoga, and helps to purify the body, mind and soul.

The spiritual interpretation of the physical ritual of sandhya vidhi can be understood through a reference in the *Bhagavata Purana* wherein Lord Narayana is narrating to his best worshipper, Narada, the importance of practice over preaching. This is what he says with regard to the sandhya vidhi:

- For the daily ritual of sandhya sadhana, the dvija should begin with purification of the mental body *(antah shuddhi)*. He is expected to rise in the fourth part of the night (before brahmamuhurta). He should sit erect, making the mind calm and serene, then do pranayama. Pranayamas are of six types *(sadhum*, *vidhum*, *sagarbha*, *agarbha*, *salakshya* and *alakshya)* and in each there are processes of *pooraka*, *kumbhaka* and *rechaka* (inhalation, retention and exhalation), based on Aum (pranava). The dvija should use ida nadi for inhalation and pingala nadi for exhalation. He should have firm faith that the Lord dwells in his heart, and meditate on Him one-pointedly.

- Thereafter, he should meditate on the kundalini form of Goddess Amba who is present in the mooladhara plexus. At six nadi centres in the body – mooladhara, linga, naval, heart, throat and eyebrow centre are situated six lotus flowers respectively with four, six, ten, twelve, sixteen and two petals. The dvija should rotate his consciousness through them and finally place it in the eyebrow centre to worship the guru in the form of the Lord.
- The next step in sandhya sadhana is purification of the physical body (tattwa shuddhi). With the consciousness fixed at the eyebrow centre, the dvija should practise *Soham* mantra japa. His body contains the elements of earth (square in shape, from the toes to the knees), water (semi-circular in shape, from the knees to the navel), fire (triangular in shape, from the navel to the heart), air (hexagonal in shape, from the heart to the eyebrow centre), and space (circular in shape, from the eyebrow centre to the top of the head).

These elements should be felt, and then he will realize the presence of maya. He should burn out the *papa purusha* present in him in the form of a dwarf (as tall as the left thumb), and smear the resulting ash over his body as *bhasma*.

- The last steps in the sandhya vidhi are achamana, arghya (symbolically offering a handful of water to Surya) and Gayatri japa. The japa should be done with full awareness of the seats of all the devatas in the body, and with full concentration on the form of Mother Gayatri.

The ritualistic procedures of sandhya are described in the Smriti texts. Condensed texts with transliteration/translation are easily available as small booklets providing the ritualistic procedures, and may be followed for daily practice.

Surya namaskara: Immediately after the sandhya vidhi, the dvija should do six to twelve rounds of surya namaskara. However, it should not be performed as just a series of postures, but as *Surya upasana* (worship of the Sun god). It involves standing erect in front of the rising sun, and prostration following specific bodily postures. One should stand facing east, preferably allowing the soft sunrays to permeate the whole body.

The upasana should start with meditation on the form of the sun, and chanting with utmost devotion:

ध्येय: सदा सवितृ मंडल मध्यवर्ति नारायण: ।
सरसिजासन सन्निविष्ट: केयूरवान् मकर कुंडलवान्
किरीटी हारी हिरण्मय वपुर्धृत शंख चक्र: ॥
ॐ आदित्यस्य नमस्कारान् ये कुर्वन्ति दिने दिने ।
जन्मांतरसहस्त्रेषु दारिद्र्यं नोपजायते ॥

Dheyayah sadaa savitri mandal madhyavarti Naaraayanah
Sarasijaasana sannivishtah keyurvaan makara kundalvaan
Kireeteehaaree hiranmaya vapudhrita shankha chakrah.
Om aadityasya namaskaaraam ye kurvanti dinedine
Janmaantarsahastreshu daaridryam nopajaayate.

I bow to Lord Narayana who is at the centre of the sun's galaxy and is adorned with luminous jewellery. He has a crown on his head, his body is shining like gold and in his hands he holds a conch and a discus.
I bow to Lord Aditya daily and meditate on him. He alleviates all our sorrow and the mental and material poverty we may have acumulated during thousands of births.

While standing with the hands folded (in front of the chest), one should try to establish a spiritual path between the eyebrow centre and the red ball on the horizon. During the process, the eyes may be kept open or gently closed as is comfortable. With every incoming breath one should inhale cosmic energy, and with every exhalation let go of all negative feelings. While prostrating before Surya, touching the earth with eight parts of the body and maintaining deep concentration on the form of Surya is of utmost importance.

With every round, one each of Surya's 12 names should be chanted aloud. On completing 12 rounds in a slow and rhythmic manner, arghya should be offered to Surya and Sarathi Aruni (his charioteer) with the chant:

आदित्यस्य नमस्कारं ये कुर्वन्ति दिने दिने

Aadityasya namaskaaram ye kurvanti dine dine

Bow in front of Lord Aditya every day in the morning to obtain cosmic energy and life force.

Bhavishya Purana mentions the spiritual benefits of surya namaskara. At the physical level, it helps to stabilize the body, mind and intellect. The result is increased and prolonged enthusiasm, a positive approach and enhanced brainpower[3].

IN CONCLUSION

To sum up, the Vedic concept of life is 'action based on sacrifice'. Since yajna represents sacrifice, it can be unequivocally nominated as the core principle of life. To adapt to yajna, one needs to undergo the physical process only after having developed a sound understanding of the basic principles. This is a mental exercise. However, intellectual appreciation alone is not sufficient. After having gained a good grasp of the principle, it has to be ingrained deeply in the mind so that every action is yajna-oriented. Samskaras help to develop such an attitude, and the pancha maha yajnas should be practised consciously so that one truly realizes the meaning of the phrase (*Kalika Purana*, 31.40):

सर्वं यज्ञमयं जगत्

Sarvam yajnamayam jagat.

The whole world is the process of yajna.

---

[3] Refer to *Surya Namaskara: A Technique of Solar Vitalization*, 2nd edn, Yoga Publications Trust, Munger, Bihar, India, 2004

ANNEXURE I

Vedic Literature: Structure & Content

RIG VEDA

The *Rig Veda* is the earliest known written text created by man. Its time of creation goes back to more than 4500 years BC. However, the knowledge existed much before it was given a textual form, being present in the ancient traditions as hymns.

The enlightened contemplators, in the course of their meditation, had revelations about the ultimate truth, and gave expression to their experiences in a poetic form. These seers were called rishis and their compositions richas. The rishis perceived the cosmic powers that governed the dynamics of the universe as the manifestation of the divine. They experienced the flamboyant divine presence as the basis of life, in the origin of worldly entities, all animate and inanimate entities – in fact, in everything. Therefore, the object of a richa is always the divine in some form or other. These forms ranged from natural powers to celestial entities. Some richas are even devoted to domestic animals.

What is the Rig Veda? *Richa* means 'hymn'. *Rik* (or rig) is a special hymn, a composition by a rishi to express an experience. They are revelations of what was perceived by the seers, and in this sense they reveal knowledge. *Veda* means knowledge. So the collection of richas is called the *Rig Veda*. Here, 'collection' implies a variety of subjects meditated upon by the rishis, and 'knowledge' implies the ultimate truth underlying everything in the universe. Therefore, it is said that the *Rig Veda* is 'total knowledge'.

What is the Rig Veda Samhita? Richas from the *Rig Veda* are used in yajnas to invoke the yajna deities. For this purpose, richas were structured using the rules of grammar (compounding words, etc.) and tone – *udatta*, *anudatta*, *swarita*. The collection of a structured richa arranged according to rishi, devata and subject is called the *Rig Veda Samhita*.

Initially there was only one Veda, and it was the storehouse of the richas of all rishis on all subjects. These were segregated into four parts, mainly to facilitate the proper conduct of yajna, as the yajnic processes use many richas. The books that go by the names of *Rig Veda*, *Yajur Veda*, *Sama Veda* and *Atharva Veda* today are the Samhitas compiled by Maharshi Vyasa and his disciples.

During a yajna, richas have to be chanted with full devotion for the concerned deity and deep contemplation. The part of the Vedas comprising prose and poetry, and used during a yajna with such an attitude is called mantra. The *Rig Veda Samhita* is also sometimes called *Mantra Samhita*. With reference to yajna, we shall use the terms *Rig Veda* and *Rig Veda Samhita* to mean *Rig Veda Samhita* unless mentioned otherwise.

Branches of Rig Veda Samhita: To begin with, yajna was simple in procedure. Individuals performed yajna as part of their household duties. The segregation of a single Veda into Veda Samhitas became necessary due to the transformation of the form of yajna from simple to complex, involving much more time, capital, energy and the teamwork of priests. Such yajnas crossed the threshold of individuals. Only those who had the capacity and the desire would undertake to perform them, and they became a social event. Around the time of the Mahabharata war, the event of yajna was at its peak.

Sage Vyasa entrusted the work of compiling the *Rig Veda Samhita* to his disciple Rishi Paila. He and his followers spread the use of the *Rig Veda Samhita* throughout the country. Over a period of time, due to location dispersion, non-availability of adequate expert support from a central point, etc., variations of the *Rig Veda Samhita* – called its branches – were developed. Their import, however, did not differ in any major way from the original.

According to the *Mahabhashya* of Patanjali, there were 21 branches of the *Rig Veda Samhita*. Recent research has discovered the existence of six more branches. However, only five are extant: *Shakala*, *Bashkala*, *Ashvalayana*, *Shankhayana* and *Mandukya Samhitas*.

Of these five branches, only the *Shakala Samhita* is currently being used in shrauta yajnas in India and abroad. The other Samhitas are either used very rarely, or are on the verge of extinction. The Ashvalayana tradition is being rejuvenated by the Yogiraj Ved Vidnyan Ashrama at Barshi in Maharashtra.

Form of Rig Veda: According to some books on tantra shastra, the form of the *Rig Veda* is described as:

ऋग्वेद: श्वेतवर्ण:स्यात् द्विभुजो रासभाननः ।
अक्षमालायुत: सौम्य: प्रीतश्चाध्ययनो द्यत: ॥

Rigvedah shvetavarnah syaat dvibhujo raasbhaananah
Akshamaalaayutah saumyah preetashchaadhyayano dyatah.

Rig Veda is fair-complexioned (crystal-coloured), has two arms, a mouth that creates a loud sound (for proclaiming his prettiest possessions), the face of a donkey, holds a rosary in one hand (exhibiting a contemplative and meditative nature), is very soft and pleasing (like the cool rays of the moon), has a preference for a studious approach, and is inviting (us) to adopt it.

Structure of Rig Veda: The structure of the *Rig Veda* can be perceived externally as well as internally.

External form: The *Rig Veda* is composed of verses which are generally in the form of hymns composed by different rishis in praise of different devatas of Vedic times. The verses are called suktas and are grouped according to subject or the devatas they praise. Care is taken to see that the groupings bring together all the compositions of a particular rishi – devata-wise. Also, while binding the Samhita, special efforts were made to establish a link between a rishi and the devata he adored.

Each sukta is composed of richas. Normally, a Rig sukta contains three to ten richas. However, a few suktas have more than 50 richas (for example, the philosophical *Asya Vamiya Sukta* (1.164) has 52 richas, more than 10 devatas, four chandas or metres, and 30 subjects). And there is also a sukta with only one richa!

The division of mantras is made in three ways: (i) the *adhyaya* method uses ashtaka (8), adhyaya (64) and varga (2024) to group 10,552 mantras, (ii) the *mandal* method uses mandal (10) and sukta (1028) to group 10,552 mantras (this method is most commonly used in studying the *Rig Veda Samhita)*, and (iii) the *Shaunaka Rig Veda Anukramani* (index) uses mandal (10), anuvaka (85) and varga (2008) to group 10,552 mantras (it is popular among yajna priests). Table 17 shows the mandal method of dividing the *Rig Veda*.

Other parts of Rig Veda: Other than the Samhita, the *Rig Veda* has two Brahmanas (*Aitareya* and *Shankhayana* – also known as *Kaushitaki – Brahmana*), two Upanishads (*Aitareya* and *Kaushitaki*), and *Ayurveda* as its Upaveda.

Internal meanings: Richas, being the expression of experiences (of seer rishis), are essentially pointers to various facets of knowledge. However, as externally they seem to be simply praising a devata, the knowledge is camouflaged. To glimpse the veiled beauty, one has to approach the verses with the simplicity and innocence of a child. It is then that a sukta will unfold knowledge beyond words.

Suktas can be grouped according to the devatas they praise. Rig devatas are many, and the majority represent the divine in the form of natural forces. Besides, there are about 35 other major devatas like Varuna, Soma, etc., some domestic animals like the horse, bull, etc., and even some

Table 17: Mandal-wise distribution of suktas in Rig Veda

Mandal	Number of suktas	Number of richas
Mandal 1	191 (19%)	2006 (19%)
Mandal 2	43 (4)	429 (4)
Mandal 3	62 (6)	617 (6)
Mandal 4	58 (6)	589 (6)
Mandal 5	87 (8)	727 (7)
Mandal 6	75 (7)	765 (7)
Mandal 7	104 (10)	841 (8)
Mandal 8	103 (10)	1716 (16)
Mandal 9	114 (11)	1108 (11)
Mandal 10	191 (19)	1754 (17)
Total	**1028**	**10,552**

inanimate entities like rivers, implements for crushing stones, etc. Two devatas, Indra and Agni, claim about 40 percent of the total number of suktas (366 out of 1028 suktas). Table 18 shows the distribution of suktas by devata.

The types of suktas include Indra suktas, Agni suktas, Vayu suktas, Usha suktas, apri suktas, khila suktas, religious suktas, philosophical suktas, spiritual suktas, etc. The suktas cover varied subjects such as general knowledge, material knowledge, creation of the universe, philosophy of life, religion, duty-bound behaviour, way of life, sannyasa, spirituality, yajna, etc.

Indra is the devata of valour. Indra suktas express qualities that support rajas guna – valour, strength, compassion, etc.

Agni (fire) is the devata of householders. In various forms he is the true friend of human beings. He is the intermediary between us and God. The rishis express friendship and closeness to this devata. They praise him and ask for the boon of welfare just as a child would seek blessings from the parents when beginning a new phase of life. In the *Rig Veda* Agni is described as the one who takes care of the family, brings prosperity and serenity, and leads at the performance of a ritual *(purohita)*. He is treated as the

Table 18: Devata-wise distribution of suktas in the Rig Veda

Type of devata	Name of devata	Related natural force	No. of suktas
Nature-related	Indra	Thunder and the fighting spirit (representing positive energy)	206
	Agni	The force that agitates particles (energy in the form of fire)	166
	Ashvinau	Positive energy in a nascent form, useful when unleashed	53
	Savitri	(Also Surya, Aditya, Pushan) Energy as life source	21
	Mitravaruna	Energy in the form of sunlight	19
	Usha	Dawn, the energy that exhilarates and enlivens the mind through impact on the related energy centre in the body (chakra)	17
	Rubhu	The seasons at the pole	10
	Dyava Prithivi	Earth and sky	6
	Ap Parjanya	The phenomenon of rain	6
	Marut	Violent energy in the form of fierce storms during rains	5
			509
Others	About 35 objects	Varuna, Soma, horse, bull, etc.	519
			1028

most adored guest of the house. Agni has two forms, *laukikagni,* used in household activities, and *yajnagni,* the form in yajna. The Agni suktas are beautifully compiled and express soft and lovely feelings.

Usha and Vayu suktas exhibit qualities similar to Agni suktas, as well as being metaphorical and ornamental in expression.

There are a large number of yajna suktas. In fact, a major part of the *Rig Veda* is devoted to yajna. As compositions, these suktas are not as poetic as the others, and being repetitive sound somewhat boring. They are spread throughout all the mandals. It is no exaggeration to say that yajna karma was the ground in which Rig Vedic poetry was cultivated. The terminology used in yajna rituals and processes is amply visible throughout the work, indicating that yajna existed in the same or similar form even in Rig Vedic times. Soma yajnas such as the ashvamedha are also described in the yajna suktas. One full chapter (Mandal 9) is devoted to soma, the principal item of oblation in soma yajna. Definitions of yajna priests (ritvijs) and descriptions of their duties are also found.

The *Rig Veda* considers all sentient beings as important. Domestic animals are treated as part of the family, and there is an equal concern about ecological balance. The Vedics were not averse to eating meat, but brahmins were expected to follow restrictions. It is quite amazing to note how this Veda goes to the utmost limit in recommending that our interactions should not affect others (fellow human beings, all members of the biosphere and inanimate beings). The welfare of others must always take priority over personal benefits.

The *Rig Veda* is vast in scope. The sheer number of richas (more than 10,000) makes it difficult to give a full coverage here, and the embedded meanings make any summary tricky. However, to conclude, a few famous richas and proclamations can be referred to:

- "Let us pray to Agni, the leader who takes us to the path of health, wealth and prosperity" (the teaching to shape one's aim in life).
- "Let noble thoughts come to us from the whole universe" (the wish that one should express).
- "Let us hear (only) the good, let us see (only) the good, and let us use our arms for (only) good actions" (the request to equip one's mind with a positive approach).
- "God is only one even though it manifests in different forms."
- "Even gods do not like people who do not work" (the caution for those who are averse to sincerity and hard work).

- "Let us make the whole universe arya" (the concept of a global village).
- *"Hiranyagarbhah sama varta ta te . . . "* (the hypothesis of the *Rig Veda* on the creation of the universe).
- "Let all united and unanimous" (the desire for a healthy nation).
- The Gayatri mantra and Mahamrityunjaya mantra are the methods to seek strength and solace.
- The path of righteousness is the direction for behaviour.
- *Shri Sukta* is the gift of the *Rig Veda* to achieve never-ending wealth of matter, mind and spirit.
- Yajna is the process suggested to accomplish purushartha.
- *Prajnanam Brahma* – Knowledge is Brahman – is the *mahavakya* (great word) or proclamation of the *Rig Veda.*
- *"Vang me manasi pratishthita . . . "* is the shanti mantra.

Commenting on the historical importance of the *Rig Veda*, Max Muller says[1], "As long as man continues to take an interest in the history of his race and as long as we collect in libraries and museums the relics of former ages, the first place in that long row of books which contain records of the Aryan branch of mankind will belong forever to the *Rig Veda*." The cultural importance of the *Rig Veda*, and its role in providing a sure way for a purposeful and happy life as purported in the 19th century by Max Muller continues to be valid even in the 21st century. Without doubt, it will remain so for all times to come.

YAJUR VEDA

The *Yajur Veda Samhita* was developed to enable the proper conduct of shrauta yajnas. Sage Vyasa assigned this work to Rishi Vaishampayana. While preparing this Samhita, the yajna mantras were picked up in accordance with the practice then prevalent for chanting and recitation during a yajna.

---

[1] *A History of Ancient Sanskrit Literature,* Max Muller, Allahabad, Bhuvaneshwari Ashrams, 1926

The yajna process requires mantras in both prose and poetry. Prose mantras are greater in number compared to mantras in the poetic form (Rig mantras). The *Yajur Veda Samhita* mostly contains prose mantras called yajus. Therefore, the Samhita containing yajus mantras is called *Yajur Veda Samhita*. Since the *Yajur Veda Samhita* is compiled to give injunctions and descriptions of the yajnic processes, a brief recapitulation of the shrauta yajna process is given here.

A shrauta yajna requires a team of priests or ritvij. One particular ritvij, the *hota,* meaning one who summons, is given the responsibility of chanting the Rig mantras with a view to invoking the yajna devata. Another ritvij, the *adhvaryu,* chants yajus (prose mantras) and performs physical actions relating to oblations. The third ritvij, *udgata,* sings the sama mantras. The fourth ritvij, *brahma,* oversees the entire yajna proceedings for correctness. The four main ritvijs are aided by other ritvijs. Depending on the type of yajna, the number of ritvijs ranges from three to sixteen. Rituals require perfect coordination and cooperation between the hota, adhvaryu and udgata for the chanting, action, etc. In addition, the yajamana (host) is required to occasionally participate in the chanting.

The *Yajur Veda* gives elaborate descriptions of the actions of each of the three main ritvijs and the yajamana. It also gives the mantras they need to use, arranging them by sequence of events and related actions by one or all four priests. First comes *adhvaryava*, the mantras useful for the adhvaryu, followed by mantras for the yajamana, and lastly the *houtra* or the mantras for the hota. The performing group in their guidebooks called *Prayoga Pustika* bind the triggers for action by the udgata.

During the yajna proceedings, some mantras are repeatedly used in various rituals. For such mantras, the *Yajur Veda Samhita* uses methods called *sakala path* and *pratika path*. The mantras are given in entirety only once, and just a few words are given subsequently. Also, when mantras are repeated, some need a few modifications. Such mantras are given with a reference to the context *(anushanga path)*.

The form of the *Yajur Veda Samhita* is described thus:

अजास्य: पीतवर्ण: स्यात् यजुर्वेदोऽक्षसूत्रधुक् ।
वामे कुलिशपाणिस्तु भूतिदो मंगलप्रद: ॥

Ajaasyah peetavarnah syaat yajurvedah aksha sootradhruk
Vaame kulishapaanistu bhootido mangala pradah.

Yajur Veda has a pale yellow complexion, the face of a goat, and is holding a rosary in his right hand. His left hand bears the thunderbolt and his gesture is pious.

Branches of Yajur Veda: As with the *Rig Veda*, over a period of time, location, vocal and traditional differences gave rise to many branches of the *Yajur Veda Samhita*. Charana Vyuha mentions that there were 86 such branches. Today only six are available: (i) *Kathaka*, (ii) *Kapishthala-Katha*, (iii) *Maitrayani*, (iv) *Taittiriya*, (v) *Kanva Vajasaneyi*, and (vi) *Madhyandina Vajasaneyi*.

The original *Yajur Veda Samhita* had an overlap between the mantras and the Brahmana text. The organization of the Samhita was also rather loose. A school of thought emerged in favour of revision. Sage Yajnavalkya, one of the disciples of Vaishampayana, disengaged himself from the mainstream, performed austerities and restructured the Samhita with the blessings of Surya, the sun god. The import of the original Samhita did not differ greatly, but the Brahmana was totally segregated and an order brought to the exposition. His branch is called Vajasaneyi Samhita. The *Kanva* and *Madhyandina Samhitas* fall in this category.

Yajnavalkya's revision is also known as the *Shukla Yajur Veda Samhita*. Since the original Samhita had a mixture of mantras and Brahmana, it came to be known as *Krishna Yajur Veda Samhita*, Krishna, meaning black, being the symbol of the 'impurity' present.

Krishna Yajur Veda: It is a massive collection of yajus mantras. The following description gives its structural details, based on *Our Vedic Literature* (Marathi version) by R.V.Vaidya.

The *Krishna Yajur Veda* (Samhita, Brahmana, Aranyaka and Upanishad taken together) has 10 chapters (kanda), which are subdivided into 82 units (*prapathaka* or *prashna*). Prapathakas are further divided into anuvaka (990). Anuvakas give kandikas (yajus/mantras). The total number of yajus mantras in the *Krishna Yajur Veda* is over 110,000. It discusses karma kanda in detail, and also covers a bit of jnana kanda, but the subjects are intermixed in the chapters. Karma kanda is expounded by rishis called *kanda rishis*, who are four in number.

Table 19: Kanda rishis and their subjects in Yajur Veda

Kanda rishi	Karma kanda subject
Prajapati	Shakhadi, Yajamana, Hotri, Hotri Vidhi, Hautra, Hautra Vidhi, Darshik Vidhi, Pitrimedha
Soma	Adhvara, Graha, Dakshin, Dakshina Vidhi, Vajapeya, Vajapeya Vidhi, Pravargya, Pravargya Vidhi, Sava
Agni	Agnyadheya, Agnupasthana, Agni, Agnihotra, Agnihotra Vidhi
Vishvadeva	Rajasooya, Rajasooya Vidhi, Kamya Pashu, Ishti, Ushanuvakya, Yajya Satrayana, Ashvamedha, Ashvamedha Vidhi, Upahoma, Kaikilee, Soutramini, Nakshtreshti, Naramedha, Pashuk Hautra, Acchidra

The *Yajur Veda* has three extant Brahmanas *(Katha, Maitrayani, Taittiriya)* and three Upanishads *(Katha, Shvetashvatara, Taittiriya). Aham Brahmasmi* – I am Brahman – is its mahavakya.

Shukla Yajur Veda: Its Samhita has 40 chapters *(adhyaya),* 303 sections (anuvaka) and 1975 mantras. All the important yajnas are covered in the first 25 chapters. It is said that the remaining 15 chapters, containing Brahmana details, Aranyaka and Upanishad, were added later.

Yajnas such as darshapoorna, pitri pinda, chaturmasya and pashu bandha are periodic yajnas and described in the first four chapters. The daily ritual of agnihotra is described in the third chapter. Soma yajnas (ekaha, ahina, etc.) are described in subsequent chapters. Chapters 22 to 25 describe ashvamedha yajna.

This Veda has two extant Brahmanas *(Shatapatha Kanva, Shatapatha Madhyandina)* and two Upanishads *(Brihadaranyaka, Ishavasya)*. Its mahavakya is *Aham Brahmasmi*. The shanti mantra of its Upanishads is *"Poornamadah, Poornamidam . . ."* The *Yajur Veda* has brought an occult meaning to words like 'vaushat', 'swadha', 'swaha' 'aum', etc. The Upanishads picked up the link, and improvised upon the significance of Aum in spiritual sadhana. From the same one-syllable word, the tantra shastras later developed the bija mantras. The *Yajur Veda* has thus earned a special place in the religious history of India.

SAMA VEDA

Although the *Rig Veda* and *Yajur Veda* attach great importance respectively to the way of life (purushartha) and ritualistic behaviour (kratvartha), the *Sama Veda* holds a unique place in Vedic literature.

The *Rig Veda* is the collection of richas. Richas become mantra when qualities like *pada* (a quarter or fourth part of a richa), *charana* (one line of a richa), *chanda* (metre) are associated with them. Some mantras can be sung too, and are called samas. The word 'sama' is formed by adding the suffix 'am' to 'saa'. *Sa* means a richa, and *am* means the note of a tune *(taal)*. Therefore, *sama* means a richa-based song composed using a specific tune. The collection of such samas is called the *Sama Veda*. It begins with the sama, "*Agna aa yahi veetaya grunano havya dataye ni hota satsi barhishi*", which is the prayer and request to Agni devata to arrive at the yajna venue to accept the havi being offered therein.

Not just any singing or song can be called a sama, because even if its words have a pada, charana, etc., it may not be a mantra. Similarly, any mantra chanting cannot become sama. Samas then are based only on richas. No other words or poetry can become their base. In view of this, sama is defined in the *Chandogya Upanishad* as *"Richi adhyudham sama"* (Ch.U. 1.6.1).

The form of the *Sama Veda* is described as:

नीलोत्पलदलाभासः सामवेदो हयाननः ।
अक्षमालान्वितो दक्षे वामे कंबुधरः स्मृतः ॥

Neelotpala dalaa bhaasah saamvedo hayaananah
Akshmaalaanvito dakshe vaame kambudharah smrutah.

Resembling a blue lotus, Sama Veda has a face like a horse. I remember him who holds a rosary in his right hand and kambu in the left.

The structure of a sama is in the tune. Brahmarshi Narada has explained the composition of an octave of a sama. This principle is adopted by the udgata to sing samas. The *Sama Veda Samhita* is the collection of richas from the *Rig Veda*. It is divided into two parts called *Prathamarchika* and *Uttararchika,* each of which has chapters or adhyaya. Sections of these chapters are called prapathaka. Elements of prapathakas are called *dashati mantra* (or sama). Mantras in the *Sama Veda* use eight metres.

The *Sama Veda* has 1875 mantras, most of which are taken from the *Rig Veda*. It is said that only about 60 mantras are non-Rig Veda mantras[2]. However, conversations with practising samavedis does not confirm this claim. Mantras in the *Sama Veda* are called sama mantras and are used to compose the sama songs sung by samavedis. There are about 4000 sama songs composed by various rishis. Maharshi Patanjali mentions a thousand different ways of sama singing. The number one thousand may be taken to mean 'numerous'. Their categorization is also sizeable. There are many branches of the *Sama Veda* – *Sama Tarpan Vidhi* of Charana Vyuva puts the number at 1000, adding that one who understands the *Sama Veda* knows the secrets of all the Vedas.

The first compiler of the *Sama Veda* was Rishi Sumantu. Today only three branches are alive – *Ranayaniya*, *Kauthumi*

---

[2] *Sama Veda Samhita,* S.D. Satavalekar, Swadhyaya Mandal, Gujarat, 1985

and *Jaimani*. They differ in the Samhita section only marginally, but differ considerably in the way of singing and pronunciation. *For example*:

Kauthumi	**Ranayaniya**
Hau	Havu
Rai	Rayi
Vajushu no (soft 'n')	Vajeshu no (harsh 'n')

Lord Krishna has honoured the *Sama Veda* by declaring in the *Bhagavad Gita* that among the Vedas, *Sama Veda* is his *vibhooti,* or divine glory.

Prose, poetry and music make different impacts on the mind. Music acts on the mind at a very subtle plane. Scientist Jagdish Chandra Bose proved this by his experiments with music and plants. Indeed, music therapy is gaining popularity as a method to heal the sick. Since the *Sama Veda* acts on a subtle level, its effect on the environment around the yajna venue as well as the devata is phenomenal. The essence of the samas is the famous Aum. Needless to say, this Veda creates immense serenity in the environment.

The *Sama Veda* has 12 extant Brahmanas and three Upanishads. *Tat Twam Asi* (Thou Art That) is the mahavakya. *Kauthumi Samhita* is more popularly used in the state of Gujarat, *Ranayaniya Samhita* in Maharashtra, and Jaimani in southern India.

ATHARVA VEDA

The *Atharva Veda* contains mainly two types of mantra rituals, which are called *atharvana* and *angiras* mantras. The form of the Veda is described as under:

अथर्वणाभिधो वेदो धवलो मर्कटाननः ।
अक्षसूत्रं च खट्वांगं बिभ्राणो यजनप्रियः ॥

Atharvanaabhidho vedo dhavalo markataananah
Akshasutram cha khatvaangam bibhrano yajanpriyah.

Atharavan is said to be fair-complexioned, with a face like a monkey. He holds a rosary in one hand and a trident-like staff in the other. He adores being worshipped.

The *Atharva Veda* starts with a prayer to all gods. It prays for ample, hygienic water that is good for drinking, bathing, etc. Compiling the *Atharva Veda Samhita* was the responsibility of Jaimini. However, the Veda is known as *Angiratharva Veda,* which could be due to the fact that Acharya Angiras made a substantial contribution to it.

The atharva mantras are used in yajna karma. The angira mantras fall in the realm of black magic and incantation. Possibly it is for this reason that this Veda has not been given the same status as the other three in religious sadhana. However, it represents the traditions in vogue among common people, and truly represents folk culture.

The atharva part of the Veda is very important for a yajna, so much so that the ritvij associated with it has earned the name 'Brahma' – he is the chief overseer of the yajna proceedings.

Several aspects of yoga shastra also derive from the *Atharva Veda*. Mantra japa, for example, is a very important sadhana of yoga shastra. The use of yantra as a symbol for instant connection with mantra, dhyana on the ishta devata, etc. find their root in the *Atharva Veda*. Tantra shastra has also developed bija mantras and related techniques using the contents of this Veda. The *Atharva Veda* also deals with various diseases and mental disorders.

Atharva Veda has two branches, one Brahmana and three Upanishads. *Bhadram karne bhi . . .* is its shanti mantra. *Ayamatma Brahma* – This Self is Brahman – is its mahavakya.

BRAHMANA GRANTHAS

Classification: Initially, the rig, yajus etc. mantras used in yajna were not in an organized form. Each group of yajna performers had their own set of mantras and procedures. Each hota had to compile/compose his own set, and therefore there was the possibility of variation. Besides, the mantras and actions of priests would yield the desired effect only if done in a perfect and precise manner. So Sage Vyasa painstakingly built the Veda Samhitas. His efforts can be said to be the first conscious recension of Vedic literature. It was an effort to organize and order the suktas and mantras according to the needs of yajna performance.

Not all Mantra Samhitas and Brahmana Granthas expounded by Vyasa and his team of researchers are extant. Many have been permanently lost. From references found in the extant work, it is inferred that there were 1130 Mantra Samhitas and an equal number of Brahmana Granthas. Today, only 14 Samhitas and 20 Brahmana Granthas are available. According to the known recension of the Vedas, each has its separate Brahmana Grantha. Table 20 illustrates this classification.

Particulars of extant Brahmanas: All yajnic processes are based on descriptions given in the Brahmana texts. They have a common structure (mantra, tantra, ahuti), but different end results. Their difference stems from (i) the resolution of the yajamana, (ii) the complexity of procedures, (iii) duration, and (iv) oblationary articles. The shrauta yajnas, in particular soma yajnas, are the most complex, involving the simultaneous and interdependent activities of 16 priests. The Brahmanas are the basic literature for yajna, describing yajnas and prescribing their procedures. The three groups of priests – hotri, adhvaryu and udgitha – represent the *Rig*, *Yajur* and *Sama Veda* respectively, and use the Brahmanas of the concerned Vedas.

In any yajna, every rite and oblation has to be performed with the chanting of mantras. The rites and rituals in (shrauta) yajnas get going on the basis of joint use of the Brahmanas. For example, invocation mantras are taken from the Brahmana Grantha of the *Rig Veda*, how the invocation is to be done is decided using processes from the Brahmana Grantha of the *Yajur Veda*, and the songs to be sung simultaneously in praise of the yajna deities come from the Brahmana of the *Sama Veda*. This also highlights the

Table 20: List of extant Brahmana Granthas[3]

Root veda	Name of Samhita	Brahmana	Associated rishi(s)
Rig Veda	1. Shakala	Aitareya (also known as Ashvalayana)	Aitareya
	2. Bashkala (non-extant)	Kaushitaki (also known as Shankhayana)	Kaushitaki
Shukla Yajur Veda	1. Kanva	Shatapatha	Kanva
	2. Madhyandina	Shatapatha (Vajasaneya)	Yajnavalkya
Krishna Yajur Veda	1. Taittiriya	Taittiriya	Tittiri
	2. Maitrayani	Maitrayani	Maitrayani
	3. Katha	Kathaka	Kathaka
Sama Veda	1. Kauthumi	1. Pancha Vinsha (also known as Praudha, Tandya, Maha Brahmana)	*
		2. Shadvinsha	*
		3. Samvidhana	*
		4. Arsheya	*
		5. Mantra	*
		6. Devatadhyaya	*
		7. Vansha	*
		8. Samhitopanishad	*
	2. Ranayaniya	Available in Sutra Granthas	*
	3. Jaiminiya	1. Jaiminiya (Arsheya)	*
		2. Jaiminiya Talawakar	*
		3. Jaiminiya Upanishad (Chandogya Brahmana)	*
Atharva Veda	1. Shaunaka	Gopatha	Gopatha
	2. Pippalada	—	

* not available

importance of the Brahmana Granthas. They are like the thread in a garland holding the flowers together. The thread is not visible, but it is not dispensable. Similarly, the Brahmana Granthas are indispensable for the proper conduct and successful culmination of a yajna.

From the geographical references found in the Brahmana Granthas, it can be inferred that they were created and developed on the banks of the Saraswati river in the area

[3] Source: *Vedic Literature and Culture,* Acharya Baldev Upadhyaya, Delhi, 1990

known as Kuru and Panchal Pranta. The association with Saraswati is particularly prominent in the *Tandya Brahmana*. Let us now take a brief look at the structure/form and contents of some of the extant Brahmanas.

Aitareya Brahmana: The *Aitareya Brahmana* is part of the *Rig Veda*. Rishi Mahidasa Aitareya is said have composed this text. Some believe that Aitareya was a shudra, and the only known one to have compiled a text of such standards. *Structure*: The text is clubbed into sections *(kandika)*, kandikas into chapters *(adhyayas)*, adhyayas into pentagonal forms *(panchika)*, and there are five adhyayas in each panchika. The *Aitareya Brahmana* has 285 kandikas, 40 adhyayas and 8 panchikas. It is the main treatise covering all the activities of the hotri group in chanting the invocation hymns in soma yajnas. Some of the important suktas and rituals are ishtis, pravargya, three savanas, shastra, etc. The compositions of the *Rig Veda* chanted during the savanas are called shastras. The *Aitareya Brahmana* covers all the shastras used in the main soma yajnas as also their variations. It also gives details of the rituals at a rajasooya yajna, and the important rite of the coronation of a king based on Indra *mahabhisheka*.

The *Aitareya Brahmana* is equally important from the point of view of religion and spirituality. Its study can give a fair idea of how the Puranic form of god – Lord Vishnu – gained prominence in Vedic society as the saviour. The famous anecdote of King Harishchandra (an ancestor of Lord Rama) and Shunahshepa appears in this Brahmana.

In general, the spiritual subjects of the Aranyakas and Upanishads and their opinion on the origin of the universe are found to have their roots in the philosophical expositions contained in the Brahmana Granthas. The *Aitareya Brahmana* also covers topics of spiritual importance leading to creation of the important *Aitareya Upanishad*.

Brahmins belonging to the Ashvalayana branch have used the *Aitareya Brahmana* predominantly. They are mostly found in the part of India lying to the south of the Narmada river from the Saihyadri mountain ranges to Andhra Pradesh.

The spiritual importance of rituals, the significance of actions and the relevance of the whole physical yajna process is sometimes brought out in the Brahmana Granthas through interesting metaphorical anecdotes. The *Aitareya Brahmana* highlights the importance of righteous behaviour for a king through such an anecdote.

King Harishchandra had been without a son for a long time. Once, when Narada paid a visit to his court, the king said, "O venerable saint, everyone (the wise and the idiot) aspires for a son and so do I. Please tell me what I should do." In reply, Narada made a general statement, "O king, he who has the fortune to view the moonlike face of a son becomes free from debt to the forefathers (pitri rin)." He then advised the king to worship Varuna devata. Accordingly, the king prayed to Varuna with all humility and faith, so much so that he promised he would donate his son to Varuna in a yajna. "So be it," said Varuna, who had appeared before the king, pleased with his prayers. When the son (Rohit) was born, Varuna came to claim him. The king pleaded that an animal was fit for sacrifice only after it was ten days old. "Granted," said Varuna and went away, only to come back on the eleventh day. Now the king made an excuse saying that an animal was only worthy of sacrifice after it had developed its first teeth. In this way, the king stalled Varuna for a long time, using one trick or another.

Finally, when the king decided to perform the yajna, the son fled to the forest. Infuriated at the king's behaviour, Varuna cursed him with leprosy. On the advice of Lord Indra, the boy stayed away from the king. Finally, after six long years he returned to the capital, but with an alternative for the yajna, a boy named Shunahshepa. This substitute was acceptable to Varuna. The story goes on to say that the boy pleaded with the Vedic gods for his life, and was liberated. He then performed a special soma yajna as a result of which the king regained good health and prosperity.

It is said that the hota tells this story to every king who performs the rajasooya yajna. The adhvaryu and the king are supposed to hear it. The adhvaryu gives his consent by uttering two words 'aum' and 'tatha'. Aum is the godly quality and tatha is human power. Thus, the king obtains both, thereby being able to conduct his duties properly and make his subjects happy and contented. Plus, he is blessed with a son.

Taittiriya Brahmana: This is part of the *Krishna Yajur Veda,* and was compiled by Rishi Tittiri, a disciple of Vaishampayana. The text is grouped into sections (anuvaka), anuvakas into chapters (prapathaka), and prapathakas into kandas. The *Taittiriya Brahmana* has 338 anuvakas, 28 prapathakas and 3 kandas[4].

The first kanda is called parakshudra. It deals with rituals concerning the establishment of sacrificial fire and soma yagas up to vajapeya. It also describes the procedures of rajasooya yajna.

The second kanda is called agnihotra. It deals with rituals concerning the maintenance of shrautagni by householders and the offering of cow's milk. The agnihotra ritual is done twice a day, every day. This kanda also gives details of rituals in yajnas like upahoma, sautramani (for Indra devata) and various satras (yagas spanning a number of days).

The third kanda, according to researchers, is an addendum from a later period. It deals with the nakshatra ishti in detail. It also gives details of the sacrificial animals in purushamedha yajna. The last three prapathakas of this kanda are designated as *Kathaka Brahmana*. The eleventh prapathaka has an anecdote that indicates the vastness of the Vedas.

Sage Bharadvaja observed austerities to gain knowledge of all the Vedas. Pleased with his sadhana, the Lord himself appeared before Bharadvaja and asked him to demand the choicest thing, *varam bruhi*. "O Lord, let knowledge of the entire Vedas come to me," Bharadvaja requested with humility. "So be it," said the Lord, and, lo and behold, the Vedas appeared in the form of a huge, luminous and shining

---

[4] *Krishna Yajur Veda,* Shrautacharya Bapat & P. Hirlekar (trans.), Amaravati, Maharashtra, 1994

mountain. Bharadvaja was overawed by the almost limitless expanse of this vision, and conceded that his wisdom and intellect were inadequate to grasp it. He then asked for only three fistfuls of the Vedas. And it is believed that only that much is extant today.

The moral of the story is that the Vedas symbolize limitless knowledge. The available, known or visible part is just a miniscule of the whole, *ananta vai vedaha*. Scientists also accept that their knowledge of the universe is equal to an epsilon (a very small value tending to zero, but not zero). The rest is a mystery.

The *Taittiriya Brahmana* also contains, in the same prapathaka, the famous story of Yama and Nachiketa in a subtle form. These legends would indicate a convergence of the *Yajur Veda* with spirituality. The Brahmana is one of the most ancient texts on yajna. The yajus mantras appearing in this Brahmana are given with *swaras* or rules of pronunciation, which is its unique quality. Other Brahmanas are generally in prose form.

While on the *Taittiriya Brahmana*, Acharya Baldev Upadhaya points out that the *Sama Veda* has been designated by this Brahmana as the topmost step of the ladder of the Vedas and Vedic literature. According to him, the Brahmana mentions that idol and vaishya (merchants) have been created from Rig mantras, movement and kshatriya (warriors) from yajus mantras, and jyoti (flame) and brahmin from the Sama Veda. In this way, this Brahmana assigns the highest importance to the *Sama Veda*. This goes well with Lord Krishna's proclamation in the *Bhagavad Gita* too:

वेदानां सामवेदोऽस्मि

Vedaanaam saamvedosmi.

I am Sama Veda among the Vedas.

During a yajna, the time, location and directional parameters of various rituals are very important. Specific things have to be done at specific times or muhurtas (auspicious times).

The *Taittiriya Brahmana* deals mainly with the prescriptions, descriptions and injunctions for ritualistic operations and actions by the adhvaryu. It also discusses jyotish shastra that enables one to decide such auspicious times and other details. Therefore, from the point of view of yajna, this Brahmana assumes prime importance.

The recensed form of the *Yajur Veda* by sage Tittiri was prevalent in Andhra Pradesh, the parts south and east of the Narmada river and the areas along the Godavari river down to the sea. Even today, yajnas performed in this part of the country make use of the *Taittiriya Brahmana* as a base for the adhvaryu's actions. The yajna procedures based on this Brahmana were so common and overwhelming in the daily routine of southern India that it was said that in these parts even cats had knowledge of the *Taittiriya Brahmana*.

Shatapatha Brahmana: It is a part of the *Shukla Yajur Veda*. There are two branches of the *Shukla Yajur Veda* – Madhyandina and Kanva. Their Brahmana Granthas are separate, but both are named 'Shatapatha Brahmana'. The *Shatapatha Brahmana* of the Madhyandina branch is also known as the Vajasaneya branch. It is authored by Sage Yajnavalkya for the most part, and co-authored by Sandilya for a few chapters.

The *Shatapatha Brahmana* is by far the most important of all the Brahmana Granthas. It is vast and exhaustive in coverage. The best of the expositions on yajna are found in this Brahmana. Hence, as a reference guide it is of unique importance to all priests vested with the responsibility for performing a yajna. According to Satyashrava, "A brahmachari who is well-versed in the *Rig Veda* never finds any difficulty in reading the other Vedas. It is easy for him to understand them. Similarly, a student who is conversant with the *Shatapatha Brahmana* is considered to be skilled in ritualism. It is easy for him to comprehend the other Brahmanas. The *Shatapatha Brahmana* is the key to the meaning of the Vedas. It clearly explains all the subjects of the Vedas, and is the correct exposition of Vedic history."

The text of the *Shatapatha Brahmana* is grouped into sections (kandika), kandikas into divisions (Brahmana), Brahmanas into units (prapathaka), and prapathakas into chapters called kandas. The *Shatapatha Brahmana* has 7624 kandika, 438 Brahmanas, 68 prapathakas and 100 kandas[5]. Why the name Shatapatha? The most common explanation is that it contains a hundred *(shata)* chapters. However, the Brahmana Grantha of the Kanva branch has 104 chapters, so the explanation is not quite apt. According to Dr. Urmila Devi Sharma[6], the term must have derived from the generic name 'Shatapathai brahmins' for the group of people who undertook the study and exposition of this text. She gives two arguments in favour of her postulation: (i) deriving a terminology from generic words was very common in Vedic literature. For example, *Taittiriya Brahmana* got its title from the name of its author, Tittiri, or Tandya from Tandi, etc. (ii) in Assam and Orissa, one finds a branch of people called 'Satpathi', who are possibly the progeny of the rishis of the Shatapatha family race.

The first nine kandas of the *Shatapatha Brahmana* cover rituals (other than pitri pinda yajna) described in the first 18 chapters of the *Yajur Veda Samhita* (Vajasaneya). The first five are the oldest part of the compilation, and the remaining four are subsequent recensions. These are attributed to Yajnavalkya, and he is often quoted as the ultimate authority for various rites. Kandas six to ten appear to be the creation of Rishi Sandilya, as there is not a single reference to Yajnavalkya in them. Sandilya is famous for expounding the secret of Agni, which is found in the tenth kanda. Thus, it can be said that the *Shatapatha Brahmana* gives details of shrauta yajna vidhis based on Yajnavalkya's exposition, and of rites such as *agni chayana* (relating to the preparation and piling of the sacred fire altar). The last (11 to 14) four

[5] *A History of Indian Literature,* A. Weber, Chaukhamba, Varanasi, 1961
[6] *Shatapatha Brahmana – Ek Samskrit Adhyana,* Urmila Devi Sharma, Meherchand Lachmandas Publications, New Delhi, 1982

kandas are in the form of appendices, as they deal with topics like the thread ceremony, vedavrata (vratadesha), swadhaya, etc., which are not in line with the subjects covered in earlier kandas. Chapter 13 gives details of purushamedha, ashvamedha and rajasooya yajnas. Chapter 14 gives the pravargya vidhi. At the end of the *Shatapatha Brahmana* is the famous and exhaustive *Brihadaranayaka Upanishad*.

As in all other Brahmanas, in the *Shatapatha Brahmana* too, yajna is equated with Prajapati, the lord of creation. Yajna is said to be the soul of all yajna implements and gods. Therefore, everything, be it material (dravya), darbha grass, implements, rites, or the people related to yajna, have equal importance and are of the same hymnic power. The *Shatapatha Brahmana* gives minute details of even apparently insignificant things. For example, it goes into a precise explanation of where the yajna patra is to be kept near the altar, and how. Should darbha grass point to the east or north? While crossing the hota, should one go around his front or back? Should the articles of oblation be poured into the fire from the north, south or centre? What should the pitch be for chanting different mantras, the sequence of rituals and actions that follow? And so on. The purpose of putting down these details goes very deep – helping to create spiritual convergence and righteous behaviour. Actions in dravya yajnas are symbolic. In order to reap the spiritual advantage, there has to be perfect harmony between internal processes and actions. The thought process and karma (cause and effect) must have resonance.

At the beginning of a yajna, two oblations are made – one for the mind and the other for speech. The first is known as *poorvadhara ahuti*, and is to be offered by the priest in a sitting posture. The other is known as *uttara ahuti* and is to be offered by the priest in a standing posture. The apparent reason is that the mind first contemplates, and then resolves upon the action to be taken. The resolution requires thought and concentration, hence the sitting pose. Action demands movement (symbolic), hence the standing pose. Without coherence between the two, no yajnic process is possible. Agni represents the male tattwa, and soma the female tattwa. In order to achieve coherence between the consumer and the consumed, a second symbolic action is performed for the benefit of the whole world – the soma juice is offered as oblation into Agni. And so it is said that the whole world is made from two principles: Agni and Soma *(Agnishomatmakam jagata)*.

A few more examples will emphasize how seemingly irrelevant or even ridiculous actions during the yajnic process carry an embedded purpose of creating spiritual convergence.

In its opening kandika, the *Shatapatha Brahmana* says that the person undertaking yajna, i.e. the host (yajamana), should seat himself between the two principal fire-pits (ahavaniya and garhapatya agni) facing east, and dip his hands in water. This is a symbolic action. If its significance is lost, the action becomes a pointless, mechanical exercise. If the significance is borne in mind, however, the action can take its performer to a different plane altogether. Flimsy explanations such as 'the purpose of this ritual is to disinfect the yajamana's hands' would then not be given. The action is aimed at purifying the mind of the yajamana. Yajna is a holy rite. One has to become pure to undertake such a rite. One has to accept that one speaks lies and therefore can be considered impure, or sinful. It is necessary to wash away such sins and become pure internally. The yajamana should think, "I am not sacred. Water is said to be pure and acceptable in the yajnic processes. Let me purify myself by coming in contact with a pure thing. I will undertake the sacred act of yajna after I become so purified. Using water, I shall wash away my impurity and then undertake the sacred act." He should touch the water with this mindset.

Another simple act is the observation of a fast by the yajamana on the penultimate day of the yajna. Rishi Ashadha Savayasa explains the reason. Gods (devatas) can read the mind of the person performing the yajna. They know that whoever undertakes a yajna will offer oblations (their food) in the morning ritual, and so they assemble there a day in advance and stay overnight *(upa vasati)*. Therefore, in general, the day prior to any religious observance is known as *upavasata* (or upavasa). If there is a guest in the house, it is also customary in India for the host not to take food until the guest has been served. To do otherwise is considered improper, or a sin of sorts. How then can the yajamana dine on the night prior to the yajna when the ensemble of expectant gods has arrived? In fact, Rishi Ashadha Savayasa makes an injunction that under no circumstances should the yajamana eat on the previous night.

Sage Yajnavalkya, however, raises a different point altogether, and puts the yajamana in a fix. He says that a householder feeds his ancestors every day before a meal (pitri yajna), and going without meals on any day would amount to denying them food! If the yajamana observes a fast, he will leave the ancestors without dinner and if he eats, he will violate the tradition of not eating before guests are fed. Whether he eats or not, he commits a sin. What should the yajamana do?

Yajnavalkya comes to the rescue of the host too. He says that the yajamana should eat only items that do not amount to a meal, such as bulbous roots grown in the woods. In this way, he does not keep the ancestors hungry, and at the same time does not violate the hosting rules with respect to gods because such items are not used in preparing the food for the yajna. Humour apart, this story underlines the mental observance of a great tradition, thus helping one to remain as pure as possible mentally. The *Shatapatha Brahmana* has quite a few such stories interspersed in between long and monotonous discussions on rituals. The Brahmana also discusses, in an interesting manner, subjects such as secrets of the creation of the universe, rules that maintain the dynamic equilibrium, ecology, union of the individual soul with Brahman, etc. It was translated into English and German by devoted researchers like Max Muller, Keith, Weber, etc., highlighting the importance of this treatise in understanding the philosophy, form and features of yajna, and thereby the theme of life of Vedic society.

The *Shatapatha Brahmana* was in use in the regions of Anga, Banga and Kalinga (currently Bihar, Bengal and Orissa), and Gujarat. It was commonly known in the regions of Punjab and Uttar Pradesh too. Great scholars like Hariswamy and Uvata were the followers of this recension of the *Yajur Veda*.

Tandya Brahmana: This Brahmana is part of the *Sama Veda*. According to Sayanacharya, *Sama Veda* has nine Brahmana Granthas. However, some researchers hold the view that these nine Brahmanas are not separate treatises, but only parts of a single *Sambrahmana Grantha*. For reasons not clearly known, they might have assumed a separate existence. The *Tandya Brahmana* is supposed to be the largest among all the Brahmanas of the *Sama Veda*.

The title of *Tandya Brahmana* is derived from its root branch, the *Tandi* branch of the *Sama Veda*. It consists of 25 chapters and hence is also known as *Pancha Vinsha Brahmana*. Because of its voluminous size, it is also popularly called *Maha Brahmana*. The series of names do not end here. Since this Brahmana is the oldest of all *Sama Veda* Brahmanas, it is also called *Praudha* (aged) *Brahmana*.

We have seen that large yajnas require four groups of priests. The udgitha group is vested with the responsibility of singing the praises in honour of the yajna devata who is invoked through mantra chanting (by the hota group) and oblations made (by the adhvaryu group) at auspicious moments. The role of the udgata ritvijs in all types of yajna, big or small, is vividly explained in this Brahmana, which has 347 kandas and 25 prapathakas.

The method of singing the praises is an important characteristic of the *Sama Veda*. They are described in the second and third chapters, and are known as *trivrit*, *panchadasha*, *saptadasha*, *stoma*, etc. The richas and the style of singing them for yajnas that span more than a year (such as gavamayana yajna) are described in the fourth and fifth chapters. The procedures for soma yagas, setting up of the audumbari, details of dronakalasha, etc. are described in chapters six to nine. The details of settings for dvadasha yagas and some ekaha yagas are given in chapters 15 to 19 whereas chapters 20 to 22 cover details of ahina yajnas. Lastly, yajnas of long duration (satra) are covered in chapters 23 to 25.

The *Tandya Brahmana* is related to the Kauthuma recension, and was prevalent in Gujarat. The tradition of using Kauthuma samas is common there even today.

Gopatha Brahmana: This Brahmana belongs to the *Atharva Veda*, and was composed by Rishi Gopatha. It belongs to the Shaunaka branch of the *Atharva Veda*.

The text is grouped into kandas. Kandas are grouped into prapathakas. It has two volumes – Poorva Gopatha and Uttara Gopatha. The Poorva Gopatha has five prapathakas and the Uttara Gopatha has six. There is a total of 258 kandas. Gopatha is considered to be a late addition to the set of Brahmana Granthas. Interestingly, it claims that its root Veda is the base from which Rig and the three Vedas were created. It is said to be the origin of pranava omkara from which the whole world has taken birth. Hence, the *Atharva Veda* is primary to the whole universe.

This Brahmana Grantha contains praise of the brahma priest. In addition, the first volume covers all the major yajnas. It also gives a detailed account of the rules for *prati veda brahmacharya,* and recommends that a student should spend a decade studying each Veda. A beautiful exposition of the Gayatri mantra is given. The third to sixth prapathakas give details of the actions of the four groups of priests who participate in a soma yajna. From the contents of the Brahmana, some researchers infer that the author belonged to the central province of India (Madhya Pradesh). However, according to Satyashrava, the followers of the Shaunaka recension of the *Atharva Veda* were mostly from Gujarat. Now its followers are few and found mostly in Gujarat.

ARANYAKAS

Like the Brahmana Granthas, every branch of the Vedas has its own Aranyaka.

Table 21: List of Aranyakas

Name of Aranyaka	Belongs to Veda	Some details
Aitareya	Rig Veda	In 5 parts: 1–3 authored by Mahidasa Aitareya, 4 by Ashvalayana, 5 by Shaunaka
Kaushitaki (also known as Shankhayana)	Rig Veda	15 chapters, 137 kandas
Taittiriya	Krishna Yajur Veda	10 prapathakas, 117 anuvaka
Brihad (Madhyandina)	Shukla Yajur Veda	Part of Shatapatha Brahmana (14th kanda)
Brihad (Kanva)	Shukla Yajur Veda	17th kanda of Kanva Shatapatha Brahmana
Chandogya	Sama Veda	Combined with Chandogya Upanishad. Only first part is Aranyaka
Jaimini	Sama Veda from Jaimini Brahmana	Has no separate identity

UPANISHADS

In general, the language of the Upanishads is very simple and lucid. The sentences are short but expressive, and understandably so because the content is not theoretical. The authors were not trying to convey carefully developed points, but were giving expression to the experiences they had actually undergone. So the language is dialogue-oriented. Because of the simplicity of presentation and depth of exposition, all categories of people – from ordinary to extremely erudite – have acknowledged them. They have been ubiquitous in all parts of India (now the whole world) in all ages. In fact, in many parts of India verses from the Upanishads are chanted daily.

The Upanishads were written by different rishis at different times, so there is variation in the thought processes, language, etc. But by and large, the philosophy propounded can be grouped into four parts: (i) knowledge about the Lord (Ishvara), (ii) knowledge about the universe, (iii) knowledge about atman, and (iv) knowledge about Brahman.

The construction of the Upanishad Granthas dates back to the Vedic times. This point is supported by views expressed by sage Panini, the Sanskrit grammarian from the 5th century BC, in his masterpiece *Ashtadhyai*. The creation of Upanishadic texts continued until the 14th or 15th century AD.

There are a large number of Upanishads, though there are different views about the exact number. The *Muktopanishad* mentions 108. Adi Shankara has written a commentary on 10 principal Upanishads, jointly known as *Dashopanishad*. Details of these and three others are given in Table 22.

Table 22: List of Upanishads

Name of Upanishad	Veda to which it belongs	Composer rishi	Shanti mantra
Aitareya	Rig Veda	M. Aitareya	Vang me manasi . . .
Brihadaranyaka	Shukla Yajur Veda	Yajnavalkya	Poornamadah . . .
Chandogya	Sama Veda	Uddalaka Aruni	Sahana vavatu . . .
Ishavasya	Shukla Yajur Veda	Yajnavalkya	Poornamadah . . .
Katha	Krishna Yajur Veda	Katha	Sahana vavatu . . .
Kaushitaki	Rig Veda	Shankhayana	Vang me manasi . . .
Kena	Sama Veda	Jaimini	Apyayantu mamangani . . .
Maitrayani	Sama Veda	Maitri	Apyayantu mamangani . . .
Mandukya	Atharva Veda	Mandukya	Bhadram karne bhi . . .
Mundaka	Atharva Veda	Shaunaka	Bhadram karne bhi . . .
Prashna	Atharva Veda	Pippalada	Bhadram karne bhi . . .
Shvetashvatara	Krishna Yajur Veda	Shvetashvatara	Sahana vavatu . . .
Taittiriya	Krishna Yajur Veda	Tittiri	Sham no mitrah . . .

VEDANGAS

The Vedas prescribe kratvartha (ritualistic actions for righteous behaviour). Following kratvartha implies action (karma). The Vedas are also called Shrutis, and therefore a karma that follows kratvartha is known as shrauta karma. In order that a shrauta karma is performed properly, perfectly and as per the Vedic injunctions, the Vedas (i.e. Samhitas, Brahmanas, etc.) have to be deeply understood and rightly interpreted. A set of six sciences (shastras) known as Vedangas helps the practising brahmins in this effort.

Vedangas explain the structure of mantras. The orderly form of Mantra Samhitas owes a lot to these shastras. The six Vedangas are: (i) Shiksha, (ii) Kalpa, (iii) Vyakarana, (iv) Nirukta, (v) Chandas, and (vi) Jyotish.

Shiksha, Vyakarana and Nirukta are used to interpret the meaning of richas and Brahmana texts. Kalpa and Jyotish help in the operational part of yajna. Chandas is used in chanting. In Vedic society, children were taught Vyakarana after the upanayana (thread ceremony) samskara. Once knowledge of varna and swara was gained and pronunciation perfected, they were initiated into the study of the Vedas.

Shiksha: *Shiksha* means phonetics. The richas have to be chanted in a particular manner. Shiksha Granthas contain in-depth discussions on how to clearly pronounce consonants, vowels, their combinations, etc. The science is so complete and perfect that it can be said that a person who has acquired mastery in Shiksha can chant the Veda richas and other stotras faultlessly. All branches of each Veda have separate Shiksha Granthas.

There is a beautiful couplet that describes how a Shiksha expert handles the consonants, vowels, words, etc. It asks "How should a varna be pronounced?" and answers, "A tigress holds her cubs by the neck with her sharp teeth while transporting them from one place to another, holding neither too tightly so as not to cause injury, nor too loosely so they do not slip out. A Shiksha expert carries the varna in his mouth elegantly and lets it out (in the form of sound) with grace." If the Vedas were to be personified, Shiksha would be the nose (the nasal cavity causes sound).

Kalpa: In metaphoric language, the Kalpa Sutras are the hands of the Veda Purusha. This indicates their importance in the conduct of Vedic yajnas.

The term 'kalpa sutra' is a combination of two words: *kalpa*, meaning vidhi, injunction, etc., and *sutra*, meaning short, cryptic formula. So, a Kalpa Sutra is a treatise that documents all the processes, sequence of operations, injunctions, moral rules for the participants of a yajna, etc. in minute detail.

Details of the mantras to be used in any yajna are available in the Mantra Samhitas, and the procedures are found in the Brahmana Granthas. One may then ask why there is a need for additional books like the Kalpa Sutras. An analogy will make this clear. In order to conduct a laboratory experiment or to install software in a computer, we always need a step-by-step practical guide. In the complex process of yajna, the Kalpa Sutras act as such a guide for the priests. In installing software, not even the slightest variation from the prescribed steps is tolerable, otherwise the end result will not be achieved. Similarly, for a yajna to yield the desired result, multiple sets of actions, concurrent mantra chanting, awareness of auspicious moments (muhurta), and knowledge of directions is very important for the priests performing the yajna.

The drill for learning such details was undergone by the would-be priests in schools where they received initiation. Initially, for every Veda there was a unique residential school. The theoretical knowledge and subtle details of practical aspects were learnt, practised and perfected under the guidance of a guru. Over a period of time, this tradition started fading out. However, simultaneously, the branches of the Vedas started to grow. In the absence of an avenue for proper training, the emphasis on perfection and correct propagation as well as the quality and precise knowledge of the performing priests began to be diluted. With such diluted procedures, naturally yajna could not yield the desired results. Therefore, a need was felt to document the finer details in the form of a guide for practising priests. For any doubt or difficulty, alternatives for materials (in the event of the prescribed material not being available), these books became the last word. Each branch of the Vedas developed its own Kalpa Sutra treatises. They are not the do's and don'ts, but the nuts and bolts of the yajnic procedure.

The Kalpa Sutras comprise four types of sutras: Shrauta Sutra, Shulba Sutra, Grihya Sutra and Dharma Sutra. Together they give a complete set of the operational requirements of a yajna. The Shrauta Sutras cover the details for shrauta yajnas (e.g. darshapoornamas or other yajnas using three fires). The Shulba Sutras give geometrical requirements and constructional details required to set up the fire altar and yajnashala. The Grihya Sutras cover the details of smarta yajnas (16 samskaras, last rites, rites for entry into a new house, and the popular tantric yajnas based on a single fire). They also cover the code of conduct recommended for a householder. An individual becomes 'samskrit' through samskaras, and is then eligible to perform kamya and other yajnas. Whereas the Grihya Sutras shape personal behaviour, the Dharma Sutras shape an individual's interactions with society. They discuss the behaviour expected of people from all varnas (brahmin, kshatriya, vaishya, shudra), the rules to be followed for inter-class mixing, expiation for wrongs done, and the punitive actions required for an offence.

The Shrauta Sutras and Shulba Sutras are inter-dependent, and there is commonality between the Grihya Sutras and Dharma Sutras. The Dharma Sutras are expansive, and not limited to yajna alone. They deal with the complete behaviour of members of the Vedic society. The Kalpa Sutras are very important for yajna. The following tables give details.

Table 23: Shrauta Sutras

Veda	Veda Branch	Name of Sutra
Rig Veda	Ashvalayana	Ashvalayana
	Bashkala	*
	Kaushitaki	*
	Mandukya	*
	Shankhayana	Shankhayana
	Shakala	*
Krishna Yajur Veda	Taittiriya	Apastamba
		Baudhayana
		Bharadvaja
		Hiranyakeshi
		Vadhula
		Vaikhanasa
	Maitrayani	Maitrayani
		Manava
		Varaha
Shukla Yajur Veda	Kanva	Katyayana
	Madhyandina	Katyayana
Sama Veda	Kauthumi	Latyayana
	Jaimini	Pushpa
	Ranayaniya	Drahyayana
Atharva Veda	Shaunaka	Vaitana

* not available

Table 24: Shulba Sutras

Veda	Veda branch	Name of sutra
Rig Veda		Nil
Krishna Yajur Veda	Taittiriya	Apastamba
		Baudhayana
		Maitrayani
		Manava
		Satyashadha
		Vadhula
		Varaha
Shukla Yajur Veda	Vajasaneyi	Katyayana
Sama Veda		Nil
Atharva Veda		Nil

Table 25: Grihya Sutras

Veda	Veda branch	Name of sutra	Main subjects
Rig Veda	Ashvalayana	Ashvalayana	16 samskaras, krishi karma, pitrimedha
	Bashkala	*	
	Kaushitaki	Kaushitaki	16 samskaras, krishi karma, pitrimedha
	Mandukya	*	
	Shankhayana	Shankhayana	Griha nirmana, griha pravesha
Krishna Yajur Veda	Taittiriya	Apastamba	Godan, griha pravesha, bali, vastu shamana, shraaddha, ashtaka, prayaschitta
		Baudhayana	Grihya Sutra, srihya paribhasha, griha shesha, pitrimedha
		Bharadvaja	Vivaha (modernized by this sutra)
		Hiranyakeshi (also known as Satyashadha)	Grihya anushthana (in great detail)
		Vadhula	Also known as Agnivesha
		Vaikhanasa	
	Katha	Kathaka	Recently found in Kashmir, also known as Laugakshi
	Maitrayani	Maitrayani	
		Manava	Chakra poojan, vadhu swapna, vastra alankara, daan, four vinayaka poojas
		Varaha	Copied from Manava and Kathaka
Shukla Yajur Veda	Kanva	Paraskara (Katiya)	Most superior of all Grihya Sutras. Daily samskaras, anna bali, monthly/annual karmas, griha nirmana, prayaschitta karma, abhichara karma
	Madhyandina	Paraskara	
Sama Veda	Kauthumi	Gobhila	General information on samskaras. Yashaskama karma, purusha-dhipatya karma, vritya vicchhiti kama karma, purshtika karma (these are uniquely found only in this sutra)
	Jaimini	Jaiminiya	Last rites, ashtaka
	Ranayaniya	Drahyayana Khadira	
Atharva Veda	Shaunaka	Kaushika	Copied from all other Grihya Sutras with some abhichara mantras added.

* not available

Table 26: Dharma Sutras

Veda	Veda branch	Name of sutra	Main subjects
Rig Veda	Authentic for all branches	Vashishtha	Rights of heirs, special duties of four varnas
Krishna Yajur Veda	Taittiriya	Apastamba	Connected to Poorva Mimamsa
		Baudhayana Hiranyakeshi	Unorganized and loose
	Katha	Vishnu	Narrated by Lord Vishnu. As old as Gautama and Apastamba sutras
	Maitrayani	Nil	
Shukla Yajur Veda	Madhyandina	Shankha	In prose form
Sama Veda	Kauthumi	Gautama	Oldest of all Dharma Sutras. Probably the only sutra available as Kalpa Sutra. Language resembles Panini. Covers all subjects
Atharva Veda	Shaunaka	Nil	

Vyakarana: This limb of the Veda Purusha is third in order, but of prime importance. It is said to be his mouth. Customarily, the beginning of a pupil's Vedic studies would start with Vyakarana.

Normally, verbal language is used to communicate and express thoughts. One needs to develop a correct understanding of the rules of language and word usage. Vyakarana shastra was developed, in Sanskrit, to create appropriate samskaras on the language. *Kru* means to do. The word 'vyakarana' is formed from this root by adding two prefixes, *vi* and *aa*. It is said that to board a punctured boat to cross the Ganges, to medicate without observing dietary restraint, and to study language without Vyakarana are all equally unprofitable and unwise propositions.

For the proper dispensation of Rig mantras in a yajna, it is expected that the gender and case be modified according to the action. This is not possible without a sound knowledge of Vyakarana, and so it was mandatory for practising priests to study Vyakarana before other subjects.

As the story goes, Brahma first taught Vyakarana to the guru of the gods, Brihaspati, who taught it to Indra, who in turn passed it on to rishis like Bharadvaja. It was then spread among all the purohitas and ritvijs (*Riktantra* 2.4).

Today, Panini's *Vyakarana Grantha* is the acknowledged treatise on Vyakarana. He achieved perfection in the subject in his *Ashtadhyayi* after minutely going through all the contemporary and older books, and improving upon their shortcomings and ambiguities.

Nirukta: Nirukta is the fourth part of the Vedangas. Metaphorically, it is equated with the ears of the Veda Purusha. Like Vyakarana, Nirukta is also associated with Sanskrit words and their meanings. However, there is a slight difference between the approaches to words. Nirukta employs a novel method of explaining the meanings of Vedic words through an alphabetical ordering, as against the method of splitting them (using case, suffix, prefix, etc.) in Vyakarana. Yaskacharya has defined this term as follows. *Nirukta – ni + (shesh tah) ukta* – means that which is explained without excluding even a single word. A grantha that takes into account: (i) the entire word along with its implicit as well as explicit meanings, and (ii) includes the word in totality for the purpose of explaining the meaning is Nirukta. It not only covers the dictionary meaning, but also includes etymology that is in congruence with the meaning. There is as much etymological equivalence as the meaning of the word[6]. This can be explained by an example.

Q: *Nadya kasmat? Nadanaaha bhavanti = shabdavatyah?* (From which root is the word nadi formed? And why it is called 'nadi'?)

A1: Nirukta: 'Nadi' is formed from the root *nad*, meaning to make noise. The rivers flow with a loud sound. According to Nirukta, this is the reason for using the word 'nadi' for river.

---

[6] *Niruktam,* Dr. Umashankar Sharma, Chaukhamba Vidya Bhavan, Varanasi

A2: Vyakarana: 'Nadee' is a feminine noun with a long ending ('ee' karant). So nadi is a nominative, singular form. It is simply a common noun designated for 'nadee'.

Yaskacharya developed Nirukta. He used an alphabetical dictionary called *Nighantu* with a collection of words to propound the nirukta shastra. However, it is said to have one drawback. Sometimes it does not take into account words like *hi*, *ho*, *tu*, *nu*, etc. while explaining the meaning of a richa, making the process of drawing a valid meaning clumsy.

Chandas: Chandas is the fifth shastra in the Vedanga series. It is equated with the legs of the Veda Purusha, a limb associated with movement. The method of arranging consonants into words, words into lines, and lines into lyrics is called *chanda,* metre. The elements of a chanda are the 33 consonants or *varnas*. Their grouping is called *pada* or *charana*. Vedic chandas do not have specific measures like *gana*, regularity, etc. The number of varnas in each pada and their short or long pronunciations decide the Vedic chanda.

The Vedic mantras are composed in chandas, which give them a structure. A chanda is made of three to five padas. The number of varnas in each pada is always fixed. Mantras derive their intrinsic power from the varnas, since each of the 33 varnas represents principles of the universe *(vishva tattwa)* or the 33 gods.

The chanda sets the mantra in motion. Mantra power is unleashed by the chanda. Mantras are sound-oriented compositions. We know that sound travels in a wave-form, and to make the desired impact at a particular point, one has to send a specific amount of wave energy in a specific way. In the case of Rig mantras, this is achieved by arranging its words following certain rules. The arrangement of varnas into words, and words into chandas gives rise to a wave pattern. Different chandas generate wave patterns of different amplitudes.

The *Rig Veda* uses more than 50 chandas. There are seven principal ones: *gayatri*, *ushnik*, *anushtubh*, *brihati*, *pankti*, *trishtubh* and *jagati*.

As mentioned earlier, each chanda has a fixed number of varnas. A reduction or increase in the total by one or two causes a modification to the structure of the chanda. Such a modified chanda is the sub-chanda of the original. For example, the gayatri chanda has 24 varnas. A gayatri with 23 varnas is called *nitchrud gayatri*, with 22 varnas *viraj gayatri*, with 25 *bhurij gayatri*, and so on. *Ganapati Atharva Shirsha Stotra* is an example of nitchrud gayatri chanda.

Chanda shastra, like many other shastras, is said to have originated from Shiva. However, its present form is owed to the effort of Pingalacharya (c. 2200 BC).

In order to chant the Vedic mantras in a pure and rhythmic manner, it is absolutely necessary for the chanter to have an in-depth knowledge of the musical notes (swara) and metre (chanda) associated with the mantra. Since varnas represent devatas, the right chanting of mantras according to chanda shastra brings about the presence of devatas. It is for this reason that one receives immense pleasure and a serene feeling when listening to perfect Vedic chants.

According to tradition, chanting of the Vedic mantras must be learnt only under a recognized authority. Self-learning using textbooks is forbidden. A pupil has to spend long years painstakingly learning the proper and perfect way of chanting at the guru's ashram. Yajna priests must have full knowledge of chandas, as specific groups need to use specific chandas. For example, in agnyadhana (a shrauta vidhi), the dvija needs to use a chanda according to his varna in the following manner:

- Brahmin: gayatri chanda
- Kshatriya: trishtubh chanda
- Vaishya: jagati chanda.

Such injunctions are not given without reason. One may dig through the Brahmana Granthas to discover it, but for the time being it may suffice to say that the injunctions cannot be diluted. Therefore, chanda shastra is of prime importance for yajna priests, and for the proper culmination of any Vedic vidhi or karma, knowledge of the chandas is essential.

Due to the importance of chandas, the tradition demands that a loud and clear mention of the chanda of a sukta along with the name of the rishi and devata be made before the chanting begins. Table 27 gives details of the main chandas.

Table 27: List of chandas

Chanda	Pada	No. of varnas in each pada and (total)		Example of chanda
Gayatri	3	8,8,8	(24)	Agni meele purohitam . . . *or* Tat savitur varenyam bhargo . . .
Ushnik	3	8,8,12	(28)	R 5,51.9
Anushtubh	4	8,8,8,8	(32)	Ramo raj mani sada vijayate . . . *or* Tryambakam yajamahe . . .
Brihati	4	8,8,8,12	(36)	R 8,87.1
Pankti	5	8,8,8,8,8	(40)	R10,64.7
Trishtubh	4	11,11,11,11	(44)	Yajnen yajnam ayajanta . . .
Jagati	4	12,12,12,12	(48)	Gana naam twa ganapati . . .

Jyotish: The sixth limb of the Veda Purusha is Jyotish. The sun god, Surya is believed to have originally propounded the basics of this shastra. The eyes have the function of seeing, but the power of vision is given by Surya. To indicate this connection, jyotish shastra is equated with the eyes of the Veda Purusha. It is one of the important ancient mathematical contributions of the Aryans. The word 'jyotish' meaning 'the science of measuring time' is found in the Puranas as well as Upanishads (*Mundaka*, *Brihad*, etc.). With reference to yajna, this science was developed mainly to decide the exact time for commencing the yajna, to decide the auspicious moments for various rituals, to decide the timespan of the yajna, to decide the position of celestial tities like the sun, moon, stars, etc. at the proposed yajna e and at specific times or time intervals, and to measure n terms of days, months, etc.

A need for this science was felt because some yajnas like the darshapoornamas ishti, etc. have to be performed on specific days (full-moon day, no-moon day, etc.). Functions such as shanti anushthana also have to be performed at specific times. It was necessary to decide the auspicious day and time for such work. Therefore, a science was developed that used five parameters (day, star, yog, karan and tithi) together with the position of various stars, the rising and setting times of the sun, moon, etc. This science is mistakenly considered as astrology whereas it is more akin to astronomy. Using positional parameters, predictions about weather, rains, overall rainfall, likely crop yields, etc. were made, but they do not form the principal purpose of the development of jyotish shastra.

Jyotish has two parts – Ganit Jyotish and Phala Jyotish. Details of this science are found in *Surya Siddhanta*, a work by Lagadha called *Vedanga Jyotish* (c. 500 BC), and in an important work by a scientist of more recent times, Varaha Mihir.

PURANAS

The Puranas contain an immense treasure of knowledge, probably next only to the Vedas. However, the large number of texts, the vastness of the subject matter, continual additions, verbosity, and above all the language (Sanskrit) used for composition, kept them away from the reach of most people. The original authentic Sanskrit texts of the Puranas are rarely to be found.

So what is a Purana? "The history of the olden times, which appears ever-novel is Purana" (*Pura api navam puranam*). The word 'purana' is found in the Veda Samhitas, Brahmanas and Upanishads. The Puranas enable one to form a realistic and true picture of the ancient traditions, civilian codes and culture. In all, there are 18 important Puranas called Maha Puranas. There is a strong view that all were composed by Maharshi Vyasa.

Table 28: 18 Puranas of Maharshi Vyasa

Agni Purana	Brahma Purana	Brahmana Purana	Brahma Vaivarta Purana	Bhagavata Purana	Bhavishya Purana
Garuda Purana	Koorma Purana	Linga Purana	Markandeya Purana	Matsya Purana	Narada Purana
Padma Purana	Shiva Purana	Skanda Purana	Vishnu Purana	Varaha Purana	Vamana Purana

In addition, there are 18 more Puranas (Upa Puranas), which are later additions to the repertoire.

Characteristics: The Puranas speak of the glory of the Lord while unfolding many stories from history. These Puranas have five characteristics: sarga, pratisarga, genealogy, the 14 Manu dynasties (Manvantaras), and the traditional way followed in the various rishi families. The subjects covered in the Puranas are the universe, its creation, its establishment in Nature, maintenance, actions (karma) as the cause, their effects, desire for action or deed *(karma vasana)*, the sequence of Manus (the representatives of each age), description of the Great Inundation, exposition on salvation (moksha), praise and prayers to Shri Hari, description of devatas, etc.

Importance: The Vedas contain knowledge about the supreme consciousness, the ultimate truth, Brahman. This is *para vidya*, and it is said in the Vedas that although this essential principle is present in everything that can be perceived or imagined, the principle itself is occult. The only way to know it is to tread the path of true knowledge. Knowledge is absence of ignorance. Ironically, the sun and knowledge have never seen their prime enemy (darkness and ignorance) because wherever they go, the enemy vanishes. True knowledge is absorbed into divine essence *(Gyanat ev kaivalyam)*.

Such formless, figureless, captionless essence is brought hin the reach of everyone through a beautiful figure h is the embodiment of grace, mercy, compassion and uch qualities. The greatness of the Puranas lies in that they have depicted God through His qualities. They have made the chanting of God's name more important than God Himself. The Puranas assure that *naam sankirtan* is the surest way to success in life. Take, for example, the mantra *Aum namo Narayanaya*. It has eight alphabets, its composer is Rishi Narayana, the chanda is gayatri and the object the imperishable Lord Vishnu. The *Narada Purana* describes this mantra as a boon in Kali yuga. Regular chanting will lead to fulfilment of all mental aspirations, good health, high intellect *(medha)*, a poetic and creative mind, contentment *(santosha)* and, above all, bliss.

The Puranas highlight the advantage of dravya yajna for material prosperity and underline its importance at the mental level for evolution. Interesting stories are found about the rajasooya yajna performed by King Harishchandra, Soma (son of Atri) and King Yudhishthira, the ashvamedha yajna performed by Rama, Bhauman (grandson of Vishvakarma), King Sagar, etc., and other yajnas performed by Sage Vishvamitra for welfare, peace and prosperity. Demon king Bali performed the ashvamedha yajna wherein Vamana, an incarnation of Lord Vishnu, asked for as much land as he could cover with just three steps. Shiva Purana gives details of the famous yajna by Daksha Prajapati wherein Sati Parvati quit her mortal body in protest.

Table 29 lists the Maha Puranas alphabetically. The numbers in column 1 shows the order of the Puranas by their spiritual (and other) importance.

Table 29: List of Maha Puranas[7]

Maha Purana No.	Name of Maha Purana	No. of slokas	Important topics covered
8	Agni Purana	15,000	Incarnations, work of agni, mantra tantra, griha, etc. yajnas
1	Brahma Purana	10,000	Life of Rama, Krishna, duties of four varnas and ashrams, etc.
18	Brahmanda Purana	12,000	Duties, formation of hiranyagarbha, Ikshvaku, etc.
10	Brahma Vaivarta Purana	18,000	Exposition of Vedic path, bhakti of Shiva & Vishnu, Ganesha, etc.
5	Bhagavata Purana	18,000	Krishna's life, Samkhya, bhakti philosophy, Kali dharma
9	Bhavishya Purana	14,000	Life story of Surya, Brahma, etc.
17	Garuda Purana	29,000	Vishnu dhyanam, last rites, etc.
15	Koorma Purana	17,000	Koorma's incarnation, Lakshmi kalpa details, duties of four varnas
11	Linga Purana	11,000	Shiva as Agni linga, 1000 names of Shiva, Daksha yajna, Gayatri, Mahamrityunjaya
7	Markandeya Purana	9000	Birds preach dharma, stories of Dattatreya, Durga, Krishna, etc.
16	Matsya Purana	14,000	Manu-Matsya dialogue, soma
6	Narada Purana	25,000	Creation of universe, ekadashi, pilgrimage places, means of salvation, Shaiva tantra
2	Padma Purana	55,000	Brahma's yajna at Pushkar, importance of daan, Shrishailya, Vishnu sahasra naam, geography, etc.
4	Shiva Purana	24,000	Shivaratri, Shiva kavacha, greatness of bhasma, importance of rudraksha and bilva
13	Skanda Purana	81,000	Legend of Harischandra and Trishanku, description of God and asuras, origin of Ganges
3	Vishnu Purana	23,000	Vaishnava Purana, stories of Dhruva, Prahlad, etc., sadachara
12	Varaha Purana	24,000	Dedicated to Vishnu's boar incarnation
14	Vamana Purana	10,000	Dedicated to Vishnu's dwarf incarnation

[7] *Bhagavata Purana and Narada Purana* (Marathi trans.), S.K. Deodhar, ...akashan, Pune, 1981

Extant or partially extant branches of the Vedas

- Vedas
  - Rig Veda
    - Ashvalayana branch – Aitareya
      - Samhita – Ashvalayana
      - Brahmana – Aitareya
      - Aranyaka – Aitareya
      - Upanishad – Aitareya
      - Kalpa Sutra
        - Shrauta Sutra – Ashvalayana
        - Shulba Sutra *
        - Grihya Sutra – Ashvalayana
        - Dharma Sutra *
  - Rig Veda
    - Bashkala branch
      - Samhita *
      - Brahmana – Kaushitaki
      - Aranyaka – Kaushitaki
      - Upanishad – Kaushitaki
      - Kalpa Sutra
        - Shrauta Sutra *
        - Shulba Sutra *
        - Grihya Sutra *
        - Dharma Sutra – Vashishtha

* not available

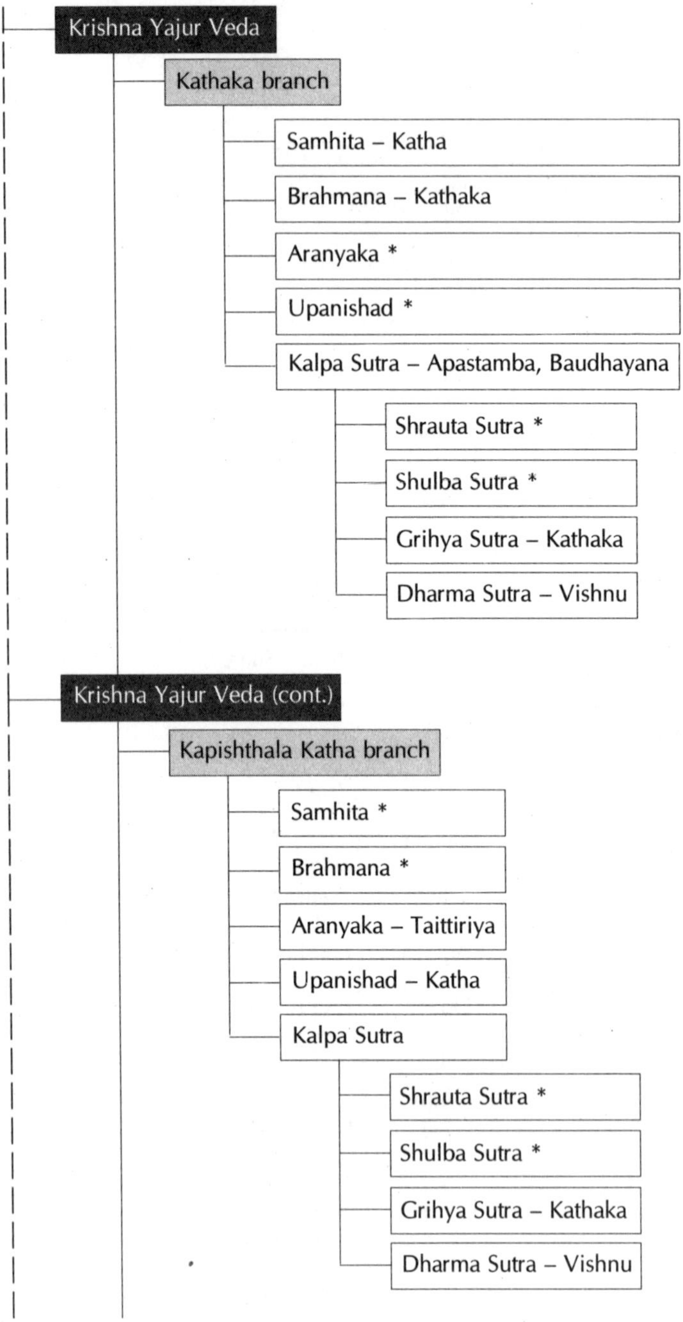

* not available

- **Krishna Yajur Veda (cont.)**
  - **Maitrayani branch**
    - Samhita – Maitrayani
    - Brahmana – Maitrayani
    - Aranyaka *
    - Upanishad – Maitrayani
    - Kalpa Sutra – Maitrayani
      - Shrauta Sutra – Maitrayani, Manava, Varaha
      - Shulba Sutra – Maitrayani, Manava, Varaha
      - Grihya Sutra – Maitrayani, Manava
      - Dharma Sutra – Vishnu
- **Krishna Yajur Veda (cont.)**
  - **Taittiriya branch**
    - Samhita – Taittiriya
    - Brahmana – Taittiriya
    - Aranyaka – Taittiriya
    - Upanishad – Taittiriya, Shevashvatara
    - Kalpa Sutra – Apastamba, Baudhayana
      - Shrauta Sutra – Apastamba, Baudhayana, Hiranyakeshi, Vadhula, Vaikhanasa
      - Shulba Sutra – Apastamba, Baudhayana, Satyashadha, Vadhula
      - Grihya Sutra – Apastamba, Baudhayana, Hiranyakeshi, Vadhula, Vaikhanasa, Bharadvaja
      - Dharma Sutra – Apastamba, Baudhayana Hiranyakeshi

* not available

- **Shukla Yajur Veda**
  - Kanva branch
    - Samhita – Kanva
    - Brahmana – Shatapatha
    - Aranyaka – Brihad
    - Upanishad –Brihadaranyaka
    - Kalpa Sutra – Katyayana
      - Shrauta Sutra – Katyayana
      - Shulba Sutra – Katyayana
      - Grihya Sutra – Paraskara
      - Dharma Sutra *

- **Shukla Yajur Veda (cont.)**
  - Madhyandina branch
    - Samhita – Vajasaneyi
    - Brahmana – Shatapatha
    - Aranyaka – Brihad
    - Upanishad – Brihadaranyaka, Ishavasya
    - Kalpa Sutra – Katyayana
      - Shrauta Sutra – Katyayana
      - Shulba Sutra – Katyayana
      - Grihya Sutra – Paraskara
      - Dharma Sutra – Shankha

* not available

- **Sama Veda**
  - Kauthumi branch
    - Samhita – Kauthumi
    - Brahmana – (8 texts)
    - Aranyaka – Chandogya
    - Upanishad – Chandogya
    - Kalpa Sutra
      - Shrauta Sutra – Latyayana
      - Shulba Sutra *
      - Grihya Sutra – Gobhila
      - Dharma Sutra – Gautama
- **Sama Veda (cont.)**
  - Jaimini branch
    - Samhita – Jaimini
    - Brahmana – Jaimini +2
    - Aranyaka – Chandogya
    - Upanishad – Chandogya, Kena
    - Kalpa Sutra
      - Shrauta Sutra – Pushpa
      - Shulba Sutra *
      - Grihya Sutra – Jaimini
      - Dharma Sutra *

* not available

- **Sama Veda (cont.)**
  - Jaimini branch
    - Samhita – Ranayaniya
    - Brahmana – Drahyayana
    - Aranyaka – Chandogya
    - Upanishad – Chandogya
    - Kalpa Sutra
      - Shrauta Sutra – Drahyayana
      - Shulba Sutra *
      - Grihya Sutra – Khadira, Drahyayana
      - Dharma Sutra *
- **Atharva Veda**
  - Shaunaka branch
    - Samhita – Shaunaka
    - Brahmana – Gopatha
    - Aranyaka *
    - Upanishad – Mandukya, Mundaka, Prashna
    - Kalpa Sutra
      - Shrauta Sutra – Vaitana
      - Shulba Sutra *
      - Grihya Sutra – Kaushika
      - Dharma Sutra *
  - Pippalada branch
    - Only Samhita available – Pippalada

* not available

ANNEXURE 2

Impressions of Vedic Society

In India, there once dwelt a society whose code of conduct was regarded as their religion. To begin with, the Vedas were the base of their religion. Later, associated literature like the Dharma Sutras, Kalpa Sutras and Smritis developed, and were also included in the religious base. The intent of the religion was twofold. At the personal level, it was aimed at progressively developing the mind, intellect and action for righteous behaviour. At the social level, it was to help each other prosper and live in peace and harmony.

A cultured, enlightened and respected individual who cared for others and was one with Nature was called 'arya'. The aim of the religion was to help individuals be 'aryan'. From this point of view, the society can be termed as one of Aryans. Since the religion of the Aryans was Veda-based, the society is interchangeably called 'Aryan society' or 'Vedic society'. Their way of life is broadly known as Vedic dharma.

According to Vedic philosophy, 'arya' is an attitude ('Udyog Parva', *Mahabharata*). "Let us make everyone an Aryan" was the manifesto of the leaders of the Vedic society. "Let noble thoughts come to us from the whole universe" was their desire for evolution.

Nobility, generosity, the principle of give and take in Nature, and interdependence and cooperation among the natural forces were the guiding principles. Nature was their role model.

The philosophers of the Aryan society saw the continuous process of creation, sustenance and dissolution in Nature as the fundamental principle – yajna in natural form. To imitate Nature, they devised prototypes of such a yajna. The natural forces and sources of energy, and their interactions were imagined as devatas. It was believed that devatas could give boons of abundance, and efforts were made to befriend them. Oblations along with hymns were offered for prosperity and peace. This was the prototype of yajna.

Some misconceptions

Although it is broadly agreed that the Vedas are the oldest available human literature and a repository of true knowledge, there are contradictory – and possibly erroneous – views about the society that fostered this treasure.

It was believed by 19th century western researchers and their early 20th century eastern counterparts that the Vedas and related texts are the literature of the 'Aryan race', which came to India from outside, defeated the local dwellers and settled along the banks of the Indus river. The people spoke Sanskrit, and followed yajnic rituals based on Vedic literature. There were three castes, brahmin, kshatriya and vaishya, and the defeated non-Aryans became the shudras.

Whatever the reasons for these beliefs, one thing is certain – they are not borne out by the facts revealed by the verses in the Vedas and other literature. Actually, there is nothing called 'the Aryan race'. Max Muller wanted an appropriate term to refer to a civilization that supposedly emerged from the Indo-European region, and became the first person to use the phrase. Later, however, he realized that the phrase was not apt, and clarified that the word arya was not to be used to refer to any race.

'Arya' denotes the quality of a person, not a race. In the *Rig Veda*, it appears only 36 times out of a total of more than 150,000 words. Such a word cannot represent a race that had the *Rig Veda* as its flagship. Further, of these 36 appearances, not even a single usage leads to the idea that

'Aryan' referred to a race. Interestingly, there is no word like non-Aryan to denote people other than Aryans.

In the *Rig Veda*, Arya indicates a cultured, learned, illustrious and honourable person. It was simply an adjective denoting the qualities of a member of society.

Colloquially, the head of a family was called Arya, and his son Aryaputra (by his wife). Learned persons were sometimes referred to as Arya X, like Arya Chanakya. *Anarya* was one who had lost such qualities; for example, Krishna refers to a confused Arjuna as 'anarya' at the beginning of the second chapter of the *Bhagavad Gita*. According to the *Mahabharata*, a person becomes arya through a virtuous attitude, not by earning wealth or knowledge ('Udyoga Parva'). Similar suggestions are also found in *Yoga Vashishtha*.

The second mistaken notion is that people of the so-called Aryan race were blue-eyed and fair-complexioned. Most famous personalities from Vedic times such as Krishna Dvaipayana Vyasa who compiled the Veda Samhitas, Lord Krishna, his most favoured disciple and friend Arjuna, the legendary lady of the *Mahabharata* – Draupadi, bluish-complexioned Lord Rama, Acharya Kanva, visionary rishis Dirghatamas, Shavya, etc. were all dark-complexioned. Whenever they were described, their complexion was not used as a contemptible adjective. On the contrary, Rig richas like *"Pishang rupah subharo . . ."* (R 2.3,9) pray for a son who has, among other qualities, a dark complexion.

However, just as arya was an adjective used for a person possessing commendable qualities, a person who had lost such qualities was also referred to as a black (dark-complexioned) person. Again, however, the word was used as an adjective for the degraded form rather than the skin pigmentation.

Such misconceptions apart, it is useful to have an idea of what various scholars have said about the origin of the Aryans, and the time period during which the *Rig Veda* assumed its form and was compiled into a Samhita.

The origins

Many researchers and scholars have studied the origin of the people who gave the Vedas to the world, but no one has been able to state the origin with clear conviction. This could be due to the absence of adequate proof or inferential links. Two opinions emerge from the findings of the studies. One school of thought believes they were the original Indians, and the second holds the view that they were immigrants. In the second group, there is no unanimity about the place from where they migrated to India.

We will take a dispassionate and statistical account of the opinions and leave the reader to draw a conclusion. This account is based mainly on:

1. Scholarly books by Dr. C. G. Kashikar and G. B. Dandge.
2. The Vedavidya section of *Maharashtriya Dnyna Kosha* by S. V. Ketkar.

The first are dispassionate and scholarly compilations. The second is a positive defence of the magnanimity of the Vedas. The *Dnyan Kosha* is a collection of views with commentary.

On the basis of some apparent commonalities in words (joan – jivah, boyos – vayuhu, serpent – sarpa, hapnos – swapnaha, mortis – mrutyuhu, etc.), some people claim that Greek, Latin, Teutonic, Celtic, Slavonic, Zend and Sanskrit are seven sisters with a single mother language. Hence, the Aryans come from somewhere in the vicinity of the places where the languages originated. However, there is no explanation of the mother language. Further, on the basis of grammatical rules and the dictionaries, this argument does not hold ground.

In 1833, Dr. Thomas Young proposed that Aryans are Indo-Europeans. However, there is no unanimity about the possible place of origin of these 'Indo-Europeans'. The diversity of views on the subject is evident from the following:

- In 1906, a German philologist, Dr. Adelong, opined that Kashmir was their place of origin. In 1920, A. G.

Rhodes inferred that it was Central Asia. This view was supported by Sheiligal, Pot, Lasen, Jacob, Grim, Picktect, Maymu, etc., but Ladem attacked it and said that the place of origin was not Central Asia but Europe.

- Cuno put forward the view that an area west of the Ural mountain ranges and north of France and Germany was where the Indo-Europeans originally came from.
- Gyner postulated on the basis of references to birch, beech and oak trees in Vedic literature that Germany was the original location.
- Views have also been expressed that parts of Russia, the banks of the Euphrates river, Scandinavia and Iceland were the place of origin.
- N. B. Pawagi proposed that 'Aryavarta' was the region inhabited by the Aryans. This view was supported by Avinash Chandra Das in *Rig Veda India*.
- C. G. Kashikar has opined that due to the racial similarity indicated through *Zend Avesta*, the Aryans were from the same place as those who spoke Zend.
- In 1898, Lokmanya B. G. Tilak mathematically proved that the Aryans came from the Arctic region. This view was not strongly opposed for a long time.
- G. B. Dandge has quoted the findings of a study of the Arctic Ocean done almost 75 years after Tilak proposed his theory. According to details in the *Encyclopaedia Britannica* (15th ed. 1973-74), there is strong evidence supporting the existence of sea ice on the Arctic Ocean during the past three million years. This refutes any theory that human civilization existed there. Dandge proposes that North India is the region and the Seven Island area (Sapta Sindhu Pradesh) the centre of the cultural development of Vedic society.

Having taken a brief look at scholarly views on the origin of the Aryans, let us see the time frame claimed to be the period of creation of the Vedas, in particular the *Rig Veda*.

The time frame

Many researchers have made concerted efforts to estimate when the Vedas were created, but no one has been able to prove conclusively even the century in which the *Rig Veda* was created. However, there appears near unanimity regarding the view that no other known literature can be traced beyond it. So one has to derive satisfaction from making the statement that the Vedas form the oldest literature in the world.

Max Muller, Lokmanya Tilak, Yakoabi, Hugo Winkler, Hatel, Dr. Keath, Dr. Bhandarkar, Dr. Das and Shri Mukhopadhyaya are some of the learned scholars who used tools and techniques such as linguistic inferences, history, comparative forms of archaeology, jyotish, astronomy, mathematics, etc. to ascertain the time of creation of the *Rig Veda*. Their estimates differ not by tens of hundreds of years, but sometimes thousands. The closest period ascribed is c. 1000 BC, and the farthest c. 16,000–25,000 BC. The majority support an estimate of about c. 4000–4500 BC.

APPENDIX

Popular Smarta Yajnas

GANESHA YAGA

NAVA GRAHA YAGA

VISHNU YAGA

RUDRA YAGA

SAT CHANDI YAGA

GANESHA YAGA

Ganesha Yantra

Moola mantra

ॐ गं गणपतये नमः

Om gam ganapataye namah

Devata dhyanam

खर्वं स्थूलतनुं गजेंद्रवदनं लम्बोदरं सुंदरं
प्रस्यन्दन्मदगन्धलुब्धमधुपव्यालोलगण्डस्थलम् ।
दन्ताघातविदारितारिरुधिरैः सिंदूरशोभाकरं
वन्दे शैलसुतासुतं गणपतिं सिध्दिप्रदं कामदम् ॥

Kharvam sthooltanum gajendravadanam lambodaram sundaram
Prasyandan madagandha lubdha madhupa vyalola gandasthalam.
Dantaaghaat vidaaritaarirudhiraih sindurshobhaakaram
Vande shailasutasutam ganapatim siddhipradam kaamadam.

He who is short in stature, is rather obese, whose face is like that of an elephant and has a vast stomach,

Whose forehead is shining from the flowing fluid licked by the black bee that was attracted by the fragrance of the fluid,
Whose body appears brilliantly red due to the smearing of the enemy's blood that oozed from its body due to the wounds caused by Ganesha's teeth,
I pray to the adorable son of Mother Parvati, Shailasuta, who fulfills all the desires of devotees.

Gayatri

ॐ एकदंताय विद्महे वक्रतुंडाय धीमहि। तन्नोदंतिः प्रचोदयात् ॥

Om ekadantaaya vidmahe vakratundaaya dheemahi.
Tannodantihi prachodayaat.

Swahakara mantra

1. From the Vedas: *Om aa tu na . . .* (ॐ आ तु न . . .) *(Shukla Yajur Veda*, 33.65–72)
2. From the Puranas: 1008 names *(Ganesha Sahasra Naamavali)*

Swahakara

In a Ganesha Yaga of more than one day, oblations are offered with the eight mantras from the *Yajur Veda* mentioned above. Alternatively, 1008 names of Ganesha are chanted. On the last day, havan is performed with chanting of 1008 names. The number of oblations is 100,000.

Articles of oblation (ahuti dravya)

The following articles are used irrespective of the type of yajna: sesame, rice, yava, sugar, ghrita, dried fruits, sandalwood powder, bhoja patra (leaves of birch tree), guggul, wood from the mango tree.

Articles specific to Ganesha yaga

Durva (a type of green grass), modaka (sweet made of rice and coconut, believed to be Ganesha's most favourite dish).

Benefits

Lord Ganesha is said to be the saviour of humankind in this epoch – *Kalau chandi vinayakau*. He is most munificent and famous for bestowing innumerable blessings on a worshipper. His worship leads to abundant wealth in the material world, and attainment of divya loka after death.

NAVA GRAHA YAGA

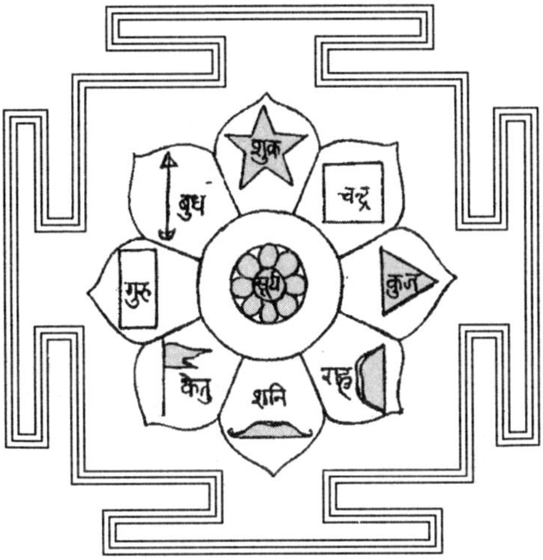

Nava Graha Yantra

Devata (42)

1. Graha devata (9)
2. Adhi devata (9)
3. Pratyadhi devata (9)
4. Kratu satgunya devata (7)
5. Protecting devata (8)

Devata dhyanam

ॐ ब्रह्मा मुरारिस्त्रिपुरान्तकारी भानुः शशी भूमिसुतो बुधश्च ।
गुरुश्च शुक्रः शनिराहुकेतवः सर्वे ग्रहाः शान्तिकरा भवन्तु ॥
सूर्यः शौर्यमथेन्दुरुच्चपदवीं सन्मङ्गलं मङ्गलः ।
सद्बुद्धिं च बुधो गुरुश्च गुरुतां शुक्रः सुखं शं शनिः ।
राहुर्बाहुबलं करोतु सततं केतुः कुलस्योन्नतिं
नित्यं प्रीतिकरा भवन्तु मम ते सर्वेऽनुकूला ग्रहाः ॥

Om brahmaa muraaristripuraantakaree bhanuhu
shashee bhoomisuto budhashcha,

Gurushcha shukrah shaniraahuketavah sarve grahaah shaantikaraa bhavantu.
Suryah shauryamathendurucchhapadaveem sanmangalam mangalah,
Sadbuddhim cha budho gurushcha gurutaam shrukrah sukham sham shanih.
Rahurbaahubalam karotu satatam ketuhu kulasyonnatim,
Nityam preetikaraa bhavantu mama te sarve nukoolaa grahaah.

Let Brahma, Vishnu (Murari), Mahesh (Tripurantaka), Sun, Moon, Mars (Bhumisuta), Mercury,
Jupiter, Venus, Saturn, Rahu and Ketu bring peace.
Valorous Sun, highly-placed moon, benevolent Mars,
Wise Mercury, great Jupiter, peace-giving Venus and welfare-giving Saturn be favourable.
Let the muscle power of Rahu help us, let Ketu help our family progress,
In this way, let all the planets shower their love on us and be favourable to us.

Gayatri

ॐ आदित्याय विद्महे सहस्त्रकिरणाय धीमहि । तन्नो सूर्यः प्रचोदयात् ॥

Om aadityaaya vidmahe sahasrakiranaaya dheemahi, tanno suryah prachodayaat.

Swahakara mantra

1. From the Vedas: Om aa krishnen rajasa . . . (ॐ आ कृष्णेन रजसा . . .) (*Shukla Yajur Veda*)
2. From the Puranas:
   a) Graha devata: Om suryaya namaha swaahaa . . . Om ketave namaha swaahaa (ॐ सूर्याय नमः स्वाहा . . . ॐ केतवे नमः स्वाहा)
   b) Adhi devata: Om rudraaya namaha swaahaa . . . Om chitraguptaya namaha swaahaa (ॐ रुद्राय नमः स्वाहा . . . ॐ चित्रगुप्ताय नमः स्वाहा)

c) Pratyadhi devata: Om agnaye namaha swaahaa . . . Om brahmane namaha swaahaa (ॐ अग्नये नमः स्वाहा . . . ॐ ब्रह्मणे नमः स्वाहा)

d) Kratu satgunya devata: Om ganapataye namaha swaahaa . . . Om vaastoshpataye namaha swaahaa (ॐ गणपतये नमः स्वाहा. . . ॐ वास्तोष्पतये नमः स्वाहा)

e) Protecting devata: Om indraaya namaha swaahaa . . . Om eeshaaya namaha swaahaa (ॐ इंद्राय नमः स्वाहा . . . ॐ ईशाय नमः स्वाहा)

Swahakara

The number of oblations is 10,000. The ratio of oblations for graha devata, adhi devata and all other devatas is 4:2:1.

Articles of oblation (ahuti dravya)

Articles of oblation common to all yajnas are given in Ganesha yaga. They are used in this yajna also.

In addition, charu and samidha are used in nava graha yaga. The type of samidha differs with the graha. The following table gives the details.

Table 30: Samidha used for each Graha

Graha devata	Adhi devata	Pratyadhi devata	Yajniya tree whose sticks are used as samidha
Surya	Ishvara	Agni	Rooyi – mandara
Soma	Uma	Apaha	Palasha
Bhouma	Skandha	Bhoomi	Khadira – khaira
Budha	Narayana	Vishnu	Apamarga
Guru	Brahma	Indra	Peepal
Shukra	Indra	Indrani	Udumbara
Shani	Yama	Prajapati	Shami
Rahu	Kala	Sarpana	Durva
Ketu	Chitragupta	Brahman	Kusha

Benefits

The *nava grahas* (nine planets) exert an influence on the whole world. It is under their control. Therefore, in order to spread their positive influence and for peace everywhere, graha yajna is performed. Since the welfare of the whole universe, *vishvakalyana*, is the principal objective of most yajnas, all shrauta and smarta yajnas include nava graha yajna as a sub-process. A person desiring wealth and immunity from afflictions must also perform this yajna.

VISHNU YAGA

Vishnu Yantra

Moola Mantra

ॐ नमो नारायणाय।

Om Namo Narayanaya

Devata dhyanam

शांताकारं भुजगशयनं पद्मनाभं सुरेशम् ।
विश्वाधारं गगनसदृशं मेघवर्णं शुभांगम् ॥
लक्ष्मीकान्तं कमलनयनं योगीभिर्ध्यानगम्यम् ।
वन्दे विष्णुं भवभयहरं सर्व लोकैकनाथम् ॥

Shaantaakaaram bhujagashayanam padmaanabham suresham,
Vishvadhaaram gaganasadrisham meghavarnam shubhaangam.
Lakshmeekaantam kamalanayanam yogeebhirdhyaanagamyam,
Vande vishnum bhavabhayaharam sarva lokaikanaatham.

He who is an embodiment of serenity, is reposing on the lord of snakes,

Has a lotus emerging from the navel and is the supreme among all,
Who is the support of the whole universe, comparable with the sky for expanse,
Is of the complexion of clouds and exhibits sacredness.
Who is the lord of the goddess of wealth, is lotus-eyed, and the object of meditation for yogis,
I bow to thee, O Vishnu, you free us from all fears and agonies, and are the singular lord of all the lokas.

Gayatri

ॐ नारायणाय विद्महे वासुदेवाय धीमहि । तन्नो विष्णुः प्रचोदयात् ॥

Om naaraayanaaya vidmahe vaasudevaaya dheemahi,
tanno vishnuh prachodayaat.

Swahakara mantra

1. From the Vedas: Om sahasrasheershaa purushaha . . . (ॐ सहस्रशीर्षा पुरुषः . . .) (*Rig Veda*, 10.90.1–16)
2. From the Puranas: 1008 names *(Vishnu Sahasra Naamavali)*

Swahakara

There are multiple forms of this yaga. The three most popular are: Vishnu, Maha Vishnu and Ati Vishnu yaga. The duration could be 5, 8, 9 or 11 days. The number of kundas depends on the number of priests offering simultaneous oblations. The number of oblations offered are: 16,000 for Vishnu yaga, 160,000 for Maha Vishnu yaga, and 332,000 for Ati Vishnu yaga.

Articles of oblation (ahuti dravya)

In addition to the articles of oblation common to all yajnas, tulsi leaves are specific to Vishnu yaga.

Muhurta

Great importance is attached to the auspicious time at which the yaga should commence. It is said to be especially beneficial if the following rules are observed, over and above the general parameters of muhurtas.

Tithi: Twelfth day of the waxing period of the moon, full-moon day, no-moon day, Samkranti, Jhoolanotsva, the occasion of samskaras like upanayana, vivaha, griha pravesha, etc. Any day from the first day of the waxing period to the fifth day of the waning period of the moon is acceptable.

Months: Chaitra, Phalguna, Jyeshtha, Magha.

Benefits

Lord Vishnu is the deity of peace, prosperity and serenity. He is the supporter of creation. Therefore, anyone who offers his mind and soul to Vishnu is said to have all desires fulfilled. This is a yaga of the highest importance and value. Vishnu yaga yields utmost benevolence for the yajamana and all participants.

RUDRA YAGA

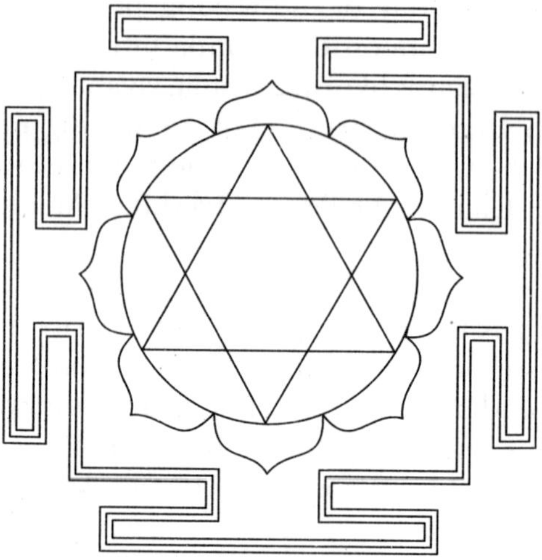

Shiva Yantra

Devata dhyanam

ध्यायेन्नित्यं महेशं रजतगिरिनिभं चारुचंद्रावतंसं ।
रत्नाकल्पोज्ज्वलाङ्गं परशुमृगवराभीतिहस्तं प्रसन्नम् ॥
पद्मासीनं समन्तात्स्तुतममरगणैर्व्याघ्रकृत्तिं वसानं ।
विश्वाद्यं विश्ववंद्यं निखिलभयहरं पंचवक्त्रं त्रिनेत्रम् ॥

Dhyaayennittyam mahesham rajatagirinibham chaaruchandraavatamsam,
Ratnaakalpojjvalaangam parashu mrigavaraabheetihastam prasannam.
Padmaseenam samantaatstutamamaraganaivyaarghrikrittim vasaanam,
Vishvaadyam vishvavandyam nikhilabhayaharam panchavaktram trinetram.

Meditate constantly on the form of Lord Mahesha, O blessed self, who resembles the snow-covered mountain and who bears the crescent like a lovely ornament,

Whose body radiates the glow that compares with the colour of a jewel, who holds a trident, has raised his arm to pronounce protection and who appears very kind,
Who is seated in a lotus surrounded by all devas who adore him, who has used a tiger skin as his cloth,
Bow to he who was present even before the universe took shape, is universally adored, is the remover of all fears and agonies, is a deity with five faces and three eyes.

Gayatri

ॐ तत्पुरुषाय विद्महे महादेवाय धीमहि । तन्नो रुद्रः प्रचोदयात् ॥

Om tatpurushaaya vidmahe mahaadevaaya dheemahi, tanno rudrah prachodayaat.

Swahakara mantra

1. From the Vedas: Om sahasrasheersha purushaha . . . (ॐ सहस्रशीर्षा पुरुषः . . .) (*Rig Veda*, 10.90.1–16). Thereafter, chanting of Rudra Sukta
2. From the Puranas: 1008 names of Shiva *(Shiva Sahasra Naamavali)*

Swahakara

This yaga has three main forms: Laghu Rudra, Maha Rudra and Ati Rudra yaga. The number of oblations offered are: 19,921 for Laghu Rudra, 219,131 for Maha Rudra and 2,410,441 for Ati Rudra yaga.

Articles of oblation (ahuti dravya)

In addition to the articles of oblation common to all yajnas, leaves of the bel tree, milk, sugarcane juice, etc. are specific to Rudra yaga.

Muhurta

Great importance is attached to the auspicious time at which the yaga should commence. It is said to be especially beneficial if the following points are observed, over and above the general parameters of muhurtas:

Star *(nakshatra)*: Ashwini, Revati, Ardra, Hasta, Punarvasu, Pushya

Day: Sunday, Tuesday

Tithi: In the summer solstice, *uttarayana*, 1, 3, 5, 6, 8, 10, 11, 13, 15th day of the fortnight (days of no study and no tithi at sunrise are to be avoided).

Benefits

The performance of Rudra yaga has many benefits. It is mainly aimed at mitigating the ills caused by animals and other creatures, fellow human beings and neighbouring countries. It remedies mental illness, mental lethargy, and is especially popular for overcoming fear of death. Those who desire salvation also perform Rudra yaga.

General procedure

Rudra yaga commences along the general lines of other yajnas. A special aspect of this yaga is that as the Rudra path progresses, a liquid is constantly poured over the idol, pinda. Whether this liquid is milk, sugarcane juice or the holy water of the Ganges depends on the resolution (sankalpa) of the yajamana. The process is known as abhisheka. The number of repetitions of the path also depends on the sankalpa. At the end of the abhisheka, the idol is installed on a place over a *kalasha* (pot). Thereafter, havan and swahakara is done to the chanting of *Rudra Sukta*.

SAT CHANDI YAJNA

Chandi Yantra

Moola mantra

ॐ ऐं ह्रीं क्लीं चामुंडायै विच्चे

Om aim hreem kleem chaamundaayai vichche

Devata dhyanam

विद्यु-ामसमप्रभां मृगपतिस्कन्धस्थितां भीषणां
कन्याभिः करवालखेटविलसध्दस्ताभिरासेविताम् ।
हस्तैश्चक्रगदासिखेटविशिखांश्चापं गुणं तर्जनीं
बिभ्राणामनलात्मिकां शशिधरां दुर्गां त्रिनेत्रां भजे ॥

Viduddaamasamaprabhaam mrigapatiskandhasthitaam bheeshanaam

Kanyabhihi karavaala khetavilasaddhastaabhiraasevitaam,

Hastaishchakragadaasikhetavishikhaamshchaapam gunam tarjaneem

Bibhraanaamanalaatmikaam shashidharaam durgaam trinetraam bhaje.

I contemplate on the form of the three-eyed goddess Durga. The glow of her limbs resembles lightning. Seated on a lion, she appears fierce,
She is being praised by maidens (goddesses) whose hands are decorated with weapons like the shield and sword,
She holds various weapons in (her seven) arms and (the eighth one) displays 'tarjani mudra' (the posture with an upward pointing forefinger),
She is luminous like fire, bears the crescent moon and is three-eyed.

Gayatri

ॐ कात्यायन्यै च विद्महे कन्याकुमार्यै च धीमहि । तन्नो दुर्गे प्रचोदयात् ॥

Om kaatyaayanai cha vidmahe kanyaakumaaryai cha dheemahi, tanno durge prachodayaat.

or

ॐ गिरिजायैच विद्महे शिवप्रियायै च धीमहि । तन्नो दुर्गे प्रचोदयात् ॥

Om girijaayaicha vidmahe shivapriyaayai cha dheemahi, tanno durge prachodayaat.

Shri Durga Saptashati Grantha has a unique power of benevolence embedded in it. It is, in fact, the very essence of Veda vidya, and has its origin in the Puranas. It is the customary path to recite at a Sat Chandi yajna. Its origin is also quite novel.

Jaimini learnt dharma shastra from Maharshi Vyasa, but even after Vyasa's revealing discourse, he had some doubts. So he went to another equally great authority – Markandeya. However, this rishi was in a deep state of meditation and had gone beyond the bodily senses, so he could not return to the mortal environment governed by maya. Realizing Jaimini's sincere desire, Markandeya appeared in his inner vision and assured him that a plan would shortly unfold wherein the 'Devi Mahatmya' story would be revealed to him, which would provide answers to all the questions hovering in Jaimini's mind. In due course, Jaimini heard the story, the glory of the goddess was revealed to him, and he passed it down to posterity. Every segment of the Devi path always starts with the words *"Markandeya uvacha"* (Markandeya said) in honour of the rishi who brought the astounding power of Mahamaya to ordinary mortals. However, since it is a valued treasure, the storytellers built a protective shield around it, and used coded words that would work like a key to unlock the treasury.

The path must be done with full devotion and faith in its efficacy. One has to pour one's mind and soul into it to experience its wonderful effects. A conscious reciter (pathi) would be like one who uses code numbers to unlock a treasure and enjoy the wealth. Therefore, great importance is attached to proper chanting of the mantras, understanding the meaning of the original words of the *Saptashati*, realizing the embedded principles, and feeling the vibrations created by the chanting.

Shri Durga or Chandi yajna has three segments: recitation of *Saptashati*, repetition such as Nava Chandi, Sat Chandi, Sahasra Chandi, etc., and dispensation, termed *path, purushcharana* and *viniyoga* respectively.

Generally, Nava Chandi is performed as a family ritual or for the fulfilment of small desires. Sat Chandi is performed for general well-being and the elimination of inherent faults arising from having taken birth on earth (*prarabdha dosha*). A larger number of repetitions (1000, 100,000, etc.) are done to remove the impurities and samskaras accumulated over multiple births and acquired by heredity.

To begin with, every day the maha sankalpa is pronounced followed by a predetermined number of repetitions. The path also has a daily sankalpa and ends with the completion of the sankalpa.

The special feature of Chandi yajna is four types of bali (offering of limbs) and kumari pooja (worship of maidens). Swami Satyananda says that maidens are a symbol of innocence, and since they become the medium to reach out to the Mother, their worship is included as a necessary ritual.

Japa, havan, tarpan, marjana and santarpan are the five parts of Chandi yajna.

Swahakara mantra

1. From the Puranas: Saptashati mantras from the *Markandeya Purana*
2. With naam mantra: 1008 names of Devi *(Lalita Sahasra Naamavali)*

Swahakara

The inverse ratio of japa, havan, tarpan, marjana and santarpan is 10,000:10000:100:10:1. If the japa is done 10,000 times, havan should be performed using 1000 repetitions of 'swaha' and so on. For Sat Chandi yaga, ten brahmins (pathi) are needed, in addition to the brahmins who act as acharya, brahma, etc.

Articles of oblation (ahuti dravya)

In addition to the articles of oblation common to all yajnas, tulsi leaves, bel leaves, lotus flowers, cardamom, cloves and dried fruits are specific to Chandi yaga.

Muhurta

Chandi yajna is performed during Karka Lagna, on Monday, Navami Tithi and under Mriga Shira Nakshatra.

Benefits

Chandi yajna fulfils the desires for personal needs and prosperity. The sankalpa to achieve the welfare of people around the yajamana, his society, the nation, or the world (animal kingdom included) is always intimately associated with it. A sankalpa for personal desires is called kama sankalpa and one with a wider frame nishkama sankalpa. A yajna with such a sankalpa is known to give immediate fruits, and its participants experience peace and serenity.

Glossary

Abhichara mantra – incantation or formula for working out a charm

Abhidhani – 1. rope for tying a cow (or accompanying calf) which is milked for yajnic purposes 2. cord binding the yoke to the pole

Abhisheka – 1. ritual where a steady stream of ajya, water, curd, milk, honey, ghee, etc. is poured over a deity's idol 2. in rajasooya yajna, abhisheka is carried out for a king with sacred water from holy rivers

Abhyudaya – 1. material prosperity 2. sunrise

Acchavaka – 'inviter', a subordinate priest of the hota group

Achamana – practice of rinsing the mouth with three spoonsful of sacred water at the commencement of a ritual by the person performing the ritual, to purify the body, mind and spirit

Acharya varana – ritual of the yajamana's giving a betel nut to the priest as a symbol of his request that the priest perform a yajna on his behalf

Adhana – establishing a sacred fire in its designated pit

Adhararani – lower plank of the arani (used to ignite the yajna fire)

Adhvara – yajna that goes on for a year, such as chaturmasya ishti adhvara, soumya adhvara, etc.

Adhvaryava – mantras used by the adhvaryu

Adhvaryu – one of the four main priests in shrauta yajna chiefly responsible for the physical act of dropping oblation articles into the sacred fire and reciting the Yajur Veda

Adhyaya – 1. study, especially of the Vedas 2. chapter or large division of a work

Adi Shakti – the primal force behind creation

Adi Shankara – credited with the revival of Vedic dharma in the 7th century, he is noted for his monistic philosophy of Advaita Vedanta and establishment of 10 orders of sannyasa (dashnami)

Adideva Shiva – Shiva perceived as the first or supreme god

Adinath Mahakala – aspect of Shiva as the primordial god of destruction

Aditi – 1. boundlessness, immensity 2. mother of the gods known as Adityas

Aditya – 1. son of Aditi 2. a god, divinity in general 3. the sun as a deity 4. a noun used for the twelve Adityas – Dhata, Aryama, Mitra, Varuna, Indra, Vivaswan, Tvashta, Vishnu, Anshu, Bhag, Pusha, Parjyanya

Advaita Vedanta – doctrine of non-duality propounded by Adi Shankaracharya

Agha shuddhi – purification required due to participation in last rites

Agni – fire, sacrificial fire, the god of fire and one of the prominent deities of the Rig Veda

Agni chayana – process of construction of uttaravedi in soma yajna

Agni chiti – a special fire-pit used in soma yajnas

Agni karya – performance of yajna by a batu (young boy) after his initiation through the thread ceremony

Agni pradakshina – perambulation of the sacrificial fire

Agnidhra – a priest from the brahma group in shrauta yajna

Agnidhriya – a sub-mandap of a shrauta yajna

Agnihotra – a small fire ritual performed daily at dawn and dusk in which cow's milk is offered in the fire

Agnihotri – person who has taken the resolve to worship the fire god throughout life

Agnishoma – Agni and Soma worshipped together

Agnishomatmakam jagata – two principles that hold the universe together – Agni takes and Soma replenishes

Agnishomiya pashu yaga – soma yaga in which an animal is offered as sacrifice on the last day of yajna

Agnishtoma – 'praise of Agni', a soma sacrifice, first of the seven soma samsthas and a model of soma yagas

Agnyadhana – rite of establishment of sacrificial fires; a sacrifice of the ishti type, also called agnyadheya

Agnyupasthana – worship of fire

Agrayaneshti – oblation consisting of the first crops at the end of the rainy season

Ahamkara – faculty of ego; awareness of the existence of 'I'

Ahavana – invocation

Ahavaniya agni – one of the three forms of fire used in shrauta yajna. Oblations are made to invite yajna devata(s) to the yajna venue (ahavana = to invoke)

Ahina – yajna lasting from two to 12 days

Ahitagni – title earned by an agnihotri through the completion of certain rituals, making him eligible to be the yajamana of shrauta yajna

Ahuti – oblations offered into the fire during yajna

Aitareya – originating from Aitareya; descendant of Itara to whom the Aitareya Brahmana and Aitareya Aranyaka are attributed

Ajayata – one who takes birth, a shudra

Ajina – deer skin

Ajnana – ignorance

Ajya – essence of butter derived from cow's milk

Akhyan – 1. legend 2. praise

Aksha – 1. unit of Vedic measurement 2. axis 3. eye

Alaja – a falcon-like bird

Amavasya – fifteenth day of the dark fortnight when there is no moon in the sky

Amba – 1. mother 2. of Durga, Shiva's consort

Amiksha – the solid substance obtained by curdling milk

Amurta – formless

Anandamaya kosha – body of bliss

Ananta – 1. endless, infinite, boundless, inexhaustible 2. name of Vishnu

Anga nyasa – ritual performed to install various devatas at different parts of the body; invoking/activating the energy body of the worshipper

Angiras – name of sage who composed many of the Rig Vedic hymns and founded the science of Brahmavidya; his descendants; certain hymns from Atharva Veda

Angiratharva Veda – another term for Atharva Veda Samhita, presumably because large parts were written by Angiras

Angula – 1. unit of Vedic measurement equal to a finger's length 2. finger
Anna prashana – rite of first solid, cooked food given to a baby
Anna-annad – 'food-recipient of food', refers to the Vedic principle that every part of the universe is food for someone and also the recipient of food from some other part
Annamaya kosha – material or food body
Anrita – unrighteous, falsehood
Antah shuddhi – internal purification of the body
Antariksha loka – space between earth and sky
Antaryajna – internalization of the yajna process
Anteyshti – last rites
Anubadhya yaga – rite in which a sterile cow is offered as sacrifice
Anudatta – one of the three tones used for chanting Vedic mantras aloud
Anushanga path – convention followed for repeated use of mantras during yajna
Anushthana – systematic performance of sadhana, e.g. mantra, undertaken with a sankalpa (resolution) for a definite period of time
Anushtubh – metre with four padas and eight syllables each
Anuvaka – 1. subdivision of the Vedas, section 2. repetition
Anuvakya mantras – richas recited by the priests hota or maitravaruna before commencement of the principal yaga, call of invitation to the deity
Anuyajya – 'after offering', series of three supplementary oblations subsequent to principal offerings
Anvadhana – first samidha offered to ignite the yajna fire
Anvaharya sthali – pot in which anvaharya rice is cooked (to be offered to priests as dakshina)
Anvarambhaniya ishti – introductory rite of darshapoornamasa
Ap – water
Apara vidya – knowledge of the manifest world
Apaurusheya – that whose creation has not had any human touch, implying it is the Lord's creation
Apoorva – something unprecedented. In the context of yajna, it refers to an effect that was not present prior to performance of the yajna

Aptoryama – seventh soma samsthaka yajna. It is believed that one can obtain whatever one desires by performing this rite

Apupa – cake of barley or rice baked on domestic fire (garhapatya agni)

Apurvadhana – first initiation of a person who is not an ahitagni

Arani – instrument consisting of two planks, a rod and a rope, used to churn the sacrificial fire

Aranya – forest

Aranyaka – third part of the Vedas

Aratni – unit of measurement in yajnic mathematics. It represents a distance equal to the length of the lower arm (between the fist and elbow) of the yajamana

Arghya – ritual wherein water is cupped in palms while chanting mantras, and then allowed to drip down the fingers

Arha Veda – one of the Upavedas

Arhaniya – worthy of worship

Arjuna – third of the Pandava brothers, reputed warrior and archer, and disciple and friend of Krishna, who revealed to him the message of the Bhagavad Gita

Arsheya – of or relating to a rishi

Arthavada – explanatory words or statements that illustrate a vidhi (ritual/rule) of a sacrifice (described in the Brahmana Granthas)

Arya – generic name used to refer to Vedic people. In Vedic parlance, 'arya' is a title given to a respected person or the head of the family

Asamskrita – uncultured

Asana – 1. steady and comfortable meditation pose in which one is at perfect ease 2. seat

Asandi – teapot-like stool used in shrauta yajna to keep soma sticks, implements, etc.

Ashram – 1. place where the spiritual preceptor, the guru, lives, works and guides his disciples for a higher aim in life 2. stage, order, or period of life, of which there are four: brahmacharya or studentship, grihastha or household life, vanaprastha or forest-dwelling, sannyasa or total renunciation

Ashta – eight

Ashtadhyai – 1. containing eight chapters 2. famous sutras of Sanskrit grammar by Panini, containing eight chapters

Ashtaka – 1. collection of three days (7th, 8th, 9th) beginning from the seventh day after the full moon 2. shraaddha ceremony to be performed on the above days 3. a division of the Rig Veda 5. the eight chapters of Panini's sutras 5. the sixth of the seven paka yajnas, where cooked food is used as oblation material

Ashtalokapala – guardians of the eight directions

Ashtami – eighth day of the lunar fortnight

Ashvamedha – 'horse sacrifice', a Vedic yajna performed by an emperor to attain a son or sovereignty

Ashvattha – holy peepal tree

Ashvinau – two physicians of the gods, represented as the twin sons of the sun by a nymph in the form of a mare

Astarana – a covering or mat

Asuras – children of Aditi , the mother of gods. Over a period of time, they came to represent evil and were classified as demons

Atharvan – the eldest son of Brahma; his descendants; his incantations found in the Atharva Veda

Atharve – mantras from Atharva Veda

Atigrahya – three extra libations for Agni, Indra and Surya during agnishtoma

Atiratra – 1. prepared or performed overnight 2. a soma samsthaka yajna, performed over a day and night

Atithi yajna – practice of feeding a stranger or unknown guest before partaking of one's own meal (also called manushya yajna and nriyajna), one of the pancha maha yajnas

Atma – pure consciousness which pervades everything; undying; self; spirit; soul

Atmabhava – experience of empathy and oneness with all

Atmashuddhi – purification of the soul

Atyagnishtoma – a soma samsthaka yajna, similar to agnishtoma

Audumbari – post made of udumbara wood, used in soma yajna

Aum – see om

Aupasana agni – form of fire used in smarta rituals

Avabhritha snanam – purificatory bathing ritual to mark the end of a yajna

Avasathya agni – one of the five forms of sacrificial fire. An agnihotri usually maintains it in his residence

Avashishta – remnants
Avidya – ignorance of true reality
Ayur Veda – one of the Upavedas containing the science of health and medicine
Bahispavaman – stotra sung by the priest udgata on the day soma juice is offered as oblation in soma yajna.
Bahu – 1. arm 2. Vedic unit of measurement
Balva – coarse grass (also called balvaja)
Barhi – type of grass
Batu – a boy initiated through the upanayana samskara
Baudhayana – an acknowledged Vedic author or sutras
Bhagavad Gita – 'divine song'; Krishna's discourse on yoga to Arjuna at the onset of the Mahabharata war
Bhagavata Purana – also known as Srimad Bhagavatam, a major Purana and primary Vaishnava scrupture, contains stories of all the incarnations of Vishnu and is replete with the aspect of bhakti
Bhairava – state of consciousness which precedes the ultimate experience of universal consciousness, or Shiva; name of Shiva in his fierce aspect
Bhakti yoga – channelling the emotional energy towards a higher reality
Bharadvaja – a Vedic sage
Bhasma – ash from a sacrificial fire
Bhautic – belonging to created or living beings
Bhava shuddhi – purification of the state of mind
Bhavak samskara – augmenting samskara
Bhoja patra – leaf and bark of the birch tree
Bhojan – 1. meal 2. that which is enjoyed
Bhoota matra – created beings
Bhoota yajna – an oblation or offering to all creatures of the lower species, one of the pancha maha yajnas
Bhrigu – the sage regarded as the ancestor of the family of Bhrigus, described in Manu Smriti as one of the 10 patriarchs created by the first Manu
Bhurij gayatri – one of the gayatri metres that has 25 alphabets
Bija mantra – seed mantra or syllable
Boucher – one of the functionaries in a yajna

Brahma – 1. cosmic creator in Hindu pantheon, one of the holy trinity 2. one of the 16 priests of shrauta yajna

Brahma muhurta – 'time of God', roughly one hour before and after sunrise, believed to be a favourable time for sadhana

Brahma samskaras – samskaras that purify annamaya, manomaya and pranamaya koshas

Brahma Sutra Bhashya – commentary on Brahma Sutras by Adi Shankaracharya

Brahma vidya – study to obtain the 'real knowledge'; knowledge of Brahman

Brahma yajna – study and recitation of Vedas

Brahmachari – 1. one engaged in studying the Vedas 2. one practising chastity 3. a person placed in the highest state of consciousness

Brahman – ever-expanding consciousness; absolute reality

Brahmana Granthas – portions of Vedas that give the origin, explanation and rules for employing hymns in various yajnas

Brahmanacchansin – a priest of the brahma group in soma yajna

Brahmanda – 'cosmic egg', the macrocosmos

Brahmarishi – brahminical sage

Brahmaudana – rice cooked in milk on sacrificial fire during agnyadhana

Brahmin – one who has dedicated his life to studying the Vedas and dispensing knowledge of Brahman. This knowledge enables him to act as a priest in Vedic rituals

Brahmopasana – study of Vedas

Brihad Devata – a treatise authored by Shaunaka focusing on different Vedic devatas

Brihadaranayaka Upanishad – one of the most important Upanishads, part of the Shatapatha Brahmana of Yajur Veda. Ascribed to sage Yajnavalkya

Brihaspati – 1. planet Jupiter 2. preceptor of gods 3. celebrated author of a smriti

Brihati – 1. large, abundant 2. a Vedic metre

Buddhi – 1. higher intellect; discrimination

Chaitra – first month of the Indian lunar calendar

Chamasa – wooden vessel used to offer soma juice during a sacrifice

Chamasadhvaryu – group of priests who offer soma oblation at a soma yajna

Chanda – metre of a verse

Chandas – 1. branch of Vedanga that deals with the arrangements of consonants into words of mantras, words into lines, lines into lyrics

Chandogya Upanishad – one of the principal Upanishads from Sama Veda. It teaches the origin and significance of Aum

Chandra – moon; the moon god (also chandrama); shining, bright; representing mental energy

Charana – single line of a stanza

Charu – rice cake used for oblation

Charvaka – one of the six systems of Indian philosophy that accepts only perceivable phenomena as valid, named after Charvaka

Chaturmasya yajna – one of the seven havi yajnas. It includes four yajnas that must be performed in a year every three–four months

Chatvala – a pit on the northern side of the mahavedi. The soil dug out of it is used to make the uttaravedi

Chayana – construction of uttaravedi using specially made bricks

Chit shakti – mental force governing the subtle dimensions

Chit – pure consciousness that lies behind all phenomena

Chiti – uttaravedi with a specific shape; e.g. 'shyen chiti' is the term for the uttaravedi shaped like a falcon

Chitta – individual consciousness, including the subconscious and unconscious levels of mind

Daan – unconditional giving

Daiva samskaras – samskaras that purify vijnanamaya and anandamaya koshas

Daksha Prajapati – one of the 10 sons of Brahma and father of Sati, wife of Shiva

Dakshin – south

Dakshina – 1. honorarium 2. mythical character, described as the twin of Yajna

Dakshinagni – one of the three forms of fire used in shrauta yajna. Oblations to forefathers are offered in this fire

Danadanyoh – simultaneous giving and taking

Darbha – a specific grass used in the yajnic processes

Darbhasana – asana or mat made of darbha grass

Darsha – 1. 'time when the moon is seen only by the sun', dark night of the moon 2. sacrificial rite performed at that time

Darshan – philosophical system of the Vedic tradition, so called because it is based on revelations or truths that were 'seen' or 'had darshan of' in a higher state of consciousness

Darshapoorna yajna – model for all ishti-type yajnas. The first of seven havi yajnas (sapta havi)

Darshayaji – one who takes a resolve to perform the darsha-poornamaseshti throughout life

Dasha pavitra – a piece of white woollen cloth used to filter soma juice

Dashati mantra – mantra from Sama Veda (also called sama)

Dashopanishad – ten principal upanishads on which Shankaracharya wrote commentaries

Data – benefactor; one who gives

Deva – divine being (devi is the feminine)

Deva yajna – a sacrifice made to the superior gods through oblations in the sacrificial fire, one of the pancha maha yajnas

Devata – 'illumined being', divine power or deity; luminous nature of spirit. According to the Vedas, anything that is made the object of prayer by seer rishis is a devata. Devatas are the subject of mantras

Devayajana – venue selected for a large-scale yajna

Devayoni – hole in the centre of adhararani

Dhanur Veda – one of the Upavedas

Dharana – 'to hold or possess', concentration; continuity of mental process on an object or idea; sixth stage of Patanjali's ashtanga yoga

Dharma – values that complement the laws of nature; right conduct

Dhishnya – small circular raised platforms with small fireplaces used for supplementary rituals at a yajna

Dhoop – incense; any fragrant substance

Dhvaja – flag

Dhyana– spontaneous state of meditation arising from the perfection of dharana; seventh stage of Patanjali's ashtanga yoga

Diksha – 1. initiation 2. specific austerity (vrata) accepted by the yajamana of shrauta yajna 3. consecration of the sacrificer at the begnning of a soma yajna

Dikshaniya ishti – oblation of purodasha to Agni and Vishnu before the diksha rite in soma yajna

Div – that which shines

Divya – divine

Dnyana – (also written as jnana or gyana) knowledge

Dohana patra – vessel used to collect milk (for use in soma yajna) while milking the cow (soma yajna uses fresh cow's milk as an oblation material)

Dori – thin cord

Dosha marjana – removal of impurities

Drashtrah – (also drashta) witness; the consciousness that knows what is going on; Atman or Purusha

Dravya – 1. money 2. liquid 3. articles of oblation in raw form (not consecrated)

Dravya shuddhi – purification of materials

Dravya yajna – yajna where physical articles of oblation are offered to devatas through the medium of sacrificial fire

Drishad – implement used in soma yajna

Drona kalasha – bowl made of vikankata wood to keep soma in

Dvadasha yaga – soma sacrifice lasting 12 days

Dwapara yuga – third time cycle of the universe

Dvarapala – 1. entrance guard 2. group of four priests in smarta yajnas who sit near the entrance

Dvi janma – two births

Dvi matri – two mothers

Dvija – twice born

Dviratra – over two nights

Dyu loka – abode of self-illuminating objects like the sun god

Ekagni karma – yajna performed using only one fire (smarta yajna)

Ekaha – yajna lasting a day

Enah shuddhi – purification required due to new arrivals and departures to/from family

Gada – mace or club

Ganapati – Ganesha; Shiva

Ganapatya – 1. worshippers of Ganesha 2. one of the priests in a smarta yajna

Ganas – Shiva's attendants; group of people

Gandharva Veda – one of the Upavedas

Ganesha – the elephant-headed son of Shiva and Parvati, god of wisdom and removal of obstacles, nvoked at the commencement of important undertakings, scribe of the Mahabharata

Garbhadhana – rite to purify the uterus of a newly married woman before she commences sexual life

Garhapatya agni – one of the three forms of fire used in shrauta yajna. It is associated with the head of the family who is called grihapati and represents earth or prithivi loka

Garmuta – type of grass or reed

Gatha – folklore; stories told in the course of description of the significance of yajna rituals in the Brahmana Granthas

Gavamayana yajna – samvatsarika satra lasting 361 days

Gayatri – 1. Vedic metre of 24 syllables 2. most famous and sacred mantra of the Vedic tradition which illuminates the consciousness; repeated during the daily sandhya ritual 3. mother of the Vedas

Gayatri japa – chanting of Gayatri mantra. It can be done as part of sandhya vidhi, in which case it is not chanted aloud, or independent of it

Gharma – havi used in the pravargya ritual

Ghee – see ghrita

Ghrita – clarified butter, i.e. ajya in liquid form ('ghee' is the colloquial term used for ghrita)

Gomedha – sacrifice of a cow

Gotra – family lineage

Graha – 1. wooden cup used to hold soma juice 2. planet

Graha balidan – symbolic sacrificial rite

Graha yajna – prototype of all smarta yajnas

Gramya dhanya – agricultural produce

Grantha – 1. binding, stringing together 2. work, treatise, composition, verse consisting of 32 syllables, written in the anushtubh metre

Grava – stone grinder used to crush soma sticks

Gravastut – a priest of shrauta yajna from the hota group

Griha nirmana – ceremony marking the beginning of construction of a house

Griha pravesha – ceremony marking entry to a new house

Grihamedhiya – offering to the Maruts who are called grihamedhina

Grihapati – master of the house

Grihastha ashram – period of life from the age of 25 to 50 when one lives a married life

Grihya – pertaining to the household

Grihya anushthana – domestic rituals

Grihya Sutras – a part of Kalpa Sutra used in household samskaras, manual of domestic rituals

Grihyagni – domestic fire

Guggul – fragrant gum resin

Gunadhana samskara – cultivating samskaras that help to expand the good qualities already present

Gurukul – educational system of ancient India where children lived in the ashram or family of the guru and were taught by the guru

Gyana – (also written as jnana or dnyana) knowledge, wisdom, cognition

Hamsi mudra – one of the three mudras made by fingers to hold the item of oblation. The mudra resembles a swan (hamsa = swan)

Harishchandra – king of the solar dynasty famous for his liberality and unflinching adherence to truth

Hariyojana – soma libation undertaken to yoke the horses of Indra for his departure from the sacrifice

Hatha yoga – system of yoga with practices for the purification of the physical and pranic bodies

Hautra – office of the priest called hotri

Havan – homa done for incidental purposes (naimittic karma) using ajya for oblation

Havani – ladle used in a sacrifice

Havi dravya – raw material used for preparing articles of oblation

Havi/havish – finished product made from havi dravya and consecrated

Havirdhana – 'oblation receptacle', the carriages on which the soma plants are placed the day before being crushed to extract the juice

Havyakavya – processes and oblations in a yajna

Heenanga – weak part

Hemanta – winter, comprising the months of Margashirsha and Pausha

Hiranyagarbha – golden womb of creation; cosmic subtle body

Hiranyakeshi – Grihya Sutra of the Taittiriya branch of Krishna Yajur Veda

Homa – ritualistic process wherein articles of oblations for devata(s) are offered in the fire by the priest/yajamana while seated

Homa purvaka adhana – ritual wherein the resolve to perform agnihotra throughout life is made

Hota – one of the four main priests of shrauta yajna. To chant rig mantras in praise of the yajna devata is his main function

Hotri – specialized group of priests who chant mantras from the Rig Veda during a yajna

Ida – 1. goddess, daughter of Manu 2. major nadi or pranic channel through which mental energy flows; lunar energy

Ikshvaku – celebrated ancestor of the solar kings who ruled in Ayodhya

Indra – king of the Vedic gods; the mind or the soul; the lord of the senses; chief of the celestial beings; the ruler of heaven; the rain god

Isha – 1. Vedic unit of measurement 2. pole of a carriage or plough

Ishana – 1. name of Shiva 2. Sun (as a form of Shiva) 3. name of Vishnu

Ishavasya – one of the 10 principal Upanishads on which Shankaracharya wrote a commentary

Ishti – a yajna performed by an agnihotri with the help of four ritvijs. The resolution of the yajamana couple is the basis of the yajna

Ishti purvak adhana – rite where the resolve to perform the darshapoornamas ritual throughout life is made

Ishvara – 1. 'one who rules', supreme being or God; state of unchanging transcendental reality 2. Shiva yajna mandap

Itihasa – 1. history 2. a body of Vedic literature (Mahabharata and Ramayana)

Jagadamba – another name of Durga

Jagati – 1. Vedic metre consisting of four verses of 12 syllables divided into two hemistichs 2. world

Jagriti – conscious realm of mind, waking state

Jaimini – founder of the Mimamsa system of philosophy

Jaiminiya Talawakar – one of the Brahmana texts of Sama Veda

Janu – 1. knee 2. Vedic unit of measurement

Japa – repetition of a mantra or name of God

Japaka – one who chants; one of the priests in a smarta yajna

Jata karma – rite performed at the birth of a child wherein the father draws an 'aum' on its tongue with a golden spatula before severing the umbilical cord

Jatavedas – an epithet of fire

Jati – caste; rank

Jiva – individual soul; creature, living being

Juhu – large wooden spoon used to offer havi into the sacred fire, with a beak like a swan

Jyeshtha – 1. third month of the Indian calendar 2. eldest, senior

Jyotish – branch of Vedanga that deals with astronomical and astrological matters with respect to Vedic karma

Jyotishtoma – 'praise of light', an ekaha whose standard form is agnishtoma (jyotishtoma is often used as a synonymn for agnishtoma)

Kala – 1. time in the absolute sense, or eternity 2. the great destroyer 3. one of the eight bhairavas or states of consciousness

Kalaka – thread without elasticity

Kalasha – pot

Kali yuga – fourth and last time cycle of the universe

Kalpa – one of the six Vedangas. Kalpa Sutras are manuals of rituals in the form of sutras (aphorisms) that provide meticulous details of the processes and rules of yajna

Kalpa Sutras – see kalpa

Kamadhenu – cow belonging to Indra, believed to yield whatever is desired

Kamala – lotus

Kamandalu – water pot used by ascetics

Kamya – desirable; request

Kamya karma – rites performed for attainment of specific desires

Kanka – 1. heron 2. a bird of prey

Kanva – name of an ancient rishi and his descendants who authored several Vedic texts, particularly parts of Rig Veda

Kapala – earthen frying pan used to roast flour used in purodasha, an oblation item

Kapishthala-Katha – one of the extant branches of Yajur Veda
Karambha – oblation prepared using roasted yava or vrihi and curd
Karira – 1. bamboo shoot 2. thorny plant that grows in the desert
Kariri ishti – kamya yajna performed for good rainfall
Karma – action in the manifest and unmanifest dimension; law of cause and effect. In Vedic parlance, karma means yajna at the physical level
Karma kanda – section of Vedas on ceremonial acts and sacrificial rites at the physical level
Karmaphala – result or merit arising from due performance of karma
Karnavedha – rite of piercing earlobes
Karpurgaura – an epithet of Shiva
Katha – story
Kathopanishad – one of the principal Upanishads belonging to the Taittiriya Brahmana of Yajur Veda. It is famous for the dialogue between Yama and Nachiketa
Kathaka Brahmana – last three parts of the third kanda of Taittiriya Brahmana (from Krishna Yajur Veda)
Katyayana – celebrated author of Katyayana Kalpa Sutra (in Shukla Yajur Veda); of Katyayana
Kaupin – loin cloth
Kaushitaki – 'descendant of Kusitaki', the group to whom several Vedic texts are attributed
Keshanta – ritual of shaving a boy's head leaving only a tuft
Khadaga – sword
Khadira – tree (Acacia catechu) whose wood is used in shrauta yajna
Khara – a platform made from clay used for yajnic implements
Kharjura – date fruit
Kirtan – practice where a group of people sing a collection of mantras
Kratu – 1. soma yagas of large dimensions in terms of duration, resolution, etc. 2. resolve
Kratvartha – performance of ritualistic actions for yajna at the physical level
Kravyad – fire used for making oblations for ancestors
Krishna – 'black', eighth incarnation of Vishnu who lived in the Dwapara Yuga, 5000 years ago, and whose teachings are given in the Bhagavad Gita

Krishna Dvaipayana Vyasa – rishi credited with compiling the Vedas in their extant form. Also known as Veda Vyasa

Krishna Pratipada – first day of the dark fortnight

Krishna Yajur Veda – original form of Yajur Veda Samhita compiled by sage Vaishampayana

Krishnajina – skin of a black deer

Krodha – anger

Kshatriya – warrior class, one of the four varnas

Kshetrapala – 'guardian of an area'

Kshudrapada – Vedic unit of measurement

Kumbhaka – breath retention

Kunda – 1. cavity 2. pit in which to kindle sacrificial fire at a yajna; copper pot to hold such a fire

Kundalini – spiritual energy; evolutionary force referred to as serpent power; primal force which lies dormant (coiled) at base of spine, awakened by spiritual practices

Kusha – type of grass used in yajnic processes

Kushmanda – kind of pumpkin

Kutumbakam – family

Laja – roasted rice flakes

Lambodara – 'big bellied', epithet of Lord Ganesha

Laugakshi – Grihya Sutra of the Taittiriya branch of Krishna Yajur Veda

Laukika – earthly, of everyday life

Laukikagni – form of fire used for domestic purposes (cooking, etc.)

Laya yoga – yogic path through which every experience is dissolved

Loka – plane of existence

Madanti – hot water specifically heated on a sacred fire for use in yajna

Madhuparka – mixture made with honey

Madhyandina – midday

Madhyandina savana – second set of stotras sung in a shrauta yajna on the day of offering soma ahuti to yajna devatas

Magha – eleventh month of the Indian calendar (January–February)

Maha soma yajna – large scale yajnas including rajasooya, ashvamedha and vishvajit yajnas

Maha vyahriti – the seven words: Bhuhu, Bhuvah, Swahah, Mahah, Janah, Tapah, Satyam

Mahabharata – celebrated Indian epic believed to be the composition of Vyasa, which describes the rivalries and contests of the sons of Dhritarashtra and Pandu (Kauravas and Pandavas)

Mahabhashya – a commentary by Patanjali on the Vedas

Mahabhisheka – coronation ceremony

Mahadhvaja – main flag

Mahamrityunjaya – 'the great one who is victorious over death', another form of Shiva

Maharshi – great sage

Maharitvijs – leaders of four groups of priests in a shrauta yajna

Mahavakya – 'great statement', profound aphorism from a script or holy person, usually used to refer to the great proclamations of the Upanishads

Mahavedi – large section of yajnashala to the east of pragvansha where the main proceedings of a shrauta yajna take place

Mahidasa Aitareya – 'descendant of Itara', name of a sage from whom the Aitareya Brahmana and Aranyaka take their names

Maitravaruna – a priest of the hota group in soma yajna

Manava – 1. relating to Manu 2. mankind

Mandal – chapter

Mandap – pavilion

Mandukya Upanishad – a principal Upanishad which explains Aum and the three states of consciousness

Manomaya kosha – mental sheath or body

Mantha – that which is produced by churning; a rod for churning the sacrificial fire

Mantra – 'that which liberates the mind', subtle sound vibration which liberates mental forces; Vedic hymns or sacred prayers addressed to a deity and chanted as per the rules of compounding of Vedic words and metre

Manu Smriti – the first concise interpretation of the codes of conduct scattered throughout Vedas, defining the four purusharthas (actions to fulfil aspirations in life) – dharma, artha, kama, moksha, as the base of life. The monograph was compiled by Bhrigu, believed to be a disciple of Manu. Manu Smriti literally means a text based on the memories of the teachings of Manu. Manu is also believed to be the father of the human race

Manushya yajna – see atithi yajna
Manvantaras – the 14 Manu dynasties, each of which constitue an age
Margashirsha – ninth month of the Indian calendar
Marjana – purifying
Marut – god of wind; relating to wind or Marut; vital air, one of the three essential humours of the body
Masi shraaddha – monthly rite performed for the souls of ancestors
Matri tattwa – mother principle
Matrika – 'little mothers', letters of the Sanskrit alphabet or root sounds corresponding to the tattwas; creative energy concealed in mantra
Maya – 'illusion', veiling power of manifest Shakti; illusory nature of the phenomenal world; ignorance of reality
Medha – sacrifice
Megha – rain-bearing clouds
Mekhala – 1. an ornament worn around the waist. 2. boundary of a fire-pit used in yajna
Mimamsa – one of the six systems of Indian philosophy. Originally divided into two systems: (i) Poorva Mimamsa, founded by Jaimini, concerned with correct interpretation of Vedic rituals, (ii) Uttara Mimamsa, ascribed to Badarayana, dealing with the nature of Brahman. Poorva Mimamsa is usually called only Mimamsa and Uttara Mimamsa is called Vedanta and ranked separately
Mooladhara (chakra) – lowest psychic and pranic centre in the human body, seat of kundalini shakti
Mrigi – one of the three mudras made with the fingers to hold an item of oblation. It resembles the face of a deer
Muhurta – a moment; auspicious time for religious or similar rituals
Mundaka Upanishad – belongs to Atharva Veda and teaches the difference between intellectual study of the Vedas and their supplementary texts and intuitive knowledge
Munja – reed grass
Mushti – fist
Naam sankirtan – chanting of names of different deities by a group of people
Naga – 1. a snake in general 2. serpent demon or semi-divine being having the face of a man and the tail of a serpent

Naimittic karma – occasional karmas

Nakshatra – lunar mansion, 27 in number

Namkarana – naming ceremony

Nandi – attendant bull of Shiva

Narada – celebrated devarishi and son of Brahma, represented as a messenger from the gods to human beings and vice versa

Narashamsa – name given to the chamasas after soma has been drunk from them and they have been caused to 'swell'

Narasimha – fourth incarnation of Vishnu as half-man, half-lion

Narayana – another name of Vishnu

Navagraha – nine planets

Navami tithi – ninth day of each lunar fortnight

Navanita – 'newly brought', fresh butter

Neshta – a priest from the adhvaryu group in soma yajna

Nighantu – Vedic lexicon that propounds the Nirukta shastra

Nirukta – branch of Vedanga that deals with etymological meanings of Vedic words

Nishkramana – rite in which a newborn child is taken out of the house for the first time

Nitya karma – routine karmas

Nyaya – one of the six classical Indian philosophical systems. Founded by Gautama, it is based on logical realism

Odan – cooked rice used as oblation in some rites of shrauta yajna

Om/Aum – cosmic vibration of the universe; the most important or complete mantra which represents Ishvara or God

Oshadhi – a medicinal plant

Pada – 1. Vedic unit of measurement 2. quarter or the fourth part of a stanza, i.e. a line

Palasha – a tree whose wood is used to make yajna implements

Pancha gavya – five outputs of a cow (urine, dung, milk, curd, ghee)

Pancha maha yajnas – the five daily sacrifices: brahma yajna, deva yajna, pitri yajna, bhoota yajna and atithi yajna, every householder is required to perform

Panchadasha – fifteen

Panchagni – 'five fires'

Panchika – consisting of five parts

Panigrahana – rite in which the groom takes the bride's hand at a wedding ceremony
Pankti – Vedic metre that has five padas
Papa – sin, inauspiciousness
Papa Purusha – personification of the sinful part of the individual
Para vidya – transcendental knowledge
Paramatma – cosmic soul or consciousness; universal or supreme self
Parampara – tradition
Paridhi – 1. fenced or marked area 2. circle of light 3. border of yajna kunda
Parigraha – acceptance of a vrata
Parikarmi – miscellaneous helpers at a yajna
Paristarana – spreading
Parjanya – 1. rain-cloud 2. rain 3. god of rain
Paroksha – beyond the range of normal vision
Parthiva – earthly
Parva – 1. occasion 2. one half of a lunar month 3. section
Parvakala – auspicious day
Parvan – periods of the chaturmasya rite
Paryavarana – environment
Pashu – animal; animal nature
Pashu yaga – yajna in which an animal is sacrificed
Pashuangas – parts of an animal
Pashubali – animal sacrifice
Pashubandha – one of the seven havi samstha yajnas in which an animal is sacrificed
Pataka – flag
Path – recitation of a sacred text
Patha – trail, road or way
Patni – wife (of the yajamana)
Patni sannyaja – offering made to the wives of gods
Patnishala – part of yajnashala used by the yajamana couple to rest and keep their personal belongings in during a shrauta yajna
Patra – 1. vessel 2. sacrificial utensils
Paurnamasa – 1. relating to the full-moon day 2. sacrifice performed on the full-moon day (also called paurnamaseshti)

Pavitraka – ring made of darbha grass, worn by the person who performs religious rituals including yajna

Payasa – rice cooked in milk

Phala – fruit; consequence

Phalguna – last month of the Indian calendar (February–March)

Phalikarina – husk obtained while pounding rice bran for darsha-poornamasa ishti

Pingala nadi – major pranic channel in the body which conducts the dynamic force, or prana shakti; solar or vital energy channel

Peepal – holy fig tree (ashvattha)

Pippalada – 1. a teacher mentioned in Prashnopanishad 2. a school of Atharva Veda

Pitamah – 1. grandfather 2. Brahma 3. Shiva

Pitri – 1. father 2. departing ancestor 3. divine hierarchy consisting of deceased progenitors and ancestors

Pitri yajna – 1. one of the seven paka yajnas performed for ancestors 2. one of the panch maha yajnas intended to express gratitude to ancestors

Pitrimedha – funeral rites

Pooja – worship

Pooraka – inhalation

Poornahuti – culminating ritual of a yajna wherein the last oblation is offered into the sacrificial fire

Poornamasa – one of the seven havi samstha yajnas performed on the full-moon day

Poornima – full-moon day

Poorti – completion

Poorva Mimamsa – prior or first Mimamsa, an enquiry into the first or ritual portion of Vedas, opposed to Uttar Mimamsa which concerns itself with Upanishads

Poorva tantra – rituals held before the path and havan at a smarta yajna

Pootika – a substitute for the soma creeper used in soma yajna

Pota – a priest of the brahma group in soma yajna

Prachi – eastern line

Pradesha – 1. span of the thumb and forefinger 2. region

Pragvansha – canopy of bamboo constructed at the westernmost part of the yajnashala. The bamboo in the roof points eastwards, hence the term pragvansha (prag = east, vansha = bamboo). The fire brought by the yajamana from his home is installed in the kunda (fire-pit) in this area

Praisha – an order, command or invitation given by a ritvij to another ritvij(s) to commence a ritual during a yajna

Prajahita – when the functions carried out in the pragvansha are over, the fire is carried to the uttaravedi. The portion of garhapatya in pragvansha is now called prajahita

Prajapati – the lord of created beings; the god residing over creation; an epithet of Brahma; epithet of the ten lords of created beings

Prakrama – Vedic unit of measurement of length

Prakriti – manifest and unmanifest nature composed of the three gunas or attributes; cosmic energy; vehicle of purusha (consciousness) according to Samkhya philosophy

Prakriti yaga – yajna in Nature that is a role model for other yajnas

Prana – life principle, vital force

Pranamaya kosha – energy sheath or body

Pranava – mantra Aum; primal sound vibration

Pranayama – yogic practices involving control of inhalation, exhalation and retention of breath; technique for expanding the dimensions of prana

Pranayana – establishing the fire in the ahavaniya fire-pit from the garhapatya kunda

Pranitah – wooden vessel in which consecrated water is stored

Pra-pitamaha – paternal great-grandfather

Prasad – blessed or divine gift; often refers to food that has first been offered to God and is thus blessed

Prashasta – another name for maitravaruna, one of the priests of the hotra group

Prastara – 'to strew', the first handful of darbha blades

Prastha – 1. Vedic measure 2. level expanse

Prastota – a priest of the udgita group in soma yajna

Pratah savana – the first set of stotras sung in a shrauta yajna on the day soma oblation is offered

Prati Veda brahmacharya – study of the four Vedas for 12 years each

Pratiharta – a priest of the udgita group in soma yajna

Pratika patha – convention followed for repeated use of mantras during yajna proceedings

Pratinidhi – representative

Pratiprasthata – a priest of the adhvaryu group in soma yajna

Pratisarga – method of classifying the contents of Sama Veda

Pratyaksha – that which is visible

Pravargya – important sub-process of soma yajna, linked with the ascent of kundalini

Pravargya khara – square mound of sand raised for conducting the pravargya ritual

Prayaja – small homa done before the main yajna

Prayaniya ishti – introductory rite of the first day of soma sacrifice

Prayashchitta – expiation

Prayoga – 1. use 2. experiment

Prayoga Pustika – workbooks created by priests to ensure that the chanting of mantras and the procedures of a yajna follow the intended sequence and method

Preyas – path of pleasure; acts that leads to material happiness and are hence preferred

Prishadajya – mixture of curd and ajya

Prithivi loka – the earth and its surroundings

Prithottar yuga – Vedic unit of measurement

Prokshana – consecration by sprinkling ajya or water over an oblation article

Punaradhana – reinstallation of sacred fires

Punya – merit

Puranas – sacred books believed to be composed by Rishi Veda Vyasa containing the whole body of Indian mythology

Purodasha – rice cake used as an article of oblation

Purodha – stand-by for the host in a shrauta yajna

Purohita – 1. 'placed in front', family priest 2. epithet of the god of fire

Puronuvakya – mantras used at specific times in shrauta yajna

Purusha – consciousness which lies dormant in the human microcosm

Purusha Sukta – sukta from the Rig Veda composed by Narayana that praises the creation and the creator who pervades it

Purushamedha yajna – a sacrifice made by a human being, referring to the sacrifice of earnings by a member of society for the overall benefit of the society and the king. Sometimes wrongly interpreted as human sacrifice

Purushartha – human attainments; the four goals to be fulfilled in life: (i) artha: material needs, (ii) kama: desires and passions (iii) dharma: ethics and duty, and (iv) moksha: liberation

Putra kameshti – kamya yajna performed to fulfil the desire of having a son

Raja yoga – 'supreme yoga', 'king among yogas'; union through concentration of mind; the eightfold path as formulated by Patanjali

Rajanya – class of society engaged in military and such like operations (also called kshatriya)

Rajasandi – specially made throne-like seat to place (king) soma on in shrauta yajna

Rajasic – related to or endowed with the quality of rajas or passion

Rajasooya yajna – yajna of large dimensions to be performed by an emperor

Ratninam havinshi – twelve offerings performed for 12 days at the houses of the officials of a king during a rajasooya yajna

Rechaka – exhalation, emptying of the lungs

Richa – single verse or stanza from Vedas expressing shades of universal truth

Rig Veda – first Veda and the oldest known literature in the world

Rik (or rig) – hymn composed by a rishi in Rig Veda to express an inner experience

Rin – debt

Rishi – seer; realized sage who meditates on the self

Rishi Gautama – sage from the family of Angiras who founded the Nyaya system of philosophy

Rishi rin – debt owed to the sages for the learning handed down

Rita – proper, righteous; eternal laws of the universe

Ritasya panthah – righteous path

Ritvij – a brahmin who, having studied Vedas, partakes in the performance of a yajna

Rudra – 1. group of 11 devatas residing in antariksha loka; 2. aspect of Shiva as the god of dissolution

Rujish – dry waste that remains after extracting soma juice from crushed soma sticks

Sabhachara – code of conduct (observed in civil conferences/meetings)

Sabhya – civilized

Sabhyata – a civilization

Sadasya – 1. a person who oversees the proceedings of a shrauta yajna and provides solutions to problems or conflicts faced by ritvijs. He must be well versed in the yajna procedures and have a deep knowledge of all the four Vedas 2. member

Sadhaka – spiritual aspirant

Sadhya devas – class of celestial beings

Sadomandap – area of the yajnashala to the immediate east of the pragvansha

Sahasrara – 'thousand-petalled lotus', spiritual centre located at the crown of the head, reprsenting enlightenment

Sakala patha – convention followed for repeated use of mantras during yajna proceedings

Sakmedha – third parvana of chaturmasya yajna

Sakshi bhava – attitude of a silent witness or seer; awareness

Sama – mantras from Sama Veda

Samadhi – culmination of meditation, state of unity of mind with the object of meditation; supramental consciousness; eighth stage of ashtanga yoga

Samagri – generic term used to refer to all ingredients (yajna dravya) and implements required in dravya yajnas

Samaropana – handing over, consigning

Sambhara – 'to bring together', collection of materials required for a sacrifice

Sambhuta – that which originates, arisen

Samhita – collection of hymns, prayers, etc. from the Vedas. The hymns in the Samhitas are structured using rules of grammar and tone, and are called stotras, suktas, etc., and are chanted at a yajna

Samidha – sticks from specific trees (yajniya tree) used as fuel in the sacred fire

Samidheni – mantras to be chanted by the hota when the adhvaryu keeps the ahaviniya agni well kindled

Samindhana – kindling

Samishtayajus – yajus formula indicating completion of a sacrifice; an oblation to the wind god

Samkhya – 1. relating to number 2. one of the six systems of Indian philosophy attributed to sage Kapila

Samradasandi – specially made stool for yajna implements

Samskara – 1. process of consecration performed on an item of oblation. 2. process of purification done on the soul after it arrives in the body of a human being 3. mental impression stored in the subtle body as an archetype

Samskriti – culture. In Vedic parlance it refers to a social environment conducive to evolution of individuals to the fullest capacity of their souls

Samstha – institution; a basic schematic form of sacrifice

Samsvatsara – 1. almanac 2. twelve months of a year 3. yajna lasting a year

Samudbhava – origin; production

Sanatana dharma – system of eternal values, followed by the Vedic people

Sandhikala – the period just before sunrise, after sunset, and noon

Sandhya – spiritual practice performed at three conjunction times: dawn, noon, dusk, required to be performed by a pupil after the upanayana samskara

Sangatikaran – to come in association with, to congregate

Sanihara – messenger sent by the yajamana to: (i) request the donations and contributions to meet the expenditure of the yajna, and (ii) to collect it

Sankalpa – spiritual resolve; positive affirmation; willpower; determination or conviction

Sannayya – item prepared from a mixture of milk and curd for use as oblation in shrauta yajna

Sannyasin – one who has renounced illusion; one who has entrusted his life to the guru; one who is dedicated to spiritual life and service

Sanskrit – 1. classical Indian language which is the source of all scriptural works and is the most perfect phonetic language 2. one who has been purified by samskaras and becomes 'cultured'

Sapta havi – set of seven cultivating samskaras
Sapta paka – set of seven purifying samskaras
Sapta soma – set of seven augmenting samskaras
Saptadasha – seventeen
Saraswati – goddess of wisdom, learning, speech and the arts
Sarathi Aruni – dawn personified as the charioteer of the sun
Sarga – 1. creation 2. chapter or canto
Sarpat – call made by the priest maitravaruna indicating that all priests should leave the sadomandap
Sarvamedha – 'sacrifice of all', a major soma yajna
Sarvato bhadra mandala – yantra for 56 devatas; a comprehensive Vishnu mandala used for all major rituals/worship
Sat – truth; reality; Brahman or supreme existence
Satra – yajna spanning more than 12 days. Sometimes a satra goes on for many years
Satsang – gathering in which the ideals and principles of truth are discussed, often in the presence of a realized person; association with the wise, the good, the self-realized
Sattwic – that in which the sattwa guna, representing steadiness, purity and harmony, is prominent
Satya yuga – the first time cycle of the universe in which righteousness predominated
Saura – worshippers of the Sun
Sava – sacrifice, pressing of soma stalks
Savana – 1. process to extract soma juice for offering the principal oblation in soma yajna 2. period in a person's life 3. fifth month of the lunar calendar, also called shravana
Savaniya sutya – fifth day of a soma yajna when the soma stalks are pressed to extract juice
Sayam homa – one of the seven paka yajnas
Sayam savana – third set of stotras sung in a shrauta yajna on the day of soma offering
Seva – selfless service
Shaiva – system followed by those who worship the supreme as Shiva
Shakta – system followed by those who worship the supreme as the Divine Mother
Shaktipat – direct transmission of energy from guru to disciple

Shala – saloon/apartment
Shalagni – alternate term for smartagni
Shamitra – butcher who slaughters the animal in an animal sacrifice
Shamya – Vedic unit of measurement 2. a yajna implement, wooden yoke pin
Shanku – peg
Shantanu – king and father to the famous Bhishma of Mahabharata
Sharabha –form Shiva assumed to kill Varaha, one of the incarnations of Vishnu, after it had fulfilled its purpose
Sharad – autumn
Sharira shuddhi – purification of the body
Shastra – 1. science or department of knowledge 2. technical term for the recitation of mantras by the hotra priest during certain processes of soma yajna
Shat Shastras – the six Vedangas (Shiksha, Kalpa, Vyakarana, Nirukta, Chandas, Jyotish)
Shata kratu – one who has performed 100 yajnas
Shatapatha Brahmana – the Brahmana textbook of Shukla Yajur Veda
Shaunaka – great sage, believed to be the author of Brihad Devata and several other Vedic texts
Shikha – tuft of hair kept by Hindu brahmins on the top of the back of the head
Shiksha – branch of Vedanga that deals with phonetics of Veda richas
Shishir – winter, comprising the months of Magha and Phalguna
Shiva – 'auspicious one', destructive aspect of Hindu trinity; destroyer of ego and duality; lord of yogis who is said to dwell on Mount Kailash; archetypal renunciate; symbol of cosmic consciousness
Shodash – sixteen
Shodashi – soma yajna in which 16 stotras are sung
Shodhak samskara – purifying rites
Shraaddha – rite performed in honour of the souls of departed relatives
Shraddha – faith, reverence
Shrauta Sutras part of Kalpa Sutras dealing with procedural aspects of yajna
Shrauta yajna – generic name for yajnas based on injunctions from Shruti texts (Vedas)

Shrautadhana – installation of sacred fires for shrauta yajnas

Shrautagni – form of fire maintained by an agnihotri and used in shrauta yajna

Shreyah sampadanam/Shreyodanam – symbolic ritual to transfer the fruits of yajna from the priest to the host

Shreyas – virtue, the path of righteous or good actions

Shri – 1. another name for Lakshmi, goddess of wealth and wife of Vishnu 2. honorific prefix meaning 'sacred'

Shruti – 1. hearing 2. Vedas (created through revelation that was heard)

Shruti paramapara – lineage or succession of karma as a way of life based on directions contained in Vedas. Also refers to preservation of Vedic mantras through the oral tradition

Shuddhi – purification

Shudra – one with a services-oriented bent of mind or engaged in such a profession. In Rig Veda, refers to the soul yet to be purified through samskaras

Shukla Pratipada – first day of the bright fortnight

Shukla Yajur Veda – rescension of Krishna Yajur Veda by sage Yajnavalkya

Shulagava – rite in which the flesh and other limbs of an ox or cow are offered to Rudra

Shulba Shastras – division of Kalpa Vedangas. Practical manuals giving measurements and procedures for constructing the sites of a yajna. India's earliest extant mathematical texts

Shulba Sutras – part of Kalpa Sutras devoted to engineering aspects of yajna

Shuna – type of grass

Shunasiriya parva – parvana of chaturmasya yajna

Shyen – hawk/falcon

Siddhi – perfection; psychic power associated with awakening of chakras

Simantonnayana – rite of parting the hair of a pregnant wife by the husband while offering ajya oblations

Smarta yajna – generic term for yajnas based on injunctions from Smriti texts, Puranas, Tantra Shastra, etc.

Smartadhana – installation of sacred fires for smarta yajna

Smartagni – form of fire around which the marriage ritual is conducted. In Vedic times a householder was expected to carry this fire home after the ceremony and maintain and worship it from marriage till death. The fire is used in smarta yajnas

Smriti – 1. memory 2. also called Dharma Shastras, monographs compiled from Vedas to make an orderly presentation of the knowledge contained therein. Topics include: (i) classification of society based on functional responsibilities, (ii) duties of each class, (iii) duties of king, (iv) duties of men and women, (v) social code, (vi) civil rules, (vii) definition of sin and corresponding punishment. The Smriti monographs are treated as the last word in social and other conflicts

Snanam – 1. bath 2. rite in which a student takes a ceremonial bath before returning home from the gurukul, marking the end of studentship

Snataka – 1. bachelor 2. one who has taken the ceremonial bath on completion of his Vedic study

Soham – 'I am that', mantra of the breath used in ajapa japa. 'So' represents cosmic consciousness and 'ham' individual consciousness

Soma – 1. moon 2. creeper whose stems are crushed to extract juice to offer as oblation in soma yajna

Soma prashana – intaking of soma

Soma purvaka adhana – rite where the resolve to perform the soma yaga ritual throughout life is made

Soma samsthaka yajna – another term for shrauta augmenting yajnas (so-called because soma is the principal object of oblation)

Soma valli – the soma plant

Soma yaga – yajna in which the principal object of oblation is soma juice

Somalata – the soma creeper

Somarasa – soma juice

Somayaji – one who has performed soma yajna(s)

Srijan – generation

Stambha – pillar

Sthali – earthen dish or bowl

Sthali paka – 'cooking in a sthali'; one of seven paka yajnas in which rice or barley grains are cooked in a dish and used as sacrificial food

Sthandila – 1. altar for domestic rites 2. temporary altar created when it is not possible to construct a kunda

Sthapana – establishing

Stoma – hymn of praise

Stotra – group of mantras sung in praise of a devata or deity. In yajnic parlance, it refers to the singing of samas from Sama Veda during a shrauta yajna

Stuta – to praise (stuti: a hymn of praise)

Subhramanya – 1. epithet of Kartikeya, son of Shiva 2. one of the priests of the udgata group in shrauta yajna, who chants mantras to invoke Indra, requesting him to come to the yajna venue

Sukari mudra – one of the three mudras made with the fingers to hold the item of oblation

Sukta – set of hymns composed by a rishi (seer) in adoration of devata(s). It is an expression of what was perceived in a deep state of meditation

Surya namaskara – 'salute to the sun'; series of 12 asanas for revitalizing the pranas

Sushupti – unconscious state of mind; deep dreamless sleep

Sutya – the day on which soma is pressed for oblation in a soma yajna

Suvrishti – good rain

Swadha – mantra used while offering oblations to ancestors

Swadhakara – process of pronouncing swadha and offering oblations

Swadhaya – self-study; reciting or reading of one's own branch of the Vedas

Swaha – mantra used while offering oblations to gods

Swahakara – process of pronouncing swaha and offering oblations

Swapna – the subtle state of consciousness, the subconscious realm, dream state

Swara – accent (raised, low, circumflex); rules of pronunciation while chanting

Swarga – heaven

Swarita – one of the three tones used for chanting Vedic mantras aloud

Swasti vachana – process of chanting specific mantras at the commencement of a rite to invoke positivity

Taittiriya Samhita – chief rescension among the Samhitas of Krishna Yajur Veda

Tamasic – that in which tamas, representing inertia and fear of change, is prominent

Tantra – process of expansion of mind and liberation of energy and consciousness from matter

Tarpan – ritual of offering oblations to forefathers, using water for the offering

Tattwa – 'thatness', essential element or principle

Tattwa shuddhi – tantric science of inner purification

Tilak – application of a paste of sacred items such as sandalwood or vermilion on the forehead

Toran – temporary and ornamental arch

Treta yuga – second time cycle of the universe

Tretagni karma – yajnas using three fires, a synonymn for shrauta yajna

Tretagni – three sacred fires – garhapatya, ahavaniya and dakshina

Tripitaka – collective name for the three groups of Buddhist scriptures

Trishtubh – metre of 4 x 11 syllables

Trisuparnam Sukta – important sukta from Pranagni Upanishad, equating parts of human body with parts of yajna

Tritiya savana – third set of stotras sung in a shrauta yajna on the day of offering soma to yajna devatas

Tritiyadhana – third repetition of agnyadhan

Turiya – fourth state of consciousness, unmanifested state of Purusha and Prakriti; superconsciousness

Tushnim – 'silent' performance of a sacrificial act without any mantra

Tyat – 1. another term for prana 2. indirect knowledge of Brahman

Ubhay swaroopa yajna – yajnas that can be classified as both prakriti and nivritti type

Udaniya – 'the last one'

Udatta – one of the three tones used for chanting Vedic mantras aloud

Uddalaka Aruni – 'Uddalaka, son of Aruna', one of the most prominent teachers of the Vedic period

Uddharana – 1. raising 2. drawing out

Udgata – one of the four main priests in shrauta yajna., whose main responsibility is to sing samas from the Sama Veda in praise of yajna devata(s)

Udgatri/Udgitha – group of priests who sing verses from Sama Veda in a shrauta yajna

Udumbara – wild fig tree

Udumbari – pole made from the stem of udumbara tree raised at the centre of sadomandap

Ukthya – 1. deserving praise 2. one of the seven soma samstha yajnas in which libations are offered in the morning and midday and verses called uktha are sung

Ulukhala – wooden instrument used for pounding the grains used in yajna

Umapati – 'husband of Uma', epithet of Shiva

Unneta – priest in shrauta yajna from the adhvaryu group

Unubhay swaroopa yajna – yajnas that are of neither prakriti nor vikriti type

Upa Puranas – group of 18 secondary Puranas that were later additions to the Puranic literature

Upa vasati – 'staying near overnight', alludes to devatas coming to stay at the host's house on the night before commencement of yajna

Upadrashta – 1. supervisor 2. priest of smarta yajna whose role is to see to overall arrangements

Upanayana – investiture with a sacred thread to initiate into sacred learning

Upanita – one who has been consecrated through the upanayana samskara

Upanshu – mode of pronunciation of yajus in which the words are murmured inaudibly (but with lip movement)

Uparava – four small pits dug in havirdhana mandap

Upasad – 1. rite in which oblation of clarified butter is offered to Agni, Soma and Vishnu into the ahavaniya agni 2. worshipping

Upasaka – one doing upasana (worship)

Upasana – worship

Upasthana – prayer in adoration of Agni

Upasya – object of upasana

Upavasatha/Upavasa – fasting day

Upaveda – class of writings subordinate to Vedas. There are four Upavedas, respectively attached to each Veda: Ayurveda to Rig

Veda, Dhanurveda to Yajur Veda, Gandharva Veda to Sama Veda and Sthapatya-Shastra Veda to Atharva Veda

Upavita – cloth or thread given to a young initiate during the upanayana samskara

Ushnik – 1. favourite of the devatas 2. Vedic metre in which the number of characters are four more than those in the Gayatri chanda

Utkara – pit dug on the northern side of the mahavedi to collect the waste generated during a yajna

Utsarga – act of passing over certain days or rituals of a satra (utsarga paksha: when chaturmasya yajna is performed only once in the lifetime of an agnihotri)

Uttara – 1. north 2. higher 3. subsequent

Uttara Mimamsa – 'later Mimamsa', the Vedanta philosophy (distinguished from Mimamsa proper which is usually called Poorva Mimamsa)

Uttara pooja – culminating worship

Uttara tantra – rituals performed after path and havan at smarta yajnas

Uttararani – upper plank of arani

Uttararchika – second part of Sama Veda

Uttaravedi – square platform constructed with bricks and mud, situated to the extreme east of the mahavedi

Uttarayana – summer solistice; northern journey of the sun (six months of the solar year)

Uvacha – to speak

Vaikhanasa – group of rishis to whom several Vedic texts are attributed

Vaishampayana – 'descendant of Vishampa', name of a teacher who compiled Krishna Yajur Veda

Vaisheshika – one of the six systems of Indian philosophy propounded by Kanada, which deals with categories as the primary means of salvation

Vaishnava – sect who hold Vishnu as the primary god and follow the path of bhakti

Vaishvadeva – 1. first parvana of chaturmasya yajna 'relating to all gods', which is the model for all parvanas. 2. offerings of cooked food to all gods, twice daily 3. four of the five (pancha) maha yajnas – deva, pitri, bhuta and atithi/manushya yajna – grouped together

Vaishya – class of Vedic society engaged in trade, commerce, agriculture, etc.

Vaitanikagni – 'expansive agni', an alternate term for shrautagni

Vaiyaktika sarvamedha – total surrender, or complete sacrfice of one's personality

Vajapeya – major soma samstha yajna, elaborate in scope and rituals

Vajina – watery part of curdled milk; god to whom this water is offered

Vajra – thunderbolt, Indra's missile

Vamana – 1. dwarf 2. Vishnu in his fifth incarnation when he was born as a dward to humble the demon Bali

Varaha Mihir – celebrated astronomer, one of the nine 'gems' at the court of King Vikrama, and author of Brihatsamhita

Varaha – third incarnation of Vishnu in the form of a boar

Varga – 1. class or division 2. class of consonants 3. section of a book, particularly sub-division of an adhyaya in Rig Veda

Varna – 1. class, especially the four classes of society (brahmin, kshatriya, vaishya, shudra) 2. Sanskrit alphabets

Varuna – 1. deity of the waters 2. name of an Aditya

Varunapraghasa – second parvana of chaturmasya sacrifice in which 'Varuna eats'

Vasant – spring

Vashatkara – the process in which the hota calls out 'vaushat', hearing which the adhvaryu drops oblation material into the fire

Vashishtha – celebrated sage, family priest of the solar race of kings, most notably Rama, and author of several Vedic hymns and ethical teachings called Yoga Vashishtha

Vasordhara – continuous pouring of ghrita into sacrificial fire using a long stick from the udumbara tree

Vastoshpati – deity of the house

Vastu shamana – rite of to pacify the forces at a building site

Vasu – group of eight devatas residing on earth

Vatavaran – atmosphere

Vaushat – the word pronounced by the hota as a signal to the adhvaryu at the end of the mantra chanting to drop the articles of oblation into the fire

Vayu – 1. the wind god 2. air
Vayu shodhak – air purifying
Vayu shuddhi – purification of air
Ved – broom made of darbha grass and used in a yajna
Veda – 'to know', oldest known form of literature in the world revealed to the seers of India which explain and regulate every aspect of life from supreme reality to worldly affairs. Four in number – Rig, Yajur, Sama, Atharva, which are further divided into Samhita, Brahmana, Aranyaka and Upanishads
Veda Purusha – Veda personified
Vedanga – a generic name for the six subjects/techniques developed to aid the study of Vedas and interpretation of mantras
Vedanta – 'culmination of the Vedas', the philosophical system based on the Upanishads
Vedi – altar, platform; place near the ahavaniya fire pit in shrauta yajna
Vedic – of the Vedas
Vibhooti – 1. ash of cow-dung used in a sacrifice 2. divine attainments
Vicchhinnagnyadhana – ritual wherein if all the three sacred fires established by an ahitagni have extinguished, the fire is established again
Vichara – thought; right enquiry; discernment
Vichitra – peculiar, varied
Vidhi – ritualistic procedure; method; sacred precept or rule
Vidya – learning, science, inner knowldge
Vighnaharta – another name of Ganesha
Vijnanamaya kosha – higher mental sheath or body
Vikriti yajna – modification of a model rite, i.e. of prakriti yajna
Vikriti – modification (of purpose, mind, form, etc.)
Vinayaka – 'remover of obstacles', another name of Ganesha
Virata – 1. Vedic unit of measurement 2. gigantic 3. macrocosm; sum total of the entire manifest universe
Vishnu – Vedic deity; preserver and sustainer of the universe; one of the Hindu trinity; supreme consciousness
Vishvadeva – a group of 10 devatas believed to be sons of Vishva; a group of devatas worshipped together
Vishvajita – 'all conquering' – a maha soma yajna, an ekaha of the agnishtoma type where dakshinas are given on a massive scale

Vishvakarma – architect and engineer of gods
Vishvamitra – royal sage who transformed from a warrior to a brahmarishi or knower of Brahman
Vishvedeva – one of the 10 Vishvadevas
Vivaha – marriage
Viveka –discrimination
Vrata – vowed observance
Vrata dharana – acceptance of observing a vow
Vrata visarjan – cessation of the observance of vrata
Vratadesha – 'imposition of vrata' – observances that a student has to keep for a certain period of time before he is eligible to learn Vedic texts
Vratapati – epithet of Surya
Vrihi – type of grain used in shrauta yajna
Vrishti shuddhi – purification of rain
Vyahriti – three mystical utterances: 'bhuh, bhuvah, swaha'
Vyakarana – branch of Vedanga dealing with the grammar of Vedic richas
Vyakta – manifest universe
Vyama – Vedic unit of measurement
Vyapara – trade
Vyavahara – behaviour
Vyayama – Vedic unit of measurement
Yaga – yajna that employs the words 'vaushat' in mantras sung by the hota, and 'yajet' or 'yajati' by the adhvaryu. The articles used by the adhvaryu for oblations are either ajya or purodasha. He drops the oblation articles in the fire while maintaining a standing pose
Yajamana – one who makes a resolve to perform a yajna, the host of a yajna
Yajniya – related to yajna, belonging to or fit for sacrifice
Yajna Purusha – yajna pavilion as personification of yajna
Yajna sadhan – yajna implements
Yajnagni – form of fire used in sacrificial rituals
Yajnartha ajna – injunctions contained in the Brahmana Granthas on the mantras to be used for different actions
Yajna samstha – the institution of yajna
Yajnashala – pavilion raised for daily worship at the yajna venue

Yajnavalkya – famed Vedic sage and author

Yajnavihara – see yajnashala

Yajnavriksha – trees recommended for use in shrauta yajna

Yajnayudha – 'yajna weapons'

Yajnopavita – upavita (sacred thread/cloth) duly consecrated to be worn by a new initiate after initiation into Gayatri mantra

Yajur Veda – second of the four principal Vedas that gives the dispensation techniques of yajna

Yajus – Yajur Veda mantras in prose form

Yajya – mantras chanted by the hota during the main process of a yajna

Yashaskama – desirous of getting fame

Yaskacharya – Vedic seer and author of Nirukta

Yava – a type of grain used in shrauta yajna

Yavajjiva paksha – kind of undertaking by an ahitagni to perform chaturmasya yajna regularly

Yoktra – belt made of darbha grass to be worn by the yajamana's wife

Yoga Vashishtha – poetic work of 24,000 verses by Sage Valmiki. It is a dialogue between Lord Rama and his teacher Vashishtha

Yuga – four time cycles of the universe: satya yuga, treta yuga, dvapara yuga, kali yuga

Yupa – pole erected near the uttaravedi at a soma yajna

Bibliography

Agni Garbha, Asharam Tripathi, O.C.R. Complex, Lucknow

Apastamba Mein Yajna Vidya, Kuvarlal Vyasashisya Acharya, Itahasa Vidya Prakashan, Delhi

Apastamba Shulba Sutram, Damodar Jha, Hoshiyarpuram, 1988

Atharva Veda, S.K. Deodhar & P.N. Joshi (ed), Prasad Prakashan, Pune, 1981

Atharva Veda, Chitrav Shastri (trans), Bharatiya Charitra Kosha Mandal, Pune, 1996

Atharva Veda Samhita, S.D. Satavalekar (trans), Swadhyaya Mandal, Pardi, Valsad, Gujarat, 1985

Bhagavad Gita Bashya, S.D. Satavalekar (trans), Swadhyaya Mandal, Pardi, Valsad, Gujarat, 1990

Bharatiya Samskriti Kosha V & VII, Mahadev Shastri Joshi (trans), Bharatiya Samskriti Kosha Mandal, Pune

Brihad Brahma Nitya Karma Samuchhaya, Durga Shankar Umashankar Thakar (trans), Valukeshwar Samskrit Pathshala, Mumbai

Brihadaranyaka Upanishad, S.K. Deodhar & P.N. Joshi (trans), Prasad Prakashan, Pune, 1983

Chandogya Upanishad, S.K. Deodhar & P.N. Joshi (trans), Prasad Prakashan, Pune, 1983

A Dictionary of the Vedic Rituals, Chitrabhanu Sen, Concept Publishing Co., Delhi, 1978

Dharma Shastra Itihasa, M.M. Kane, Bhandarkar Oriental Research Institute, Pune, 1990

Four Chapters on Freedom, Swami Satyananda Saraswati, Yoga Publications Trust, Munger, Bihar, 2000

Graha Yajnaha, Keshav Shastri Joglekar, Anamol Prakashan, Pune, 1982

Grihyanushthano ka Samskritic Anveshan, Reena Ashthana, Nag Publishers, Delhi, 1986

A History of Ancient Sanskrit Literature, Max Muller, Bhuvaneshwari Ashram, Allahabad, 1926

A History of Indian Literature, A. Weber, Chaukhamba, Varanasi, 1961

Internal Yajna, S.K. Ramachandra Rao, Kalpataru Research Academy, Bangalore, 2002

Ishavasya Upanishad, S.K. Deodhar & P.N. Joshi (trans), Prasad Prakashan, Pune, 1983

Ishavasya Upanishad, Swami Satyananda Saraswati, 1st edn, Bihar School of Yoga, Munger, Bihar, 1975

Katyayana Yajna Padhati Vimarsha, Manoharlal Dwivedi, Rashtriya Samskrit Samsthan, Delhi

Krishna Yajur Veda Part I & II, Shrautacharya Bapat & P. Hirlekar (trans.), Amaravati, Maharashtra, 1994

Maharashtriya Dnyana Kosha II – Ved Vidya, Shridhar Venkateshwar Ketkar, Maharashtriya Dnyana Kosha Mandal, Nagpur, 1986

Mind – Its Mysteries and Control, Swami Sivananda Saraswati, Divine Life Society, Rishikesh, 2001

Mundaka Upanishad, S.K. Deodhar & P.N. Joshi, Prasad Prakashan, Pune, 1983

Nine Principal Upanishads, Swami Satyananda Saraswati, 2nd edn, Yoga Publications Trust, Munger, Bihar, 2004

Niruktam, Dr. Umashankar Sharma, Chaukhambha Vidya Bhavan, Varanasi

Nitya Karma Puja Prakash, Lal Bihari Mishra, Gita Press, Gorakhpur, 1994

Paraskar Grihya Sutram, Om Prakash Pandeya, Chaukhamba Amar Bharati Prakashan, Varanasi, 1995

Principles of Yajna Vidhi, S.K. Ramachandra Rao, Kalpataru Research Academy, Bangalore, 1991

Puranas – 18 volumes, S.K. Deodhar, (trans), Prasad Prakashan, Pune, 1981

Purusha Sukta, Gajanan Balkrushna Dandge, Maharashtra Grantha Bhandar, Mahadwar, Kolhapur, 1908

Rig Veda, S.K. Deodhar & P.N. Joshi, Prasad Prakashan, Pune, 1981

Rig Veda, Chitrav Shastri (trans), Bhartaiya Charitra Kosha Mandal, Pune, 1996

Rig Veda Darshan, R.G. Kolangade, Joshi & Bros, Sadashiva Peeth, Pune

Rig Veda Mantra Samhita, Dr. R.L. Kashyap, Shri Aurobindo Kapali Sastry Institute of Vedic Culture, Bangalore, 2003

Rig Veda Bhashya Bhumika, Sayanacharya, Chaukhamba Orientala, Varanasi

Rig Vediya Brahmano ka Samskrit Adhyayana, Dr. Balcir Acharya, Vidya Nidhi Prakashan, Delhi, 1991

Sama Veda, S.K. Deodhar & P.N. Joshi (trans), Prasad Prakashan, Pune, 1981

Sama Veda Samhita, S.D. Satavalekar (trans), Swadhyaya Mandal, Pardi, Valsad, Gujarat, 1985

Samskrit Sahitya cha SopaPattik Itahasa, Vinayak Vaman Karambelkar, Shri Sharada Prakashan, Nagpur, 1988

Sarva Darshan Sangraha, R.P. Kangle, Maharashtra Rajya Sahitya Samskriti Mandal, Mumbai, 1992

Satyartha Prakash, Maharshi Dayananda Saraswati, Arya Samaj, Delhi, 1984

Shatapatha Brahmana, with commentary by Vedarth Prakash, Shri Hari Swami, Nag Publications, 1990

Shatapatha Brahmana – Ek Samskrit Adhyana, Dr. Urmila Devi Sharma, Meherchand Lachmandas Publications, New Delhi, 1982

Shatapatha Brahman (Kanva), Indira Gandhi National Centre of Arts, 1994

Shrauta Dharmachi Swaroop Chikitsa, Dr. C.G. Kashikar, G.J. Abhyankar, Pune University, Pune, 1977

Shrauta Yajna – Devata Dhyana Vichara, Ahitagni Nana Kale, Yogiraj Ved Vidnyan Ashram, Kasarwadi, Barshi, Maharashtra, 1998

Shri Manusmriti, K.M. Bapat Shastri (trans), Joshi Bros., Appa Balawant Chouk, Pune, 1985

Shulba Sutras, Dr. Raghunath Purushottam Kulkarni, Maharashtra Rajya Sahitya Samskriti Mandal, Mumbai

Solah Samskar, Pradyumna Kumar Shastri, Rajasthan Patrika Prakashan, Jaipur, 1995

Tantra Darshan, Swami Niranjanananda Saraswati, Sri Panch Dashnam Paramahamsa Alakh Bara, Deoghar, Jharkhand, 1993

Trisuparna – Sartha, Gangacharya Tuljapurkar, Dwimitra Prakashan, Mumbai, 1908

Vajapeya Yajna, Shrautacharya Dhudiraj Ganesh Dikshit Bapat, 1994

Vedic Culture, Ganga Prasad Upadhyaya,

Our Vedic Literature, R.G.Vaidya, 1930

Vedic Literature and Culture, Acharya Baldev Upadhyaya, Delhi, 1990

Vedic Mythology, A A. Macdonell, trans by Ram Kumar Rai, Chaukhamba Vidya Bhavan, Varanasi, 1963

Veda Navaneetam, Dr. Urmila Devi Sharma, Astha Prakashan, Ram Kutir, Jaipur, 2000

Vedic Sacrifice, Swami Harshananda Saraswati, Ram Krishna Math, Bangalore

Vedic Samaj, Gajanan Balkrushna Dandge, Maharashtra Grantha Bhandar, Mahadwar, Kolhapur, 1985

Ved Shastra Parichaya, Moreshwar Shastri Joshi

Vedic Vangmaya Vishleshan, Dr. Krishna Lal, J.P. Publishing House, Delhi

Vedic Yajna Samstha (I & II), Shripad Damodar Satavalekar, Swadhyaya Mandal, Pardi, Valsad, Gujarat

Yajna Kunda Mandap Siddhi, K.M. Bapat Shastri, Joshi Bros, Pune, 1982

Yajna Maha Vijnana, V.V. Vedvijnanacharya, Veda Sadan, Maharani path, Indore

Yajna Mimamsa, Veniram Sharma Gaud, Chaukhamba Vidya Bhavan, Varanasi, 1999

Yajna Parijatah, Devi Prasad Mishrah, Chaukhamba Amar Bharati Prakashan, Varanasi, 1995

Yajna Rahasya, K.M. Bapat Shastri, Joshi Bros, Pune, 1982

Yajna Tattwa Prakash, P.N.Pattabhiram Shastri, Motilal Banarasidas, Varanasi, 1950

Yajur Veda, S.K. Deodhar & P.N. Joshi (trans), Prasad Prakashan, Pune, 1981

Yajur Veda Subodh Bhashya, S.D. Satavalekar (trans), Swadhyaya Mandal, Pardi, Valsad, Gujarat, 1985

Notes